# LIBERTY'S DAWN

EMMA GRIFFIN is Professor of History at the University of East Anglia and an expert on the social and economic history of Britain from 1700 to 1870. She is a frequent contributor to BBC Radio 3's *Night Waves* and is the author of three previous books, including *A Short History of the British Industrial Revolution* (2010) and *Blood Sport: Hunting in Britain since 1066* (2007).

EMMA GRIFFIN

# LIBERTY'S
# DAWN

## A PEOPLE'S HISTORY
### *of the*

# INDUSTRIAL
# REVOLUTION

YALE UNIVERSITY PRESS
NEW HAVEN AND LONDON

For information about this and other Yale University Press publications, please contact:
U.S. Office: sales.press@yale.edu    www.yalebooks.com
Europe Office: sales@yaleup.co.uk    www.yalebooks.co.uk

Set in Adobe Caslon Pro by IDSUK (DataConnection) Ltd
Printed in Great Britain by Hobbs the Printers Ltd, Totton, Hampshire

Library of Congress Cataloging-in-Publication Data

Griffin, Emma.
   Liberty's dawn: a people's history of the Industrial Revolution/Emma Griffin.
      pages cm
   ISBN 978-0-300-15180-0 (hardback)
1. Industrial revolution—Great Britain. 2. Great Britain—Social conditions. 3. Great Britain—Economic conditions. I. Title.
   HC253.G75 2013
   330.941'07—dc23

                                                                          2012050618

A catalogue record for this book is available from the British Library.

ISBN 978-0-300-20525-1 (pbk)

10 9 8 7 6 5 4 3 2

*For David, Benedict and Anna*

An ample theme: the intense interests, passions, and strategy that throb through the commonest lives.
—Thomas Hardy, *The Life and Work of Thomas Hardy,* ed. Michael Millgate (London, 1884), p. 158


The most remarkable century ever known in the history of the World, for progress in Education, inventions, Engineering, Electricity, Farming, everything tending to the betterment of the Nation and the Welfare of the People and making life worth living.
—Richard Cook, p. 26, Lincoln Reference Library

# CONTENTS

# ACKNOWLEDGEMENTS

MANY FRIENDS AND colleagues have been kind enough to offer advice and criticism on this project at various stages. I would like to thank Silvia Evangelisti, Tim Hitchcock, Jane Humphries, Gareth Stedman Jones and Leigh Shaw-Taylor for discussing this project. I am particularly grateful to Gregory Claeys, David Craig, Christopher Ferguson, John Hatcher, Richard Huzzey, Jo Innes, Steve King, Peter Mandler, Sarah Pearsall, Heather Savigny, Anne Secord, Patrick Wallis and Andy Wood for reading and commenting on work in progress. Carolyn Steedman let me read her work on Joseph Woolley and that and the communications that followed have been of immense value. Robert Poole has helped me out with queries about Samuel Bamford, and Christopher Ferguson has set me straight on points of detail concerning James Carter. I am grateful to all for countless corrections and for helping me to improve my argument and expression in significant ways.

I have had the opportunity to present ideas to seminar audiences at the Cambridge Group for Population History; the Local Population Studies Society; Robinson College, Cambridge; Southampton University; Gonville and Caius College, Cambridge; the Institute of Historical Research, London; All Souls College, Oxford; and St Anne's College, Oxford. I must thank the organisers of these events for their invitations and the audiences for invaluable criticism, advice and encouragement. What follows is certainly the better for its engagement with so many critical listeners.

The actual completion of this book was made possible only by a research fellowship from the Arts and Humanity Research Council and a year's study leave from the University of East Anglia. My thanks are due to both institutions for these much valued periods of research leave.

My greatest debt goes to my husband, David Milne, who discussed the big ideas of the project and pored over the smallest details of countless draft chapters, all the while sharing equally in the running of a home and the raising of our two small children. This book is dedicated with love and gratitude to David, Benedict and Anna.

# CHAPTER ONE

# Introduction: 'A Simple Naritive'

A T THE DAWN of the nineteenth century, a subtle and little-noticed social change began to take place in Britain. As the industrial revolution picked up pace, a growing number of ordinary working people picked up pen and paper and wrote down their memories. Some, such as the poet Robert Anderson, overcame impoverished origins to acquire considerable literary skills. His 'Memoirs of the author' were published in 1820 as a preface to a volume of his poetry.[1] Others scratched out their stories without artistry, apologising as they wrote for their poor spelling, explaining that their schooldays had ended before they 'learned the points and stops'.[2] Regardless of literary merit, these writers bequeathed an extraordinary collection of historical sources, hundreds of evocative tales of everyday life during one of the most momentous transitions in world history. This book tells their story, an unexpected tale of working people carving out for themselves new levels of wealth, freedom and autonomy. Let us begin by opening the pages of one such notebook.

In the vaults of the Norfolk Record Office lie the memoirs of John Lincoln. Written in the 1830s, the memoirs were carefully passed through his descendants from one generation to the next until they reached the local historian, Patrick Palgrave-Moore, who wisely deposited them for safe keeping at the Record Office. The eighty pages of Lincoln's notebook are fragile and torn, filled with the untidy hand of a self-taught writer. The closely written, margin-less pages remind us that Lincoln lived at a time when paper was a precious commodity. They comprised what he called his 'simple Naritive', a detailed account of his life from his earliest childhood recollections to the present. Lincoln was nearly sixty when he wrote his memoirs. He is not listed in the

1841 Census, so it seems likely that he did not live for many years after their completion.[3]

From his notebook, we learn that John was born into a life of crushing poverty, even by the depressed standards of the late eighteenth century. His father died shortly after his birth, leaving his mother destitute. To keep her small family of two children together (down from the ten she had given birth to), John's mother 'would go a washing 5 days in the week'.[4] Mother's work and a little assistance from the parish kept a roof over the family until John was seven. At this point, though, the parish decided that the seven-year-old would have to earn his own way. John never lived with his family again. He was first dispatched to work for a hemp manufacturer that the parish had found. The placement did not last long. His mistreatment at the hands of his master's wife escalated until she cracked John's skull open with a wooden hemp reel. It was too much even for his lukewarm guardians, and the parish officers lost little time in finding him a new situation. Over the next decade, John moved from one post to the next, choosing his employments so as to keep close to his sister and 'dear mother'; he felt uneasy, as he said, without a 'friend to tell all my little sorrows' close by.[5] The circumstances of this little family were far from ideal, yet the bonds between mother and son were clearly strong and meaningful. Despite living apart since the age of seven, John found the death of his mother a shattering blow. Plunged into a sorrow he could not articulate, he described himself simply as 'very unsettled' and of a 'Roveing dispassion', unable for a number of years to settle in one place or one position for long.[6]

Perhaps these traumatic experiences help explain the unsatisfactory relationships he entered soon after. His first was with Ann, a fellow servant at Oxborough, an excellent cook but a woman with 'a hot and Violent Temper – she was a very stout person and ten years older than myself'.[7] Within little more than a year, Ann found herself in a delicate condition. A wedding was the only solution. The nuptials took place in January 1799, but the marriage was neither long-lived nor successful. As soon as she had a ring on her finger, Ann left their employers' household and headed back to her own family, with John reluctantly following shortly after to work with her father at 'hedging and ditching' and to live in the family's humble home. He admitted in his notebook that his reception there quickly left him wishing he had followed his master's advice and never married at all. In July, Ann presented John with a son, but in the winter she fell ill. Weeks later she lay dead. With her parents unwilling to take care of the child, John was left alone to manage as best he could. He found a nurse to watch the child while he toiled in the fields during the day but suspected her of neglect. The 'feet of my dear child was almost Rotted up' through long hours of confinement to a cradle, he recalled, and when he returned from his day's labour his son 'would leap from joy at my appearance'.[8] John removed his son to a second nurse, but the child's pitiful life was cut short at eighteen months. Two years had passed since John had married. Both his wife and son had died and, as John laconically observed, he 'was far from being happy'.[9]

The seasons rolled by, with John constantly shifting from one employer to the next. In his memoirs, John made a careful note of each of his employments and the petty fallings-out that had terminated many, but did not touch again upon personal matters until he 'formed an acquaintance with a young woman' while working in Brandon.[10] Though she never intimated as much, John soon suspected his unnamed acquaintance was pregnant. In sharp contrast to the usual desires of unmarried women in her predicament, however, she seemed to care little for John's involvement. When he moved away from Brandon in search of work, she brusquely terminated the relationship. John's suspicions were confirmed months later when she wrote to inform him that she had given birth to his son and requested that he return to Brandon to make her his wife. He hastened back and readily published the banns, perhaps hoping for a happier outcome for this family than his first. He was soon disappointed. A month after his return 'she took in her head to deny me Coming to her house and Resolved not to Marry'.[11] Unable to persuade her otherwise, John moved on, first to Wimblington to work at the plough, and then into Essex, ending up finally at the Royal Arsenal at Woolwich where for a number of years he enjoyed plenty of work at good wages, thanks to the government's insatiable need for munitions triggered by the wars with Napoleon's France.

It was at Woolwich that Lincoln once more 'began to think of trying another partner for life here was plenty of Choice'.[12] He met a young woman living with her family in Woolwich and although John said little about their courtship it was clearly conducted along similar lines to his previous two. His new wife gave birth to their first child just four months after the wedding. During the course of their marriage, she bore ten children in all. The memoirs provide scant detail about the nature of their married life or the fate of their children. Of his marriage, John declared that he had never 'repented of our Union', but he said little about their life together, and indeed did not even note her name. (From the baptism registers we learn that she was called Sarah.) The record of his children was also incomplete: the parish registers reveal that the family suffered at least one infant death that was not mentioned in the memoir.[13] And despite the care with which John described his own childhood and entry to the workforce he wrote very little about his children and nothing about when and why they started work. After his marriage, John's memoirs wandered on to other themes – his struggle to find employment following the downscaling of operations at the Royal Artillery and, above all, his religious conversion. He returned to family matters only sporadically and inconsistently.

Here then is an example of the kind of record we will use to unlock the meaning of working-class life: detailed in certain aspects, frustratingly incomplete in others, heartbreaking in some of its recollections, and hopeful in others. John Lincoln's story belongs to a remarkable set of records going under such titles as memoirs, life histories, autobiographies, notes, sketches, recollections and adventures, as well as many others more idiosyncratic.[14] I have turned to them in order to think about a question that has animated observers for the best part of two centuries: what was the impact of the world's first industrial revolution on the ordinary men, women and children who lived through it?

Stating the question so baldly instantly raises a problem: what exactly do we mean by the 'industrial revolution'? It is hard to imagine a term that has been more bitterly contested. Not only are historians divided about how it should be defined (was it the emergence of new technology? of new commercial systems? of new forms of fuel?); they also fail to agree on when the great event is supposed to have occurred. There are even a few sceptics who question whether such a 'revolutionary' event occurred at all.[15]

Yet no matter how much we dispute the fine detail, it is clear that something momentous happened in Britain between the end of the eighteenth century and the middle of the nineteenth. 'Revolution' is an unavoidable and apt description of these events. At some point, the nation stopped trying to make all its goods by hand, and started to burn fossil fuels to drive machinery to do the work instead. In the process, large numbers of families gave up working the land, and moved to towns and cities to take up employment in factories, mills and mines. As each decade of the early nineteenth century passed it became increasingly obvious that Britain had left behind its pre-industrial past and was travelling on an entirely new trajectory. What these changes meant for the nameless individuals who formed part of that exodus from the country to the town, from the land to the workshop, remains a question of innate human interest. And it is one of enduring relevance in our own times as other parts of the globe industrialise at a galloping pace.

As the moment when one small European nation left behind its agrarian past and entered decisively on the path to modernity, the industrial revolution has quite rightly attracted the attention of generation after generation of historians. But most of this work has focused on the great men and machines that turned Britain into the workshop of the world: James Hargreaves, Richard Arkwright, James Watt, George Stevenson, Isambard Kingdom Brunel; the spinning jenny, the water frame, the steam engine, the locomotive engine, the railways. These individuals and their achievements transformed Britain into an industrial nation and fully deserve the attention they have received. But so too do the ordinary men, women and children who worked the machines, hewed coal for the steam engines, and built and drove the trains. It is too often assumed that workers like these left little mark on the historical record and must for ever remain voiceless. But as John Lincoln's tale shows, the workers in Britain's fields and factories were not always so silent as has generally been supposed.

It is hard to characterise the memoirs and 'simple Naritives' that John Lincoln and others have left behind, beyond indicating that in each, the writer and the subject are one and the same. They are works that we would today recognise as autobiographies, though the word 'autobiography' only entered the English language in the early nineteenth century, well after the culture of life-writing had taken root. I have consulted over 350 items, both published and unpublished. Most of the autobiographies that have survived appeared in print during or soon after the author's lifetime. A few were even commercial successes. James Dawson Burn's *Autobiography* was published in 1855, and by the end of the decade had gone into its fourth edition. Others were published in very small numbers by obscure provincial printers, more for the writer's satisfaction than in response to any public demand. John Robinson's *Short Account of the Life of John Robinson* was as short as its title promised – just one page long. Robinson was a printer and probably published his short account himself. It seems likely that the copy held by the Torquay Central Library in Devon is the only one now in existence. Some of the autobiographies I have consulted were not written for publication at all. Their authors' motivations defy all attempts at simple categorisation. They vary from recounting a religious conversion to retelling a career of modest political achievement (and perhaps wistfully hoping to appear in print). For these authors, life-writing was a private exercise in writing and composition, perhaps intended as a record of family history for the amusement or edification of their children. Some have since been brought to light by their authors' descendants; the others still remain locked away gathering dust in the strongrooms and vaults of local history libraries and county record offices.[16]

In turning to autobiography to think about the impact of industrialisation on the poor, one inevitably soon hears the criticism that there is something exceptional about the man who wrote an autobiography. It has often been suggested that the ability to write, combined with the desire to do so, was so rare in the working class during this period that the few hundred who wrote down their life history cannot be taken as representative of the silent majority.[17]

Yet it is my belief that the autobiographies capture a broad swath of working-class life. If we take the working class to be those who had no income other than that which they earned, those working as manual labourers, and those sufficiently close to the margins of a comfortable existence that a stint of ill health or unemployment posed serious difficulties, we find that the autobiographies do indeed capture the life experiences of this group. The skilled and unskilled; agricultural, urban and industrial workers; the reasonably comfortable and the desperately poor are all represented. Of course wealthy families purchased better educations for their children, but there was nothing exceptional in a labourer knowing how to write. There were opportunities for the most impoverished to receive some schooling, particularly following the creation of the Sunday schools at the end of the eighteenth century. The ubiquity of 'dame schools' – small schools run by women which combined childcare with schooling – held out the prospect of basic literacy to the children of very poor families before their working lives began. As we shall see in the pages that follow, it is undeniable that many of our authors began life in the most abject poverty. Furthermore, this period witnessed the creation of a wide range of opportunities for learning to write later in life and it was this adult learning which proved particularly important for the writing of working-class autobiography. And this raises an intriguing possibility: that many writers were able to describe an earlier time in their life when they had been wholly unable to read or write. As a result, this diverse set of memoirs contains reflections and detail about those born into poverty and who had remained poor and illiterate for a part of their adult life.

In inviting people to think about the social origins of the autobiographers, I have sometimes suggested they imagine a large bus with seats for working-class families only. All my writers started out on the bus – they were raised in poor families, on scant fare, with limited or non-existent schooling, and turfed out to the workplace at the earliest opportunity. But as the time passed, some of the autobiographers stepped off the bus: between a third and a half left behind their working-class origins and either made money in business or rose to some kind of prominence in politics, the arts, or the Church. This still left plenty of writers who spent their lives as labourers so far as we can know. Men like John Hemmingway, who grumbled that after a life of hard work as a weaver, a soldier and a carter, in old age he and his wife were forced to sell their furniture and wedding rings, move into a miserable cellar dwelling, and live off a small dole from the parish.[18] Yet even where writers did alight from our working-class charabanc, this poses far less of a problem than is often assumed. We need only turn to their writing to establish whether they are describing their working-class self or their life as a self-made success. This book is not about the ease with which men stepped on and off the bus, or what happened to them after they did so. It is resolutely about the time spent as a labouring man.

In fact, the greatest drawback in working with these records stems not from their inability to capture the lives of poor working men, but their failure to say much about the life experiences of women. Very, very few were written by women. Perhaps some female autobiographies remain to be found, but even the most careful trawl through the archives is not going to fill this absence. There were unavoidable practical difficulties that stood in the way of female life-writing. Girls' educational opportunities were more limited than those of their brothers; women had less money to spend on notebooks, pens and ink. But there were also a range of cultural forces muting the female voice. Poor women were far less likely to achieve the kinds of accomplishments in the workplace, in the arts, in the Church, that provided the motivation for some of the men who wrote a life history. And a woman's domestic work was most certainly not the stuff from which a marketable autobiography was made. Family legend has it that Elizabeth Oakley abruptly abandoned her autobiography before its completion, worn down by the jeremiads of her eldest son. 'Who ever will want to read about your poor boring life?' he would ask.[19] The low status of poor women, at least until 1850, was a far more powerful check on female life-writing than the combined forces of illiteracy and poverty.[20]

This is not of course to suggest that autobiographies offer the perfect vantage point for understanding working-class life, a window through which we may unproblematically peer at the life and loves of the down-trodden. Men and women writing their own histories raise problems of their own. Long and complex lives were condensed into a matter of pages,

sometimes by authors with very little experience of writing and composition, and decisions had to be made about what to discuss and what to leave
out. So much is already evident from the memoirs of Lincoln, who wrote
considerably more about his one year of marriage to Ann than he did of his
twenty-two years with Sarah, and who dealt very unevenly with the twelve
children he fathered. The same problem is visible in many of the other
memoirs which we will look at here.

Doubtless, some of the omissions reflect experiences that writers lacked
the stomach and vocabulary to address. John Tough, for example, in less
than half a page outlined his two marriages, the birth of his eleven children,
and the death of ten of them – seven as infants and three as adults. He
concluded, 'I have had to contend with many vicissitudes in course of my
time, having buried a wife and ten children'. But Tough did not pause for
long on these losses. He swiftly proceeded: 'having given an account of my
parentage, my birth and marriages and offspring, I now give some of the
incidents which I recollect to have seen in the course of my life. The first is,
the straightening of the Denburn and building the Bow Bridge . . .'[21] Then
follow several pages of recollections, mostly of notorious criminal trials and
hangings he had witnessed, all addressed at far greater length than the
harrowing events of his own life. One can only speculate upon the reasons
for Tough's lack of commentary on the repeated loss of family members,
losses that were unusual, even in the high mortality regime of the early
nineteenth century.

In some of the autobiographies prepared for publication, it was the very
fact of publication that caused writers (or their publishers) to remain silent
on certain aspects of their life. More than one writer had chalked up experiences that they had little relish to publicise. Take, for example, the writer
and Radical, Thomas Frost. Although he did refer to his marriage to his
first wife in his *Recollections*, he did not mention that he married a second
time, following her death. Nor did he describe how he subsequently left his
second wife and cohabited with another woman for many years.[22] When
Ellen Johnston described the birth of her illegitimate daughter, she was
censured by a reviewer in the *Glasgow Sentinel* for discussing incidents 'that
it would have been better to keep back'. All mention of the affair was duly
excised from the second edition published a few years later.[23] Middle-class
notions of decency governed the publishing world and helped to ensure
that many writers censored themselves before going into print.

Even those who wrote for personal reasons without a view to publication still had an audience in mind influencing their decisions about what

merited inclusion and what did not. The reasons underpinning the exclusion of some experiences were not always deep or profound. John Bennett was born in the quiet Wiltshire village of South Wraxall, but left as an adolescent in search of work in Bristol. In old age he succumbed to the wishes of his children, and wrote down for them an account of his 'walks through life'.[24] Having recorded some recollections from his childhood, he informed his family that 'many things ... happened during the time I was in the country, which I don't think it worthwhile to repeat'. He added though that they would, 'if so inclined find them in a bundle, somewhere about'.[25] If his children ever did find the bundle of childhood reminiscences, the historians have not. For many reasons, then, the account of working-class life contained in the autobiographies should not be thought complete or comprehensive. There are always omissions stemming from reticence, prudery and the chance survival of some records and not others. Life histories do not give a glorious Technicolor view of working-class life; they give glimpses of reality, with some parts left obscured in the shadows.

Not only is much left out, but there is a host of difficulties concerning what was put in. Failures of memory, inherent subjectivity and the retrospective imposition of meaning and order on events experienced without meaning or order are inevitable.[26] These problems have seemed so insurmountable that some have gloomily concluded that autobiographies are a form of literature – even fiction – revealing how working-class writers chose to present themselves, but not to be trusted as a window on the 'reality' of working-class life.[27]

Such head-scratching would no doubt seem curious to our autobiographers, who refused to be detained too long by the possibility that their writing might be found wanting in terms of truth and objectivity. In the eighteenth century, John MacDonald prefaced his colourful memoirs of life as a footman with the declaration that he would write 'with perfect impartiality'.[28] William Hutton informed his reader that he had 'adhered to facts ... there is not a statement either false or coloured'.[29] In the nineteenth century, James Nye believed that 'many people will tell the bright part of their life, but I will be honest and put it down black and white, if there is any white'.[30]

We might smile at the innocence of our pre-modern writers and are certainly not bound to accept their claims of neutrality. Yet we should take seriously their attempts to present a truthful and accurate account of their lives, and to shed light more generally on the lives of the unlettered communities from which they sprang. In the preface to his handwritten

'Worldly Experience', John Hemmingway admitted to his daughter that she would not find 'every word and sentence grammatically correct'. Yet he continued that she would find an informative narrative, written for the 'vulgar class of society', that was 'both plain and legible'.[31] Hemmingway and others believed they had given their readers material to understand their world. Working towards this understanding is not always easy or straightforward, but there is much to be gained by the endeavour.

Above all, we should work with these autobiographies because we can. In our enthusiasm to show awareness of their shortcomings, we have sometimes overlooked their value. And the value of life-writing to the historian is very real indeed. These autobiographies and memoirs represent a very special set of records in which working people set out to describe their lives in their own words and for their own purposes. Of course there are other places to which we may turn if we want to know something about working-class life – the mountain of papers generated by the administration of the Poor Law, the criminal courts, or parliamentary commissions, to name a few. But such documents were always the outcome of an uneven encounter between those who had power and those who did not. And in this respect, life histories and autobiographies are both unusual and unique. Here is a collection of personal stories freely narrated by the ordinary men and women we wish to understand and it is worth emphasising the rarity of historical testimony of this kind. For all their shortcomings, the autobiographies offer the best way – indeed the only way – to examine the lives of working people during a critical epoch in world history.

In looking at the encounter between industrialisation and the working poor, this book takes up a theme – that the industrial revolution degraded and exploited workers – that has exercised writers and thinkers since the first quarter of the nineteenth century. Not that there was anything new about poverty and exploitation. Toiling away for scant reward had been the lot of mankind since the dawn of time. Yet thinkers and intellectuals were, by and large, content to file away destitution as an ordinance from God, a fact so universal that it hardly called for serious investigation. Until, that is, the early nineteenth century. As Britain rose to global pre-eminence, educated elites paused to ponder the continued existence of so much seething misery at the heart of a modern country blessed with unprecedented wealth. With characteristic style, the historian Thomas Carlyle deplored the degradation of the 'working body of this rich English Nation'.

And writers from across the political spectrum took up their pens to join Carlyle in debating the 'Condition of England'.

The educated few had been muttering about the failure of the nation's increasing wealth to better the condition of the labouring poor since the end of the eighteenth century. In the 1790s, Thomas Malthus' gloomy predictions concerning the consequences of unchecked population growth, and the investigations of the Rev. Mr David Davies and Sir Frederick Eden into the hardships created by rising food prices, opened a new line of enquiry into the living standards of the poor. By the early nineteenth century, interest in the question extended beyond political economists. Poets may be found searching for ways of capturing the dramatic changes to landscapes and social life from Blake's evocative lines on the 'dark Satanic Mills' to Wordsworth's critique of the 'outrage done to nature' by the growth of urban industry.[32] These ideas found their fullest expression in the industrial novels of Benjamin Disraeli, Elizabeth Gaskell and Charles Dickens, published in the 1840s and 1850s. In *Hard Times*, Dickens depicted a workforce that was not only desperately poor, but also degraded and dehumanised by the advent of machines.[33] Disraeli's *Sybil* drew attention to the gulf between rich and poor – the 'two nations' that formed the subtitle of his novel.[34] Popular writers such as William Cobbett chimed in, regretting the disappearance of merry England and the gentrification of farmers as their 'labourers became *slaves*'.[35] And as the discussion moved back into the more measured realm of political economy the same bleak assessment prevailed. John Stuart Mill concluded that society's mechanical inventions had done no more than 'enable a greater proportion to live the same life of drudgery and imprisonment'.[36] By the middle of the nineteenth century, a broad and unlikely alliance of poets, novelists, philosophers and political economists, conservatives and Radicals united in lamenting the failure of recent economic change to improve the lot of the labouring poor. The critics of industrial society had found their voice.

Yet the most enduring legacy came not from these English writers but from a German visitor. The young Friedrich Engels spent two years in Manchester in the early 1840s. His father had organised the stay to give his son a chance to complete his training in his own line of business – the cotton industry. But Friedrich, already deeply involved in the German Radical movement, seized upon the trip as an opportunity to conduct a first-hand study of the lives of the workers the factory employed. The result, *The Condition of the Working Class in England*, shone a bright light on the most unsavoury consequences of England's industrial transformation.

Engels based his account on the borrowed notion of a more primitive, but more contented, past where cottagers had enjoyed a material condition 'far better than that of their successors'.[37] For Engels, the working-class losses extended beyond the material. He conceived the industrial revolution as a rapid, large-scale social transformation, involving the change from one way of life to another and placing novel strains on the human condition. And in this scheme the workers' losses were cultural as much as financial, entailing the disappearance of stable family and community relationships; of homes in the clean rural environment; and of health and contentment.[38]

It perhaps goes without saying that much of the vitality of the Condition of England debate derived from the few dissenting voices that pictured the working class enjoying new levels of prosperity and contentment. The defenders of industrialisation constituted an equally diverse alliance of writers and thinkers – Harriet Martineau, Andrew Ure, Edward Baines, John Rickman, to name a few – although they lack the profile of the critics. Edwin Chadwick, whose pioneering research into the living conditions of urban slums formed the basis of the nation's earliest public health measures, nonetheless believed that in strictly monetary terms, the new town dwellers were sharing in the nation's newfound wealth: 'wages, or the means of obtaining the necessaries of life for the whole mass of the labouring community,' he wrote, 'have advanced, and the comforts within the reach of the labouring classes have increased with the late increase of population.'[39] Yet for the most part his contemporaries were not convinced. Just beneath the veneer of Victorian economic and cultural progress, they feared, lay a mass of unnecessary human suffering. Worse still, their comforts were bought at the expense of the workers' well-being.

With the passage of time, the industrial revolution gradually slipped from lived experience to historical event. As it did so, the task of dissecting its social consequences fell into the hands of historians. Throughout the late nineteenth and early twentieth centuries, a succession of writers, inclined towards the Left and successfully marrying a scholarly interest in the poor with active engagement in the social problems of their own times, tackled the big ideas of this transition. Arnold Toynbee, Sidney and Beatrice Webb, and John and Barbara Hammond stand out as key figures in the consolidation of the dark interpretation of working-class life with their numerous books and pamphlets easily accessible to readers outside the academy. All were broadly sympathetic to Engels' views, and his template – declining living standards accompanied by a deterioration in social life – resurfaced time and time again in their work.

First, Arnold Toynbee. The circumstances surrounding the publication of Toynbee's short book were far from ideal. Following his premature death from meningitis aged just thirty, his *Industrial Revolution* was published from the notes taken by students who had attended his Oxford lectures in the 1880s. The ease with which historians have criticised his account for inaccuracies and inconsistency is therefore hardly surprising. Yet whatever its shortcomings, there can be no disputing its immense influence. Here is Toynbee describing the advent of industrialisation:

> We now approach a darker period – a period as disastrous and as terrible as any through which a nation ever passed; disastrous and terrible because side by side with a great increase of wealth was seen an enormous increase of pauperism [and] the degradation of a large body of producers ... The steam-engine, the spinning-jenny, the power-loom had torn up the population by the roots ... The effects of the Industrial Revolution prove that free competition may produce wealth without producing well-being.[40]

Toynbee ushered the expression 'industrial revolution' into the English language, and his social interpretation of that newly named event continued to inform opinion through much of the twentieth century.

Toynbee's ideas passed first to the Webbs, and from them to the Hammonds, the pioneer social historians whose trilogy, *The Village Labourer* (1911), *The Town Labourer* (1917) and *The Skilled Labourer* (1919), unpacked the consequences of the industrial revolution for different sections of the labouring poor. Over three volumes and nearly a thousand pages, the Hammonds gave a far more ambitious, wide-ranging and detailed account than any hitherto attempted. But whilst the research and scholarship that underpinned their books was original, their interpretation was essentially derivative. The Hammonds' account repeated the well-tried formula that industrialisation was a catastrophe for the generations of ordinary workpeople who lived through it. It was Engels repackaged for the early twentieth century's popular history market.

There was, of course, the occasional dissenting voice. John H. Clapham, Professor of Economic History at Cambridge, turned to the emerging field of statistics to dispel 'the legend that everything was getting worse for the working man'.[41] Taking a well-aimed swipe at the 'historians who neglect quantities', Clapham sought to demonstrate that wages had 'risen markedly' and concluded that his predecessors' 'excessive concentration on the shadows of the historical landscape' had led them to ignore 'the patches of

sunlight'.[42] But whilst the historical profession was broadly appreciative of
Clapham's effort, the Cambridge professor never quite managed to lift the
gloom that had by now taken hold of the popular imagination. His *Economic
History* cost more than double the Hammonds' popular histories and the
qualities that academics prized – his 'comprehensive, well documented
statements' gathered from 'the harvest of years of austere research', his 'ripe
mastery of the sources of economic history', and his refusal 'to simplify or
to generalize' – did little to endear him to the general reader.[43] In any case
Engels' capacious understanding of social change during the industrial
revolution allowed the pessimists to shift ground away from 'quantities' and
back to the lived experience. When John Hammond wrote: 'Let us take it
that so far as statistics can measure material improvement there was
improvement', he was not suggesting that Clapham had resolved the
matter.[44] Instead, the statement prefaced an attempt to move away from
the quantifiable to those social and cultural experiences upon which
statistics could never 'throw a great deal of light'.

The assault on Clapham's optimistic interpretation continued in the
post-war years with a new generation of socialist and Marxist historians
confident that recent advances in the science of economics would finally
decide the matter. Within the pages of the learned journals, academics,
sharply divided into the 'optimist' and 'pessimist' camps, conducted one of
the most acrimonious and polarised debates in the profession's history. Not
for nothing did Eric Hobsbawm describe the terrain as a 'battlefield'.[45] Yet
quantification failed to end the debate, and R. M. Hartwell, Hobsbawm's
chief opponent, later reflected that it would never be resolved, 'no matter
how much evidence is ultimately brought to bear on the issue'.[46] The fragmentary data and the uncertainties and complexities surrounding its
manipulation posed insuperable difficulties. Economic history could not, it
turned out, deliver its promise of an objective measure of the workers'
welfare during the industrial revolution.

It was at this point that E. P. Thompson made an appearance. His
*Making of the English Working Class*, published in 1963, was very quickly
recognised as a work of rare quality and insight. The demand for copies
from the growing university sector and interested general reader appeared
insatiable, and the publishers were no doubt as surprised as they were
delighted by the runaway commercial success of a book written by a little-
known lecturer in the Extra-Mural Department at the University of Leeds.
In 1968, Pelican Books bought the rights to *The Making* and published a
revised version as the thousandth book in their list. In less than a decade it

had gone through a further five reprints. *The Making* is still in print and still hailed as a canonical text, gracing the reading lists of history courses in Britain and beyond, both within and without the university. It is a very rare history book that stands the test of time so well.

Despite the furore in the journals about the fate of real wages, Thompson refused to be detained too long by the question of measurable, monetary gains. As he calmly noted, 'it is quite possible for statistical averages and human experiences to run in opposite directions'.[47] Instead, he focused on those 'human experiences', sketching out the lives and values of the little people that great works of history had hitherto ignored. And although historians found plenty to criticise in Thompson's landmark book, the broader framework – the exploitation, the immiseration, the oppression, the human suffering – was largely immune from criticism. As a result, Thompson produced an extraordinarily powerful restatement of the dark and bleak interpretation.

In the fifty years that have passed since the publication of *The Making*, historians have never lost interest in the impact of the industrial revolution on ordinary people, though the terms of debate have shifted considerably. Whereas Thompson sought to understand 'experience' (a word he used eight times in his six-page preface), the focus in recent years has been on quantification. In pursuit of definitive answers, historians have turned increasingly to economics and statistics. Measuring the real wage, for instance, continues to occupy a small body of economic historians, who remain active in mining the archives for more data and refining their equations.[48] Others have sought to evaluate such things as working hours, the extent of child labour, and death rates.[49] A new line of enquiry has also been opened on well-being and food welfare, with estimates of calorie consumption and adult heights.[50] Producing graphs and tables is more in vogue than asking how the workers felt.

Yet though today's historians search for new ways to answer the questions that Thompson posed, there is rather less that is new about their conclusions. For all these writers (and there are more than a few) tend to see the industrialising world in the same way.[51] However living standards are measured, historians report stagnation or decline. Evidence of modest rises is gloomily dismissed as a paltry recompense for the labouring families that had done the most to create the substantial economic growth that occurred over the period. And even these modest improvements are reduced to nothing when the deteriorating industrial environment is brought into the balance. Today's intellectuals understand the industrial revolution in much the same way as the educated elites who lived through it. Historians, like contemporaries, evince a degree of guilt over the price that others paid for the comforts and privileges that we enjoy in a mature industrial society. It has been a very long time since the critics of industrialisation could plausibly deny the long-term benefits of industrial growth. Nonetheless, even the most circumspect continue to claim that these gains must have been bought with the blood, sweat and tears of the workers who experienced at first hand its grinding effects.

The only difficulty is that the autobiographies, those rare and unique records in which the labouring poor retold their stories, refuse to co-operate. It is surely surprising that in spite of ongoing interest in how the industrial revolution was experienced by the poor, no one has opened the pages of the books and notebooks where the poor wrote about just that. Historians have measured wages and working hours with meticulous care, yet none has sought to listen to, or make sense of, the messy tales that the workers left behind. In the pages that follow, we shall do precisely that. And as we shall find, if we listen rather than count, we shall start to see the industrial revolution in a very different light.

Time and time again, our working-class writers describe complex and untidy lives, irreducible to one common theme or overarching narrative. Of course these people sometimes endured bleak periods involving material hardships or emotional difficulties. Yet no matter how we try, it is not possible to frame the autobiographical literature within the dark interpretation without imposing a wilful distortion upon the messages our writers are seeking to communicate.

Let us turn back for a moment to John Lincoln. John certainly knew plenty about privation. Poverty blighted his childhood, splintering apart his family and breaking his health. Quite apart from the crack in his skull caused by a flying hemp-wheel, the work in one of his childhood placements was, in his opinion, so hard that 'it stunted my growth'.[52] The few years of prosperity he enjoyed while working in the Royal Arsenal at Woolwich – 'the work was very Light and the pay very good' – proved to be transient. The war came to an end, the government's orders for weapons fell away, and John, now remarried, soon found himself scraping around for work in the fields and the farmhouses once more. There was rarely enough to keep the wolf from the door.

In 1816 his life sank to its lowest ebb. John and Sarah still lived close by the Royal Arsenal at Woolwich, but John was unable to find regular work and Sarah was too busy caring for their daughter and baby son to look for work outside the home. Perhaps the love of their two small children was a drop of consolation for a life of penury, but whatever domestic satisfactions they enjoyed were soon to be shattered. In January measles, a highly contagious childhood disease, infected the household. Their elder child fell sick first; in the space of two weeks both children were dead. 'If we were unhappy before,' recalled John, 'we were duble unhappy now.'[53] The couple's misery was compounded by poverty in the following months as John 'was chifely out of imploy and the winter came on was miserable for we had sold and pawned all our furniture and all Sunday Clothes – for bread – some times we went the whole day with about two or three potatoes twice in that time.'[54] Is this not the kind of immiseration that critics have long argued was caused by industrialisation? Might not the harrowing events endured by this family in 1816 be used to support the claim that the industrial revolution did nothing for the first few generations of working families that lived through it?

Yet we cannot leave John in the winter of 1816, bereaved, unemployed and hungry. Moreover, linking his misfortune to the process of industrialisation is simply dishonest. The root of John's poverty was not industrialisation, but its absence. The counties of Suffolk and Norfolk in which Lincoln spent most of his life were left almost entirely untouched by mechanisation, industrialisation and urbanisation, and the difficulties that John experienced in earning a living during the dull winter months were timeless and universal in pre-industrial Britain. It might be true that economic progress did not bring many gains for the first few generations, but the poverty of a family in rural Norfolk does not prove the point.

And the difficulties of situating John's experiences in the pessimistic view do not end here. As critics have long argued, the industrial revolution was above all a social phenomenon, touching not simply the economic sphere, but also 'moral and other non-material territories'.[55] Yet attention has been focused for so long upon the way change destroyed older and valued ways of life that historians have largely failed to notice the gains that many working men wrought for themselves out of the turmoil. John may have worked in an agricultural village, but he lived in a changing world, some aspects of which he experienced directly in the arms factories at Woolwich. In the pages that follow, we will see how the urban growth and social reorientation of these years changed the fabric of British society in subtle and myriad ways. For the present, I want to suggest that one consequence of industrialisation was to broaden the mental horizons of those who had traditionally had little to contribute to the intellectual life of the nation. At least in the case of

John Lincoln, it certainly opened new avenues for cultural and personal expression.

John's 'Simple Naritive' was never conceived as a critique of economic change. It was most certainly not a lament for the simplicity of a lost, pre-industrial life. In describing the depths to which he and his wife sank in 1816 John sought to highlight the poverty he had experienced at first hand, but these dark sufferings were not intended to define his life. The defining event was yet to come. John's story continued, and out of the depths of personal and economic misery he eventually found solace in hearing the preaching at the Baptist Chapel. The dull services of the Church of England had done nothing for John. The years passed by, but John rarely stepped inside a place of worship aside from the 'Naming our children and at their Burial'.[56] He liked to sing, he admitted, but in alehouses not churches. In any case, for much of his life John was so poor that he lacked the respectable Sunday clothes that the Church's clergymen expected their flock to wear. And then, at some time after the privations of 1816, John began to turn the matter of religion over in his mind. The lady of the village bought him a nice bible and prayer book and his master had provided him with some 'tidy Cloaths', so he decided to go to church on Sunday – though he did so, he confessed, more from 'curiosity and Pride' than from religious conviction. Once there, however, the minister touched 'my eyes, my ears, my heart'.[57] He started to attend weekly services. His religious commitment grew and within a few years he had begun to preach the occasional sermon. Then, back in Oxborough where he had embarked on married life with the stout and hot-tempered Ann many years before, he opened his 'humble Cottage' as a meeting house, determined 'to bring the inhabitants of Oxborough under the sound of the Gospel'.[58] This, then, was not a man oppressed by poverty. It was a man who had found freedom and even a small drop of power, despite his poverty.

It is worth emphasising how far John Lincoln pushed against traditional cultural boundaries when he opened the doors of his cottage and began preaching the Gospel to his neighbours. There was a long tradition of dissenting religions in Britain, which had always been far more open than the established Church to preachers from humble backgrounds. Yet even allowing for these precedents, a man like Lincoln was not supposed to teach the Gospel. John fathered his first child out of wedlock. His second son bore the taint of illegitimacy. His third child too was conceived before marriage. John Lincoln did not conform to the Church's notions of sexual propriety and respectability. John was also a poor man. He was poor at his birth and remained poor throughout his life, never rising above his station as a day labourer, living from one day to the next by the labour of his hands and frequently unable to earn enough to support his family decently. In fact, that 'humble Cottage' that he turned into a preaching house was not his at all. It was provided by the parish as his income was too low and too precarious for him to find lodging for his family without help. Yet here he was. Not sitting in the pews designated for the poor at the back of the parish church, listening to a religion which taught that the poor will always be with us, but standing at the front, delivering his interpretation of God's teaching. John had a voice in his own community, and because he wrote down his memoirs his voice can still be heard today. It is time to take voices such as his more seriously.

The downbeat narrative of working-class life during the industrial revolution may be cathartic for some. But it is not good history. John Lincoln, like many of the authors whom we will get to know, was an exceptional man. The opportunities that he grasped were not. John lived in a time of economic growth and social flux and one outcome of these forces was the throwing open of opportunities for those at the bottom of the social pile. Industrial growth provided the labouring poor with a degree of personal freedom that the poor in the eighteenth century and before had rarely enjoyed. This is not to dismiss the pages of evidence documenting low wages, long hours, poor diet, unsanitary housing and all the rest that several generations of outraged and apologetic historians have produced. It may all be true. Nonetheless, this dismal litany of industrialisation's failure to adequately recompense working men must be tempered by an appreciation of their own sense of empowerment. Economic exploitation and political oppression could live side by side with newfound and much-valued personal freedoms. Or (to borrow from E. P. Thompson) statistical averages and human experiences can run in opposite directions.

So here is an alternative account of labour and the industrial revolution. My goal is not to root out some 'patches of sunlight' in the name of historical novelty. Nor do I wish to replace one simple story (things were bad and getting worse) with another (they never had it so good!). The pattern was complex. Just as statistical averages and human experiences can run counter to each other, so too can the experiences of different people. Men, women and children, we will see, felt the advent of industrialisation in very different ways. The patches of sunlight certainly shone more brightly on men than on their wives or children.

Above all, we need to listen more carefully to what our first-hand witnesses are trying to tell us. In recounting their journeys to adulthood and self-understanding, in the sheer fact of writing an autobiography at all, our writers communicated something about their place in a changing world. It is time to think the unthinkable: that these writers viewed themselves not as downtrodden losers but as men and women in control of their destiny; that the industrial revolution heralded the advent not of a yet 'darker period', but of the dawn of liberty.

# PART I

## EARNING A LIVING

The labourer's appetite works for him; his hunger drives him on.
(Proverbs, 16: 26)

Sweating, slaving, and tormoiling,
When in the midst of all their toiling,
When most they thought to reap the pleasure,
And sattisfaction of their treasure

Just at the instant they propose,
To have the blessings of repose,
Some most unlucky thunder shower,
Come down from heaven upon the poor.
(John Hemmingway, p. 27)

IT IS TO work that we turn first, inevitably and necessarily. The poor spent most of their lives working hard to keep the proverbial wolf from the door. With work starting in childhood and continuing for as long as one had the health to perform it, it was, without a doubt, the central experience of any labourer's life.

But the nature, necessity and rewards of work were experienced by different members of the working-class family in very uneven ways. At the head of the ideal family stood the male breadwinner. Men were called upon to take up the hardest, dirtiest and most dangerous occupations. But with this responsibility came certain compensations – the possibility of learning skills, of earning better wages, of improving one's status and even of deriving a measure of satisfaction from work. How different the purpose and rewards of work for small children. The prospect of earning status, satisfaction, or even a fair reward for their labour was almost non-existent for these most vulnerable members of the workforce. And for women, matters were different yet again. Paid employment did not mix well with the running of a household and the care of small children. Not of course that the endless scrubbing, cooking, washing, and all the rest required to keep the workman's family clean, fed and clothed do not constitute work. The point rather is that many women spent much of their lives performing the unpaid work of the home rather than in paid employment for the market.

This then determines the format of the three chapters that follow. We consider, in turn, the experience of men, children, and women in the workplace. How did the individuals within each of these groups procure the wherewithal to eat? How did the experience of work vary according to age, gender and class? And how were these working lives disrupted or changed by the onset of the industrial revolution?

# CHAPTER TWO

# Men at Work

Week after week, and month after month, and season after season, for a period of nine years, the very prime of my manhood, did I thus drudge [in a tan-yard] . . . My past reverses and pressing necessities had taught me the value of regular employment. ('Jacques', 1 November 1856)

As a miner I did very well and made my earning about seven pounds a month. (Oliver, p. 18)

SINCE THE MOMENT that the term 'industrial revolution' entered our language, most writers have believed that the process went hand in hand with the destruction of older, more benign, working patterns. Engels' *Condition of the Working Class in England* gave an unflattering, and hugely influential, account of the newly created factory system. He informed his middle-class readers of the ill health, physical deformities and accidents caused by very long hours of work at machines; and the discipline, oppressive and petty in equal measure, that subjugated the hapless worker to fines for lateness, but also for activities as innocuous as singing, whistling and laughing.[1] Of course, there were the factory apologists who found social progress and happiness for all in the move towards mechanised industry. But claims (such as those of Andrew Ure) that factory workers enjoyed light labour in pleasant conditions and that whatever ill health they suffered stemmed from their tendency to consume the wrong sort of bacon and too much tobacco and gin displayed such ignorance and insensitivity that they failed to make any impression on subsequent assessments of work during the 'Bleak Age'.[2]

If the outlines of the dark view were first sketched by Engels, historians of the twentieth century added much of the subsequent shading. A succession of pioneering social histories painted an unremittingly grim picture, with the imposition of longer hours, the subordination of the individual worker, and the introduction of work that was more monotonous, more intensive, and less meaningful.[3] As E. P. Thompson summarised with his usual eloquence: 'It is neither poverty nor disease but work itself which cast the blackest shadow over the years of the Industrial Revolution ... long hours of unsatisfying labour under severe discipline for alien purposes'.[4] More recent academic judgements slot neatly into the same framework, providing a little more detail, illuminating the odd unexplored corner, but not, ultimately, disturbing the perceived wisdom. Yes, working hours were extended.[5] Yes, the position of the traditional artisan and skilled labourer was eroded.[6] Yes, factory discipline and new working methods rendered workloads more intensive and relentless.[7] And yes, punitive criminal sanctions were used to coerce labour from a supposedly 'free' labour force.[8]

At first blush, the autobiographies seem to amply confirm the historians' grim assessments. Take William Dodd's account of his life as a factory boy. Starting work at a Cumbrian woollen mill at the tender age of six, William's life entered a period of 'uninterrupted, unmitigated suffering'.[9] The long hours and unnatural posture at the spinning machines soon left him with seriously bowed knees. By early adulthood, William was (in his own words) a 'miserable cripple'.[10] The noxious smells, deafening machines, unnatural rhythms, extremes of heat and cold, and deformed bodies – all were recounted in careful detail. The injustice of 'toiling and sweating day after day for the bare necessities of life [while] the manufacturers were amassing immense wealth' left William disgusted with the system.[11] He quit in his early thirties, in search of a better life outside the confines of the factory walls.

But using life-writing to retell the dark story of the industrial revolution is not quite such an easy or straightforward matter. William Dodd, after all, was active in the factory reform movement, so it would surely be naïve to imagine that his political convictions did not colour his account of life as a factory child. He was also describing experiences from childhood. Writers tended to remember their *adult* years in the mill, mine or forge in a far more positive light. Recalling his seven-year apprenticeship in a Lancashire factory, one anonymous writer declared that he 'was never as happy as I was at that time'.[12] Still working at the mill during the early years of his marriage, he and his new wife enjoyed plenty of money and good furniture. No wonder then that 'things went on very smoothly for a long time'.[13]

In Scotland, the cotton mills held out similar attractions to Charles Campbell. By any measure, Campbell led a chequered life. He spent his childhood working in a cotton mill in the lowland town of Johnstone, but as a young adult decided to exchange the monotony of Johnstone for a life on the seas. There he certainly found the adventure he sought. When his captain and most of his crew were killed by yellow fever, he ended up spending two years working in the West Indies. The experience was enough to persuade him to make his living once more on British soil. On his return to Scotland he gained enough medical training from Glasgow University to establish a small medical practice in a west Highland village. But when this failed to pay its way, Campbell decided to seek out a 'more congenial situation'.[14] What did he choose? What, for a man who had spent his youth in a cotton mill, could be more congenial than a small country medical practice? Campbell knew of something better. He became a spinner in one of Glasgow's many cotton factories, where he earned a hefty 30 shillings a week. For these workers, the good wages and regular work that could be found in the factories more than compensated for the clatter of the machines. Some writers, it seems, simply refused to tell the story of working lives blighted by the advent of mechanisation.

These difficulties are compounded by the slant of our sources. Some writers took up the pen precisely because they had been born into a life of illiteracy and hard, manual labour but managed by dint of perseverance to escape the life mapped out at birth. They became teachers, preachers, poets, scientists, politicians: at some stage leaving behind their overalls and smocks and taking up a more comfortable job sitting down in the warm. For these men manual labour was effectively a life stage, rather than, as it was for most ordinary workers, a continuous state that lasted as long as their capacity to perform it. Then there is the uneven spread of records over the pre-industrial and industrial eras. As we move back in time, fewer autobiographies survive, and those that exist become ever less concerned with temporal matters. The result is that working lives before the industrial revolution are usually discussed in the most cursory of terms. So despite the relative abundance of our source material, there are gaps and imbalances that make it difficult to get at the truth about the nature of work for the labouring poor and the way in which it changed with industrialisation.

Difficult, but not impossible. Making sense of our autobiographers' stories requires defining with care the questions that need to be answered.

It is my belief that opportunities in the workplace were brighter for adult men in the late eighteenth and early nineteenth centuries than they had been at any other time in the eighteenth century or before. Work, and more particularly the wages that went with it, was a powerful tool for raising a man's status within his family and his community. The trouble historically has been that there simply was not enough work to go around. Not enough, at least, to provide workers with much independence from their employers or to allow them much autonomy in their personal lives. Autobiographies can shed light upon some of these issues. With nearly 350, it is possible to identify genuine developments in the extent and nature of work available in the eighteenth and nineteenth centuries.[15]

An idea of the scope of the autobiographies can be captured by looking at Edward Barlow's 'journal', a handwritten memoir of the early eighteenth century which recounts his successful career as first sailor, then captain. Barlow was born in 1642 in Prestwich, then a village about five miles from Manchester, now a settlement physically connected to the city through urban sprawl and subsumed administratively by the metropolitan county of Greater Manchester. Barlow was not the only autobiographer who 'never had any great mind to country work'. Ploughing, sowing, haymaking, reaping, hedging, ditching, threshing and dunging amongst cattle were all, in his opinion, 'drudgery'.[16] But his prospects for quitting the plough in mid-seventeenth-century Lancashire were not bright. His parents lacked the means to provide him with an apprenticeship, and in any case, nobody in the neighbourhood seemed to need an apprentice. Eventually an opening with a whitester came up. The work involved bleaching yarn for the weaving trade. He went on a 'liking' – a trial period – but returned two weeks later informing his parents that he did not in fact like it at all, and persuaded them to let him come back. But resettling at home was not straightforward. Returning to his village after refusing to be bound apprentice to a trade he did not like, he faced his father's displeasure and comments from the neighbours, 'asking why I could not stay at my place . . . [and] hitting me in the teeth'.[17] The good folk of Prestwich, it seems, did not take too kindly to the return of a neighbour who had turned down work in Manchester and had nothing better to say for himself than that he did not like it.

Several clues in Barlow's account indicate that work around mid-seventeenth-century Prestwich was in short supply. Prior to his apprentice-ship to the whitester, Barlow was clearly not fully employed – he described himself as 'troublesome' to his parents when 'out of work'. And even when in work, he earned 'but small wages'. Yet despite his small and irregular

earnings, he continued in Prestwich for some years as nobody in the neighbourhood was hiring apprentices: he stayed with his parents until 'at last'
his father heard of a man 'willing to take an apprentice'. This small whitester's business was not even at work the year round: during the winter they
'worked but little at the trade', so they did threshing, hedging, ditching and
'other country work' instead. Then there was the response of his neighbours
when he turned down work with the whitester and returned to the
village. Their hostility to the return of one of their own suggests they did
not welcome another pair of hands competing for work in the village – too
many workers posed a serious problem when one day's work bought the
next day's meal. Using autobiographies to capture the changes in men's
working lives during the period of industrialisation is not straightforward.
Nonetheless, Barlow's account of trying to earn a living in the seventeenth
century offers a clue to some of the questions that we might ask in order to
make sense of the ways in which working lives changed over the following
two centuries.

Let us begin by looking at the world of skilled labour – the shoemakers,
carpenters, blacksmiths, butchers and other artisans who formed the back-
bone of the pre-industrial, urban economy. Though the factories and mines
provide us with the most dramatic manifestation of industrial growth, large
numbers continued to find employment in a raft of occupations whose
processes were changed hardly at all by new working methods. The traditional way of learning such trades was by apprenticeship, worked according
to a legally binding contract between master and apprentice, with obliga-
tions on either side. The usual expectation was that the master would
provide lodging, board, training, and often wages as well, for a set period of
time, typically seven years. In return for this training, the apprentice's family
paid an upfront fee, or premium, and the apprentice himself was bound to
work for his master, accepting below-market wages or sometimes even no
wages at all. At the end of the specified term, the apprentice's indentures
were cancelled and he obtained his 'freedom': the freedom to leave his
master and to work at his trade for whomever he pleased. The Statute of
Artificers, 1562, had limited the practice of most skilled trades to those
who had served their time, so despite the expense an apprenticeship had
the potential to secure very real long-term advantages in the workplace.[18]

The skeleton of the apprenticeship system was still visible in the late
eighteenth century, though much had changed since Barlow's time. Over
the century, terms were becoming shorter and by the century's end the
prohibition on trading without an apprenticeship was in many trades a

dead letter, though it was not until the repeal of the relevant clauses of the Statute of Artificers Act in 1814 that it was formally abolished.[19] The autobiographies let us sketch out the ways in which these changes altered the daily life of skilled artisans. Above all, our working-class writers illustrate how the unmaking of some elements of the apprenticeship system introduced a new degree of fluidity and openness to the world of skilled labour, especialy in two of the most common and easily learned trades – shoemaking and tailoring.

In the 1760s, Thomas Hardy was the first of several autobiographers to take advantage of easier, cheaper and more flexible ways of learning a skilled trade. Hardy's family had fallen upon hard times following his father's death, so his mother, unable to pay the premium for an apprenticeship, sent young Thomas to learn shoemaking from her father. When he had taught him all he knew, Thomas moved to Glasgow to improve his skills by working in a better-class establishment.[20] Within a matter of years, Thomas was making his living as shoemaker, despite never having served an apprenticeship. In subsequent years, these kinds of stories about the learning of shoemaking and tailoring resurface many times.[21] Thomas Carter, for instance, learned the tailoring trade in this way. His father was a day labourer with a heavy drinking habit, and there was no question of his summoning the means to pay for an apprenticeship. But Thomas' parents did manage to find him a position as an errand boy to a prosperous woollendraper who employed twelve men in his tailors' shop. By rising early and spending the first hour of the day assisting one of the tailors, Thomas learned just enough about clothes-making to subsequently set himself up in business as a tailor.[22]

By the early nineteenth century, tailors and shoemakers were more likely to learn their skills outside an apprenticeship than within. They picked up the rudiments of their trade while working as a dogsbody in a workshop.[23] Some perfected their skills later by paying for teaching from a more highly skilled, urban craftsman. A similar route was taken by many of the bakers, butchers, carpenters, coopers, metalworkers and shipwrights.[24] Other more unusual trades were also accessible outside the apprenticeship system. Amongst those who became skilled labourers without ever mustering the means to pay their master a premium were a coach-trimmer, chair-maker, knife-grinder, shopkeeper, and a maker of pearl ornaments.[25]

The creation of new ways to learn a skilled trade has sometimes been dismissed as evidence of the 'deskilling' of the independent artisan that occurred during the industrial revolution.[26] But the beauty of skilled labour is very much in the eye of the beholder. Of course, the protected status of those who had served an apprenticeship was valuable to the fortunate few; but it did little for those who by dint of poverty were left outside. From their perspective, the relaxation of entry to the trades was wholly advantageous. Take, for example, the experiences of Thomas Dunning. Thomas' family was never going to pay for him to learn a skilled trade. His father had chosen to remain in service following his marriage, leaving his wife to raise their two sons alone. Given Mrs Dunning's desperate attempts to earn a little money, it seems unlikely that her husband was sending much, if any, of his wages home. When he lost his place in service, his contribution to the family's welfare deteriorated further: he stole his wife's linen and other household goods, then found Thomas at work and begged him to give him what little money he had. Thomas' 'poor dear mother', meanwhile, was so reduced in circumstances that she had left her youngest son in the care of a friend and returned to service. It seems highly unlikely that this man would willingly pay for his son's apprenticeship, while his wife was clearly unable to do so. So at the age of twelve, instead of entering an apprenticeship, he 'had to turn out ... to earn a few shillings and a bit of food'.[27]

But following the death of his father, matters for Thomas began to look up. His mother married a 'shoe manufacturer' and rather than see her son depart as a merchant sailor for the East India Company, she persuaded her new husband to teach him shoemaking instead. This he did, and Thomas quickly became proficient in his stepfather's line of business – rough shoes for the workpeople of Lancashire. As Thomas wished to 'master the best class of ladies' boots and shoes', however, he left off working for his stepfather and went to lodge with the Cooke brothers, excellent shoemakers who agreed to teach him 'to finish best goods suitable for the first-rate shop in town' in return for payment. From these men he learned how to make fine ladies' shoes, and worked at this for several years.[28] Through most of the eighteenth century, the poverty and misfortune of Thomas' family would have prevented him from entering an apprenticeship and closed down the possibility of his ever becoming a shoemaker. In the 1820s, by contrast, he was able to take advantage of well-established alternative routes to the world of skilled labour.

It was only in the most skilled and complex trades that apprenticeships remained the norm. Almost none of the many printers amongst the autobiographers, for example, had learned their work outside a formal, seven-year apprenticeship.[29] None of the wood carvers and gilders, or cutlers had.[30] Elsewhere, skilled workmen sought to keep the doors to their ranks firmly closed to those who had not served their time. Trade societies were stripped of their legal power to restrict the practice of their trade by the new legislation of 1814. Nonetheless, determined and united workmen could be a powerful force keeping the unwelcome out, as the future leader of the Chartist movement, William Lovett, found to his cost.

Lovett had been born in the Cornish fishing town of Newlyn, a mile from Penzance, in 1800. His mother raised him alone following the early death of her husband and somehow found the means to pay for her son's apprenticeship. Their choice of trade – the dying Cornish rope-making industry – could hardly have been more unfortunate. Even before the end of his seven-year term, the trade had become so bad that his master was unable to pay his wages. His indentures had to be cancelled and Lovett was forced to find alternative employment, working first on the fishing boats, and then with a carpenter. But the sight of a poor boy learning the carpentry trade without being apprenticed was enough to arouse some of the local apprentices' jealousy. Two young men from Penzance came to Lovett's employer and muttered enough about the 'legal consequences' of hiring an untrained carpenter for his master to break the engagement.

Unable to find work in Cornwall, Lovett made the long trek to London. Either the country carpenter had taught him well or Lovett was especially talented, for soon he was busily employed by a firm of cabinetmakers, working in the most skilled branch of the trade. But no sooner had he found himself a position in one of the finest cabinet-making shops in London than the hostility of carpenters who had served their time surfaced once more. His new workmates took a very dim view of the arrival of a man who had never been properly apprenticed to the trade and agreed to set 'Mother Shorney' at him. As Lovett explained, this meant 'the putting away of your tools, the injuring of your work, and annoying you in such a way as to drive you out of the shop'. Lovett responded by deploying the skills that would later prove such an asset to the Chartist movement. He called a meeting with his workmates, explained how he had wasted his youth learning a trade that was 'comparatively useless, and appealed to their sense of justice to determine whether it was right to prevent me from learning another'.[31] Needless to say, after Lovett had put his case justice won the day. But Lovett was a remarkable man and his entry to the highly skilled world of cabinet-making without serving an apprenticeship was unusual: he was certainly the only one amongst the autobiographers to do so.

So tradition and protectionism kept the gates barred to those who had not served an apprenticeship in a handful of trades; but a practice that had once been usual and enshrined in law had now become exceptional, a right tenaciously (and illegally) held on to in pockets of the most skilled trades. For most of the rest, access to the world of skilled labour had never been easier to obtain.

The experiences of learning a trade in the early eighteenth century and before could hardly have been more different. Only one writer before 1750 learned a trade without serving an apprenticeship. This was Benjamin Bangs, who had entered an apprenticeship in Norfolk in the 1660s but never completed it, as his master had gone bankrupt within his first year. He travelled to London and there found a shoemaker willing to take on a cheap, but unqualified, worker.[32] But Benjamin Bangs was unique in learning a skilled trade in this way and it is probably significant that it was in London rather than Norwich that he found a master willing to teach him shoemaking outside the apprenticeship system. Otherwise, for writers in the pre-industrial period, access to the trades was gained by apprenticeship only.

The rise of informal apprenticeships is no less than we should expect in a society undergoing the kind of growth seen in Britain over the late eighteenth and nineteenth centuries. This was an era of rising wealth, and even if the lion's share was greedily swallowed up by the middle classes, their burgeoning incomes inevitably increased demand for goods such as shoes, clothes, bread, buildings and furniture. At the same time, rapid urbanisation made the kinds of control that the trade societies had previously exercised over entry to their ranks impossible to enforce. Industrialisation certainly did carry a degree of social turmoil along with it in much the way that many of the pessimists have maintained. It may also have led to the 'deskilling' of some trades. Yet many at the bottom of society proved extremely adept at grasping opportunity from the chaos.[33]

No matter how skills had been acquired, the learning of a trade could usher in a more comfortable and prosperous working life. In even the humblest branches of skilled labour the ability to work a trade carried the promise of better-paid and more regular employment, which together represented a very significant advantage indeed. Almost all the autobiographers who had learned a trade reported earning sufficient to keep themselves and their families in a degree of comfort.[34] Several recalled 'good wages'.[35] Another recurring theme is the satisfaction that young men experienced once they had started work as a journeyman and could afford to buy decent clothes and a few books of their own.[36]

Nor can this be explained away by suggesting that those who wrote their memoirs were either life's victors or too proud to admit to personal or business failure. After all, it is not as if low wages, poverty and hardship were themes that the autobiographers were reluctant to discuss. Indeed they form the mainstay of the skilled labourers' accounts of learning their trade, whether formally apprenticed or not. Many experienced serious privation, even to the extent of regularly going hungry. John Gibbs recalled crying himself to sleep 'for hunger'; another was 'much afflicted'; Joseph Burdett described himself as 'miserable' and 'almost naked for clothes'.[37] Many others expressed bitter resentment that they had been forced to work such long hours for a pittance. Yet once they became adults with a skill to their name, their complaints about low wages, insufficient food and lack of clothes simply faded away. A skill was enough to ensure a reasonable living. As James Dawson Burn commented: 'I knew I never could be badly off while I could work at my business.'[38]

The material well-being of many skilled workers had less to do with the wages they received than with the fact that they were at work week in and week out throughout the year. One whitesmith boasted that since arriving in London he had never been out of work.[39] Never 'have I been unemployed,' wrote a London printer.[40] Samuel Hick had work 'pouring in' following the end of his apprenticeship.[41] More modest writers still referred to 'plenty of employment'.[42] As a young man John Bennett gave up trying to earn a living in the sleepy Wiltshire village of South Wraxall and moved to Bristol. It was fair time on the day he arrived and no one was hiring. It was not long, though, before the fair left town and everyone was back at work. As John watched the men going into the shipyard a workman cried out 'Can you saw?' John replied, 'Yes ... top or bottom.' The workman shouted, 'Come along then', and so began John's life as an urban carpenter.[43] He spent the rest of his adult life in either Bristol or Bath and appears never to have been out of work.

It is likely that there was a regional dimension to the employment patterns of skilled workers which is obscured in the autobiographies. London and other large cities no doubt offered better prospects for employment than smaller provincial towns.[44] Similarly, the flow of work throughout the year and over the years was probably more varied than writers recalled. Yet whilst autobiographies do not allow us to sketch regional and temporal patterns with the degree of detail we might wish, they nevertheless make clear the *relative* ease with which skilled workers found employment. When work dried up they were rarely plunged into the desperate poverty that had blighted the lives of some as they learned their trade. They simply moved on to a larger town, where they invariably found someone willing to hire them.[45]

It comes as little surprise to find that those who encountered the greatest difficulties in finding regular work were employed in the most easily entered of the skilled occupations: the shoemakers and above all the tailors. Allen Davenport was raised in a poor family as one of ten children. In his late teens he joined the army and during a stay in Aberdeen befriended two young shoemakers who encouraged and assisted him in making a pair of shoes for himself.[46] Following his discharge, he settled in Cirencester, and found his friends had taught him just enough about making shoes for him to set himself up as a shoemaker. But the people of Cirencester did not have sufficient call for his services to provide him with much of a living. Davenport was faced with the same dilemma as many other skilled workmen trying to earn their way in villages or small provincial towns: to stay put and face declining living standards or move somewhere larger in search of better prospects. And in opting to move rather than stay put, he made the same decision as most of the other writers who found themselves in this position. After four years he gave up plying his trade in Cirencester and moved to London, quickly going on to establish a prosperous business.[47]

The difficulties for the tailors were more acute. It was not uncommon for tailors to move on to a larger town in search of work only to find none there either. Even in the cities, almost all of the tailors suffered from unemployment, paying the price for working in an industry that had become extremely easy to enter.[48] The problems with the trade were captured by Robert Lowery, who started his adult life as a tailor but later emerged as a key figure in the working-class political movement. When Lowery became a tailor's apprentice in 1825, the trade 'was then very good – wages were high, and it was considered a very respectable employment'. But even within the time it took to complete a short apprenticeship of just two years the situation had deteriorated. As Lowery explained, 'there had been a rush into it, from its being considered an easy and genteel business with good wages, there was soon a surplus of journeymen, and, except for a few, there was but little chance of regular work for more than six months of the year'.[49] And so indeed it proved, not just for Lowery, but for almost all of the tailors who have left behind a life history.

Yet the tailors stand alone amongst skilled labourers in encountering chronic difficulties in making ends meet. It was rare for artisans to be unable to find enough work to make their business a going concern and those who failed usually pointed at some exceptional reason. The boot-maker Dan Chatterton found he could only earn a 'precarious crust', but this he blamed on his ill health.[50] A number of writers indicated that heavy drinking had undone their attempts at business. Miles Watkins, for instance, had enjoyed a prosperous start to his career as a bootmaker, but became 'enslaved to the drinking customs', fell into debt and soon found himself staring poverty straight in the face.[51] In fact even the drunkards occasion-ally possessed skills in such high demand that they were able to remain fully employed. John Colin was a skilled leather-dresser. He learned his trade in Scotland and spent nearly two years living in Paris where he learned some of the most valuable and lucrative branches of the trade. His drink problem made it impossible for him to derive much profit from his skills: he was frequently turned away from his work and 'always ... through my drunkenness'.[52] But although Colin could not hold on to employment, he had no difficulty finding it. In Worcester, for example, he had 'many places offered me'.[53] In order to keep him at his place, one of his employers ordered a three-gallon bucket of beer each morning and had it 'placed beside me, with a half pint cup to drink it with'.[54] It must be admitted that John Colin was unusual in combining a successful working life with a drinking habit he could not control. But his experiences indicate something that was shared by many of the skilled artisans amongst the autobiographers: high levels of employment with all that that entailed.

Once again, it might be countered that those who wrote their life histo-ries were more likely to have made a success of their lives, or at least to emphasise their successes. But the autobiographers were not unremittingly cheerful and upbeat. Poverty, ill health, unemployment, low wages and suffering were themes they were only too ready to discuss. More generally we should never underestimate the seriousness of ill health in a society with little in the way of a safety net for those who fell upon hard times. John Buckmaster was learning to be a carpenter when he deserted his master and ran away to nearby Salisbury in search of a better future. In fact he fell ill with smallpox which not only left him unable to earn, but landed him with a large doctor's bill when he recovered.[55] The autobiographies contain heart-rending tales of families reduced to dire straits by such appar-ently innocent misfortunes as a 'great Boil', an unexplained loss of sight in early adulthood, an infected cut, a cold that could not be shifted, a slip while getting off an omnibus, and a leg that was so badly injured by a stick thrown by a boy that it eventually had to be amputated.[56] When skilled workers found themselves unable to work, they were no better off than anyone else.

Life was hard for working people in early nineteenth-century Britain, extremely hard, and it is not my purpose to deny the crushing poverty and suffering endured by far too many of those at the bottom of the pile. But if life was hard, life was also changing, and if we look carefully enough we can glimpse in these changes an unmistakable upturn in the fortunes of the skilled labourer. The decline of the apprenticeship system caused by rapid urban growth created new opportunities for learning a skilled trade, and with the economic expansion that occurred over the century 1750 to 1850 those with skills were in demand. It became both easier to learn skills and easier to find work no matter how those skills had been learned. In other words, social flux and economic growth created a scenario in which many working men stood to gain.

Nor was this the only way in which working men gained. Better wages filled out wage packets, but they also enhanced the status of skilled workers in more subtle ways. Shining through the autobiographies is the fact that complex working lives cannot be reduced to simple measures of pounds, shillings and pence: abundant employment also changed the balance of power in the master–servant relationship. Artisans frequently and fondly retold stories about the time when their younger selves had had enough of their master's petty tyrannies and retorted in no uncertain terms that they would no longer submit. James Lackington was twenty-one, a shoemaker just out of his time, when he fell out with his master's wife about where he should buy the milk. His mistress ordered him to purchase it from a customer of the shop, but as Lackington had a 'smart little milk-maid of my own', he refused to comply. He 'left without hesitation' that very day.[57] The errant shoemaker took a circuitous route to Bristol, collecting his sweetheart, the 'beautiful Nancy Trott', before deciding that travelling with Nancy was perhaps not such a good idea, and proceeding to Bristol alone. Having finally reached the city, he 'got work the same evening'.[58] Although Lackington could not have known that his search for employment would be quite so straightforward, he probably grounded his hasty departure in a sound knowledge of the buoyancy of the labour market in nearby Bristol. The demand for labour gave workers meaningful choices and this in turn helped to shape the relationship between master and servant in tangible ways.

Although Lackington was the only writer who walked out on his master over a quarrel about milk, he was just one of several who threw up perfectly good employment for a relatively minor matter. The leather-dresser John

Colin may have been frequently dismissed for drunkenness, but he was not slow to walk away from positions he disliked. He quit one master because he was 'such a tyrant'; another because he cut his wages for going to a lecture against the Corn Laws; and another simply because he 'got sick of the job'.[59] William Swan left a good bake-shop rather than 'beg pardon' from his master after the pair had had some 'high words'.[60] Another London baker handed in his notice rather than waste one more of his precious Sunday mornings at his pious master's family services.[61] There was no doubt some degree of story-telling going on here: men whose lives had been devoted to serving other men's needs seem to relish recounting the moment when the tables were turned. Yet even allowing for some rhetorical flourish, there is no reason to discount the essential truth at the heart of these accounts. And stories like this remind us that work is about more than pay and hours, important as such things undoubtedly are. All working relationships are defined by a disparity between master and servant, an inequality that is rendered more palatable if we are well remunerated for our services and can leave at will.

With so much evidence that learning and practising a trade became easier in the century after 1750, it will surely no longer do to parrot the oft-repeated claim that the rapid economic growth of this period brought nothing but misery for the working man. An unintended, and largely unnoticed, consequence of economic growth was a liberalisation of the workplace, with the creation of new opportunities for growing numbers amongst the poor to acquire the skills, and with them the advantages – above all more work and better-paid work – that artisans had always enjoyed. Entering the ranks of skilled labour ushered in a very welcome enhancement in men's material lives but it also improved their status in ways less obvious but no less important. It widened their choices, strengthened their hand, and bestowed a drop of personal power.

The first half of the nineteenth century brought brighter prospects for skilled workers. But what about those who did not follow this route? Not only did economic growth make it easier for the poor to gain skills, it also made it much easier for them to earn a decent living without acquiring any of the skills that had formed the traditional path to advancement. The growth of cottage industry, factories, mills, mining and towns all, in their different ways, increased demand for male labour. This in turn helped to raise both the wages and the status of the unskilled worker. With industrialisation came a raft of new occupations, none of which called for exceptional skills or training that could not be picked up at the workplace. The result was that the unskilled labourer also had better prospects than at any earlier time.[62]

Much of the expansion in unskilled labour came from the growth of cottage industry. Sometimes also called domestic manufacture or 'proto-industry', this refers simply to production that takes place within the home. It can encompass a variety of processes. In Britain the most vibrant cottage industries were in spinning, weaving, knitting, metalworking, basket-making and straw-plaiting. Small-scale domestic production of this kind had existed for hundreds of years, but the eighteenth century witnessed significant expansion, particularly in the textile sector.[63] At the forefront were the handloom weavers, using hand-operated looms to weave thread into cloth. Weaving thrived in Lancashire, Yorkshire and the Scottish borders, with smaller centres in East Anglia, the West Country and the east Midlands. Also important was the framework knitting industry centred in Nottingham and Leicester and in the many villages thereabout.

Weaving and knitting sit somewhere between the worlds of skilled and unskilled labour. Some entered the trades by serving an apprenticeship, though as both trades could be learned quickly and the apprentice was therefore soon able to earn an income for his master, the terms were short (typically two years) and entry costs were low.[64] Many others learned how to weave or knit from their family, the skill being passed from parents to children, as might be expected given that most worked their looms or frames within the home.[65] And, of course, the handloom weavers and stockingers occupy a special place in the mythology of the industrial revolution, frequently cast as independent labourers who dovetailed their industrial avocations with wholesome work in their garden. In the dark interpretation, these domestic workers figure promi-nently as traditional artisans ground down by the remorseless spread of machines, the hapless victims of the dismal process of industrialisation.[66]

It would be hard to deny that the weavers have been romanticised by posterity, but like all good historical myths this one contains a kernel of truth. Weavers and knitters often did combine textile production with farming a small garden, and this life of dual occupation did provide a higher income than could be gained from agriculture alone.[67] Weavers were able to earn, during the good times at least, more than they could ever earn on the land. Several of those engaged in the handloom industry recalled periods of prosperity during which they had enjoyed good wages.[68] In Glasgow in the 1840s, for example, William Hammond earned 35 shillings a week.[69] When this wage is contrasted with the nine shillings a week that Joseph Arch earned as an agricultural labourer in the Warwickshire village of Barford in the same decade, it is not hard to understand why workers were so ready to quit the land and work the loom.[70]

There is also real substance to the claim that the weavers enjoyed a degree of independence. Most of the autobiographers engaged in domestic manufacture regarded their work as preferable to agriculture, and the autonomy that came with weaving formed part of its appeal. Weavers were for the most part self-employed, either owning their own loom or renting it in a shop. Either way, they set their own hours, which gave them the very welcome option of trading work for leisure. Samuel Bamford approvingly noted that on exchanging his position in a Manchester warehouse for a loom, he became 'master of my own time', with the liberty to partake of 'country amusements with the other young fellows of the neighbourhood', a liberty which would quickly have led to his dismissal had he tried it at the warehouse.[71] Hardly less importantly, it also paved the way for working long hours when prices were high. A few of the autobiographers could hardly contain their surprise at the riches that weaving occasionally allowed them to amass. When Ben Brierley and his family took to weaving satin shawls they thought they had 'found a silver mine'. Ben was earning 24 shillings a week and his father 30: 'such an income was enough to turn our heads, We seemed to be rolling in wealth.'[72]

But if we can agree that the weavers did enjoy periods of high wages, did often tend a cottage garden, and did appreciate the independence associated with working the loom, there are other parts of the myth that we cannot accept. For all its attractions, there were intractable problems associated with the weaving industry. Even in the good years, the demand for woven cloth could fluctuate wildly from one season to the next, and as quickly as weavers remembered the good wages, memories of periods of acute hardship came flooding back. During the trade depression of the 1840s, William Hammond saw his weekly earnings plummet from 35 shillings to 12 shillings a week. 'During bad trade all the prices for work fell, and slim diet was the order of the day.'[73] And Ben Brierley's 'silver mine' was soon exhausted, his prosperity lasting 'only for a time'.[74] Thirty-one of the autobiographers turned their hand to weaving at some stage in their life, and over half recalled periods of falling demand and its predictable consequences.[75] Others had experienced the same effect as children raised in weaving families.[76] In fact, this helps to explain why so many weavers continued to tend a cottage garden. The weavers did not pursue farm-work through love of the wholesome fresh air, but as part of a necessary survival strategy when working in such a volatile and precarious industry.

The position of the framework knitters was broadly similar. George Calladine became an apprentice framework knitter in 1805 when the trade was prospering. After two years, he could complete his master's work and also 'with ease earn four shillings a day' for himself. With hindsight, George considered that the custom of paying by the task rather than the hour encouraged the apprentice to become 'almost independent of his master . . . very apt to idle away a day or two at the beginning of the week'. In his own case, he regretted that 'too much liberty' had led him into bad company.[77] But as those who stayed in the trade could testify, such problems were not usually long lived. Outside a few years of exceptional prosperity, most of the knitters were unable to generate steady year-long earnings. All those involved in the knitting industry encountered the same difficulty, one moment enjoying the boom times the next plunged into poverty when demand for their goods fell sharply and rapidly away.[78] Most retained some footing on the land for no other reason than to cushion their fall during the hardest times.

So here is the context in which we should situate the long-term pressures on the handloom and knitting industries that resulted from the spread of mechanisation. By the 1820s, new 'power looms' were beginning to rival handlooms in the quality and quantity of cloth they could weave. As the machines were refined and improved they became ever more attractive to manufacturers. Inevitably, the growth of factory-based weaving in the 1830s and 1840s had serious ramifications for those who continued to weave on a small scale in their own home.[79] Most of the autobiographers born in the nineteenth century at some point abandoned their attempts to earn a livelihood from the handloom industry. For some, moving out of weaving was a painful transition.[80] Joseph Gutteridge described the desperate conditions he endured in the 1830s during long intervals without employment: 'some of our experiences were bitter indeed'.[81] In the same decade, William Thom's family was plunged into crushing poverty when the Scottish weaving industry collapsed, silencing 'in one week, upwards of six thousand looms in Dundee alone'.[82] Entirely out of employ and unable to feed his children, Thom took the road with his family. On their travels, the family's youngest member, a small baby, passed away. Some of the weavers have bequeathed heart-rending accounts of horrendous suffering, a salutary reminder of the harshness of life in the absence of an adequate safety net; a reminder too that the autobiographers were not simply the 'winners' of industrialisation, but came from all walks of life.

What is less obvious is how we should fit the handloom weavers into our narratives of the industrial revolution. For those committed to the dark view, the matter is clear cut. The weavers were tragic victims of the dismal process, their misery stamped on the back of the new capitalist coin. But there are at least two problems with connecting the weavers' distress and the industrial revolution in this way. In the first place, the problems with the weaving and knitting industries were apparent decades before the mechanisation of either process. Here were trades easily learned and easily entered. As willing workers crowded in, the slice of the pie that each could take got smaller. In many respects, the weavers' position was no different to that of the tailors: casualties not of that mythic beast 'the industrial revolution', but of a rather more prosaic force – a surplus of workers. At the very least, this was not the first generation of domestic workers to find that supply outstripped demand. In 1747, William Hutton was forced to look for a new master as a stockinger following the death of his uncle. Unfortunately, at this time 'trade was dead'. The hosiers could not employ their own workers, still less a newcomer like him. He tried several warehouses, but 'all proved a blank', and Hutton was reduced to tears to think he had served seven years as an apprentice to a trade 'at which I could not get bread'.[83] Almost a century before the rise of mechanised weaving, Hutton was in much the same situation as Gutteridge and Thom, the victim of an endemic problem that pre-dated industrialisation.

In the second place, the autobiographies suggest a far more complicated relationship between the old and the new ways of weaving cloth than the black-and-white view permits. After all, the new factories needed workers too. It is true the factory owners exhibited an unmistakable preference for employing women and children, regarding them as a cheaper and more submissive source of labour.[84] But adult men, especially those living in Lancashire, Yorkshire and the Scottish Lowlands, can also be found taking up new opportunities in factories and warehouses. Indeed the factories were the most common destination for the unemployed handloom weavers among the autobiographers. Those living in Lancashire or Yorkshire were particularly well placed. Seven moved from weaving to factory work, a further six moved into warehouses, dealing or travelling.[85] Three more set themselves up as small-scale shopkeepers: living in areas with large populations of working people made such enterprises viable, though not necessarily profitable.[86] All of the weavers living in the heartlands of the industrial revolution found alternative employment once they had decided to give up their loom.

Outside the industrial regions, the situation for the weavers was very much worse. John Castle in Essex, John Leatherland in Northampton, and

Joseph Gutteridge in Coventry all hung on to the weaving industry more tenaciously than their northern counterparts. They suffered a very serious reduction in living standards when their local industries failed. When finally cast out of employment with thousands of others, their options were virtually non-existent.[87]

But in the industrial districts the situation was very different. Factories provided a real alternative to handloom weaving and the autobiographers moved seamlessly from one line of work to the other. The only writers to voice consistent dissatisfaction with the transition were the poets and writers, and they perhaps had rather different concerns to the run-of-the-mill early industrial worker.[88] Nor is these weavers' enthusiasm for the factory system too hard to fathom, for there were some very real compensations for adults who worked in the factories. First and foremost were the high wages. We noted in the opening pages of this chapter Charles Campbell and the anonymous autobiographer who appreciated the good wages they could earn in the factory.[89] They were not the only writers to express pleasant surprise at the pay they received. Samuel Catton spent his early years as an agricultural servant, but in his twenties he moved to Stratford where he found employment at the chemical works for 'very good wages'.[90] In Preston, Benjamin Shaw found 'good work & wages'.[91] Other writers stopped short of describing their pay as good, but nonetheless indicated that their factory wage had enabled them to save fairly considerable sums of money. Working as a machine grinder and glazier in Heywood, William Marcroft saved £20 in two years and eventually retired from manual labour altogether.[92] Adam Rushton stashed away enough to contemplate emigrating to the USA.[93] Even William Dodd, whose childhood experiences in the factories were so harrowing that he became a reformer, was forced to concede that his working conditions and pay picked up when he reached adulthood.[94]

And although factory work could never offer the same degree of independence as cottage industry, it did hold out the offer of more stable and continuous earnings. Many of those who worked in factories stayed relatively long periods with the one employer. Positions which spanned a decade or more were not unusual and a few men spent almost their entire working life at one mill. Robert Collyer's father, for example, worked at one factory, 'man and boy', for thirty-two years.[95] John Tough spent thirty-seven years with a hosiery manufacturer in Aberdeen.[96] William Wright's father was a weft manager at a mill for 'somewhere about half a century'.[97] A position at the factory could last for several unbroken years. Of course not all were so lucky, and those working in factories sometimes found themselves in the trough of a trade cycle, experiencing cuts in their wages or even finding themselves out of work altogether. But this should not be permitted to obscure the fact that factories and mills promised steady employment over many years, and that those who found such work had very few complaints.

In some parts of the industrialising north, the mills were emerging as a major source of employment, but the new towns offered much more than the chance of employment as a factory operative. After all, mill owners had needs that went beyond the making of goods. One common alternative to working in the factory was working in the warehouse. With better wages and pleasanter working conditions, most of our writers regarded this as something of a promotion.[98] Thomas Wood found work repairing the machines in the factories of Oldham rather than working them.[99] And in Preston, Benjamin Shaw made a living fixing spindles and making fly frames, mules and other parts of the machines that kept the town's cotton industry going.[100] Others kept the books or collected accounts for mill owners.[101] As George Hanby found, goods needed to be weighed as well as made.[102] Then there was work to be done moving raw materials and finished goods around. William Smith minded a turnpike gate.[103] John Hemmingway carried goods on his horse and cart for a fustian manufacturer.[104] James Watson had the charge of a saddle-horse for a Leeds warehouse.[105] Yet others found work on the railways, or delivering mail.[106]

In addition to the employment to be found servicing the factories, there was a mountain of work to be done providing for the needs of a large population. The urban workforce required bread, clothes, shoes and furniture; as we have already seen, their demand for the staples of life generated plenty of business for skilled tradesmen. Those without a skilled trade to their name could also take advantage of the growing urban economy. One option was to set up as a small shopkeeper. George Cooper, for example, was unable to find employment in the Stockport cotton mills following his role in leading the strikes in 1848, so he set up a very small grocer's shop instead.[107] One autobiographer gave up manual labour to sell tea. Another sold 'cheap cheese' in very small quantities to his neighbours; yet another, his own sweets, cakes and gingerbread.[108] To the dismay of many a polite commentator, the urban workforce had an insatiable appetite for alcohol, so setting up a beer shop was yet one more alternative for workers seeking a new way to make a living.[109] The urban poor had a taste for entertainment, providing an opening for a handful of singers, ballad-writers, sellers of cheap literature, and actors.[110] They also needed policing, or at least so it was thought by those who governed them: just another example of the new opportunities emerging in the towns.[111]

Many of these businesses were initially conducted on a very small scale funded by no more than a few borrowed shillings. George Cooper, for example, began his store with eight shillings lent by two friends; and Joseph Livesey, the seller of 'cheap cheese', started trading on a borrowed sovereign and a pair of borrowed scales. Nor were they always successful. The difficulties of making money in poor communities can be easily imagined. The beer-sellers usually found that working in the beer trade did far more to ruin their health than it did to make their fortune and many of the quacks and entertainers carved out a living that was at best precarious. Shopkeepers sometimes prospered, and sometimes not. At the end of a year's trading, John Hemmingway 'was very glad to get out of the shop at any price, a ruined man'.[112] So these activities should not be held up as examples of how urban growth permitted a flourishing of entrepreneurial genius or facilitated social mobility.[113] We are on safer ground using them simply to suggest that Britain's growing towns increased the amount and variety of employment available to the unskilled urban worker, evidence of yet one more way in which city life opened choices to the working man.

The sheer variety of opportunity that was opening up in many industrialising areas is captured in the life history of John Tough. Between the ages of seventeen and thirty-nine, Tough turned his hand to no fewer than ten different jobs. He began his working life as a gardener, three years later he moved into land surveying, and next he became a traveller for a hosiery manufacturer. He then had a succession of office-based jobs; first as an assistant clerk at a cotton mill, next as a bookkeeper for a brewery, and then as the 'Collector of Freights' for the London Shipping Company – though this proving to be 'a very disagreeable situation', he soon left. Finding himself without work, he filled in a little time by hiring a vessel and travelling to Danzig to collect a cargo of wheat, before returning to Aberdeen and trying to eke out a living with a horse and cart and three cows. When this small enterprise failed, he travelled with his family down to the central belt of Scotland to work first in a mill and then at an ironworks, before finally returning to the hosiery business in Aberdeen.[114] He stayed at this company for the next thirty-seven years.

As with the skilled labourers, the combination of good wages and abundant employment produced a very real rise in unskilled working men's status and sense of self-worth. Those who worked in the most vibrant parts of the economy were also the most likely to be found leaving their work for minor considerations. James Powell, for example, gave as his reason for quitting the mill no more than a 'trivial act of oppression' which caused him 'considerable annoyance'.[115] As a young man, Thomas Whittaker left 'profitable employment' because of what he lamely summarised as 'a little temper on the part of the master, with too much defiance on the part of the servant'.[116] Some industrial workers were prepared to leave work over the frequency of their 'drinkings', or tea breaks as we now call them. Joshua Dodgson, a dyer in Halifax, left a good position after just two weeks when he realised that the drinkings he had been promised were to be discontinued.[117]

Benjamin Shaw and his workmates went even further. Shaw's master, David Ainsworth, had decided that his workmen should 'not go out to [their] drinkings' and when the men continued to leave work for their breaks in defiance of his order, he fined them all two shillings of their wages. The men responded by combining and summoned Ainsworth before the mayor. This got their two shillings returned, but it also got them the sack. According to Benjamin, 'some submited & Beged their work again' but not him: he found himself a new employer.[118] And all this over a matter that that Benjamin himself described as a 'trifeling thing'. There was no doubt more than a little pride at stake in such instances, and our slighted workmen did not always move on to find work at such preferable rates. But, and this I think is the important point, find work of some kind they did. These employed and healthy adult workers were clearly not on the breadline and this allowed them to exercise some control over whom they would work for and what conditions they would (or would not) tolerate. So long as levels of pay and employment were relatively good, workers would reap the benefit.

The same pattern is evident in other areas of the industrialising economy. In mining, for example, wages were generally good and unemployment relatively rare.[119] Almost all of the miners recorded earning good wages as adults.[120] As Thomas Oliver summarised, 'as a miner I did very well'.[121] The fact that mining was a growing industry with good prospects for finding employment also enhanced the industry's appeal. Very few of the miners suffered serious unemployment. Some indeed appear never to have been out of work, though they frequently needed to migrate short distances in order to remain in full-time employment.[122] This is not of course to suggest that mining provided an easy living. The work was hard, the conditions unpleasant and often dangerous, and there was expense and inconvenience involved in moving in search of new work. By the same token, however, our writers did not expect life to be easy or comfortable. The decision to move a short distance for a full week's work was taken in a heartbeat, too inconsequential to merit much retrospective analysis.

One final way in which industrialisation improved prospects for the working man was in the rapid extension of navvying (unskilled building work). A growing population and economy ensured that there was a lot of such work to go around. Throughout the first half of the nineteenth century, workers drifted out of agriculture and into construction, working on projects ranging from the building of canals, roads, factories and ware-houses to drainage projects and (from the 1840s) the railways. Emanuel Lovekin described himself as 'a bit given to roaming about' so working as a navvy held considerable appeal. 'Railway tunneling was very rife, at this time,' he continued. 'But my mate and I, had the getting of quirry stone for putting in the Locks in the Severn reiver between Stourport and Woscester.'[123] The life of a navvy was summed up by Joseph Arch as 'hard work, good wages, rough quarters'.[124] Much of the attraction of navvying undoubtedly lay in the higher wages it paid: one autobiographer noted that his wages doubled overnight when he left the farm and started work as a navvy.[125] And when Lovekin and his mate went navvying they found 'very good jobs and plenty of money'.[126] It all amounted to one more option for men who had been raised to expect to spend their lives devoted to earning a subsistence wage in agriculture.

The navvies must have appreciated the good money they could earn, but as with most of the developments we have looked at here, moving into construction involved more than the prospect of better wages. Navvies enjoyed a private life that was remarkably free from supervision, and this must have formed a very palpable benefit for farm servants who were used to living under their master's roof. As one farm labourer recalled: 'men living in the house were not expected to leave the premises without the master's permission'.[127] Such restrictions could prove irksome to adults. One anonymous writer took up navvying following a quarrel with his master about his visiting the public house.[128] Once the transition from servant to navvy had been made, a man's days of having his trips to the public house monitored had truly come to an end.

Even at work, the relationship between navvy and gangmaster was quite different to the traditional master–servant relationship, as John Wilson described:

My father being a navvy, and the railway system in this country being in its early development, there was a great demand for workmen at high wages, and he, being a strong vigorous man, was sure of employment wherever he went. Being, however, of a very sharp temper, he would throw up his work at the first sign of harsh treatment or fault-finding, and thus he and I were very often on the move, for I was his constant companion where possible.[129]

It is worth emphasising that our writers do not suggest that they found their employment in the mills and towns pleasant, easy, enjoyable, worthwhile or anything else that we might seek from our work today. Many of these jobs were physically demanding. The hours were invariably long. Being a navvy could be particularly difficult, with dangerous work, constant movement in search of the next job, and occasional spells of unemployment when the demand for navvies dried up. Most men tired of this existence in the longer term, especially once settled with a family. Nor in our haste to stress the gains that many working men found in the booming economy should we neglect to point out the very serious difficulties that many workers experienced when the economy hit the buffers. The first half of the nineteenth century was haunted by deep trade depressions, with unusually severe downturns in the winter of 1831–2 and again in 1841–2.[130] In addition to these periodic downturns was the constant risk of commercial failures and strikes. Any and all could throw the mill-hands out of work and threaten the livelihoods of those connected to the mills' good fortune. In no time, families that had been enjoying a measure of prosperity were pawning their furniture and living on short rations. The grim struggle that the labouring poor faced throughout our period to make ends meet should not be underestimated.

Yet repeatedly our writers tell us that work in cottage industry, factories, mines, warehouses, large cities and construction was better than the labour that had consumed their fathers' energies – and often their own early labours as well. And however much this might jar with our own expectations of earning a living during the industrial revolution, it is probably worth our while to take these comments seriously. Implicit in the accounts of good wages and plentiful work is a relative judgement about the alternatives that were available. In other words, making sense of this view requires us to look at those who tried to earn a living before the emergence of the new industrial economy.

Understanding the nature of manual labour in the pre-industrial era is difficult. The answers to even the simplest questions about wage levels or employment are obscure, as early writers usually spent very little time dwelling on the material aspect of their life. Most life histories before about 1750 were framed around religious conversions. A working life might be summarised in no more than a couple of paragraphs, the brief prelude to a narrative describing the author's journey from sin to salvation. Yet even with such unpromising material, it is clear that many adult men, including skilled craftsmen, suffered endemic unemployment and underemployment. This had formed part of Edward Barlow's objection to being bound to that whitester in Manchester. There was really not much demand for bleached yarn, so the whitester made up his living by farming a small plot of land. Throughout the year, looking after the animals formed a part of his apprentices' daily workload. In fact during the quiet winter months they worked very little at 'the trade' and spent most of their time ploughing, ditching and doing other 'country work'.[131] In a similar fashion, the coal mines in early eighteenth-century Durham were not busy enough to keep the miners fully employed. Christopher Hopper worked driving horses on the wagon-ways connecting the district's coal mines, but he was also employed in 'various branches of agriculture'.[132] And given that many men needed to turn their hand to more than one occupation in order to make a living, it is little surprise to find that others complained that there was simply too little work. William Chubb stayed with his master at the end of his glove-making apprenticeship for, as he glumly noted, he 'had no *better*, or indeed no *other* way, to get a livelihood'.[133] He spent a further four years with him, despite his fear that the close work was destroying his eyesight.

And just as buoyant employment prospects strengthened a worker's hand in the master–servant relationship, so insufficient work had the reverse effect. Consider the choices that James Ferguson made when two employers in succession failed to keep their end of the bargain. In the early 1730s Ferguson went to work with a miller, hoping to improve on his previous position in service. He was quickly disappointed. His master was a heavy drinker and failed to provide Ferguson with adequate food, leaving him 'almost starved . . . for want of victuals'. But Ferguson had entered into a year-long contract and so stayed until the end of his time. When he returned to his father at the end of the year, he was 'in a very weak state' and had to rest there a short while, to recover his strength.[134] His next situation with a country doctor promised to be better, but soon proved to be even worse. Ferguson's new master kept him 'constantly to very hard labour' and early in the placement the overwork injured his arm. But once again, Ferguson did not leave. It was only when the injury became so bad that he was unable to continue working that Ferguson finally left his master. As he had broken his six-month contract, his master refused to pay him anything for the three months of service he had completed.[135] Ferguson may have been unlucky in meeting with two such miserable masters, but his response was not unreasonable. What other choices did he have? His family could not take him in – 'I could not think of staying with my father, who I knew full well could not maintain me' – and there was little chance of finding alternative employment before the next round of hiring fairs.[136] Both times, his best chance of obtaining a meal and keeping a roof over his head lay in staying where he was. And this was just what he did.

I would not suggest that Ferguson's experience was normal for his times. Even in the early eighteenth century, most workers did not leave their master half starved or with their health seriously impaired, and most were paid for the service they completed. Deciding how common such experiences were is simply impossible. The autobiographies cannot tell us this, and it is hard to imagine any other kind of evidence which might. What can be said, however, is that Ferguson's experience lay within the range of the expected. Although the evidence is incomplete and difficult to interpret, the autobiographies indicate that work was in short supply in pre-industrial Britain. It was certainly more scarce than it would become once the industrial revolution took off. And so long as this was the case masters had a very powerful hold over their employees. Low levels of employment not only left large numbers of manual workers uncomfortably close to the breadline but also rendered them powerless to challenge their masters' authority.

The suggestion that it was the amount of work available which did the most to influence workers' living standard is reinforced by the experiences of men living in areas largely untouched by industrialisation. The uneven and piecemeal nature of early industrial growth left large pockets of rural workers working in conditions that resembled those of earlier writers more than they would have liked. All through the first half of the nineteenth century, the same package of low wages and insufficient work remained the lot of those trying to earn a living on the land and there is little to indicate that farm workers were sharing in the gains made by workers in the larger towns and cities.

Most of the men working as agricultural labourers described taking home wages that were too low to provide a decent living for their family.

'Small wages' that were not raised 'for a long time', as the wife of one farm labourer recalled.[137] We were 'very hard off' and 'very bad off' wrote another.[138] 'Starvation wages' and 'in very narrow Circumstances', lamented others.[139] Of course, the weekly wage does not quite do justice to the farm worker's income, as the grandees of the parish often provided their villagers with small non-monetary gifts. Richard Cook remembered how 'the Laides bountiful' of his Lincolnshire parish sent baby linen and cordial to the newly delivered wives of working men in the parish.[140] Elsewhere auto-biographers wrote about gifts of cast-off clothes, blankets and the occasional plate of broken meat.[141] But these exceptional acts of largesse did little to alter the fact that almost all of those who described ongoing difficulties in earning a living were working on the land.

Shortage of work lay at the root of the problem. Many agricultural labourers simply could not find constant employment, year in, year out. Their lives were composed of interludes of steady work followed by leaner times, scraping by without the blessing of a regular weekly wage. In Cambridgeshire, James Bowd found that after an accident at work, his master 'did not care for having me much more'. Inevitably, there was nobody else in the parish who needed the services of a lame man, so Bowd had 'sometimes work and sometimes none and that ment not much for a man and two Children to live upon'.[142] And in Buckinghamshire, unemployment reduced Joseph Mayett to gathering 'old raggs', selling 'laces, thred and Cotton &c', and taking work from the parish overseers for as little as six shillings a week. Let us put six shillings in context: Mayett's rent and fuel cost 3s. 2d. a week, and a loaf of bread 2s. 4d. This was a man in a desperate situation.[143]

Agricultural historians remind us of the great regional diversity that existed in rural England, of the differences in working patterns and wages between pasture and arable, uplands and lowlands, areas of good soils and poor. They emphasise that conditions for rural workers deteriorated with the return of large numbers of unskilled workers to the countryside following the end of the Napoleonic wars in 1815. But such differences across time and space are hardly visible in the autobiographical material. What stand out are the things that agricultural workers had in common. The perennial problem in rural areas was that the demand for labour was much lower during the quiet winter months than in the spring and summer, leaving a glut of hands with little choice but to take whatever work they could at whatever wage was offered.

Low wages and insufficient employment obviously depressed the living standards of agricultural workers and their families, but farm workers were

not the only ones who felt the pinch. Their poverty also made it very difficult for others in their community to earn a proper livelihood. Villages
needed their bakers, shoemakers, carpenters and small shopkeepers, yet
tradesmen often found it difficult to keep afloat when their neighbours
were so poor. As one man wrote of his father, who was working as a shoemaker in the Scottish border village of Longnewton in the late eighteenth
century, there were 'plenty of feet requiring comfortable shoes, though too
little money in circulation to pay for them'. His father turned to the land to
supplement his income, keeping a cow and a sheep, growing vegetables,
and skinning horses.[144] Many of the skilled workers in rural areas were
forced to supplement their income by a range of agricultural pursuits. So
we find amongst the autobiographers a tailor in County Antrim running
a farm;[145] carpenters in Cornwall eking out their income by brewing,
gardening and keeping cows;[146] and a glove-maker in Sussex digging graves
and wells, harvesting, skinning horses, making cider, growing potatoes, and
performing countless other tasks.[147] In agricultural areas, skilled workers
were rarely fully employed and so turned to field work to make ends meet.
The root of the problem was that the land could not provide sufficient
wealth to maintain all its workers in comfort. In nineteenth-century
Britain, as the world over, those at the bottom fared worst.[148]

Most of the dissatisfaction with rural life stemmed from insufficient
income, but many writers also commented on something in the master–
servant relationship that they found restrictive and distasteful. The
scarcity of employment in rural areas inevitably influenced this balance
of power and could be a powerful tool for employers seeking to extract
obedience from their workers. Ann Oakley remembered the trouble that
had followed when her husband, an agricultural labourer, managed
to upset his master just after their marriage. She recalled that he had
'vexed his master so much' by applying to the parish for relief for his
elderly mother that he lost his harvest work – a very serious penalty
when the wages from harvest work were vital for paying off debts and
buying essential items such as clothes and shoes.[149] Samuel Catton spent
a year living on a farm where 'he was very uncomfortable, and cruelly
treated, as his master and mistress were both drunkards, and the only son
was very often deranged'.[150] Nonetheless, he stayed out his term. When he
was next hired to a farmer he noted he 'worked hard and did not live
well', but he still stayed until the end of the year's term.[151] Nothing did
more to keep a servant in his place than the prospect of unemployment
if he left.

Farm servants could of course leave an unreasonable master. But in the small and relatively closed community of the village, a disgruntled master was never far away, as Joseph Mayett could testify only too well. Mayett and his master both belonged to Quainton's newly formed Baptist church, and along with others in the congregation they helped to pay his stipend. Mayett gave one of the nine shillings he earned each week towards the stipend. A few months into this arrangement, Mayett's rent was increased and, much to his master's displeasure, he could no longer afford to make the weekly one shilling payment. From that point on there was, as Mayett laconically noted, 'no peace'. The months rolled by and Mayett's payments for the minister fell deeper into arrears until his master finally 'fell in a passion and said he would have it then'. Mayett responded that he 'would not pay it at all'.[152] The pair agreed to part and as it was harvest time, Mayett had little difficulty finding a new employer. But this did not mark the end of his old master's interference in his life. Six months later, in the dead of winter and out of work, Mayett started claiming relief from the parish. When his old master heard of this he instructed the parish to stop paying him, giving as a reason no more than the fact that Mayett had 'left his Service'. The parish complied, heedless of the fact that it put them in breach of the law. Mayett had to go to the magistrates to compel the parish to pay the relief he was due. And when Mayett did find a new position, his old master went and spoke to his new one and 'perswaded him to discharge me which he did'.[153] Farm workers lived in small, deferential communities. New employers could sometimes be found, but old ones could not so easily be lost. Not for nothing did James Murdoch grumble that as a child in rural Scotland he had been 'taught to look forward with humble submission to a life of rustic serfdom'. As he never could 'learn to like submission to the authority of a master', he left off farm service as soon as he could.[154]

With too little work to go around it is not surprising to find that auto-biographers tended to be rather less than romantic about rural life. For the most part, rural roots were something to escape, not something to glorify. Many of the autobiographies devoted considerable attention to describing the whys and wherefores of their leaving. About fifty of our writers migrated from rural areas in order to seek work in industry, towns and commerce, usually leaving as an adolescent or young adult. Their experiences were predictably diverse. About twelve left the land as part of the process of becoming a skilled labourer, leaving either to take up an apprenticeship or in search of a position once their rural apprenticeship was complete.[155] The same number left in order to become a soldier or sailor.[156] A few of these left tolerably comfortable lives and appear to have been driven by a spirit of adventure, but most were mired in the most oppressive rural poverty and a life on the seas or in the armed forces obviously represented their best hope for a better life.

By far the largest group, thirty in all, took up work as navvies or moved directly to a nearby town, trading in effect unskilled agricultural work for unskilled urban, industrial or construction work. Once settled, they moved into the same set of occupations already described in this chapter. Several managed to learn a skill outside the apprenticeship system: tailors, shoe-makers and ironmongers figure repeatedly.[157] Hard labour in quarries, mines, canals and railways provided employment for yet more.[158] Others took up work in factories, mills and warehouses.[159] The autobiographers skipped off without a backward glance, never regretting the step they had taken, never lamenting the health or simplicity of their earlier life, and almost never returning to the scene of their birth.

It is interesting that many of those retelling the story of their departure dwelled upon the moment when they took their final leave of their master. Here, for example, is George Mitchell's account of leaving his Somerset village of Montacute. Mitchell had been born there in 1827, and (as a consequence of his father's low wages and love of cider) was raised 'in the greatest poverty and misery'.[160] He started work when he was five and by the age of nineteen he was working for a local farmer for a subsistence wage. He 'was certainly very discontented with my lot'. Following a partic-ularly onerous day's work ending in a quarrel with his master, Mitchell resolved to leave. He rose the next morning to give his master a fortnight's notice and informed him he would go to neighbouring Ham Hill to work in the stone quarries, adding that 'fourteen shillings a week was better than seven', a presumption that caused his master to scoff.[161] On the day of Mitchell's departure at the end of the fortnight, his master gave him an extra two shillings, telling him he had worked hard and deserved it. However, Mitchell did not bow his head and say thank you, but turned to enquire whether his master thought the five shillings he had been paying him until then constituted an adequate wage. A discussion ensued, with neither man giving ground. Mitchell continued to refuse to play the part of the deferential servant and eventually brought the matter to a close by telling his master that he would spend the extra two shillings on 'shoeleather to carry me away' from the village.[162]

If the story of Mitchell's departure was long-winded, that of Isaac Anderson was exceptionally brief. When railway-building began near his village in Essex he gave his master one week's notice. This astonished his master, who asked him where he was going. Anderson replied that he did not yet know, saying only 'I can't stand this work any longer'.[163] And where Anderson was brief, an anonymous writer in the *Working Man's Friend* was self-important. He thought the farmer he worked for 'somewhat tyrannical, ordering me up at four o'clock in the morning, and requiring other things which I considered an infringement of my rights. I told him plainly I would not submit, and took it upon myself at once to become my own master.'[164]

Maybe our autobiographers spoke these words; maybe these are the words they wished they had spoken. Either way, it is significant that they were inserted into their stories. In the usual order of things, farm servants could not expect to criticise their masters without unpleasant repercussions. Most of the time quiet submission was a far wiser option than speaking one's mind. Perhaps these writers retrospectively associated leaving the land with finding their voice. Certainly most of those who moved on found higher wages and better living standards. Yet it is interesting to note how much time the writers spent telling us that leaving the village marked the end of that 'humble submission' that Murdoch had so reviled.

Of the fifty men who left the land as young adults, just three returned later in life. Their accounts provide us with a rare opportunity to place experiences of rural and urban life side by side. One, Joseph Mayett, we have already met, falling out with his master over payments for their minister's stipend. Mayett was then in his mid-thirties, back in the village of Quainton after a twelve-year stint in the army between 1803 and 1815. Mayett's situation continued to deteriorate over the next two decades. Unable to find regular work, increasingly dependent on handouts from the parish, and in declining health, he died in poverty in the village of his birth in his late fifties.

Then there was John Lincoln, born in Suffolk in 1777. By the age of twenty his search for work had taken him no further than across the county border into Norfolk. Following the death of his wife and child, Lincoln turned his hand to whatever rural Norfolk could offer. Between 1801 and 1807, his jobs included minding horses, harvesting, well-digging, driving a 'Mail Cart', managing a garden, ploughing, and working as a footman.[165] In 1807, however, he received a letter from a friend who had moved to Woolwich and found him work at the Royal Arsenal. Lincoln left without hesitation. At Woolwich, he had no reason to regret the life he had left behind. At the Arsenal 'the work was very Light and the pay very good', and at one point his earnings rose as high as 38 shillings a week.[166] But sadly for Lincoln the good times did not last. Following the peace with France in 1814, the government downscaled production at Woolwich and Lincoln was laid off. He moved back to Norfolk, but returned to Woolwich soon after in the hope of finding a new opening at the Arsenal. Disappointed, he returned to Norfolk once again, giving up all hope of work at the Arsenal and settling down to a life as an agricultural day labourer, his paltry earnings eked out by a small dole from the parish.[167]

Finally George Mockford. Unlike Mayett and Lincoln, Mockford spent the whole of his life in east Sussex, never moving much further than fifteen miles from the village just outside Lewes in which he was born. He started work as a bird-scarer but got a glimpse of industrial life when he found work in a soap factory in Lewes. He continued there for a number of years, but when his master went bankrupt, Mockford's stint of factory work came to an abrupt end, there being few factories in Lewes. Mockford was back to picking up what casual and intermittent work he could find as an agricultural labourer – a 'little employment, for a time' here and there, at tasks such as haymaking, harvesting, hop-picking and gardening. He and his wife 'struggled on' trying to make a living from a smallholding, the annual harvest work, and the charity of his friends in the church.[168] The experiences of Lincoln and Mockford turn the pessimistic interpretation on its head. No mention of machines or monotony, of 'unsatisfying labour . . . for alien purposes'.[169] No regret for the supposedly wholesome or meaningful toil of farm work. Returning to agricultural work implied returning to low wages and unemployment. All in all, it is not surprising that leaving the land was so common and returning was so rare.

Only twelve of the autobiographers born in rural areas remained in agriculture well into adult life, which is much fewer than we would expect, given what the censuses tell us about the structure of nineteenth-century society. The under-representation of rural workers is a useful reminder that the autobiographers are not a reliable cross-section of working-class society. Working-class autobiographers may have been born into ordinary lives, but at some point they tended to diverge from the expected path. Clearly, life-writing was associated with adventure and achievement, and these things were more likely to occur if one moved away from the village. Yet if relatively few of our writers lived out their lives on the farm, there is nevertheless no reason to think their experiences particularly exceptional. And here there is little to add beyond what has already been said. Until at least 1850, many of those who stayed faced an ongoing struggle to make ends meet: low wages, insufficient work, and positions or masters that they disliked yet could not leave.

It is time to end this chapter; but this, perhaps, is where any attempt to understand the impact of the industrial revolution on the working poor ought to begin. Since the moment when commentators recognised that Britain was undergoing an irrevocable transformation, informed opinion has betrayed an unshakeable uneasiness that those at the bottom did not share equally in the advantages. Running like a thread through more than a century of historical analysis is the belief that the ordinary worker enjoyed a healthier, simpler and less frenetic life before the smoke and steam of the industrial revolution.

The trouble is that our autobiographers simply refuse to tell the story we expect to hear. Work was central to any labourer's life and was a theme to which the autobiographers frequently returned. But piecing together their thoughts and observations leaves us in little doubt that many working men saw substantial improvements in their living standards, not in spite of industrialisation, but because of it. Of course, much of the reason for this lay simply in the fact that the pre-industrial economy had been so poor at providing for its workers. In most places, there was just not enough to go around, and this left workers with irregular wages that covered little more than the bare essentials of existence, and too often not even that. And low incomes had cultural as well as economic consequences. Nothing gave meaning to the words 'master' and 'servant' more fully than low levels of employment. Deference and submission were part of the natural order of things when the servants' need for work outstripped the masters' ability to provide it.

With industrialisation some of the unskilled got to taste good, regular wages and the kind of independence that reliable earning power could bring. It is hard to unpack precisely when matters began to change, but dramatic changes had taken place between the late eighteenth and mid-nineteenth centuries. Nor is it easy to pinpoint exactly why industrialisation had the effect that it did, but the sheer demand for the backs and hands of adult men must stand out. Mills, factories, mines and quarries needed large numbers of men, not only to produce goods but to perform a range of tasks to ensure that raw materials and finished goods were to be found in the places and at the times they were needed. The rise of industry, the growth of towns and the development of new forms of transport increased the demand for construction workers. And towns housed large populations, forming a ready market for a wide range of goods and services.

It all helped to increase the amount and variety of work that needed to be done and this had myriad and far-reaching effects. Even the humble shoemaker, fashioning his shoes from materials and with methods not substantially different from those in use hundreds of years earlier, found himself drawn into this brave new world.

# CHAPTER THREE

# Suffer Little Children

The food of the family had to come through the fingers of the family
... The consequence was, that as soon as a shilling or two a week could
be earned by any of us, we had to do it. My term of toil began when but
a few months over six years of age. (Whittaker, p. 36)

THE DOLEFUL IMAGE of the Victorian child forced to work long hours
from a very young age is one of the first things that come to mind
when we consider Britain's industrial past. Poets, novelists, essayists and
reformers have all played their part in immortalising the plight of the child
worker. Children crowd the margins of several of Charles Dickens' novels,
most memorably, perhaps, in the form of Oliver Twist with his narrow
escape as the apprentice of Mr Gamfield the chimney-sweep; and in David
Copperfield, Dickens' semi-autobiographical hero, sent to work as a
'labouring hind' in the warehouse of Murdstone and Grinby at the age of
ten.[1] A little later in the century, Charles Kingsley's *Water Babies* took up
the theme of the chimney-sweep once again and, whether intended or not,
the novel became part of the last push to outlaw the use of boys as chimney-
sweeps in all its guises. And besides the great canon, a host of more ephem-
eral novels such as Frances Trollope's *The Life and Adventures of Michael
Armstrong, the Factory Boy* and Charlotte Elizabeth's *Helen Fleetwood*
exposed the suffering of child workers to the middle-class reader. The
industrial novels are perhaps not the finest examples of Victorian literature,
but it is nonetheless remarkable that privileged writers were so ready to
take up their pen for the most powerless members of society.[2]

Nor was it just the poets and novelists who were offended by the
employment of the very young in factories and mines. Many of the period's

most vocal and prolific commentators turned their attention to these voice-less victims – the 'white slaves' of England, as they were evocatively and effectively named by the Ten Hours campaigners – those agitating for a limit of ten hours on the length of children's working day.[3] The situation of child workers entered the political heart of the nation when reformers such as John Fielden and Lord Ashley, the Seventh Earl of Shaftesbury, took up their cause in Parliament. The year 1833 witnessed the passage of the nation's first major Factory Act, prohibiting the employment of children in factories under the age of nine and limiting the hours that older children could work. Legislation in the mining industry followed soon after, and the Acts were consolidated and amended down the century to further restrict and control the use of children in the workplace.[4] As part of the process of reform, a series of parliamentary select committees were established to investigate the extent of child labour. Their reports, along with the reformers' pamphlets and the lively public debate in the newspapers, generated a mountain of documents that none but the most short-sighted of historians could fail to notice. And throughout it all runs a sad tale of exploitation and cruelty, enough to break the spirit of the hard-worked child and the heart of the modern reader.

For all that our image of the emaciated child worker has been distilled from Victorian novels and half-remembered history lessons, it nonetheless contains more than a grain of truth. There may be a little mileage to be gained in claiming that novelists, poets and campaigners were not particu-larly informed or impartial witnesses: but this line of argument will not go very far in silencing their message. Nor will it do to suggest that children had always worked and that the Victorians at least possessed the humanity and wisdom to ameliorate their lot. They were after all slow to respond to the problem and many a mill owner made good profits from the children's nimble fingers before anyone was moved to act. That earlier and poorer societies had also connived in the practice must surely have offered no more than the smallest crumb of comfort to those who suffered.[5]

Even the most superficial trawl through the autobiographies quickly dredges up plenty of evidence to suggest that these bleak assessments of the impact of industrialisation on the children of the poor are not simply the bad dreams of doomsayers and pessimists. Time and again, the autobiog-raphers describe a depressingly familiar story of a childhood brought to a premature end by work that was arduous, unpleasant and often dangerous; by work that started at far too young an age. Here for example is Edward Rymer describing his first foray into farm work at six years old: 'I was sent to tend the herds of cows and flocks of sheep belonging to Squire Clough . . . my work being some distance from the village, I sometimes lost my way in a fog, and wandered miles shouting and crying for my mother half-blind and nearly heart-broken.'[6] Or Robert Collyer, starting in the factory at the age of eight 'with many more children of my age or older, standing at the spinning frames – "doffers" they called us – thirteen hours a day, five days of the week, and eleven on the Saturday – rung in at six in the morning and out at eight in the evening, with an hour for dinner and a rest'.[7] The former child miners provided some of the most distressing accounts of their early lives, telling of how they felt uncomfortable and frightened, working in rough conditions alongside rough men. The hours were so long that they saw no daylight for days on end during the winter months – little lives of darkness, in every meaning possible.

But we can do more with the autobiographies than pile up examples of writers saying what we already think they ought to be saying. It was a rare autobiographer who did not devote considerable attention to his experiences from early life. Almost all the writers had something to say about their father, mother and family circumstances. Most described their first experience of paid employment and some wrote at length about the family decisions that lay behind their entry to the workforce. In a sample of 350 autobiographies, this amounts to a very rich seam of information, enabling us to put some figures to the incidence of child labour as well as to probe the social context in which it occurred. Our writers not only stand testimony to the dark interpretation, they also enable a much deeper understanding of the complex forces that motivated parents to send their small children out to work.

Let us start by looking at the ages at which the young started work, a crude but very useful way of contrasting the experiences of children during the industrial revolution. Despite the long passage of time that had usually elapsed before our child workers took up the pen, the age at which they started work was clearly remembered and diligently recorded by the majority of writers, a sign no doubt of the significance of this event in any working person's life. Admittedly some were uncertain about timing. Those, for example, who inform us that they started work at 'about this time', 'now' or 'at a proper age' are not so helpful as they perhaps intended.[8] A handful of writers did not specify the date of their birth, which makes piecing together the most rudimentary chronology of their working life impossible. But for the most part, the transition from school or home to the workplace was something that few forgot and most writers had little difficulty pinpointing the moment when this important step towards adulthood occurred.[9]

When the ages at which children started work are plotted on a graph, they fall neatly into the bell-shaped curve that one would expect. One child started work at the age of four, a few more started at five, and then the number of children in each age group rises steadily until the age of ten, at which point the number starts to fall again. The average age at which the autobiographers started work was also ten years.[10] The only slight interruptions to the curve occur around the age of twelve, when the number rises modestly again. This age was a very common time for starting apprenticeships, so the clustering suggests that some writers may not have bothered to note the more casual employments that preceded their apprenticeship. Had they done so, the average age for starting work would be pulled slightly downwards, though as the rise is small the effect would be slight.

So ten years old was the average age for starting work. It is slightly younger than other historians have found, probably because I have been more ruthless in excluding children who did not belong to families that can be accurately labelled 'poor' or 'working class' (our criteria, it might be remembered, cover those whose only income was derived from manual labour and those whose income was sufficiently scanty for a period of ill health or unemployment to pose serious financial difficulties).[11] It is also striking that the average age at which children started work changed very little over the period. All through the eighteenth century and until 1850, ages for starting work fluctuated widely around the age of ten, falling as low as four and rising as high as seventeen. But the average age always hovered about ten.[12] Given the relatively small number of autobiographies that have survived before about 1750 we should not place too much weight on the figures for the earlier period. The wide variation in the ages does, however, call out for analysis. What determined the age at which our autobiographers entered the workforce? Why did some start at five or six and others in their mid-teens, or even later? And how can these children's experiences be fitted more broadly into the social history of the industrial revolution?

Conventional wisdom dictates that the age at which children started work was connected to the poverty of the family, and the autobiographies lend some support to this idea. Amongst those starting work at the youngest ages were to be found some living in the most desperate poverty, and writers often linked their family's poverty to their own early entry to the workforce. Edward Davis, for example, 'lacked even the bare necessaries of life' as a small child owing to his father's heavy drinking habit and the fact that he 'disliked work exceedingly'. Edward gave this as the reason he was 'compelled to join the ranks of the bread-winners of the family' at the age of six years and eight months.[13] At the other end of the distribution the reverse also appears true. Large incomes and small families helped to delay the moment at which a child was cast out to earn his daily bread. Richard Boswell Belcher and his two brothers were raised in relative affluence by their grandfather, following the death of both their parents. He sent them to 'good schools as boarders, our racket being too much for him'. Richard's last school was a 'first class school for tradesmen's sons', where he remained studying the three Rs, history and geography until, at the age of thirteen, he was taken away to become a draper's apprentice.[14]

But there are also some problems with the commonsense view that variation in the age at which children started work can be explained by the wealth of their families. For there amongst the autobiographies, alongside families like Davis' and Belcher's, behaving just as they should, were many others who failed to act in the way that common sense predicts. The experiences of George Mockford and John Taylor illustrate the problem. A fair few of the autobiographers had very little that was good to say about their father, and George Mockford may be counted as one of their number. 'The great ambition of my father', he opined, was 'to save money [and] his children's little strength and time should be all put to such an account as would be conducive to this end.'[15] But even leaving aside the meanness or otherwise of George's father, it is certain that he was a very poor man – struggling to feed a family of twelve children on the piteously small wages he earned as a shepherd. As a child, George's diet consisted largely of potatoes with a little bacon fat, and it is doubtful that his father often ate a finer meal than potatoes with the bacon. Not only was George's family desperately poor, his father had very little care for their welfare. Nevertheless, George did not start full-time work until the age of ten – young to us, but not unusually so for the period.[16]

On the other hand, John Taylor had nothing but praise for his parents. They were 'creditable, industrious, managing persons', he wrote; there were 'few like them of common working people'. Nor was this simply family conceit, he hastened to add, for it was 'hardly my place to say'. No, it was the considered opinion of their neighbours in the village, by whom 'it was often said that they were the best housekeepers in Northowram [particularly] in regard to that principal branch of it, the bringing up of children'.[17] His father worked tirelessly to provide for his family's wants. During the summer he was 'frequently doing thrice as much work as any man ought to do', ultimately working himself to an early grave owing to his 'excessive fondness' for his wife and children. John's assessment was clear: his father was a loving and industrious man and his family was nowhere near the bottom of the social heap. Yet these qualities notwithstanding, John and his brother Dan were sent to work many years earlier than George Mockford: the brothers were sent down the local coal mine at the ages of six and four.[18] Nor are these isolated cases. The autobiographies allow us a unique insight into the relationship between hardship and the age of starting work and so permit us to explore the connections a little deeper.

With children often only vaguely aware of their parents' earnings, there is no way of measuring the breadline in the autobiographies, but writers did provide rich contextual detail about their childhood and were usually acutely aware of, and commented upon, the position of their own family relative to their neighbours. Some writers gave a graphic account of their impoverished beginnings, describing their families as 'poor', 'destitute', 'desperate', and their childhood selves as lacking the most basic necessities – food, clothing and shoes. We also know that some kinds of families were likely to be much poorer than others. Mothers had very few options for earning an income outside the home, so the death or departure of a child's father invariably plunged a family into serious financial straits. The figure of the drunken father regularly appears in the autobiographies, with bruised bodies and empty bellies usually to be found close by. It is probably fair to assume that children raised in large families were more likely to suffer from want. So let us also mark all the children who mention single mothers, drunken fathers or large families as impoverished, regardless of whether they actually specified this. If our child workers are sorted into two groups along these lines, those that showed signs of extreme poverty and those that did not, some rather unexpected patterns emerge.

Let us begin by looking at the children who started working at the youngest ages. Fourteen of the twenty-six children who started work before the age of seven described poverty in their family, but the other twelve gave no indication that the level of need within their family was particularly high. In other words, although a little over half of the children who started work at a young age appear to have done so because of poverty, an almost equal number failed to connect their early entry to the workforce with an unusually acute level of hardship. What is yet more surprising, however, is that the number of children from deeply impoverished families did not fall away as the age at which they began work started to rise. If we use exactly the same qualities to mark out the children who started work at the age of ten as impoverished – reference to acute poverty, large families, and drunken or absent fathers – the level of need appears almost as great as it was amongst children who went to work several years younger. Just over half of the children who started work before the age of seven described impoverished backgrounds, yet amongst those who started work at the age of ten that figure still hovers just below the 50 per cent mark.[19]

It is only as the children become older that the connection between family circumstances and starting work becomes more clear cut. Amongst children who started work at the age of fourteen or older, none provided evidence of acute hardship within their family, so a higher income does appear to have played an important role in delaying a child's entry to the workforce. At the younger ages, though, the picture is more complex. Regardless of the actual age at which their working lives began, the level of need was high in many of these families: between 50 and 70 per cent of the children in each year group offered distinct signs of acute hardship and, given the nature of the sources, we can probably assume that the real figure was even higher. Yet parents were responding to this need in different ways, some sending their children to work as young as five or six, others delaying for a number of years. The question inevitably arises: why did not all the parents take advantage of such an obvious way of raising the family's income?

To make sense of the different choices made by parents in broadly similar material circumstances we need to look at the options that were open to them. As anyone who has spent much time with children would probably testify, putting a child of six or seven to gainful employment is not straightforward. Nor is the unemployability of young children a phenomenon unique to modern society – the consequence of our cosseting of children, lax parenting, the decline of discipline, or anything else that might be indicated. There are far more fundamental developmental impediments that stand in the way of small children earning their own living. A six-year-old lacks the strength, concentration, co-ordination and stamina of an adolescent or young adult, and this places serious limits on the willingness of employers to take such workers on. As one autobiographer recalled, he was 'only about six years old' when his father had the good fortune to find a chimney-sweep ready to hire him. Yet his new employer found he was 'really too young for the work, so they made me do odd things about the house, such as lighting the fires and nursing the baby'.[20] In other words, neither the needs nor the desires of their family are the only forces controlling a child's entry to the workforce. Parents had to find employers for their children, and we should not be too quick to assume that in poor, pre-industrial societies these employers were readily to be found.

So let us sort our workers for a second time along a different set of lines. This time we shall place each child worker into one of three groups, according to the kind of employment opportunities that existed in their neighbour-hood. In the first group are all those children raised in rural areas with no domestic industry, indeed with very little employment of any kind outside agriculture – villages such as Pagham in Sussex, described by one of its inhabitants as a place where 'there was literally nothing for young men to go at, only remain upon the land and displace the old, or be a sailor or soldier'.[21] The second group comprises those children living in market towns, where trade rather than manufacturing predominated. Towns such as Cheltenham, Banbury, Wellingborough, Cambridge, Chichester, Hull and Chester figure in this group. The third and final group encompasses those who lived close to centres of industry or manufacture. By the nineteenth century, industriali-sation took a very wide variety of forms, so this group represents a corre-spondingly heterogeneous collection of settlements. The mining and factory districts of the Midlands, Lancashire and Yorkshire, the north-east and the Scottish Lowlands are included here, as are many of these regions' emerging towns and cities. Areas of cottage industry are also counted in this group, so plenty of villages are to be found in its midst. How do matters look when our child workers are divided into three groups along these lines?

There are no real surprises when we look at the children who lived in agricultural areas: with an average age for starting work of ten and a half years, these children broadly conformed to the national pattern. For those living in towns, paid employment started on average one year later, at almost eleven and a half. The most startling result, however, comes from those children living in the industrial regions. The average age of starting work in this group was just eight and a half years – fully two years younger than the children in agricultural areas, and three years younger than the boys in traditional market towns. Almost all of the very young workers were also found in this group: nearly 70 per cent of the children at work before the age of eight lived in industrial areas.[22] Living in an area with industrial employment was therefore closely correlated with entering the workforce at a younger age. But of course, simply demonstrating that industrialisation and young workers were found in the same places is a far cry from proving that the two events were related. We will need to look at what our writers tell us about their entry to the workforce in more detail to understand why work started earlier in the industrial districts than elsewhere.

In agricultural districts there was, inevitably, very little for children to do outside the farm, so almost all the children in this group began work on the land. As a result, their entry into the workforce was heavily determined by the ability of local farmers to provide work for small hands. At the younger ages, boys were employed at a relatively simple level – scaring birds, keeping sheep out of the roads, and herding cows.[23] Their work was seasonal and often part-time. With increasing age, the children's responsibilities and workload increased. From the ages of eight or nine, they started to help in the fields, performing such tasks as helping with harvests, picking potatoes, sowing turnips, ploughing, and looking after horses.[24] Some went to live with their employers though most remained at home with their own family. A few more bypassed agriculture altogether and left their village in order to embark on an apprenticeship in a nearby town.[25]

Yet pervasive difficulties stood in the way of putting children to work on the land, no matter what age they actually started work and no matter how serious the poverty of their family. As David Barr astutely noted, his parents' search for employment for his childhood self had been a 'difficult task', as the family were 'cut off from the world in a remote hamlet that presented little opportunities for employment beyond agricultural labour'.[26] If we look at the stories our writers told about their early childhood and the moment that they started work, it becomes clear that many small children were kept at home because nobody in the neighbourhood had any need for their services.

This was certainly the experience of John Gibbs. John spent the early years of his childhood in the most abject poverty. His mother had died, his father taken to drink, and poor John was left roaming the village with 'a hungry belly and a ragged back ... at times in cold, in hunger, and almost in nakedness'.[27] Despite occasional spells helping out at harvest time, John remained out of work for the rest of the year. Employers in the small west Sussex village of Bolney were thin on the ground, however much one might need them. At the age of ten, he made a bid to escape his father's neglect by travelling to find a relation living nearby and asking her to help him find a position in service, though he entertained no real hope that any such place would be found. 'To my great surprise,' however, she 'informed me that a lad had run away from a small gentleman's house that morning.'[28] Enquiries were made and in no time the hopeful young John was standing in front of the household for inspection. The family looked him over, certain members casting doubt on the ability of the malnourished ten-year-old before them to perform the work of the house – 'some said, I was much too small, others, that I was altogether unacquainted with the business'. The situation was saved only when one of the daughters of the house spoke up and indicated her approval of the lad.[29] Even John realised that their agreeing to employ him was more an act of charity than of economic self-interest.

The utter neglect and deprivation of John Gibb's early childhood was unusual. Many of our writers suffered poverty, but most had at least one parent with more than a passing concern for their welfare, and many had much more than that. His difficulty in finding full-time employment in a rural area, however, was anything but unusual. In fact on close inspection we see that many of those who appeared to start work at a young age were not actually entering paid employment at all. There is frequently a discrepancy in these accounts between the moment when the writer's schooling stopped or at which he felt childhood had ended and the moment when wage-earning began, time that was usually filled with some form of unpaid service to parents or more distant family members. Joseph Jewell was kept from school at the age of eight so that he could help his father look after horses. John Bethune started herding cows for his father at the same age. But neither received any payment for their labour for a number of years: Jewell was paid only when he took up a position in service at the age of thirteen and Bethune when he was put to stone-breaking when he was eleven.[30] One child in the Scottish Highlands was initially paid in kind rather than in cash: James Hogg's payment for herding cows at the age of seven came in the form of a 'ewe lamb and a pair of new shoes'.[31] Another, living at home with his widowed mother, was threatened with a parish apprenticeship, 'to be a drudge in a farm yard, without any remuneration until I had reached the age of twenty-one'. He refused to take up the apprenticeship on these terms, but he did start working for a widower 'for my food' rather than for wages.[32] The rural autobiographers also convey the impression that there was a limited number of openings and possibilities, with children remaining in school or idle until an opportunity became vacant. John Bennett's childhood had comprised intervals at school and intervals 'kept at home to do what I could' and there is little doubt it would have continued along these lines had his elder brother not died. This was a 'sad job' for John, he later recalled, as he was then taken from school 'to supply his place'.[33]

As employment was hard to come by, positions were jealously guarded, no matter how unsuitable they subsequently proved to be. Parents living in agricultural districts displayed an unmistakable reluctance to remove their children from a place of work, even in the face of heartbreaking cruelty. This at any rate was the experience of James Bowd, who found himself driving a plough for a horse-keeper who oscillated between leaving him to 'do as I liked' and 'floging' him mercilessly. James knew there was no point in asking his parents to find him a new position. As he explained in his unpunctuated prose:

> My father was very firm with Children working with him he used to tell those that his Children worked with to Yank us if we did not do as they wanted us and so it was no use to go home and tell my father how this man had been serving me and so I had to keep on going with the treatment for one year and then Came Micklamas which was the time for servants Changing their situations and he left and you may be very sure I did not shed many tears after him.[34]

When Joseph Jewell quit his position in the midst of winter with a carter 'who used me ill' he also knew he would not meet with sympathy at home. But with nowhere else to turn, he returned to his father's house and hid in a barn for a few days. There he lived off scraps of food brought out by his sister; they both knew their 'father would near kill me if I did not go back to my place'. When his father discovered him he fell 'in a great passion, shook his stick over me, but I sopose my pittyfull apearance prevented his beating me'. But Joseph's 'pittyfull apearance' did not weaken his father's resolve to return him to his master. The father's plan was to tie Joseph to a horse ridden by his brother while he followed behind and whipped him there. It only failed because he learned that another boy had already taken Joseph's place in the few days that he had been missing.[35]

The sufferings of James Bowd and Joseph Jewell might be blamed on their fathers, as neither father appears to have had the slightest concern for his son's welfare. But responsibility for the abuse that some children encountered in the workplace cannot always be placed so neatly at the door of the uncaring, hardened father. Even parents who did care very much about their children's welfare ultimately reached the same decision, choosing to return their children to their employers, whatever the treatment they received there. Roger Langdon, for example, was nearly killed by the drunken ploughman under whom he worked on the farm, but as 'every other place in the parish was filled and my parents could not afford to keep me in idleness', back to work for the brute he went.[36] James Hogg was 'often nearly exhausted with hunger and fatigue' with one of his masters while he was a shepherd; but once again, there was no question of leaving before his term was out.[37] When William Milne ran away from his place in service his mother remonstrated with him and 'let out at me with a big stick'. She missed, but before William could escape 'I was seized and laid across my mother's knee!' Still unable to effect the blow she desired, she resorted to reason, pointing out that 'she was not able to provide for herself and me, if I were to be idle on her hands'. Before the day was out, William was back with his employers.[38] Time soon taught William what a bad employer really looked like. The rations he received in his next position were so scanty they left him seriously malnourished. Yet he still remained there for the term he had been hired. On returning home at the end of his term and resuming a normal diet, he was taken ill and the family concluded that his 'organs of digestion had been damaged' by the recent privations he had had to endure.[39]

These parents should not be grouped with those guilty of neglect and abuse. Each had made a reasonable decision from the very unpalatable range of options available. Many of these parents were simply unable to feed their growing children adequately. James Nye was one of a family of eleven children raised in rural Sussex in the 1820s and did not start work until the age of twelve. He recalled how 'the young ones' in his family went 'very short of food and clothing'. Despite his mother's best efforts, he rarely had more than 'half a bellyful' at mealtimes, and ate scarcely anything other than bread: 'I was such a white weakly boy that people used to say I never should come to nothing, and no wonder so hungry I used to be nearly all day'.[40] Paid employment gave children the best chance of enough to eat, even though it might have to be bought at the price of harsh words, cruel taunts and violence, and even though employers occasionally failed to provide even that. Clearly, though, the scarcity of employment in most rural areas was a double-edged sword. It certainly delayed children's entry to the workforce, but did very little for their welfare once they were there.

The situation for families living in market towns was broadly similar. Those raised in towns often recalled how their parents' plan to put them to work had hit the buffers when nothing suitable could be found. Here for example is Thomas Wallis' account of his search for work as a boy in Hull in the 1830s. His father's cabinet-making business had failed and the family were living in extremely straitened circumstances, but although William's parents removed him from school at the age of nine, they could not find a suitable position for him until he reached eleven. The first job they found for him involved helping his father make bristles for brushes from whalebones. But the work proved 'too heavy for so young a boy', so this enterprise was soon abandoned. William next received a little money first for passing tools to a 'kind old stonemason' as he needed them and then for travelling to the country to help a coal dealer sell his wares. Neither venture came to anything though, for the family were still looking out for 'more congenial and continuous employment' for their son several months later. Their hopes were raised when they learned of a quack doctor seeking a messenger. Dressed in his smartest clothes, William walked with his mother to the doctor's house to apply for the situation. Unfortunately, the young William 'failed to find favour in the eyes of the young lady [the doctor's daughter], who urged that [he] was too young to be entrusted with the duties required from the "Doctor's" assistant!'[41] A permanent position at last came at Ellison and Sons' Mustard and Blacking Manufactory. William's job was to walk an 'old blind horse' in an endless circle to drive the plant's machinery. He was paid two shillings a week.[42] William stayed here for three months, before finding work as an errand boy, first for a shoemaker, then for a doctor.

William Wallis ended up working where most of his peers in small towns began – as an errand boy. But as his family found, potential employers did not see much value in the service of a young child, and this helped to ensure that very few of the boys raised in towns were at work before they were nine, and many of these were working as unpaid helpers to their parents or employed on an occasional basis by a local farmer.[43] The problem of finding work as an errand boy was captured by one autobiographer living in the small Highland port town of Dingwall. His mother had the good fortune to find him a position at the age of eight, but when his master married, one of his new wife's first acts was to get rid of the errand boy. Our writer continues:

> Go home I hardly could; my poor mother was not able to support me. A place I would and must have, but where to get one was a mystery. I could not obtain a place where I could be of such service as to [e]nsure myself even 'dog's wages' – my daily food.[44]

This was the problem that kept so many of the children living in market towns in school or at home through their early years. When John Hemmingway's mother was unable to feed her family during the 1802 trade recession in Norwich, she sent John and his elder brother not to work, but to collect nettles – almost certainly a reflection of the reality of the situation rather than a desire to shield her sons from an early entry to the workforce.[45] Peter Taylor found work as an errand boy in Paisley at the age of eleven and a half, but only because his elder brother had fallen ill, so he 'was sent to take his place'.[46] And just as in rural areas, once a position had been found, parents and children made sure to hold on to it, no matter how serious the mistreatment a child encountered.[47] Most employers found that the expense of feeding and clothing a growing boy younger than ten or eleven outweighed the profit that could be made from his labour. It spelled bad news for family incomes, but helped to protect children from the long hours and exploitation that so often haunted the experience of very young workers.

The industrial areas form a stark contrast to the more traditional parts of the economy. The autobiographies provide considerable evidence that work here was easily found, and this must go some way to explaining why young children in these areas were more often at work. Here as elsewhere, the work that children performed reflected the needs of the local economy, so factories, mines, handloom weaving and other forms of production dominated the working landscape.[48] With the growth of these industries, there was lots of work that needed to be done and children were hustled into economic activity at ever younger ages. Factories and mills were the largest source of employment for young children, and with no effective lower age limits before the passage of the Ten Hours Act in 1833, mills routinely hired children from the age of six. Most of these young workers entered the factories as piecers, standing at the spinning machines repairing breaks in the thread. A few started as scavengers, crawling beneath the machinery to clear it of dirt, dust or anything else that might disturb the mechanism.[49] From piecing they progressed to 'doffers' or 'fillers', their task being to remove the full bobbins from the spinning machines and replace them with empty ones.[50] As they grew older, they moved into jobs of greater responsibility.

No less importantly, the children were supervised by a system of 'overlookers' – older, male workers who patrolled the inside of the factory monitoring their work. As one factory child recalled, 'a rope with a knot at one end was hung over the steam pipe, and a very trifling effort indeed brought the rope from its resting-place to be laid on the shoulders of the poor little piecer'.[51] Inside the factories, therefore, a combination of simple tasks and overlookers ensured that even very young children could perform work that was of some value to their employer.

In the coal-mining districts, a similar framework was in place, with boys starting out on light tasks befitting their abilities, under the eye of a more experienced worker.[52] As Emanuel Lovekin remarked on being sent to the mine at the age of seven, 'it was little I could be exspected to doo except open a door for wagons to pass through'.[53] Several of the child miners started out like Emanuel as 'trappers', minding the trapdoors in the tunnels underground.[54] Others began by picking over the coals at the pit mouth, carrying picks for the miners, or pushing coal-laden trolleys along underground.[55] Their tasks were simple, required relatively little strength, and were usually carried out under some supervision by the more experienced miners. As the boys' strength increased, new opportunities unfolded. Emanuel, for example, was soon 'Promoted to drive a Donkey', whilst his younger brother, who had now reached the age of seven, took over the work of minding trapdoors.[56] Boys progressed to driving wagons, working with the pit ponies, and eventually hewing coal from the coalface, each time moving on to work with greater responsibility and better pay – though none of it, in the understated opinion of one former child miner, 'could be termed congenial'.[57] Most of the boys employed underground worked in the coal industry, but the copper- and tin-mining industry in Cornwall also found early employment for some.

Domestic industry, handloom weaving in particular, was another important source of employment for children in industrial areas. Young family members could be made useful from the ages of six or seven winding the bobbins for their parents.[58] And alongside the major employers were a host of small workshops willing and able to put young fingers to work. Amongst the autobiographers were those who had started work in a brickyard, for a button-stamper, at twine-making and thread-bleaching, and at walking horses in circles to turn wheels to drive machines.[59] In each case, a similar set of forces were at work. Industrialisation was generally associated with higher levels of employment and this helped to increase the demand for child workers. But industrial employers also had tasks that required little skill or responsibility and the scale of their operations made it possible and economic to establish a network of monitors and supervisors. So it was not just economic growth in itself that increased the use of small children in the workforce in the industrial regions. There was something in the nature of the economic growth that occurred at this time that was peculiarly well adapted to exploit the capacities of small children.

Although industry was the most important source of employment for the children living in industrial areas, a sizeable number also worked in agriculture. In many areas, particularly in centres of cottage industry, manufacturing and agriculture existed side by side, and the demand for industrial workers created a shortage of young people to help till the land. The situation was nicely described by John Struthers, who spent his childhood in East Kilbride, just outside Glasgow. He noted how the rise of handloom weaving in the area had caused men of all professions – the ditcher, the quarryman, even the ploughman – to desert the land, creating 'a scarcity of boys for agricultural purposes'.[60] So of course his parents had no difficulty finding him a position as a live-in farmhand. John was not alone in finding agricultural work in the heart of an industrial district. Other autobiographers started their working lives clearing dung off the turnpike roads, herding, harvesting, and milking cows, clearing out brushwood from 'a long, wild clough below the canal basin' and planting potatoes.[61] The picture that emerges for the industrial regions is one of plentiful employment. The new industries offered a range of jobs designed to make the best of the capabilities of very young children, but they also reduced the pressure on jobs in agriculture, thereby easing entry to work on the land as well.

There is also something significant in the fact that the children in industrial areas had nothing to say about *how* their parents had managed to find them a place of work. Whatever the reasons for parents wanting to put their children to work, the outcome was always the same. A trip to the mill, to the mine, or to a small local manufacturer and the matter was resolved. Within days mother was walking her child to work in the morning with a parcel of food for the day. Here, for example, is William Marcroft's recollection of how his mother went about looking for a situation for her son when she had decided that he 'must not work in the cotton mill any more':

A looking out was begun to find another job ... Fustian cutting at that time was very busy. Application was made to Jacob Ashton, of Cowbourne Lane, Heywood. Did he want a lad about twelve years of age? He said he did. An agreement was entered into ...[62]

None of the children living close to centres of industry provided any hint that their family's designs had been frustrated or delayed owing to difficulty in finding a suitable situation. Instead the finding of work was presented in extremely straightforward terms, with families moving into the factory districts and finding work for their children 'immediately' or 'almost immediately'.[63] When the young John Hemmingway ran away from his master in Pendleton to Manchester he was just 'rambling along one of the streets' when a 'small Manufacturer from Bolton ... accosted me with the words, well, my boy, are you in want of a place'.[64] The ease with which parents translated their desire for work for their children into a position of paid employment forms a marked contrast with the obstacles encountered by parents living outside the industrial regions.

The suggestion that work was easily come by in the industrial districts seems to be supported by the ways in which parents reacted if they discovered that their children met with rough usage in the workplace. Parents were quick and emphatic in responding to suspicions that their children were being mistreated at work. John Wood, for example, started at the cotton factory at the age of six and his overlooker lost little time in treating him 'in a most brutal manner'. Within weeks, his mother had noticed the 'discoloration of my back as the result of a flogging I had received': she removed him immediately and returned him to school – where, Wood added with no apparent sense of the contradiction, he was taught to 'knit stockings'.[65] Joseph Hodgson started down the mine at the age of ten, but was 'severely buffeted, whipt and kicked' by his supervisors. His mother noticed the mark of a whip-crack along the side of his face, and both parents immediately decided that he 'should go no more'.[66] More unusually, when George Marsh worked with his elder brother for 'Mr. Willie Jubb', his brother used him 'so cruelly, that one day I could not walk home, so I laid in a coke basket beside a fire until midnight when my mother came and found me'. His mother did not let the constable take her older son away and 'lock him up' but that was the end of George's employment with his brother at Mr Willie Jubb's.[67]

It did not even need to be a matter of bruises, welts and floggings to persuade parents to reconsider their choice of employment. George Smith was taken away from the flax and hemp mills after a few weeks because the work made him 'so wet that my parents thought it would injure my health'.[68] The child miner Thomas Oliver returned to school because he could not stand the cold.[69] And David Whitehead's mother repeatedly came and took her son back home for matters far less weighty than the violence, overwork and stinted rations that some of the child workers in agriculture had to endure. A false accusation of drinking the new milk, a mistress who suspected him of dishonesty, a quarrel with his master over a piece of bodged weaving – each time his mother agreed to take him home, though not always with quite the degree of sympathy that her son might have wished.[70] There was no reason not to when a new position could be easily found, as indeed proved the case over and over for these children. After their move to Manchester, one day at the cotton mill was enough for John Hemmingway's parents to 'make up their minds not to send me to that mill again'. Over the following two years, John worked in several of the town's mills – though he ruefully noted that from his perspective he 'could very rarely find any difference in their mode of treatment'.[71] The ease with which new positions could be found created a very different situation to the non-industrial areas, where low levels of employment meant that parents often sympathised with their children, but rarely removed them from their tormentors. The simple fact that work for young children was so easily come by must go some way to explaining the younger than average age for starting work in industrial districts.

So parents played a complex role in the extension of child labour that occurred in the heartlands of the industrial revolution. We know that most parents took care to monitor their children's welfare in the workplace. Yet it must also be admitted that many were careful to ensure their children were economically active in the first place. In reality, we cannot fully grasp the history of child labour in industrialising Britain unless we acknowledge the place of children's work in the cultural horizons of the labouring poor. 'Child welfare' was not yet a meaningful concept. Many adults simply believed that children should be sent to work as soon as they were able. William Dodd did not know 'the predisposing circumstances' that had induced his parents to send their four children to work in the factories at very young ages. He thought that they went 'as we could meet with employers'.[72] John Hemmingway started work at the age of ten, following his family's migration from Norwich to Manchester. On their arrival, his father found work as a spinner in a cotton factory, and it is hard to imagine that he earned less than he had as a weaver in Norwich during a period of recession. Yet it was at this moment that John and his siblings entered the workforce: 'it followed as a matter of course, that his children, such as were able must also be employed to assist . . . I for one was doomed to become an operative'.[73]

The situation was much the same for the child miners. One anonymous writer recalled that he had started work at the age of six. His mother and father, he noted, had 'passed me off as seven years and a half; so they got my wages'.[74] Joshua Dodgson went down the mine at the age of nine for no other reason than that his widowed mother had become acquainted with a coal miner who was well placed to find work for her sons. Joshua wrote that 'as he was a miner, he soon had my oldest brother and myself' in the pit.[75] What emerges a number of times is that parents put their children to work not simply because they had to, but *because they could*.[76]

Something more of parental attitudes was captured by Henry Hughes, who was sent down the mine to mind a trapdoor for his father at the age of nine. His stepmother 'did not see much value in education', he wrote: 'learn to work and work should be the proper object and business of children and young people'. Young people 'should break coal or dig peat or other manual labour and then they would never lack bread. Therefore to the work underground, I was sent early in life.'[77] Nor was this simply a case of a wicked stepmother who could not get rid of her husband's children quick enough. After all, it was Henry's father who actually found him his first job and Henry was fond of his stepmother – they later emigrated to America together.

His parents were not alone in the value they placed on honest, hard work. John Harris' father took a dim view of his son's love of books. He 'appeared to dislike it, saying he did not think I should ever earn my living'.[78] The carpenter, Peter Gabbitass, admitted that his schooldays had been short. His father had had 'a good business', but also 'believed in boys going to work early'.[79] In many poor families, child labour was simply part of the natural order. The rights or wrongs of putting small children to work was not too deeply questioned. This was just the way things were. As John Clifford ruefully remembered, his father did 'not seem to have thought it any hardship that I should have to get up at four o'clock when I started work in the factory. He used to do it as a boy, therefore there should be no reason why I should not rise at that time.'[80]

How far these views were typical is impossible to establish. Alongside the fathers who liked to see their sons at work and did not think it 'any hardship' if they had to rise early to get there, were many mothers who were sorely troubled that their children were compelled to go to work so young.[81] Whether the stern fathers outweighed the soft mothers is anyone's guess. Part of the difficulty is that for many writers a lot had changed between the time they started work and the time they wrote their autobiography. Within the space of a few decades, child labour had became a political issue. The employment of very young children in factories and mines became first morally repugnant and then illegal. The shift in values that had occurred between our writers' childhoods and the moment at which they wrote about it clearly posed difficulties for some adult writers. Men found themselves bound to explain something that in reality had called for no special explanation at the time.

The problems are compounded by the fact that all the discussion of parental motivations comes from children second-guessing, excusing, or simply seeking to understand their parents' choices rather than from the parents themselves. The tendency of autobiographers to write at length about their childhood but to say little about parenthood or their own children is widely recognised, and this is certainly true of the working-class writers looked at here. Despite the crystal-clear memory that many writers had of the age at which their own working life had begun, they were almost uniformly silent about the ages at which their children entered the workforce. And though our writers were far better placed to explain why they had put their children to work than to comment on their parents' reasons, almost all of them had absolutely nothing to say under this head.

One exception comes from the 'Family Records' written by Benjamin Shaw, which range over his own life and the lives of other members of his extended family. He declared it was written 'Partly for his own use & Partly for his Children' and he wrote at length about each of his eight children, even little Mary who had died of measles when less than a year old. The family grew up in Preston in the first quarter of the nineteenth century and all started work in one of the town's many factories before they were adults. Shaw's 'Family Records' promise to shed a little light on one of the darkest corners of Britain's industrial history.

Benjamin Shaw did not know that factory children would later become a historical oddity that subsequent generations would seek to understand, so he did not worry too much about explaining the place of the factory in the life of his own young family. Of his first son, Joseph, Shaw wrote simply that 'he went to the factory to work young, was mostly in the Card room'. His second son, William, was also 'Sent to the factory young, & wrought in the yard at Horrocks in the Card room'. His first daughter, Isabella, was a 'fine, Strong & healthy child, & good Humoured': she also 'went to the factory young'. On the other hand, his second daughter, Hannah, being 'a Small and Puny child', remained at home 'employed in the House with her mother' until the age of about fourteen, only then joining her brothers and sisters in the factory. Thomas, their next child, also suffered from ill health. He was 'a troublesom Child from his Birth, Cross, & Peevish … with a Bad Stomach, & every way full of trouble'. Perhaps this was the reason why he was 'Sent to the School when young', when his older siblings had been sent to the factory. But Thomas followed them when he was nine, so 'young' for the elder children presumably meant starting work at age eight or younger. There, 'still he continued to be full of trouble to us, for he came home nearly every day, with his fingers or hands or cloaths torn &c …' Shaw's youngest two daughters, Mary and Agnes, he described as 'mostly' healthy. Mary started in the card room when 'about 9 years old' and Agnes went to school 'when little' and to the card room 'when young'.[82]

How can we interpret the evidence Benjamin provides? He did not even state exactly how old his children were when they entered the factory, still less leave clues as to why they entered when they did. It is tempting to suggest that the Shaws sent their young children to the factory because poverty left them no other choice; but poverty provides only a partial explanation. The family certainly suffered from downturns in trade in some years. His second-youngest daughter, Mary, for example, was 'brought up rather hardly, for Bread was deer'. But such hardship was not constant and at other times Benjamin 'had good work and wages'. In some years 'things seemed to prosper'.[83] The family did not perceive themselves to be in great need. His wife, Betty, refused to mend the children's clothes and always bought new ones. She told her husband she did not like 'to see them in mended clothes ... she did not like to be poor & seem so'.[84] Why patch clothes? Why not just buy new ones? Benjamin did not expatiate on the whys and wherefores of his children's entry to the factory because there was simply nothing to explain. His children went to work at young ages because the work was there. That was the way things were done in poor families like his. That was how the family were dressed in decent clothes rather than rags.

In fact it is not necessary to pass judgement on the parents who sent their children to work at unusually young ages, for this line of thinking implies that the labouring poor were uniquely responsible for the use of small children in the workplace. A tacit acceptance of child labour ran through this society like a fault-line from top to bottom. If the poor were ready to send their children out to work, their social superiors were no less ready to take them in. Aristocratic mine owners, middle-class factory owners, farmers great and small, doctors, clergymen and other professionals, small businessmen and women, skilled craftsmen and unskilled labourers, all played their part in the exploitation of very young children. Men and women from all walks of life emerge in the autobiographies offering employment, tendering food, lodging and a few pennies in exchange for long hours of work from the small and vulnerable. And in the absence of parents, children were taken in by the parish, housed and fed until the age of seven or so, and then discharged to earn their own living. Most of the autobiographers raised by the parish were at work by the age of seven – considerably younger than the average for children raised by their parents. Before the emergence of agitation in the second quarter of the nineteenth century, the desirability of work for poor children had almost universal acceptance.

We see this yet more clearly when we look at the choices made by earlier generations. After all, there was nothing new in sending small children to work. Families before the industrial revolution had done just the same when they could find willing employers, which usually meant if they lived somewhere that offered industrial opportunities. The boys who started work at young ages earlier in the eighteenth century were all employed in some branch of industry. Those starting work before they were ten assisted parents in domestic weaving, worked in silk mills, or down coal and copper mines.[85] As Samuel Sholl, whose parents were both weavers, explained: 'as I could assist early in my parents' business, they took me home [from school]'. He was probably about five at the time.[86] In other words, young child workers were to be found wherever there was work for young children.

Just like Benjamin Shaw, these writers did not indicate that they came from especially large or impoverished families. Nor do they hint that there was anything unusual, or even unpleasant, in entering the workforce when they did.[87] This is not, of course, to deny the unpleasantness of their experiences: it is highly doubtful that they were any better than those of later generations. The point simply is that it was not something they thought to write about. Decades before the emergence of campaigns to restrict the use of children in the workplace, the earlier autobiographers saw their task simply as recording the moment when their working life began, rather than reflecting upon why their parents had put them to work so young, the treatment they met with while there, or the morality of employing small children. They provided the same kind of unreflective and impenetrable account of childhood labour as Shaw's. And their silence suggests a weary resignation as regards the place of child labour in the lives of the poor.

The pattern amongst those who went to work at older ages also mirrors what happened later. Some of the better-off families kept their children at home because they had the resources to do so.[88] Other poor families also kept their children at home, but only because they could find nothing for them to do. In many rural areas, the chronic shortage of employment meant that gainful employment for poor children was a hopeless chimera. Edward Barlow, for example, described his parents as 'but poor people' working the land. As soon as he and his brothers and sisters were able, they had to 'provide for ourselves or else want our bread'.[89] Yet Edward was not at work full-time until the age of twelve or thirteen, almost certainly because of the lack of work in his Lancashire village. James Ferguson's father had to support a large family with nothing but 'his daily labour'. As he 'could not afford to maintain me', James was put to minding sheep, but it was not until he was ten that he was thus employed.[90] In terms of wealth, status or attitude there is little between those families who sent their children to work in mills and mines at the ages of six, seven or eight, and these families who kept their children in school or at home for many years longer. The only real difference was that in some areas the work was available, whereas in others it was not.[91]

Poor families had always made the most of whatever employment opportunities existed for their children, and those living through the industrial revolution did no differently when presented with the same choice. Yet assuming an unchanging cultural fabric risks painting this period in false hues of comforting continuity. Benjamin and Betty Shaw may have acted in the same way as their grandparents, but they were no longer living in the same world. With industrialisation came lots of jobs, many of them suitable for the small hands and fallible concentration of very young children. So putting the old logic to work in a new world did not lead to the same outcomes. Framed in this way, the industrial revolution had serious and significant welfare implications for children.

In the first place, the persistence of old patterns of behaviour meant that far more children were at work. This may seem a rather elementary point, but I think it deserves emphasis. Throughout the pre-industrial era, the sluggishness of the economy had placed a cap on the extent to which children were used in the workplace. Centres of industry were relatively undeveloped. A few parents could find work for their offspring at a loom or underground, but the vast majority could not. This meant that most children were shielded from the rigours of the workplace. When the industrial revolution began to take off, this cap was prised off and many more very young children found themselves earning their bread.

It is also doubtful that this change brought many welfare benefits to the children concerned. It is likely that parents grasped at the chance to send their children to work because they saw in it the opportunity to feed and clothe their children decently. Most mothers probably did spend the pennies and shillings that their children brought home on more and better-quality food, both for the children who had earned then and for other, younger family members still at home. Indeed, there is even the occasional child worker who made favourable comparisons between the family's living standards before and after they started work. One writer, for example, contrasted the poverty of his home life when his father spent a year away at sea and failed to send any money home with the prosperity they all enjoyed when he got work at a flax-spinning mill a couple of years later. Jobs for all five children were found in the same factory, and their 'joint earnings amounted to a handsome sum weekly, which kept us all very comfortable'.[92]

But comments of this nature were made extremely infrequently. Though many writers anticipated the transition from schoolboy to wage-earner with some excitement, most soon discovered that the reality fell very far short of their childish hopes. With hindsight, our writers conceded the importance of the hard-earned contribution their labour had made to their family. As Thomas Wood observed, 'small as it was, it was a sensible and much needed [addition] to the family store'.[93] Yet very few writers interpreted their entry to the workforce as having enhanced their lives. Time and again, the autobiographers' memories centred upon the long hours, tiredness, distress and harsh treatment that had characterised the early years of their working life. Joseph Townend described his seven-year-old self at the mill as 'sorrowful and dejected in spirit'.[94] Richard Weaver's early years down the coal mine had been 'a life of dreadful suffering'.[95] If the transition from child to child worker had also been accompanied by a little more bread and butter, any memory of this had long been lost in the mists of time.

No less important than the overall rise in the extent of child labour is the change in its nature. Work in factories and mines was dangerous. Whilst we should not overlook the risks associated with more traditional forms of work – in agriculture, children were vulnerable to accidents from livestock, and outdoor work in all seasons could damage health – factory work stands out as particularly injurious to children's welfare. Long hours spent in unnatural postures damaged growing bones. Machines were unfenced and tore off small fingers, hands, and sometimes worse, at an alarming rate. Accidents were notorious and crop up regularly in the autobiographical writing. Benjamin Shaw's family had not escaped. His 'little Brother Joseph, got catched in the wheels in the factory, and got his hand ill crushed, & cut, one finger taken off, & the other Broken & Sadly mangled'.[96] Benjamin also noted that one of his daughters was 'rather deaf' which might, he speculated, have been caused by the 'noise of the factory'.[97]

Added to this were the long hours. One of the most depressing themes that runs through the autobiographies is the very long hours worked by many of the young children in industrial areas. Before the introduction of the Ten Hours Bill, children in factories and mines usually worked a twelve- or thirteen-hour day and almost all of the autobiographers who entered such work before the legislation paused to comment on the crushing effects of working such long hours at so young an age.[98] Many recalled feeling very, very tired. Who can fail to be struck, for example, by the image of Moses Heap, who was so tired and so young when he began at the factory that he was carried back and forth upon his father's back?[99] Or here is Robert Lowery, picking the brasses out of the coals at the mouth of the Tyneshire coal mines at the age of ten:

> I had to rise at 4 a.m. every morning and walk nearly two miles to work, which continued from 5 a.m until 6 p.m. and well I remember how I longed for the 'day of rest', when the voice of the 'caller' no longer broke in on the sound slumbers of the morning.[100]

Through many months of the year, the hours of daylight placed a limit on the number of hours that children could drive ploughs, pick potatoes, sow turnips and perform the sundry other tasks required to till the land. In industrial employment these kinds of limits did not exist, and their absence increased the burden of work for the very young.

For the children of the industrial revolution, it was not just long days that ratcheted up their hours at work. When children went to work in factories or mines they were entering a world that offered steady employment throughout the year. Rural districts had their fair share of children starting work before the age of ten, but those who did so were rarely embarking on full-time work. As one Suffolk farm boy explained, he 'partly left school' at the age of ten to scare birds off the seedcorn, but as 'this kind of work lasted only a few months in the year ... I still had some time for school'. In this case, full-time employment was delayed until the writer was twelve.[101] And the difference between the age of first starting work and the age at which full-time work began could be quite considerable. Take, for instance, Adam Todd and Thomas Irving. Both started farm work when aged nine, but as their employment was seasonal they continued to return to school in the winter. They both carried on in this vein until they were fourteen.[102] This had the effect of allowing them a far more gradual entry to the workforce.

We have already noted that ten and a half was the average age at which children in rural areas started their working years. But if we substitute the age at which children first started work with the age at which they began full-time work, the average increases by a full year, raising their starting age to eleven and half. This takes it to the average age at which children in towns started working, and is more than three years above the average for

the children in industrial districts. At the root of the rural child's experience of work was the ongoing difficulty of finding full-time, year-round
work. This helped to soften the transition from home or school to work,
and meant that there was a very real difference between the child who
started work in the fields at the age of six and the one who began in one of
Manchester's mills, working twelve hours a day, six days a week, week in
and week out, year in, year out.

There were also tangible differences in the nature of the work expected
of young children in different parts of the economy. In agriculture, a boy's
early jobs were often light and although the hours could be long during the
summer, the line between work and leisure was far less clearly drawn. When
Joseph Robinson started work at the age of six, for example, he was set to
bird-scaring and 'similar light work that a little boy could do'.[103] And when
William Lea was put to work scaring birds from the newly sown or ripening
corn at the age of seven he found that 'the work was light and recreative to
me, for I amused myself by building small sheds under the hedges ... I
found some pleasure ideally in the midst of my employment.'[104] The possibility of play while at work was something that other writers remarked upon.
During his first year at work for the local farmers, Joseph Arch 'found a
good deal to do, what with bird-nesting, trespassing, and other boyish tricks
and diversions'.[105] Herding cows, Alexander Somerville 'made water-mills
and wind-mills, built houses large enough to creep into'.[106] Out in the fields,
the youngest children were often left largely unsupervised and this created a
very different experience to that of the mill-hands and child miners whose
work was closely watched by a man carrying a large strap. One writer even
confessed that he had not thought it 'much hardship' when his parents'
poverty had him exchanging schooling for bird-scaring at 'an early age'. 'At
the time,' he pointed out, he had been 'fonder of an open-air life.'[107]

We should not be too quick to romanticise the lot of the farm lad. The
stubborn truth is that most of the boys who started work young disliked
their labour, and that was no less true in agriculture than it was in any other
sector of the economy. Even in agriculture long hours, lonely work, bad
weather or cruel co-workers could make the experience miserable in the
extreme. So it should not be imagined that industrialisation marked the
passing of the good old days, the substitution of easy and wholesome labour
in the open air with the unrelenting and unnatural patterns of the factory.
All child workers were vulnerable to abuse and exploitation. The point
rather is that agriculture was very poor at extracting sustained and valuable
work from small children. With little work available suited to their

capacities and no mechanisms for monitoring the labour of inherently unreliable workers, most farmers looked elsewhere when they needed a job done.

It is time to draw this chapter to a close. Enough has been said to suggest that a new interpretation of the rise in child labour during the industrial revolution may be in order. For the most part poor families have been presented as passive players, sending their children to work through lack of choice, ground down by mechanisation, immiserated by capitalism, victims of the great impersonal economic forces that were taking shape around them.[108] It is all true to an extent. But painting the poor as the faceless victims of sinister economic forces does not take us far in understanding why so many small children were being thrust into the workplace at ever younger ages.

So here is an alternative way of understanding the rise in child labour which occurred at this time. Child labour had a very long taproot in Britain. Society had always viewed putting poor children to work as an answer to the miserable poverty in which their families lived. The trouble was that the pre-industrial economy was ill equipped to give most families any hope of earning income from their children's labour, no matter how much they might need it. This situation changed rapidly and dramatically with the onset of industrialisation in the early nineteenth century. Early industrial Britain was a booming economy with an insatiable appetite for strong backs and nimble fingers. We saw in the last chapter the many advantages this brought to adult men. We can now see the disaster it heralded for children.

Industrialisation unleashed a wave of economic growth, and when faced with the prospect of gainful employment for their children families responded in the way they had always done. Industrial Britain offered more (and more intensive) employment for young children, and many working parents, who remembered the gnawing hunger of their own childhood only too well, grasped eagerly at these opportunities. The outcome? Children were thrust into the workforce at ever younger ages. Above all, the British experience reminds us that different members of society experienced industrialisation in very different ways. Rapid, unregulated growth opened up welcome opportunities for adult men, but the gains for the smallest and weakest were very questionable indeed.

# CHAPTER FOUR

# Women, Work and the Cares of Home

The cares and claims of home bounded her ambition and fully occupied her thoughts and hands. (Edwards, p. 8)

How it was that my mother was able to fulfil all the duties which she undertook, I can scarcely conceive; giving birth to a child upon an average every two years, and never having any assistance in the management of her family, except that of a nurse during her confinement. Not only was the food of the family from day to day prepared by her hands; but the stockings of her husband and children were of her knitting; their linen was spun by her hands, and bleached under her direction; and to keep these articles of clothing in constant repair was no easy matter. (Jackson, p. 10)

L IKE NOT A few of the autobiographers, Benjamin North, the eighth child of a day labourer in Thame, Oxfordshire, was born into a life of poverty. From a young age, North was spending his days working long hours in the cold as a bird-scarer and ploughboy, all on a diet that consisted of little more than bread and lard, a little cheese and 'once a week a mite of meat'.[1] But North's greatest regret for his childhood concerned not the long hours and scanty rations, but the fact that he returned home each night to a home 'without a mother . . . to look after me'. His mother had passed away when he was four, and with her he lost all 'the advantage and love' that only a child's mother can provide.[2]

Perhaps North's motherless childhood helped to shape his views on the respective roles of men and women in the working-class family. Fathers, in his opinion, were breadwinners. Their role was to work outside the home, building, making, and earning the wherewithal to maintain the family. Man, he wrote, 'was intended to subdue the earth, and to take upon him the responsibilities of life. He is organised to take the lead, clear the land, till the soil, raise the stock, build houses and bridges, make railways, provide for and defend his family.' A mother's position in the family was altogether more complex. Although North was quick to stress that 'woman has her place and work' too, that 'place' straddled the workplace and the home in awkward and undefined ways. Women, he thought, were especially qualified to 'keep a shop, a post-office or a bookstall, to sell goods, to make and mend wearing apparel, to write and copy, to wash and nurse, to keep the house and mind the family'. Should any of his audience remain uncertain, he added that 'Christ Jesus the Lord was a carpenter, Paul a tent-maker, Peter and John fishermen, Matthew a penman at the "receipt of custom", Luke a physician, and Martha a good housekeeper and cook'.[3]

It is scarcely an exaggeration to suggest that North's view of the division of labour between the sexes was almost universal amongst the autobiographical writers. The narrow range of jobs that he thought suitable for women, the emphasis on cleaning, caring, mending and selling, and his inclusion of the unpaid work of the household under the heading of a woman's 'place and work' were all typical, reflecting both men's attitudes and the reality of women's lives. Cultural expectations about natural and proper roles were a powerful force, fixing the horizons within which working women lived out their lives. There can be no question of simply assuming that the gains that many men wrought out of industrialisation were shared by their wives and sisters. And it is to wives and sisters that we must now turn. It is time to consider how life changed for those North designated the 'helpmate of man'.[4]

Looking at the 'helpmates', though, presents fresh challenges and difficulties. Few autobiographies were written by women and few of those provided any useful detail about such workaday matters as how they put food on the table. Christian Milne wrote two versions of her autobiography, yet in neither did she say anything about how she was employed beyond mentioning that at the age of about fourteen she 'went to service', and that as a mother of eight, her 'work' consisted of baking, washing and rocking the cradle.[5] The only clue in Margaret Davidson's autobiography to how she earned a living is contained in a story she tells about a man who attempted to rape her. The man's daughter was a friend, and the two women spent their days 'spinning together'.[6] In all, there are only around a dozen autobiographies that were written by women and contain substantial evidence about the work, whether paid or not, they performed. We will mine this evidence as thoroughly as we can, but such a small body of sources is not going to be sufficient to permit large conclusions about the impact of industrialisation on women's lives.

For the most part we will have to fall back upon the testimony of sons and husbands, which closes down some lives of enquiry. Most obviously, sons and husbands tended to write about the lives of their mothers and wives, and had much less to say about women who were childless or single. This may seem a relatively minor distinction, but marriage and mother-hood involved fairly major upheavals in a woman's relationship to the world of work. It follows then that this chapter is primarily about the working lives of married women rather than of their single cousins.[7]

Sons and husbands were not always the most reliable or conscientious of witnesses. Many male writers did not regard the work performed by the women around them as central to or significant in their own life history, or indeed as being of any possible interest to anyone. In his memoirs, Alexander Murison described his wife as 'an excellent worker at all kinds of work', and in his writing he paused several times to record some of the various roles she performed. But when his son edited the memoirs for publication he replaced most of what his father had written about his wife's work with dots, explaining that these signified omissions of material 'being of no particular interest'.[8] And even where unedited accounts of women's work have survived, the fact that they were seen through the eyes of a male observer means that much was missed out. Men did not expound upon such details as how long a woman worked or how much she earned. They were almost entirely mute about how women felt about their labours. Of course, the lack of interest that sons, husbands and sometimes women themselves displayed in reporting the nature of female employment is itself revealing, speaking volumes about the low regard in which women's work was held. Nonetheless, this is the material that we have to hand and for all its limitations it is a rich and untapped seam of evidence about women's work, sufficient to shed meaningful light on women's working lives and how they changed during the period of industrialisation.

Let us begin by gathering together the information that the autobiographies contain about the different ways that women earned their living. If we make a note of every job that a woman is recorded as performing, it becomes evident that female employment was concentrated in a very small number of low-paid areas. If every mention is noted, then about 80 per cent of women's work falls into in just five areas: textiles, agriculture, domestic service, retailing and needlework. Each area encompassed a variety of different tasks. Cloth manufacture, for example, ranged from spinning on the humble spinning wheel to working as a skilled weaver on a handloom, to operating a vast power loom in a factory. Domestic service might refer to a lady's maid in an aristocratic household or to a woman going out to char for a neighbour only marginally better off than herself. But with so much women's work shoehorned into just five areas of the economy and with so little change over the period, it is clear at the outset that women were experiencing the industrial revolution in very different ways to their husbands and children.

These ideas may be explored more fully by looking at each of these five sectors in more detail. Let us start with the largest sector: cloth manufacture. Despite the great variety of tasks that needed to be performed to turn raw cotton or wool into dyed and woven cloth, most of the work done by women was concentrated in the least skilled and lowest-paid areas. Spinning on the spinning wheel was the most common occupation for women, an employment that was particularly widespread in rural Scotland.[9] Winding thread on to bobbins for use by weavers was only slightly less common.[10] But neither of these did much to enhance women's income or status. Many of those who worked a spinning wheel were spinning in order to clothe their family, rather than for wages. John Younger recalled that his mother had risen between five and six every morning while the rest of the family lay in their beds in order to spin yarn to 'provide clothes for the family'.[11] In other words, spinning simply added to her labours, and did little to enhance either her income or her independence.

Even where women were spinning or winding for the market rather than their families the remuneration they received for their labour was paltry. William Fairburn's mother kept her spinning wheel 'constantly in motion'. Yet when her absent husband was unable to send any money home one summer, she and her family were sunk 'almost in a state of destitution'.[12] Another writer's mother tried to keep her family on the income of her spinning when her husband went to sea one year and failed to send her any money. But her earnings were only sufficient to keep herself and the two youngest children – the elder three had to be sent away to work or to stay with relatives in better circumstances.[13] The profits from winding bobbins were no better; in fact only a few appear to have received any payment at all for this work.[14] Most of the women who wound bobbins and pirns did so for their husbands and there is no evidence that they were paid for the privilege. As a young man, the Radical Samuel Bamford considered winding bobbins suitable for old women, and when his asthmatic aunt put him to work beside her in the 'bobbin-winding department' he objected that it was 'a piece of bondage ... abhorrent to my feelings'.[15]

Spinning and winding accounted for the lion's share of women's employment in the textile industry, but a few women are also found working in the more skilled branches as weavers or cloth-dyers. Weaving certainly offered better reward than spinning or winding. Following the birth of her illegitimate son, Sally Marcroft had to get by as best she could. She must have earned more than the spinners as she was able to keep her own house and raise her son without support from his father.[16] But once a woman had married and had responsibility for a house and children, most found it difficult to earn much of an income from weaving. William Farish's mother tried to delegate 'household management' to her eldest daughter so that she could work on her handloom, but in her son's recollection her weaving 'came to very little'.[17] Some women simply got rid of their loom when they married. When John Wood's father remarried, his new wife's handloom was transferred to John and she took over the running of the house.[18] Female cloth-dyers were even scarcer than weavers, and most of those described as dyers were either helping their husbands or dying cloth on a very small scale for their family's needs rather than for the market.[19] For the most part, entry to the more skilled echelons of textile production was difficult to achieve and, once a woman married, even more difficult to maintain.

Alongside the traditional avocations of spinning, winding and weaving, the recently built factories were starting to offer new opportunities to working women.[20] From around the 1780s factories began to spread in south Lancashire and south Yorkshire. As Benjamin Shaw noted of the factories that sprang up around his village of Dent, 'this was a change of employment for the women', offering 'rather better wages' than the knitting and spinning that had traditionally kept women busy.[21] Yet although factory work undoubtedly offered work at much better wages than women could command elsewhere, very few women continued this work after marriage. Benjamin's own wife, Betty, for example, had worked in a number of factories in Dent and Preston in her teens, but never returned to factory work after her marriage. The only income she earned as a married woman came from a little bobbin-winding and a short-lived attempt to earn money by baking oatcakes at home. Thirty-five autobiographers spent at least some part of their childhood working in a factory or mill. A few mentioned that their mother had worked at the mill *before* her marriage, yet only one indicated that his mother worked there *after* his birth.[22] So the high wages that women could command in the factories were for the most part a transitory experience. Once women had families to care for, their days at the factory were usually over.

Second in importance to the textile industry was agriculture. Once again, this broad umbrella term encompasses a variety of roles, though none required high levels of skill or commanded good rates of pay.[23] A small number of families farmed their own land, sometimes a small commercial farm, sometimes a few acres that the family tended to meet their own subsistence needs. Either way, the women in the family were kept busy helping to till the land, care for animals, or occasionally run a dairy.[24] Such smallholdings were becoming rare, however, and most of those working in agriculture were employed on somebody else's land. Given the difficulty that men experienced in finding year-round employment on the land, it should occasion no surprise that women's work in rural areas was highly seasonal in nature and largely confined to helping out at the busiest times of year. The wife of one Glasgow handloom weaver spent the harvest shearing alongside her husband, but of course her work in the fields only lasted for as long as the harvest season.[25] In William Clift's village, Bramley in Berkshire, the women and boys came in to help with bean-setting every February. The work lasted about a month.[26] For most of the rest of the year, these women were not at work. And of course, the income that could be earned from such short-term employment could do no more than provide a small supplement to the husband's wage. William Clift recalled that a woman with two children could earn about 12 or 13 shillings a week during the bean-setting season and he thought that such women were usually 'well pleased' with their earnings. Doubtless they were 'well pleased' with the money, but it was no substitute for the year-round earnings that the men in the village aimed for.[27]

Ranking alongside textiles and agriculture in importance was domestic service. I use the term here to denote all forms of cooking, cleaning and washing, whether as a servant living with an employer or in any other capacity.[28] Many families sought out positions in service for their daughters in the hope that they might learn skills which would prove useful later in life.[29] And although women only rarely returned to work as a live-in servant after marriage, many found that what they had earlier learned could be put to good use both in running their own household and as a source of extra income when the need arose.[30] Taking in laundry was one of the most common ways in which mothers earned an income throughout the period covered by the autobiographies. The work could be fitted around caring for a family and called for little in the way of materials that a married woman did not already possess. Robert Spurr's wife usually assisted him in his shoemaking, but in 1837 trade was at a standstill and there was no work for her to do. According to her husband, she 'took in some washing' instead.[31] When the father of Francis Place, the future Radical, lost all his money on the lotteries, his mother paid a visit to her old neighbours and asked them to give her their clothes to wash. Several agreed and it provided just enough income for Mrs Place to scrape by.[32] And if laundry work did not appeal, there was always cleaning. Several other married women who had fallen on hard times went out to char for their wealthier neighbours in order to help make ends meet.[33]

But if washing and charring could be combined with family responsibilities, they also involved hard work and long hours. Place remembered his mother working late into the night and rising early in the morning to pursue her occupation as a laundress, and carrying the large bundles of clothes between her customers' homes and hers upon her head.[34] It was the corns and calluses on his grandmother's hands that William Adams recalled.[35] And like almost all of the work available to married women, doing other people's washing and cleaning was not well paid. When Thomas Sanderson's father was away fighting in the Peninsular War, his mother and sister 'made a living at the wash tub'. Although his mother did the washing 'for the best families in the neighbourhood' she was unable to earn sufficient to maintain herself and her two small children and it was only thanks to four shillings from the parish that she was able to keep her small family afloat.[36]

Fourth in importance was shopkeeping and small-scale selling. Like the other broad sectors in which women worked, retailing encompassed a wide variety of enterprises. At one end, a few women managed to run successful small businesses, sometimes combining their selling with the making of goods. Joseph Townend's mother, for example, made sweets and gingerbread and sold them in a small shop which she ran from her home.[37] David Binns' mother sold 'drapery goods ... grocery, meal and flour' and also 'made up garments' for her customers.[38] Shopkeeping at this level (our writers make plain) was held in much higher regard than most other forms of female employment. Before the extent of her husband's losses on the lotteries became clear, Mrs Place had 'urged him to let her take a shop and deal in any thing she could'. It was only once she realised that her husband had gambled away the nest egg that was supposed to fund the enterprise that she turned to her neighbours and asked them to give her their clothes to wash instead.

This was the genteel face of trading. At the other end of the scale were forms of selling that rivalled laundry work and charring for low pay and low status. Hawking and peddling were widely regarded as very humble occupations. One successful pedlar admitted that it was a 'mean calling'.[39] Women working as fish-sellers were surely under no illusions about the low regard in which their work was generally held.[40] When John James Bezer's mother bought three shillings' worth of hot-cross buns to sell with her son, he was mortified that the route she had mapped out for him was on a leading thoroughfare and close to his home and Sunday school. Indeed her own bun-selling had come to nothing for soon after setting out she had 'met a person she had known years before'. Her courage had failed her, and she returned home without selling a single bun.[41] More than most occupations, retailing referred to a wide array of occupations with a correspondingly wide set of rewards and social connotations.

The fifth and final major source of employment for women was needlework. This, like service, was regarded as a valuable skill that women might put to good use through life, both in clothing their own families and as a possible source of income. William Hanson and his wife put their eldest daughter to dressmaking, believing it to be a useful business and hoping she would teach it to her younger sisters.[42] Timothy Mountjoy counted his blessings that his wife 'was a good needlewoman ... and [knew how to] cut out and make her husband's shirts well, and make the children's garments, without putting it out to be done'.[43] Dressmaking required very little in the way of capital or materials and could easily be done within the home. It gave women the potential to earn extra income should the need arise. It was also the closest that women's work got to being skilled. One autobiographer described his wife Jane, who had been put to learn dressmaking in Glasgow when ten or eleven years old. As a young woman she moved to the small Ayrshire town of Maybole to 'establish herself in trade'. She soon 'obtained abundance of employment, and had secured the most respectable customers in the locality'.[44]

But dressmakers suffered from exactly the same kinds of problems as the tailors whom we saw in Chapter 2. Dressmaking was easily entered and the demand for goods was sensitive to the broader economic climate. As a result, many women found it difficult to earn a good living from their needle when the economy failed to prosper. When Mary Ann Ashford was orphaned at the age of thirteen, her family proposed placing her as an indoor apprentice to a dressmaker or milliner for five years. She sought the advice of a family friend and was told 'that is all very well for those who have got a home and parents to shelter them, when work is slack; but depend upon it, many clever women find it, at times, a half-starved kind of life'. Her aunt shared this opinion, so Mary Ann opted for service instead.[45] And her friends' predictions proved only too true for many of the women who did seek to earn a living from their needle. Dressmaking could be a valuable source of income added to that of the male breadwinner. But those married women who sought to earn a living from needlework in place of male wages were invariably left struggling in miserable poverty.

Cloth production, agriculture, domestic service, retailing and needle-work accounted for 80 per cent of the female employment mentioned in the autobiographies. Three other areas of the economy – education, medi-cine and helping husbands – made up most of the rest. Education is a rather grand term for the small day schools, or 'dame schools', which a few women ran in their own homes. John Leno's mother added to the family fund by running a dame school, though as her son rather apologetically observed, 'her scholastic qualifications would fail to commend her to the School Board authorities of today . . . a little education among the extremely poor went a long way' in those days.[46] She was one of a small number of women in the autobiographies who managed to raise a little income by teaching poor children. The work possibly offered women a little more in the way of status and autonomy than most female employments, but inevi-tably, given the small scale of these establishments and the poverty of the clientele, dame schools were not a route to riches.

A similar number of women earned income by providing some aspect of medical care, usually on a small, local scale. A handful of the wives and mothers mentioned in the autobiographies practised midwifery, an occupa-tion that seems to have been held in the highest regard. Samuel Bamford, for example, reported that his grandmother had been one of only two 'this side of the country who then practised the obstetric art'.[47] Hamlet Nicholson's mother had worked as a midwife and 'ultimately became known as such, all over the town'. Indeed, she became so successful, he proudly continued, that the local doctor entrusted her 'with cases of well-to-do ladies when he could not attend'.[48] Nicholson's mother was one of a very small number of women who managed to carve out a role for them-selves in their community as a medical practitioner. In addition to her midwifery, she had a 'good practice' in the application of leeches. Richard

Cook's grandmother was another. His 'Granny Jackson' sold a number of medical concoctions – a 'Popular pill', medicinal waters made from worm-wood, yarrow and parsley, an eye water made of rainwater collected in the month of June – and applied leeches, bound limbs and bled the sick.[49] As we might imagine, however, the number of women who managed to find much success as either a midwife or a female healer was small. It is also unlikely that they made much money from their medical enterprises. At the same time as Granny Jackson sold her pills and June water, bled, blis-tered and bound the sick, she also spun and knitted goods for her house-hold, gathered dried cow's dung to burn in place of coal and gleaned after the harvest – hardly the activities of a woman of great means.[50]

Considerably more common than both midwifery and medicine was 'nursing' – a term used to cover both tending to the sick and caring for healthy babies and small children. Such work was usually short term and temporary in nature. It is likely that the work employed far more women than the autobiographies suggest. We only learn that Thomas Pointer's wife cared for a 'nurse-child' (a one-week-old baby girl whom she took in a few months after burying her own first child) because she became so attached to the baby that the couple later adopted her.[51] How many other mothers and wives took in 'nurse-children' whom they did not subsequently adopt we can only speculate. But if the number of women who found employment in nursing is unknown, the low pay and low status of the work is more certain. The transient nature of most nursing work and the low regard in which it was held probably encouraged male writers to pass silently over the income earned from nursing by their mothers and wives more systematically than any other occupation.

Finally a small number of the women in the autobiographies worked alongside their husbands, though as ever in the world of women's work the range of options was fairly limited. Shopkeeping and innkeeping were both clearly regarded as enterprises that required work from both halves of a married couple. The autobiographers who kept public houses always enlisted the help of their wives and those who ran shops almost always did.[52] It was also common for women to help their husbands in shoemaking and clothes-making.[53] But outside these four lines of work, none of the skilled tradesmen reported receiving any kind of assistance from their wives, except in the retailing side of their businesses.[54] Women were certainly not working alongside their husbands as carpenters, furniture-makers, metalworkers, or in any of the other skilled trades that men followed. With the exception of shoemaking and tailoring, women, whether married or not, remained firmly shut out from all skilled occupations.

When teaching, medicine, and assisting husbands are added to the five areas already mentioned about 95 per cent of all female employment is accounted for. Most of the last 5 per cent of the female employment mentioned in the autobiographies involved small-scale manufacture in the home.[55] Thomas Cooper's mother, for instance, made 'pasteboard boxes . . . entirely by hand', which she sold as workboxes and storage boxes.[56] Women living in Hertfordshire were to be found employed in the local straw-plaiting industry and in Buckinghamshire they worked at lacemaking.[57] In the coal districts, some women found work in mining, until the Mines Act of 1842 forced women out of underground work.[58] More unusually, George Holyoake's mother for a while ran a successful business manufacturing horn buttons in a workshop attached to the house. According to her son, she 'received the orders; made the purchases of materials; superintended the making of the goods; made out the accounts; and received the money'. One of the most unusual things about Catherine Holyoake's business was that she 'employed several hands' – she is one of just two mothers in the auto-biographies to appear as both a worker and an employer.[59] But with few exceptions, the financial rewards of this work were fairly limited. Thomas Cooper's mother, for instance, 'toiled hard' and 'was not a woman to sink for lack of effort'. Nonetheless, for all her efforts it was 'difficult for her to make a livelihood' and during the worst winters she and her son lived on barley cakes and potatoes and handouts from their wealthier neighbours.[60]

Here then are the major contours of women's employment down to about 1850. It is obvious that women's experiences differed from those of men and children in a number of significant ways. In the first instance, when looking at men we noticed that industrialisation threw the door to skilled labour wide open. There is next to no evidence to suggest that women shared in this process. Unlike young male apprentices, women did not work for below-market wages in the hope of learning a skill that would earn them greater rewards at some unknown time in the future. They worked to get money for the here and now. Our collection of autobiographies contains just one exception to this – Eliza Mitchell. Eliza was working as a domestic servant in Bristol in the 1840s and (according to her future husband) 'thought she would like to learn a trade instead of service'. She left her place, and spent two years living with her aunt and learning 'the little fancy shoe making for little children'.[61] Once she had learned the trade, she moved on to a better position. She followed a trajectory which resembled that of the many men we saw in Chapter 2 who managed to learn a trade without serving a formal apprenticeship. But Eliza was the only woman described as learning a skill in this way in over 350 autobiographies.

In noting that women did not become 'skilled workers', I am not suggesting that there was no skill involved in the work that they did. It was rather that those skills were not considered so abstruse as to call for much in the way of formal instruction. Mary Ann Ashford was the only woman who was offered the opportunity to learn a skill formally – a two-year apprenticeship to a dressmaker was proposed. She thought the idea was pointless as she could already 'work at my needle very well'.[62] By contrast, while working in service, universally classified as an unskilled occupation, Mary Ann was peeved when one of her mistresses placed obstacles in the way of her learning the more difficult parts of her work. Not only did this mistress do 'all that required any art or knowledge herself', she would even send Mary Ann 'out of the way' so that she could not learn how more complex domestic work was done. Mary Ann clearly did recognise the concept of 'skill' in her work, but she understood that concept in a very different way to the men we met in Chapter 2. And for this reason, the unmaking of the system of apprenticeship, which brought many gains to working men, had very little significance for the women who worked for a living.

It is also striking that the participation of married women in the work-place was far from universal. Only about 40 per cent of the autobiographers provided evidence that their mother worked. We should not attach too much importance to this figure. Some writers had almost nothing to say about their mothers or wives, so we cannot read much into the fact that they did not record them as working. Others almost certainly failed to mention the work performed by the women in their life. We only learn that the wife of James Bowd worked, for instance, because when the couple fell into debt it was the woman that she 'used to go charring at' who paid it off.[63] We can safely assume that there were other mothers and wives who went out charring without an incident occurring that made it worth mentioning. There is something telling in William Adams' comment that although there was no shame in his grandmother's laundry work, some people 'would perhaps consider that it was a fact to be concealed'.[64] So 40 per cent is best regarded as the lowest estimate for mothers who worked. Nonetheless, we have two clearly discernible groups of women – those who did some form of paid employment after marriage and those who did not – which inevitably prompts us to ask: what determined whether or not women went out to work after they had married?

One of the most curious features of married women's retreat from the workforce is the fact that it was not related to the opportunities that existed in their area. The previous two chapters on men and children revealed that industrialisation substantially increased the amount and variety of work available, resulting in higher wages and fuller employment in the industrial districts. Yet when looking at married women's work it is difficult to discern any kind of improvement in employment prospects. Indeed, living in an area undergoing significant economic growth appears to have reduced rather than raised the likelihood of a mother going out to work. The auto-biographies reveal that the proportion of working mothers in industrial areas was lower than average – just under a third earned some income for their family. In provincial towns about 42 per cent of mothers were at work. Rural areas noted the highest levels of female employment, at around 46 per cent. As ever, we would probably be wise not to attach too much weight to these figures. Many of the women in rural areas were doing no more than spending a few weeks of the year gleaning or helping with the harvest, so their working lives were not so very different to the lives of those living (and not working) in the industrialising regions. Nonetheless, this is a very different pattern to the experience of men and children, for whom economic growth translated into higher rates of participation in the work-force in a fairly straightforward, though not always desirable, fashion.

Not only did industrialisation fail to increase the chances of married women working, it also did little to change the kind of work they did. Despite all the economic upheavals that we know occurred between the late eighteenth and mid-nineteenth centuries, the profile of women's work hardly shifted at all. With the exception of the factory districts, which did offer a distinctive new form of employment, most women remained employed in the same old sectors, very often doing much the same work as their own mothers and grandmothers. Once again, this forms a very marked contrast to men's experiences. As we saw earlier, the factories offered men one type of employment, but along with this came many more – building, navvying, and working in warehouses and transport. The urbanisation that accompanied the growth of factories created a buoyant demand for the goods and services of many skilled labourers. Those making bread, cakes, food, furniture, cloths, shoes and a host of other goods found their services in demand no matter how traditional their processes. But women had very few opportunities to improve their income and prospects outside the mills, even in the factory heartlands. No doubt dressmakers had brighter prospects in the large industrial towns than those living in the country, but needlework still remained a fragile industry with poor prospects for full employment throughout the year. The opportunities for women seeking to make money by doing other people's washing and cleaning were also likely to be good in large towns and cities, but the low pay meant that even though finding employment was easier, the benefit of that employment was in reality very small. The combination of low pay and limited opportunities effectively ensured that even in the most economically thriving parts of the country the chances for women to earn a good livelihood were limited. Little surprise, then, that so many married women stayed out of the workplace altogether.

It all poses something of a puzzle. It is undeniable that much more work was available in the cities than in the country. This was why the population was migrating towards the towns. This was why many adult men were starting to enjoy full employment and taste all the benefits that came with it. This was why children were being hustled into the workplace at ever younger ages. Yet married women did not move into the workforce en masse to take advantage of these opportunities. As the chance of earning a good wage improved, families clung more tightly to the traditional model of a breadwinning husband and a homemaking mother. We are led, therefore, to an inescapable conclusion. There was something about marriage and motherhood that militated against women making a sustained contribution to the labour force, even in areas where there was clearly a need for nimble hands and strong backs. What was that? Why did marriage and motherhood do so much to curtail women's paid employment?

To answer these questions, let us begin by looking in detail at the experience of one woman living in the heartland of the industrial revolution. Betty Shaw was born and raised in south Lancashire. She had started life as a domestic servant, but soon did what most women in the region did: she traded service for a place in a local mill. By her late teens, she was living in lodgings and working as a factory girl in Preston. The moment she married she gave up her position and moved to Dent, where her new husband was learning the machine-making trade. She gave birth almost immediately after her wedding so she was soon kept busy enough. Over the next two decades, Betty gave birth every two to four years and the responsibility of caring for this large family severely limited, though did not entirely suppress, her attempts to earn some income. When her first child was in its second year, she took 'some [bobbin] winding into the house' to help make ends meet, but the bobbin-winding did not last long, and after the birth of her second child she had to give it up, as 'now her hands was compleatly tied'.[65] For the next fifteen years she devoted herself to the household, but in 1807 the family fell upon hard times. Trade was bad, work scarce and wages low. To make matters worse, Benjamin's health failed the following year and he was soon unable to work at all. It was then that Benjamin mentioned that Betty had begun working: she was taking in some winding once more. In 1810, Benjamin took over the winding and Betty began baking 'oat cakes for the neighbours', which she continued to do, on and off, for the next two years. Betty's eighth, and final, confinement in 1812 appears to have put an end to her baking, and indeed to all her attempts to make any addition to the family's income.[66]

For Betty Shaw, marriage did little to alter the sectors in which she worked. Her baking of oatcakes drew upon the cookery she had learned in service. Her bobbin-winding belonged to the textile industry, just as her earlier factory work had. But Betty's relationship to the world of work did change significantly from the moment she was married. She left her position at the factory, and after that she worked on a very casual and intermittent basis, early in the marriage because she was able to and later because poverty left her little choice. She was also employed on different terms. As a single woman she had worked outside her own home and had been paid for her time. After her marriage, all of her work was performed within the home rather than outside, and she was paid by the piece rather than the hour.

Betty's first response to marriage was to stop working altogether, and there was evidently nothing unusual in this. The simple fact of marriage was sufficient cause for many women to hand in their notice, particularly if they had been in domestic service. When Robert Oakley asked Elizabeth to marry him he also told her she was to leave her situation. Elizabeth was only too ready to oblige, and immediately 'gave notice to my mistress that I was going to leave and she would have to suit herself with another servant'. She left her position before the wedding took place and moved in with Robert and his mother. The three had to struggle by on Robert's piteously low wages.[67]

The opportunity provided by marriage to leave a position in service seems to have been heartily welcomed by many women. At the age of twenty, Mary Porteus despaired that 'if every mistress be as bad to please as this one, my life will be wearisome' and resolved to marry, concluding that it would 'be far better to have a home of my own'.[68] On the other hand, when Mary Ann Ashford's suitor proposed marriage he told her that 'he should wish me to remain in my place for some time afterwards'.[69] His mealy-mouthed suggestion perhaps set the alarm bells ringing and helps to explain why Mary Ann later called the wedding off. Remaining in service as a married woman was certainly not the norm. The usual expectation amongst working people was that marriage was sufficient grounds for a servant to hand in her notice.

Yet despite the enthusiasm with which many domestic servants quit their place in service, this did not necessarily mark a complete retreat from the workforce. The reality for poor families living on the margins of existence was often very different. Elizabeth Oakley enjoyed recounting how Robert had instructed her to give her mistress notice so they could get married, but she was soon squeezing in such work as was compatible with her new role as a wife. She spent the late summer making rush lights with her mother-in-law.[70] Mary Porteus too did indeed give up service and move into a home of her own when she married, but she and her husband opened a small shop so she was soon working in a new capacity.[71] Mary Ann Ashford had not thought much of the idea of being told by her husband-to-be that she should continue in service after their wedding, but later in life she married a tailor and put her excellent needlework skills to good use by helping him complete his orders.[72]

Many other women, especially those who were not working in service, did not give up work at all when they married. Benjamin North's bride-to-be was a domestic lacemaker. After her marriage, she worked in the new home she shared with Benjamin rather than in that of her parents. In their first year of married life she 'was able to earn her own livelihood', allowing him to save part of his wages, he approvingly noted.[73] Less felicitously, one anonymous writer indicated that his wife kept at her straw-plaiting after their marriage. Arguably she did not have much choice in the matter, as her husband admitted he was keeping the best part of his own wages and spending them at the alehouse. Joseph Wilson's mother Sarah lived in Great Horton, just outside Bradford, and 'in the early part of their married life, [she] would go out charring or would take in washing, and so add a few shillings per week to the family income'.[74] Yet others were busy helping their husbands to run shops or inns, or assisting in their shoemaking or tailoring businesses.

In fact, it was not really marriage that had women retreating from the workplace. It was motherhood. In a childless household, work and house-keeping could be easily combined; once the children began to arrive the

juggling became more difficult. Betty Shaw had given up work so soon
after her wedding not because of her newly married status, but because she
was very heavily pregnant. Her first child arrived just six weeks later, and
that made continuing at the factory impossible. So long as she had just the
one child, she did take on a little work; it was only after the birth of her
second child, when her hands became 'compleatly tied', that the effort was
abandoned. This pattern was repeated by many other women in the autobiographies. Arnold Goodliffe's wife must still have been helping in their
shop after the birth of their first child as her husband remembered an incident when she was serving in the shop and their baby fell from the makeshift bed she had made for her. But Anna's children kept coming, and she
soon gave up her work in the shop in order to attend to them.[75] John
Britton's mother had 'managed the whole domestic arrangements' and
helped to run her husband's bake-shop. As she had ten children, this second
role soon became impossible to fulfil, and in time the business failed.[76]
William Hart and his wife set up a shop selling haberdashery goods, and
women's and children's shoes. It answered well at first, 'but we soon found
it impracticable, for my wife having young children to attend to had but
little time for business'.[77] Even the enterprising Eliza Mitchell, who had
made the effort to get out of service and learn children's shoemaking, found
that her skills were largely useless once she had a growing family to care for.
After her marriage, Eliza continued to make children's shoes and helped
manage the shop that her husband had taken. When the children started to
arrive, she added childcare to her workload, but within five years both 'her
strength . . . and her spirits' were failing. Their little shop was soon neglected.
'Eliza did her best but her weak health and the care of the children was
more than she could do'. They gave the shop up, and Eliza became a full-
time mother and housekeeper like many others in the autobiographies.[78]
The autobiographers told the same story over and over again. No matter
what a woman's energy, enthusiasm and skills, the demands of a large family
always prevailed.

And just as large families undermined, and often completely foiled,
mothers' attempts to work, so small families and working mothers proved
remarkably compatible. Women with no or few children nearly always
carried on with some form of paid employment. In 1822, John Brown, a
shoemaker, married a seamstress. Like many a newly wed seamstress, Mrs
Brown continued with her work. Besides attending to her domestic duties,
she 'nimbly ply[ed] her needle', whilst her husband worked at his lapstone.[79]
But two years into their marriage Mrs Brown was still childless, so at just

the moment when many married women were abandoning their attempts to earn a living, Mrs Brown developed new skills, learning how to close the boots her husband made.[80] After four years of marriage, James Murdoch and his wife were also childless, so she 'commenced doing field work to the neighbouring farmers, by which means she earned most part of her own living'.[81] John Leatherland's wife worked as a silk weaver, Samuel Bamford's as a cotton weaver, and Robert Lowery's ran a small bookselling business. In each case, the fact that they had no more than two children to care for made it possible to combine motherhood with paid employment.[82]

In fact, the autobiographies can be used to demonstrate the relationship between motherhood and work more formally. Over 200 writers mentioned the size of their families and this makes it possible to assess whether the size of a woman's family influenced the likelihood of her being at work. The results may be easily imagined. Small families and paid employment could be, and usually were, combined. As a woman's family grew in size, the chance of her being at work rapidly diminished. In families with just one child, over 80 per cent of the mothers worked. About 70 per cent of the mothers with two children worked. Of those with between three and four children, the participation rate hovered around 50 per cent, and as families increased in size that figure steadily declined. Almost none of the mothers with between eight and nine children did any paid work at all, though interestingly, as families grew yet larger, the number of mothers working crept up slightly again, a hint perhaps that after a certain point the combination of many mouths to feed and the presence of older daughters able to take over the running of the house paved the way for a limited return to the workforce. Nonetheless, the basic trend is very obvious. Work was far from unusual for the mothers of small families, the great majority of whom were at work, but as families grew, mothers sooner or later abandoned their attempts to earn extra income.

The autobiographies also show that most husbands tended to be enthusiastic about their wives' attempts to earn a little money so long as their family remained small. As the numbers at home increased their enthusiasm began to wane. Once mothers had five or six children to care for, husbands usually wished to see their wives devoting themselves fully to domestic matters, with perhaps just the odd seasonal work, such as harvesting or gleaning, permitted. John Pearman's wife Elizabeth bore eleven children and raised eight. John did not consider that her contribution to the household should go beyond keeping 'the house and the Children straight'. His wife, he mused, was 'a most hardworking woman' and she looked after

domestic matters 'to her great Credit'.[83] Husbands whose wives sought to
do more than take care of the house and children usually despaired. William
Swan, for example, was far from pleased when his wife Harriet began going
out to work 'at Washing and Ironing, – at both of which she was expert'. At
this time she had five children; a sixth had died the previous year. She went
'without my consent', William stonily noted. He 'endeavoured to persuade
[her] otherwise, feeling sure a wife can do her best duty at home, – to
which she would not agree'.[84] A year later, Harriet had exchanged going
out to work for taking in laundry to do at home. But this too failed to gain
her husband's approval: 'small houses are not suited to laundry work and a
family to live in . . .' he grumbled.[85] Benjamin Shaw was similarly unim-
pressed by Betty's attempts to make a little money by baking oatcakes in
their small kitchen, declaring it 'a very disagreeable Business in a house, &
very ingurious to health'. He was pleased when she was 'at last forced
to drop it'.[86]

It is interesting to note that when mothers could find suitable carers for
their children, they often did continue to work. Early in her marriage,
Elizabeth Oakley's mother-in-law took care of her son so that she could
work at the harvest. Living just outside Manchester, Joseph Burgess' mother
had the benefit of her own mother living close by. His son recalled that she
went out to work 'while Grandmother nursed her children'.[87] One woman
married to a Norfolk labourer recalled how the children 'came fast' during
the early part of her marriage. 'Mother came to us, and nursed me when the
babies came, and in between I worked as hard as my husband; not such
heavy work in course, but as much. Mother stayed at home and looked after
the children'.[88] In the 1850s, Roger Langdon's wife had six small children
to care for, yet she still 'kept a school and had several neighbours' children
to teach'.[89] Her daughter wondered 'how mother managed to keep the
school going with such a large family of her own', but she provided the
answer to her own question, adding that her 'mother's mother was a
frequent visitor and would also be at work all day long'.[90]

But most women did not have their mothers living nearby, and it was
not easy to find suitable alternatives. Thomas Cooper's mother made and
sold small workboxes, and when she had to travel further afield to sell them,
she left Thomas for the day 'in the care of such of the neighbours as would
consent to have me', usually either Will Rogers, who kept a small boarding
house, or a pensioned solider who had lost his sight.[91] At least Thomas
appears to have been relatively safe in the hands of the innkeeper and blind
soldier. More commonly, mothers left their children in the care of a

daughter – their own or a neighbour's – sometimes with tragic results. William Cameron, for example, was left 'in the charge of a girl not six years of age' when he was three so that his mother could go to work at the harvest. As he noted: 'At such an age she could not be expected to take care of herself; to her I have no grudge, but during that harvest my right leg caught damage, and left me a cripple for life'.[92] As a small child, Joseph Townend and a friend had been alone 'mending the fire' in the house when Joseph's apron caught fire and he was seriously burned. His life was despaired of, and although he survived, he lost the use of his left arm.[93] Such sad tales illustrate how difficult it was for mothers to undertake full-time paid work without a trustworthy family member to take over the care of their children. The absence of effective childcare emerges as the most significant obstacle in the way of women returning to the workforce. Small families and employment could be combined, but caring for larger families required considerable time and energy. Unless a woman's mother or mother-in-law was able and willing to do this, paid work was almost impossible.

There is one final point that deserves consideration, and that is the casual and intermittent nature of much of the work that women performed. We have seen that about 40 per cent of married women worked, but what was meant by 'work' could differ dramatically from one woman to the next. Let us think once more about Betty Shaw. She would be counted as one of that 40 per cent, but she did not really do much work throughout her married life – just a little bobbin-winding in the early years and those oatcakes that irritated her husband so much between about 1809 and 1812. These were brief interludes of employment. Yet much of the female employment described in the autobiographies was similarly fleeting in nature. In agricultural districts, married women usually worked only at harvest time, so their employment was inevitably short term and amounted to little as the years rolled by. In rural Sussex, George Mockford's wife earned highly valued extra income by hop-picking, haymaking and harvesting most summers.[94] Often in their married life, George and his wife desperately needed more income, but outside the harvest there was simply no work that she could find.

Married women, especially those with families, not only tended to work on an intermittent basis, they also evinced a marked preference to stay out of the workplace altogether. Amongst families who lived rather too close to the margins of a comfortable existence, small twists of fate could quickly plunge solvent households into desperate poverty. The death, desertion, unemployment or ill health of a husband could leave a woman without the necessary income to keep herself and her children, and force her out to work. But the preference in working-class families for mothers to devote their energies to housekeeping and childcare was very strong, and it usually took a fairly serious crisis to get married women back in the workplace. Betty baked her oatcakes when the ulcers on her husband's leg had become so bad he had had to have his leg amputated. He was unable to work for almost two years and the family were trying to subsist on their children's wages and a small pension from the parish. Matters were not quite so serious in Harriet Swan's household, but her husband had suffered recurring bouts of sickness and unemployment in the years before she began her laundry work, which may have served to strengthen her resolve.

Several autobiographers made the connection between a family crisis and their mother's entry to the workforce quite explicit. The mothers of John Bates and David Whitehead only returned to their looms when their husbands died. Andrew Carnegie's mother opened her small shop when her husband was thrown out of work during the catastrophic failure of the hand-weaving industry in Scotland.[95] Robert Lowery's mother opened up her dame school when her husband 'became ill with a pulmonary disorder' and was unable to work.[96] It is evident that all of these women had marketable skills, yet they only began exploiting them when a domestic crisis forced their hand.

Their reluctance to re-enter the workplace is not hard to understand. After all, paid work did not replace a woman's domestic work: it just added to it. After the death of her husband, Hugh Miller's mother spent her evenings working as a seamstress to her neighbours 'after she had sent my two little sisters to bed . . . and her hands were set free'.[97] William Hanson used to think of his mother and the 'toiling life she led', with her ten children and a dairy to run.[98] Alexander Somerville recalled that his mother's 'out-field labour' was added to her 'domestic toil' – he thought she was remarkable for the 'labour she encountered and overcame'.[99] When George Mockford's wife joined in the hop-picking each year she had to do her 'washing, baking &c, at night, so that she had but little rest'.[100] It is not surprising that many women continued with paid labour only until a better solution could be found.

To make matters worse, the income that women could earn from all this extra effort was meagre. No matter what work they did, very few women could earn enough to maintain their family. Most had to resort to other strategies to make ends meet – they usually sent their children out to work (or off to relatives in happier circumstances) or called on the parish for assistance. Women balanced these alternatives in their own, unique ways. Edward Rymer's mother worked 'in the barn and the field' when her husband deserted her and their four children, but her sons were also at work at a young age. John Castle's mother took her seven shillings from the parish, did some nursing, and sent John to work at the age of nine.[101] When John Lincoln's father died, his mother took a small dole from the parish, but she also took in washing. John James Bezer's mother received four shillings a week from the parish once her husband had entered Greenwich hospital, to which she added two shillings a week from her cotton-winding. Unsurprisingly, John James was at work by the time he was nine.[102]

When women had more than six or seven children, paid employment often ceased to play any part of their strategy, no matter how straitened their circumstances. Instead, they usually sought to make up lost income by turning to the parish and sending their oldest children out to work. George Marsh's mother was a widow with eleven children and dependent upon support from the parish. When George was six, she went to the parish officers with five of the children, requesting 'some further relief', and when she was denied she left the children with them, saying 'keep them!'[103] The children were soon returned with bread, flour and treacle, but when that was used up, they had to go begging. George's mother found work for her children as soon as possible, and as she lived in Penistone, just outside Barnsley, finding employment for her children was not a difficult matter.

Given that women were paid so poorly for their work, many of those who found themselves without their husband responded by trying to track the errant man down. When William Adams' father wandered off to London leaving his wife with four young children, she 'set out . . . on a three days' journey in a wagon for London to search the great wilderness' for him.[104] She did not find him, so left her youngest child with her aunts in London instead. Others sought a new breadwinner. Thomas Preston's mother was left with 'three little boys' when her first husband died. She quickly remarried, but the new husband obviously did not want to raise these three boys and Thomas was placed 'under the care of a strange nurse, through whose negligence [he] was made to suffer an accident creating lameness'.[105] With hindsight, we can see the hopelessness of many women's attempts to find themselves a male breadwinner. But with so many obstacles in the way of going it alone, it is not difficult to understood their efforts.

We are forced to conclude that wives and mothers experienced the industrial revolution in very different ways to their husbands and sons. The first half of the nineteenth century was a period of significant economic growth, yet this did little to create employment opportunities that could be grasped by women. The only real exception to this was the unmarried women living in the factory district, who certainly were able to earn higher than average wages. But even these gains were transitory, for once a mill-hand had married and had the care of a family, she was very unlikely to return to work. Elsewhere, new opportunities were simply not forthcoming. Towns and cities may have offered more dressmaking, more laundry work, more charring, but such work was so badly paid that the offer was far from enticing. It is hardly surprising to find that women's employment patterns changed so little throughout this period. The industrial revolution was undoubtedly a time of economic opportunity, but the weight of existing social structures and cultural expectations kept women firmly shut out.

# PART II

## Love

Therefore shall a man leave his father and his mother, and shall cleave unto his wife: and they shall be one flesh. (Genesis, 2:24)

As I HAD become a Man and what must I do now been about twenty four years of age, what did I do but followed the advice that is given to us in the Second Chapter of Genesis Verse twenty four Therefore shall a Man Leave his Father and Mother and Cleave unto His Wife and they shall be one flesh and now I Began to Make known Myself to this person and in Corse of time She became my Lawfull wife. (James Bowd, p. 296)

My first love ... deserted me, but another soon after offered me his heart – without the form of legal protection – and in a thoughtless moment I accepted him as my friend and protector, but, to use the words of a departed poet –

When lovely woman stoops to folly,
And finds too late that men betray,
What can sooth her melancholy,
What can wash her guilt away?

The only art her guilt to cover,
To hide her shame from every eye,
To wring repentance from her lover,
And sting his bosom, is to die.

I did not, however, feel inclined to die when I could no longer conceal what the world falsely calls a woman's shame. No, on the other hand, I never loved life more dearly and longed for the hour when I would have something to love me – and my wish was realised by becoming the mother of a lovely daughter on the 14th September 1852. (Ellen Johnston)

L OVE AND SEXUAL desire are intrinsic to the human condition. Be it the adolescent Samuel Bamford, swept off his feet by 'heart-gushings of romantic feeling'.[1] Or Robert Anderson, unable to concentrate at church because of that girl with rosy cheeks sitting across the aisle.[2] Or Elizabeth Oakley, whose heart quickened when she first spotted the new man on her employer's farm: 'he was the nicest looking young man I had ever seen . . . he had dark eyes and his hair was black and hanging in shining ringlets around his head'.[3] In different ways, the autobiographers captured the possibilities of meeting and falling in love. We might be separated by two centuries or more, but each of these writers described something that is instantly recognisable to any modern reader.

Nor is there anything too difficult to fathom in the sexual desires bound up in their stories. Along with these heart-gushings, and minds distracted by rosy cheeks, dark eyes and curly hair came powerful physical urges. You know the kind I mean. Samuel Bamford's expression of 'romantic feeling' with one unnamed girlfriend had him paying maintenance for an illegitimate son for several years. Strong desires, weak wills. You do not need to turn to history to read stories such as these.

But if love and sex are timeless constants, the space within which these drives and emotions are allowed to operate is not. Our autobiographers lived in a time when very different values on such matters as courtship, marriage, illegitimacy, extramarital affairs and homosexuality prevailed, values diligently upheld by parents, neighbours, employers, and even the young themselves. And it is this, the clash between desire and culture, which we shall look at here. First love; then sex. In the following two chapters we shall explore how a society in flux maintained control over the most intimate parts of other people's lives.

# CHAPTER FIVE

# A Brand New Wife and an Empty Pocket

We thought one house would do for us both and, as soon has we got ready, we went to Leeds parish Church in 1833. (Spurr, p. 284)

JOHN HARLAND WAS an ordinary working man. Born in the north Yorkshire village of Askrigg in 1792, by his late teens he and his family had moved to Clayton, a village a few miles from the centre of Bradford, to take advantage of the town's thriving woollen industry. As a young adult, John learned wool-combing – an easily learned and monotonous trade which involved preparing the raw wool for spinning into yarn. Like most people, though, John had interests beyond work. His growing commitment to the Methodist faith emerges as his abiding concern, but scattered among his pious reflections is evidence that John also shared the more earthly concerns common to many young men. In October 1812 he confided to his diary that he had shared with an unnamed female his 'views and feelings on the subject of a matrimonial connexion'. Three years later, John and Olivea had still not married, though a connection of a different kind had most definitely taken place. Having now traded wool-combing for a career as a Methodist preacher, John was stationed at Liskeard circuit in Cornwall, awaiting a vessel to take him to Nova Scotia, where he would soon set to work converting heathen souls.

It was at this point that the consequences of his connection with Olivea became unmistakable and inescapable. The Methodist authorities sent John back to Bradford to 'make what reparation I could to Olivea by making her my wife'. Three weeks later the couple married and moved in with her parents. Within months their child, Richard, was born. John's dream of a life devoted to overseas missionary work was in tatters. Back in Bradford, he resumed his work as a lowly wool-comber and his life fell back into its original groove. Work, parenthood and poverty filled his existence – a more humble life than that of the Methodist missionary, but one not without its compensations. As John generously noted, Olivea proved to be his 'greatest blessing'. Of his small children, he wrote simply, he 'found in these an unknown source of enjoyment, when almost destitute of worldly goods'.[1]

Courtship and marriage open a fascinating vista on to the interior lives of the poor and unlettered, and in this chapter we look at stories such as this in greater detail. As the tale of John and Olivea demonstrates, the creation of new families is a topic of innate human interest. But looking at marriage is worthwhile for more than the salacious stories of unsanctioned sexual activity, broken hearts and shattered dreams that we might hope to uncover. As even this spare outline of John and Olivea's courtship shows, sexual behaviour and marriage were expected to conform to certain social codes. John may have managed to get Olivea pregnant before they married, but a birth outside wedlock was more than they (or their church) could stomach. When John and Olivea found themselves outside the bounds of acceptable behaviour they quickly brought themselves back in. Their hasty marriage reveals the unspoken values and expectations that guided and governed the behaviour of the labouring poor. Looking at the processes by which working people went from 'walking out' to walking down the aisle illuminates aspects of working-class culture that are usually hidden from view.[2]

It would be difficult to exaggerate the place of matchmaking, wooing, and walking out in the lives of the working poor. Some of the autobiographers admitted to spending much of their early adulthood falling in and out of love, making and breaking vows of fidelity, and generally devoting the best part of their attention to matters of the heart. Undoubtedly, emotional attachments and sexual intrigue brought interest and excitement to lives characterised above all by long hours of hard work. But courtship was not all fun and games. Choosing a spouse was a serious matter. There were after all no legal routes out of marriage. This was a decision that was permanent and final; quite literally, till death us do part. So it is hardly surprising that finding a partner formed an important element of young working people's lives and filled page after page of many of their autobiographies.

Marriage was a step with heavy consequences, yet for all this the young enjoyed a surprising degree of freedom to find their partners for themselves. Among the labouring poor, there were no introductions, no matchmakers, no chaperones. Parents are noticeable only by their absence. Ordinary life teemed with opportunities to meet and get to know members of the opposite sex, and families played little or no role in guiding their children towards suitable or desirable matches. The occasions for meeting and mixing in the large cities will not require much imagination, but it was not just in the towns and cities that the young enjoyed the privilege of finding partners. Domestic service and harvest time threw the sexes together in rural areas, and the custom of young men and women gathering to socialise on summer's evenings and Sunday afternoons was simply part of the normal order of life. The printer's apprentice, James Roper, kept a detailed diary of his time in the small market town of Atherstone, Derbyshire, and described how the young people of the town gathered on the commons after work was finished on Sundays. One Sunday evening he 'ran with the Damsels up the hill and down', while the next he took long walks around the town as 'Miss Allan lighted my cigars for me, nice looking Damsel she is to!'[3] Young people met at work, on the village green, in the Sunday school, on the pews of their local Methodist church, and made their own decisions about their compatibility and the kind of relationship they sought. Everyday life provided all the social interaction necessary for young people seeking suitable partners, most of it free from the watchful eye of parents, employers and social superiors.

Working men and women had ample occasion to size each other up as they went about their ordinary business, but custom dictated that certain codes needed to be respected before couples started 'walking out'. Relationships were initiated when the young man in question plucked up the courage to declare his intentions to the object of his affections. As one writer recalled, he chirpily informed his wife-to-be, 'If ever you do want one [a sweetheart] I'll keep you company.'[4] Women were not supposed to articulate their preferences so freely. Joseph Terry's autobiography was longer than most, and he included a lot more detail than others did about the passage from meeting his sweetheart to 'keeping her company'. Here is what he tells us. In his early twenties, he joined his local Methodist chapel and started to help teach at the chapel's Sunday school. There, being 'quite free from any love engagement', he naturally enough 'began to look about for a suitable girl'. Having selected Sarah Ann as his choice, he wrote her a letter 'on the subject' and enlisted the help of a mutual friend 'to intercede for me and bring about an interview'.[5] Sarah Ann signalled her interest in his suit by asking her friend to relay the time and place they could meet a few weeks hence.

Although our male writers tended to present women as the passive recipients of their opening moves, women were of course scarcely less active when it came to looking out for suitable partners. They kept a watchful eye on the men they worked with and used friends and intermediaries to gauge and communicate their interest. Elizabeth Oakley recalled that one of her roles when in domestic service was to take the men their lunch in the fields, and so 'I had the opportunity of seeing afar of as it were what sort of men they were or if they were steady or not'.[6] She was struck one day to find 'the nicest looking young man I had ever seen' helping out at harvest. Weeks later they met again at the Baptist Chapel's harvest, and when the harness at the rear of their cart broke she and the young man had to switch seats. In their new seats, they finally got 'into talk'. Robert began to accompany her as she walked between her parents' and her employers' home, but true to form, their relationship developed only when he had 'expressed a wish to keep my company'.[7]

Once couples had agreed to walk out, they were largely left to get on with it. At the heart of many relationships lay the exchange of letters and tokens. Several of the autobiographers described how they kept relationships alive by writing letters – some even cited this as the spur to their learning to write. Even for those unable to hold a pen, letter-writing could play an important role. So long as James Lackington was unable to write, he employed his friends to write for him; occasioning their praise, he claimed, as a 'good inditer of letters'.[8] And along with the letters, young lovers exchanged other small tokens of their affection. One young printer received a 'lock of hair very neatly braided', a silk purse and many 'affectionate notes' from one girl, all the while busily giving nosegays and scraps of poetry to another.[9] Richard Gooch gave his sweetheart 'a stick and pocket handkerchief as a lover's relics'.[10] Our autobiographers had complex love lives, juggling the attentions of more than one woman at once, and sometimes (and less satisfactorily) finding themselves involved with a woman who was juggling several suitors at a time.[11] Above all, these writers described an unsupervised world in which young people followed their heart wheresoever it led.

Parents and employers generally allowed their young charges considerable privacy to get on with matters. When couples began 'walking out', they could meet alone, usually out of doors, but away (they hoped) from the eyes and ears of their neighbours. So Sarah Ann, once persuaded by her friend to meet with her Sunday school teacher, Joseph Terry, arranged a meeting 'at the bottom of the garden' the following Sunday evening. She and her friend arrived together at the appointed hour, but the friend then left them alone to enjoy 'a long and serious conversation' together.[12] At the beginning of James Roper's diary, he may be found joining in the fun and games with the other young men and women of Atherstone. But after matters with the beautiful Kitty had taken a more serious turn, the pair spent their time alone in the garden bowers and on 'delightful' long walks around the town and along the canal.[13] The Northumbrian poet, Robert Story, remembered pleasant summer's evenings walking out alone with a lady's maid called Anna.[14] Time and time again, the autobiographers recalled enjoying the freedom to be alone together in whatever quiet and secluded corners they could find. What went on between them was unknown to parents, employers or any other authority figures in their lives.

The liberty to spend time alone together carried risks as well as pleasures. In male eyes, walking out is presented as harmless and enjoyable. The occasional female autobiography hints at the darker side of unsupervised courtship. Very few working women penned their life story, yet one recurring theme in the small body of writing they have left behind is young women's fear of, and near encounters with, male sexual violence. Here for example is Elizabeth Oakley, working as a domestic servant before her marriage to Robert. One Sunday afternoon while she was in the house alone a young man from her village came knocking at the door and tried to gain entry. Elizabeth thought he was a 'libertine' and was sufficiently concerned about what he intended to do to her to 'lock the door and run upstairs'.[15] There she cowered for several hours, before her unwelcome visitor eventually abandoned his trip. When stormy weather forced Margaret Davidson to spend the night alone at her friend's house, the father of her friend assaulted her as she lay in bed and attempted to rape her.[16] Mary Saxby recalled a lucky escape from assault by a band of sailors who had 'fixed their eyes on me, and forced me along with them'. She was rescued by a farmer who heard her cries and set his dogs upon the sailors.[17]

Mary Ann Ashford was another domestic servant and, like most servants, she was sometimes free to spend her Sunday afternoon with whomever she wished. Decades after the event, she wrote a vivid account of how a Sunday afternoon spent walking with the man she had agreed to marry took a very sinister turn. As Mary Ann's suitor led her down 'a lonely footpath' through a wood, he began talking about the injustice of the recent execution of a young man for rape. The isolated spot he had taken her to and the tone of his conversation left Mary Ann feeling 'dreadfully alarmed'. She resolved never to 'go walking again without knowing what sort of road I had to go ...'.[18] She called the wedding off, though not without experiencing more threatening behaviour from the man.[19] In these autobi-ographies, private courtship appears in a far less benign light than it does in the narratives that men have bequeathed. Clearly the beauty of privacy could lie in the eye of the beholder.

Although couples attempted to enjoy their courting in private, some obviously struggled to obtain quite the degree of privacy they wished. Young, unmarried working people did not live in homes of their own: they lived under a roof shared with parents or employers, so new relationships could be difficult to conceal. When Nathaniel Bryceson started walking out with Ann Fox, they regularly crossed paths with people they knew, despite trying to keep their relationship under wraps by walking about parts of London far from where they lived.[20] And when he took to surrep-titiously inviting Ann to the empty lodgings he usually shared with his 'Granny Shepard' on Sunday afternoons, it was not long before his granny, mother and stepfather had all passed Ann on the stairway as she left and begun to wonder 'how matters stood'.[21]

In early eighteenth-century Somerset, John Cannon faced similar diffi-culties in obtaining privacy for his personal affairs. Working for his uncle as a farm servant, John developed a relationship with the maid, Mary Rose. The pair must have managed to enjoy some time alone for he recalled 'kissing and toying when together in private'.[22] But like other later writers, he also noted that cramped living conditions made it difficult for them to conceal the relationship from those around them, despite their best efforts. He ruefully noted that the 'odd doings' that occurred between him and Mary Rose each night as Mary passed his bed on the way to her own were 'difficult to be kept long a secret, by reason of the boy' with whom he shared a bed.[23]

The lack of genuinely private space meant that new attachments would sooner or later fall under the purview of chattering friends and neighbours. And there can be little doubt that neighbours kept a very keen eye on other people's courtships. The twists and turns of each liaison formed the substance of story-telling that sustained local communities for weeks at a time. Several of the writers told long tales about the interference of 'busy' people – either their friends or those of their partner – in their courtship. Joseph Terry's relationship with Mary Dinton, for example, had fizzled out when Joseph's health failed and Mary 'got rather cold'. He later learned that her coldness was 'caused by a base calumny' concerning the cause of his ill health.[24] Richard Gooch's courtship of Mary Foreman came to an abrupt end when 'the iron tongue of slander began its work' in his absence.[25] The breach caused between the pair by tales of his infidelity was not repaired and the relationship soon came to an end. Working-class couples may have been able to spend time alone together, but their courtships were nonetheless conducted in the full glare of gossip and idle village chatter.

The extent of local interest in matters of courtship is brought to life in the diary of Joseph Woolley who was as forthcoming on the romantic, sexual and marital relations of his neighbours as he was silent about his own private life. His diary included an account of a 'sore despute' between William Barber and his wife, after she had seen him visit the barn 'that the old Slut Lives in'; a fight between Thomas Bilby and 'is whife'; and a battle between Mary Hardy and William Reckless over the father of her illegitimate child. Then there were all the whisperings about Joan Francis who was supposed to have married on the Tuesday before Easter Thursday, but called the wedding off. All was not as it seemed, according to Woolley, as 'people knew she had been [pregnant] if she was not then but a very little time before'. This couple had 'secretly Cohabitted together for some years but as it is not openly seen they Can Carey the fars on under the mask of religion and when she happens to be prignant she can take sumthing to Cause abdoration [abortion]'. Woolley also seems to have known everything about what happened between Tom Shore and Sall Holt, who accused him of assault. According to Woolley, the truth of the matter was that Sall had in fact laid a false accusation against Tom because 'he would not be naughty with hir'. Finally, Henerey Allin returned back to the village from London, 'turned away from is place for Being too free with the Cooke or as people say he was Caut with hir in such a place as was no Credit to them'.[26] Evidently, young courtships were not entirely private from the prying eyes of their neighbours. But Woolley's comments are just the musings of a prurient and nosy neighbour, with great interest in, but no control over, the events he described.

Courtship was a form of play, lacking responsibilities and without serious consequences. It could be relished and enjoyed (as well as dissected by the neighbours) because new relationships were easily entered and quickly terminated. But at some point, many a courting couple began to turn their thoughts to marriage and when they did so the tenor changed perceptibly. A marriage could not be terminated quickly, slowly, or in any other way. Of course, given the relatively high death rate, many marriages were not long-lived, and broken families and step-parents scattered the social horizon in much the same way as they do today.[27] But death could hardly be relied upon to offer a route out of marriage to those who needed it. The only option for the unhappily married was to desert (an option that in reality was far more accessible to husbands than to wives) or to agree to live apart, though that left no legal opportunities for starting anew.[28]

Marriage was not only difficult to exit – it was not even particularly easy to enter. Tying the knot was a costly business. Newly wed couples did not move in with their in-laws. They had to set up a household of their own, and this required a little thought and money. Even the simplest wedding called for a modest outlay – rings had to be bought, the clergyman paid, and a celebratory glass or two raised. And the wedding was just the start. If the newly-weds were to set about housekeeping, they also needed money for rent and to purchase the few pots and pans and sticks of furniture that made running a home possible. Young couples found many different ways to make all of this happen. Some set aside a part of their wages each year, building up a small nest egg that could be put towards the expense. Others reached a stage in their lives where they felt confident in their ability to earn a living. George Smith, for example, turned his thoughts to marriage once he had 'succeeded in opening up a tolerable trade as a carpenter and builder'.[29] The future Chartist leader, William Lovett used his talents as a carpenter to prepare for marriage 'by making my own furniture, and by otherwise providing for her a comfortable home'.[30] Occasionally couples were helped out by families and friends who provided money, housing or furniture. The routes to marriage were various, but the idea essentially the same. A separate household had to be formed, and couples needed to pool their resources and ingenuity to make that happen.

The expectation that young newly-weds would move into a home of their own helped to keep the age of marriage relatively high. Studies of parish registers suggest that men married at twenty-seven at the start of the eighteenth century, the age falling to twenty-five by the early nineteenth century; women at twenty-six falling to twenty-three.[31] Even allowing for the fall in ages, marriage occurred long after the onset of both sexual maturity and courtship. For most people, the expense of housekeeping lay behind the delay. Israel Roberts met his wife-to-be in January 1845 when he was not yet eighteen, but did not marry her until June 1851. For six long years, Israel could 'never persuade my sweetheart that I could keep a house and home together. In reply to my entreaties she used to say, when you can make salt then we'll talk about it.'[32] As Israel learned, the necessity of setting up home following one's wedding ensured that marriage rested not simply upon the state of one's affections, but also upon the contents of one's purse.

And the fact that a couple's wedding plans were connected with their prosperity raises the intriguing possibility that the industrial revolution was the cause of the steady fall in marriage ages through the eighteenth and early nineteenth centuries.[33] We saw in the last three chapters that industrialisation generally brought better prospects for earning a living for many unskilled workers. Were these improvements sufficient to permit young people to embark upon marriage and housekeeping at a younger age? Or, more generally, did the emergence of new working patterns have the power to influence the decisions that people made in this, most intimate, corner of human life?

The autobiographies reveal that there had always been considerable variation in the ages at which different kinds of workers had married. Throughout the years covered by the autobiographies, the most prosperous workers always married the youngest. Prior to industrialisation, this meant that young marriage was largely the privilege of those who had learned a skilled trade. Alexander Mather, for example, had been taught the baking business by his father and following a move to London he presumed his prospects were bright enough for marriage at the age of nineteen.[34] Also amongst the young grooms in the eighteenth century were a razor-grinder, tailor, mason and shoemaker.[35] Right through the industrial revolution, skilled labourers continued to stand out for the ease with which they made it down the aisle. The carpenter, John Bennett, having abandoned his attempt to carve out a living in the quiet Wiltshire village of South Wraxall and moved to nearby Bristol, married at the age of twenty.[36] Several shoe-makers reported marrying in their early twenties, having just completed an apprenticeship and begun life as a journeyman.[37] A couple of blacksmiths, a cutler, whitesmith, tailor, painter, shopkeeper, cabinetmaker, printer, ship-wright and sailor also figure amongst those who married in their teens or early twenties.[38] It was no doubt for much the same reason that there was a relatively high incidence of young marriages amongst those living and working in London, where work tended at least to be regular, if not also well paid.[39]

By the end of the eighteenth century, however, a range of new industries was helping to raise the incomes of those who had not learned a trade. As a result, unskilled industrial workers were increasingly likely to be found in the ranks of the young marriers. The youngest groom amongst the auto-biographers was Joshua Dodgson, who had started work in a cotton mill in Sowerby, West Yorkshire, 'when a mere boy'. He married at the age of seventeen, while employed as a dyer in Halifax for 15 shillings a week.[40]

The flax-dressing industry in Dundee provided one of its young workers with enough to deposit 'from time to time my surplus earnings in the Savings' Bank', permitting him to marry at the age of twenty.[41] In fact, young marriage was common throughout the factory districts.[42] Thomas Whittaker was one of eight brothers, all of them employed in the factories around south Yorkshire, all but one of whom were married by the time they were twenty – one had married when just sixteen years old.[43] Whittaker believed that early marriages were very common amongst the mill workers, and he described the reasons for this as follows:

> Two young people look at each other, they are sixteen or eighteen years of age, they can each earn a pound or twenty-five shillings a week. Two twenty-fives are fifty, and that is a lump of money and a temptation to people who can live on ten or twelve shillings a week. They put themselves together, and their wages too, and for a time there is abundance, but usually this is not long lived . . .

The relatively good wages that could be earned in the handloom trade (prior at least to its decline in the second quarter of the nineteenth century) helped to encourage early marriage amongst the weavers as well. At the age of twenty William Hanson decided that he 'would get married, and be settled in life . . . the prospect seemed very nice and inviting. I got married in March 1825, and we set up house near the bottom of Steep lane, in Sowerby.'[44] Joseph Livesey held firm to the principle that 'no man should take a wife till he has a house furnished ready for her to come to', and although his efforts in that respect were helped by a small bequest from a family member, his and his wife's labour as a weaver and spinner must also have helped.[45] The weaving industry helped to encourage younger marriage in Lancashire, Yorkshire and the Scottish Lowlands, but its effects could also be felt in Taunton, Devon, and Colchester, Essex.[46] For much the same reason, young marriages were common in the mining districts. George Marsh, despite a miserably poor childhood following the death of both his parents, enjoyed relatively regular work and good wages in the coal mines around Barnsley by his late teens, and was able to marry at the age of twenty.[47] And Anthony Errington's work as a wheelwright repairing the wagonways at various Tyneside collieries provided him with the where-withal to marry and start housekeeping at the age of nineteen.[48] Other miners from Staffordshire, Durham and Scotland's Central Belt were also amongst those who married in their early twenties.[49]

It is noticeable how closely these marriage patterns dovetail with the changes in men's working patterns described in Chapter 2. As we saw there, those who had learned a skilled trade enjoyed significant advantages because of their ability to find regular and relatively well-paid work. This suggestion now appears to be reinforced by the relative ease with which skilled workers traded the freedoms of their single life for the comforts and responsibilities of the married man. Furthermore, from about the 1790s unskilled workers were beginning to share in these gains as ever more mill-hands, weavers and miners were to be found amongst those with the resources to marry young. Of course, how far young marriage can really be understood as advantageous is very much open to question. In the absence of effective birth control, young marriage meant larger families, which imposed a drain on a family's resources and a strain on the mother's health. It is worth repeating Thomas Whittaker's observation that the abundance which characterised the newly-weds' early life together was often 'not long lived'. But these were not considerations that detained our young spouses for too long. Rising wealth gave many working people the power to set a wedding date at the time of their choosing, and if early marriage entailed certain inconveniences, from our writers' perspectives these were more than outweighed by the ability to exercise autonomy in this crucial area of personal life.

Just as the advantages enjoyed by skilled workers and those living in industrial areas were mirrored in their marriage preferences, so were the disadvantages experienced by agricultural workers visible in their choices. Skilled work, or access to relatively well-paid unskilled work in industrial areas, helped to encourage younger marriage; the absence of these opportunities in rural areas had the opposite effect. Very few of the men working in agriculture had accumulated sufficient resources to set about housekeeping by their early twenties.[50] In the early 1840s, Joseph Arch married when barely twenty-one, though he and his father already possessed a house; as he frankly admitted in his autobiography, they sorely needed a housekeeper to look after it following the death of his mother.[51] The only other agricultural worker to marry young was Joseph Ricketts, who married at the turn of the century while working as a gamekeeper in his native village of Castle Eaton in Wiltshire: they 'scrabled along as well as we could' on his earnings of eight shillings a week.[52] Without access to the brighter opportunities provided by a skill, those working in agriculture, fishing and other forms of rural day labour simply waited – their marriages were uniformly spread from their mid-twenties to their early thirties, and occasionally beyond.[53]

By delaying marriage until such time as they felt confident about their ability to set up and maintain a home of their own, all of the writers we have been looking at were essentially adhering to the old way of doing things. But there is a further possibility that we ought to explore. After all, we have already caught a glimpse of one couple who did not go about marriage in the time-honoured way. John and Olivea, whom we met at the start of this chapter, did not get married after figuring out a strategy for financing the big event. Following their hasty wedding they did not move into a home of their own at all: they moved in with her parents. Let us go back for a moment and re-examine their story.

John was living and working as a Methodist preacher in Cornwall when he was abruptly recalled from his post and ordered to marry Olivea and spare her the shame of baptising a bastard child. Unsurprisingly, given the unplanned nature of their wedding, this young couple lacked the means to set up a home of their own. After the wedding they moved in with Olivea's parents, and there they stayed for the next three years. John returned to his old life as a wool-comber; Olivea forged a new life as a mother to their children – by the time they left her parents they had three, so we can assume her new life kept her fully occupied. This was not the way that things were supposed to be done. The normal expectation was that marriage (and therefore sex) should be delayed until such time as the couple in question could entertain a realistic hope of setting up a home of their own. What is more, John and Olivea were not unique. They were just one of many couples whose hopes for marriage (or sexual desires) had run far ahead of their means to pay for a wedding and a home. And this suggests that there is something more to the history of marriage that needs to be explored.

A recurring story in the autobiographies is that of newly-weds returning from the church without a penny left in their pockets. Once the parson had been paid and a celebratory drink or two bought, our shame-faced autobiographer admits he had nothing left to embark on the journey of married life. James Nye, for example, recalled that 'when I agreed to be married I had only one sovereign in my pocket to do everything with . . . Well off I went to church with my bride and was married as big as anybody with an empty pocket; at least I came home so, for after I bought a wedding ring and a wedding dinner and paid the parson my money was gone'.[54] With 'no work and winter coming on', James and his new wife found themselves in just the same predicament as John and Olivea: married, but with 'no house furnished'.[55] Or there is James Hawker who declared that after returning on foot from the ceremony he, his wife and his brother had just threepence between them, and a pint of ale later 'I stood with a Brand New Wife and an Empty Pocket'.[56] Meanwhile David Love, unable to finance the wedding at all, followed the Scottish custom of a 'pay-wedding': 'Some make free weddings, with great feasting, music, and dancing, and nothing to pay; but the poorer sort make pay-weddings, every man and woman who are bidden, give one shilling for their eating, and also pay for their drink: such a wedding ours was ...'[57] Of course, if the wedding alone depleted a couple's savings, the prospects for their housekeeping did not look bright.

Christopher Thomson decided to marry at the age of twenty, with employment 'very slack', and 'neither a home, nor the means to purchase one'.[58] Then there is Robert Spurr, an unskilled labourer living in Yorkshire who got married at the age of twenty-three, when his 'wages was very small. I seldom had any or very little in my pocket'. He quickly 'found I had been very foolish for i soon began to learn the cares of the world ...'[59] Joseph Mayett, an agricultural labourer living in Buckinghamshire, took the decision to marry at the relatively advanced age of thirty-one: yet at the time he had been reduced to selling rags and his employment prospects were at the lowest ebb they had been for several years.[60] John Leno and his wife 'got mated young, too young many would say', and like many young newlyweds 'were poorly off, and had not the wherewithal to furnish a room'. They were helped by a friend who lent them the furniture he had managed to get together when his own marriage was postponed – but when that marriage took place, the Lenos had to return the furniture and sleep on the hard floor.[61] Elsewhere writers can be found admitting they had married when 'all the money I was worth was eightpence;'[62] 'without any legitimate prospect of obtaining a living';[63] or with hopes for keeping a wife 'of a very hazy character'.[64]

For some, funds were so low they were unable to move into a house of their own. The 'Journeyman Baker', for example, whose life story was published in the *Commonwealth*, remembered that 'The joint finances of my partner and myself were very limited indeed ... on the morning after our marriage, our whole stock of funds amounted to the sum of one shilling and sixpence sterling. As we had nothing in the shape of furniture, we lived for a short while at my mothers.'[65] James Bowd, an agricultural labourer living in Swavesey, Cambridgeshire, got married with a bed and a 'very good Family Bible', but very little money – 'only three shillings not much to start in Life', he confessed.[66] The couple lived with his parents for the first eight and a half months of marriage, 'so we had a chance to gather a few sticks together', during which time their first child was born, which suggests that a pregnancy might have hastened the marriage.[67] John Lincoln left his place in service to marry the fellow servant he had made pregnant, a woman with 'a hot and Violent Temper – she was a very stout person and ten years older than myself'.[68] As they had not the means to furnish a room, they moved in with her parents instead.[69]

Many other marriages described in the autobiographical literature had yet bleaker prospects, for the couple lacked both the resources to start housekeeping and any real chance of future well-being. Take, for example, John Colin, a drunkard who in his early twenties married a girl two years younger; it is possible that she was still in her teens. After the wedding he left his wife and moved to Ipswich for work, but she followed him and soon after gave birth to a boy. John's drinking was already spiralling out of control and in the face of these family responsibilities he fled a second time. This time he moved to London. Once again his wife followed him, finding him in the great metropolis out of work, 'drunk, dirty and ragged'.[70] At this point the marriage broke down. She and the child returned to her family in Hitchin and were not reunited with John until he had taken the pledge, many years later.

Mary Saxby, one of very few female autobiographers, provides a rare account of the marriage decisions of an unwed mother. After an illegitimate birth, Mary Saxby endeavoured to persuade her child's father to marry, even though the couple 'had not money enough to discharge the expense', and despite the fact that (in her own estimation) 'he did not promise to prove the best of husbands'.[71] Such was their poverty that they had difficulty persuading a clergyman to perform the wedding service. The prospects, both emotional and material, for this union could hardly have been worse.

John Harland wrote in muted terms about his hotfoot trip to the church to wed Olivea. Yet clearly, there was nothing unusual about his story. They were not that rare exception to sensible marriage-planning that proves the rule; just one of many couples whose desires were larger than their pockets. In fact it is possible to establish this more firmly by making a rough tally of the number of such marriages that occurred throughout the eighteenth and early nineteenth centuries. The custom of couples delaying marriage until they had the wherewithal to set up a home of their own appears firmly entrenched until about the 1790s. Before this date the evidence of working people marrying without the means to keep a house of their own is virtually non-existent. Only one writer – Mary Saxby – admitted to this error and at the time she wed she was a vagrant travelling with the gypsies, living largely outside the bounds of conventional society. Between the 1790s and 1850, however, somewhere between 10 and 15 per cent of all the marriages described by the autobiographies resembled in some way the unplanned nature of John and Olivea's union, with writers either admitting that the material outlook for their marriage had been poor, or indicating that they had lacked the means to set up a house. We are left then with a fairly sharp break in marriage customs around the 1790s, with almost complete social conformity before that decade and a sizeable minority of couples rejecting traditional values afterwards.

In drawing attention to the break that occurred around the 1790s, it should not be assumed that these couples went on to experience greater poverty than those who had married earlier in the century.[72] Most working people in the eighteenth century were extremely poor, and though they might have delayed marriage until they could set about housekeeping, in reality many did so in the meanest of styles. After their wedding ceremony in February 1759, for instance, Robert Barker and his new wife 'had but ten-pence left ... part of a cold sheep's head that was dressed the day before', and a pile of recently printed ballads to sell.[73] Their hopes were pinned on the pile of ballads; but still, it was not much with which to embark upon married life. The morning after James Lackington's wedding to Nancy Smith in 1770 the newly-weds found they had 'eatables sufficient for a day or two', one halfpenny, and some orders for new shoes (they were shoemakers) which they hoped would see them through.[74] This was not fine living, but there was one point which both writers took pains to emphasise. When they wrote about the event years later, both Robert and James let their readers know that when they had married, they had also set up a household and made plans to maintain it.

It was this that had changed by the nineteenth century. Many of those who regretted the poverty of their early years of marriage went on to live tolerably comfortable lives. Yet they never forgot how they had disregarded society's expectations when they tied the knot. Robert Lowery, the Newcastle Chartist, forged a successful career in public life, but he had married at the age of eighteen while still a poorly paid tailor's apprentice. In his memoirs, he noted that 'in a prudential sense we both afterwards perceived that it would have been more prudent for us to have waited until we had been older, and I had time to fix myself in something, whereby a better provision could have been made for our wants'.[75] Lowery and his wife held to the belief that marriage should be delayed until a degree of financial security had been obtained, yet also realised they had failed to implement this ideal on a personal level. And with so many writers sharing the Lowerys' sentiments we are looking at a very significant shift in values. Right in the heart of the industrial revolution, social customs which had been respected by generation after generation started to unravel. And the timing of this development is suggestive, raising the possibility that older customs began to unravel not simply at the same time as industrialisation, but because of it.

To explore this possibility a little further, let us think once more about the ideals that so many couples were starting to reject. The expectation that newly married couples should move into a home of their own had helped to delay marriage for most women until their mid-twenties. This in turn served to limit the number of children they would bear. Most pre-industrial societies have evolved a set of expectations surrounding sex and marriage, one role of which is help to keep the size of the population down. Britain was no exception. Society frowned on illegitimate births and demanded that new life should be created within the context of marriage. But marriage was difficult to enter because it required the setting up of a new home. Together, these expectations helped to limit the number of births, and the number of mouths that needed to be fed. So when Sarah brushed off Israel Roberts' marriage overtures for a number of years, telling him that when he could 'make salt' then she would talk about it, she not only revealed how far she had internalised her society's values, she was playing an active role in limiting the size of her family – for in the absence of reliable birth control, the later she married, the fewer children she was likely to bear. If enough young people internalised these values and put off their wedding until such time as the groom could 'make salt', they had the potential to raise the age of marriage and so keep a tight lid on population growth.

We might imagine that many would find these restrictions on sex and marriage oppressive and so seek ways to get around them. Yet most adults found security in the restrictions. Take the parents of courting couples. When newly-weds' housekeeping plans failed, they were likely to return to the homes of their parents. So quite aside from the genuine concern that parents might have for their children's conjugal happiness, they had more self-interested motives for steering their children towards suitable partners and delayed marriages. Next in the line of defence came employers and parish notables. In the absence of family willing or able to help out when feckless marriages hit the rocks, the parish would be called upon to help raise the small children such unions produced. So those who paid the parish rates also took an interest in the marriage plans of humble neighbours.

Even the young themselves were motivated to take these cultural norms seriously. Although parents might in principle be willing to help their adult children should their efforts at housekeeping fall apart, their own poverty meant that the level of practical assistance they could provide might be extremely small. And one would hardly expect the parish to treat its poorest members willingly or generously should they marry without due regard for society's values, and then run into financial difficulties. With so little to fall back on should things go wrong, young couples had very good reason to pay more than lip service to the advice of their parents and neighbours.

When we look at the autobiographers who married before the 1790s, we find children remarkably compliant with their parents' wishes. Roger Lowe's courtship of Mary Naylor foundered when her father declared himself against the match: 'such actors and abetters against it as her father and others!' thundered Lowe hopelessly in his diary.[76] Her father's disapproval was grounds for the pair to keep their relationship secret and in due course it petered out. Matters with Ann Barrow ended no better. Roger believed that 'if shee thought her father would dye soone she would waite for me'. But her father did not die and no marriage took place.[77] Clearly the fathers of both women considered Lowe an unworthy match, and their opinion was enough to prevent his marrying either. Lowe eventually did wed Emm Potter, after a courtship of nearly four years. She, by contrast, had no living parents – or at least none that Lowe ever mentioned.[78]

An alternative illustration of the potency of parental power is the unusual case of James M'Kaen's private marriage, which took place at some time in the early 1770s. In early adulthood, M'Kaen had 'fallen into acquaintance' with a young woman and wished to marry her. The difficulty was that his mother had a different woman in view for him, one possessed of a little money. For this reason, M'Kaen, who still lived with his mother, married '*privately*, for fear of her interference'.[79] He continued to live with his mother for several months, keeping the marriage a secret all the while, until the news of it 'broke out'.[80] If parental disapproval was not always sufficient to prevent offspring from tying the knot, it was certainly sufficient to circumscribe their movement. The wishes of parents were a powerful force throughout most of the eighteenth century and played an important role in guiding and restricting the marriage plans of the young.

It is difficult to establish the influence, if any, of the wider community in sanctioning or thwarting the marriage plans of its younger members. The autobiographers do not refer to any broader communal involvement in marriage plans, though of course their silence cannot be read as proof that no such involvement existed. We are on stronger ground when looking at how children responded to the wishes of their parents and those of their intendeds' parents. Perhaps one of the most interesting things to emerge from the eighteenth-century autobiographies is the relative willingness of most writers to accept the obligation of securing parental approval for their wedding plans. Samuel Bownas, after completing his apprenticeship as a blacksmith, not only solicited the approval of his partner's family before engaging to marry but also felt duty bound to respect their wishes. Although his suit was received by her parents, when an uncle got wind of his intentions he 'seemed much averse to it; and would have his niece left at liberty' until such time as the marriage could actually take place. Bownas noted that he 'very readily complied' with the uncle's wishes and the question of marriage was dropped for a number of years.[81] In the 1770s, Samuel Hick was successfully warned off marriage by the parents of his sweetheart.[82] Thomas Johnson simply took it for granted that Mary would 'never marry without [her uncle's] consent', and duly went about obtaining this before expressing his interest in her.[83] When William Hutton asked a young woman if she cared to spend an evening with him, she tartly replied that she would never 'keep company with anyone, without my father's consent'.[84] Hutton thought this went beyond the bounds of duty, and lost interest. And as we have just seen, James M'Kaen did not obey his mother, but he nonetheless wanted to appear as though he did.

In a similar vein, there is no evidence of apprentices attempting to marry without the permission of their masters. Indentures routinely included a clause forbidding the apprentice to marry, and for most of the eighteenth century, the fact of being apprenticed was sufficient to stymie even the most ardent of passions. Lackington, for example, had fallen 'desperately in love with [a] farmer's handsome dairy-maid' in the 1760s; but as he calmly noted, 'my being an apprentice, prevented me from marrying at that time'.[85] Love-struck apprentices simply waited. Nor should their conformity occasion too much surprise. As we saw in Chapter 2, through most of the century there was just too little work to go around, even for the most skilled workers. In this context, the logic of marrying against one's master's wishes was extremely weak, no matter how inflamed one's heart might be.

When looking at the ways in which marriages were formed in the eighteenth century and earlier, we can see that not only did most people respect social norms, but they did so for good cause. When men and women delayed marriage in deference to the expectations of family and friends they were behaving in a way that made sense for the world in which they lived. Poverty extracts obedience. Penury was the reason why men like James Ferguson stayed with masters who almost starved them. It was also why adult writers did not complain about the forces that had had them at work at the age of six or seven. Poor people do what they need to do in order to put food on the table. And poor societies do what they need to do in order to make sure there are not too many people sitting around the table. Throughout the eighteenth century, Britain was still a traditional society, with most working people engaged in an unending struggle to earn the money needed to pay for their weekly rent and their next meal. Poverty encased working people and made their culture what it was. It powerfully discouraged young couples from pursuing risky marriage strategies without the support and consent of those around them. Parents and children cleaved to the same customs as their best means of survival.

By the end of the eighteenth century, the economic growth associated with industrialisation began to ripple through society. And as working people stepped away from the harsh struggle for subsistence that had ever characterised their lot, the rationale for restrictive marriage customs became less compelling. New forms of employment, more work, and higher wages all helped to make the outlook for young parents hoping to raise a child brighter than ever before. In a more benign economic climate, parents did not need to be so vigilant in patrolling the sexual activity of their children and the young could be less risk-averse in the timing and circumstances of their marriage. Gradually, old customs waned. If we examine more closely the behaviour of both parents and children when courting couples turned their thoughts to marriage, we find that all those involved were interpreting their duties far more loosely than ever before.

Parents, for example, were increasingly likely to open the doors to their married children, even when they had manifestly failed to scrape together the resources required for housekeeping. Between about 10 and 15 per cent of newly wed couples resided with one set of parents after their wedding, usually for a relatively short period of less than a year, though sometimes longer. All but one of these couples did so in the nineteenth century. (The eighteenth-century exception was Christopher Hopper though he, interestingly enough, was living on the Durham coalfield and working as a miner, and so shared the brighter economic prospects usually associated with the later period.) As employment prospects for working people improved, parents became more ready to countenance providing their newly wed children with a roof over their heads, regarding it as a temporary expedient rather than an admission that that their offspring had failed to form a viable union.[86]

In some families, lodging with parents immediately after marriage was evidently accepted as part of the established order of things. We have already met Benjamin and Betty Shaw a number of times. We first met Benjamin in Chapter 2, working as a machine-maker in Preston and taking his employer to court when he refused to allow his men their 'drinkings'. In Chapter 3 we met Benjamin and Betty's seven children, all but one at work in the factories by the age of seven or eight, in part because Betty thought this a better option than dressing the children in second-hand clothes. And in the last chapter we met Betty once more, baking cakes in the family kitchen much to the consternation of her husband. In the next chapter, when we turn to illegitimacy, Benjamin, Betty and their seven children will, you may well guess, all appear once again. For the present, however, we are looking at parents opening their home to adult children in order to get them started in married life, and the Shaws both received such help from their parents and in turn offered it to their children. Following their wedding in 1793, Benjamin and Betty lived for a short while with her father; and all but one of their seven children spent some time back in the family home (or in that of their in-laws) after their marriage. John and Olivea Harland were also first recipients and then givers of such assistance. They found themselves in much the same pass as their own parents had been when their second son Edward announced that his girlfriend was expecting their first child.

Such outcomes were accepted with resignation, though usually without much enthusiasm. Benjamin Shaw complained endlessly about the problems his children gave him as young adults. John Harland, meanwhile, referred to Edward's indiscretion as a 'source of much grief'.[87] Yet parental disapproval was confined to angry words rather than actions. Living in the heartland of the industrial revolution, the Shaws and the Harlands had no reason to fear that these arrangements would become permanent. They regarded sharing their home as an irritating but short-term solution rather than a life sentence of poverty and insecurity.

Just as parents were becoming more relaxed about the circumstances of their children's marriages, young people were becoming very much less concerned about what their parents made of their choices. Some of course courted their parents' blessing. James Roper, for example, having resolved to settle for 'a steady life, no more fun with the girls, no, after having about a dozen different sweethearts', lay in bed 'and wrote a very long letter to my father, asking his consent to our marriage'.[88] Only when an agreeable reply came back did James and Kitty proceed with their wedding plans. According to Anthony Errington, when he asked his second wife Mary 'wilt thou have mee? She Answered, Shee would see what her Mother said . . . She returned on the Sunday night. They was agreeable whereon wee got married.'[89] Others, however, cared very little for their parents' opinion, and either failed to inform them of their upcoming nuptials, or flatly disobeyed them if they refused to give their consent.

William Hollingsworth, for instance, made an elaborate show of seeking the consent of the parents of his bride-to-be prior to their wedding, but did not seek any from his own parents, who remained unaware of the marriage until after it had taken place.[90] John Colin's bride's 'relations were greatly set against our marriage, as I was such a sad drunkard and my wife's family were all religiously disposed' – not that their opposition did anything to prevent the wedding, which took place on 30 October 1820.[91] Neither his parents nor the 'crones of the neighbourhood' held any sway over Christopher Thomson: 'Love and poverty were the last to try the issue; the contest was brief, and – love prevailed!'[92] Finally John Hall described how his courtship with Mary faltered when her 'father requested me to desist', on the grounds of her 'extreme youth'. This he would not do, reasoning that his 'affection was too deeply rooted to be extinguished, and the prospect of happiness too bright to be given up for trifles'. In response, her parents whisked her off to a friend's house ten miles away (though this 'only increased our attachment'), where the couple managed a clandestine meeting before being interrupted by her parents' arrival. Hall noted approvingly that Mary would not agree to marriage without her parents' consent, but the pair's persistence eventually paid off. Her parents finally relented and the couple married two years after first meeting, in August 1806.[93]

Some parents could be persuaded, others stood firm: but if their children were determined, in the end it made very little difference. Francis Place's story of his marriage to Elizabeth in late eighteenth-century London reveals the relative ease with which children could disobey their parents. In Place's version of events, he had initially received a warm welcome from his intended wife's family, but her mother had subsequently been persuaded by a sister and 'other gossiping women' against the match – though as her daughter was sixteen and Place a struggling breeches-maker just three years older, she may not have required much persuasion.[94] When Place made it plain that he did not intend to respect the mother's wishes, matters quickly came to a head, with Elizabeth's mother seizing a poker and threatening to knock Francis down with it. Place observed that this simply 'precipitated our marriage . . . I put up the banns of marriage at Lambeth Church without the mother's knowledge.'[95] In the event, the bride's mother got wind of the impending wedding and proceeded to the church before them to inform the clerk that her under-aged daughter was coming to the church to be married without consent. The clerk advised her that she might stop the ceremony if she wished, but following a last minute change of heart she chose not to do so. No doubt she had realised that the pair would simply go and marry elsewhere.[96]

In fact Place's experience of unsanctioned marriage was perhaps somewhat wider than he cared to admit. Just months earlier he and his mother had strenuously opposed the wedding plans of his elder sister, and the following year mother and son mounted a formidable campaign against those of his younger sister. In both instances their opposition proved ineffective, and his sisters married in defiance of their family's wishes, just as his own wife had.[97] In Place's retrospective account, his fears about his sisters' marriages were well founded as both subsequently failed. His own refusal to respect parental authority, by contrast, could be exonerated as his marriage proved long and successful. But whatever the truth of the matter, his story reveals the powerlessness of working-class families when it came to halting marriages they disapproved.

Nor were these opportunities to marry in opposition to one's parents the unique privilege of those who lived in London. Like all respectable young men, Joseph Terry sought the permission of Sarah Ann Darley's father for her hand in marriage. The trouble was, Sarah's father 'resolutely refused to consent'. Following the unhappy interview between the two men, Joseph reported to Sarah that it was 'of no avail talking to your father' and asked 'are you willing to be married in a month from now?' Sarah replied that she was. According to Terry, once Sarah's sisters had heard of their father's intransigence, they all agreed that they would 'never ask his consent' when their time came.[98] In Long Calderwood, East Kilbride, John Struthers and his bride faced similar opposition from her mother and 'an old aunt', who went so far as objecting when the banns were first read. They had the banns read the following two weeks at Barony Church in Glasgow and married there instead.[99] And in Coventry in the 1830s, Joseph Gutteridge and his wife-to-be tried to marry in their teens and in spite of the fact that the terms of Gutteridge's apprenticeship forbade marriage. They managed to obtain her mother's consent, but his relatives remained implacably opposed. When the young couple went ahead and published

the banns anyway, they intervened on the grounds that he was still inden-
tured. Once again this did no more than briefly delay the wedding, as
Gutteridge simply published the banns at another church and there they
married a few weeks later.[100]

With parents unable to do much to hinder their children's wedding
plans, it is hardly surprising to find that masters and employers also lacked
any real authority. In the 1790s, John Britton walked out of his apprenticeship months before its end, driven (he claimed), 'by that all-powerful stimu-
lant – love'.[101] His uncle and employer viewed this as 'an act of disobedience,
and an impudent dereliction of duty', but they still agreed to cancel his
indentures so that Britton could head for Plympton in Devon and pursue
his (ultimately unsuccessful) marriage plans with Elizabeth.[102] Other examples abound. Benjamin Shaw married in the same decade, with over a year
of his apprenticeship left to run. In the nineteenth century, James Dawson
Burn, Joseph Gutteridge, Robert Lowery and Thomas Sanderson all
married before being out of their time.[103] None of these men even reported
what their masters had thought of their early marriage; perhaps they considered their opinion of too little consequence to mention. Certainly, though,
an almost qualified apprentice did not need to curry his master's favour in
the way that an earlier generation had. A booming economy ensured good
prospects for a young man nearing the end of his apprenticeship, and this of
course reduced the premium on obedience to one's master.

Most of the evidence from the autobiographies is seen from the
perspective of young people forging ahead with marriage, but occasionally
autobiographers included detail about the role they had played as parents.
William Hanson, a handloom weaver working in west Yorkshire, had
himself married young – not yet twenty-one – and his children expected to
do the same. 'Among our five daughters and two sons, were some who had
reached a critical period of life', he noted, and they now 'began family trials
of a different character'. Their eldest daughter got into favour with 'a neighbouring man, a little older than herself ... he did not much like work.
Efforts were made to break the connection but without avail. At length her
mother said to her, that if she would have him, she would have to work her
life out for him. Her reply was, that she had to work now and it would only
be the same then.'[104] Needless to say, the marriage went ahead. The Hansons'
daughter had been at work in the factories since early childhood and was
now employed as a dressmaker. With a decade of wage-earning under her
belt, she knew enough about life to feel confident in her ability to start
making her own way in the world.

William Hanson's daughter is an obscure historical figure. We do not even know her name. But the defiant actions of this nameless woman capture historical forces that went far beyond the Hanson family. There had always been wayward individuals who refused to fall into line, young people who rejected the commands of parents or employers, and turned their back on the values of society. But the young adults now marrying without their parents' sanction were not standing in defiance of society: they simply belonged to a different society altogether. The young people in Hanson's Yorkshire could earn their way – or at least they believed they could – and this upended the old balance of power between themselves and their parents. When young working people could earn enough to raise their children, they could set out their own timetable for marriage and procreation.

The unmaking of centuries-old marriage customs that occurred during this time is one of the great, overlooked consequences of the industrial revolution and reminds us that industrialisation was an event of cultural, as well as economic, significance. The oppressive and unmoving poverty of the great bulk of the population throughout Britain's pre-industrial past cast a pall over social relationships, and set a mould for customs and culture that changed very little from one generation to the next. The need to share scant resources underpinned a set of values that limited the number and size of families, and poverty powerfully discouraged individuals from transgressing these norms. From the late eighteenth century, rising wealth made the logic for the old traditions that had hindered the poor from making it down the aisle far less convincing. The effect was most pronounced in the factory districts, but was not confined to them. Social change may have originated in the areas of greatest economic and social upheaval, but it trickled and spread beyond.

The change that occurred is captured in the story that Thomas Whittaker told of his marriage to Susan Scholes. Thomas Whittaker was born on the Lancashire–Yorkshire border in 1813, one of nine children in a close-knit family, all set to work in the cotton mills early in childhood. In his early twenties, he traded his work on the factory floor for the life of a temperance missionary, but his first marriage occurred before he took the pledge and embodied the values of the factory community in which he lived and worked. Thomas never specified his age at the time of his marriage – he described himself simply as 'very young'. He must have been twenty or younger, as he was married before the birth of his first son and this was the age at which he buried this son. Writing in his seventies, after an adult life devoted to spreading sobriety and respectability amongst the working classes, Thomas clearly deplored the shambolic circumstances of his youthful first marriage, yet he provided a fairly detailed and colourful account, perhaps as an education to his reader in what he now regarded as the social chaos and decay of early industrial Britain.

While working as a cotton-dresser in a factory in Glossop, he had fallen in love with a 'bonny little creature', who to everyone's surprise was equally enamoured with young Thomas. They wished to marry, but Thomas' friends taunted him that her 'father would not allow it'. His friends were quite right. When the banns were published, Susan's father 'in hot haste forbade them; we were both under age'. In their taunts, though, his friends had overestimated the power an unreconciled parent could wield. Having taken a liking to Thomas' sweetheart, his elder sister obtained a three-pound loan, which Thomas spent in travelling twelve miles to Stockport and marrying by licence, thereby circumventing the need to read the banns. As he lacked a decent suit for the occasion, he took a brother's Sunday clothes as he lay in bed sleeping. Of course, a man who had neither money nor clothes for his wedding was unlikely to have the wherewithal to pay for a home – 'that was out of the question' – so on the couple's return from the church they moved in with his parents.

But although Thomas was young and lacked everything he needed for his wedding, he was not poor in the way that working people had been poor in the eighteenth century and before. As a mill-hand, he was able to earn good money, and so could those around him. The three pounds that his sister borrowed represented a sizeable sum and Thomas could count not only on his own wages but also upon those of his wife to repay the debt. The day after their wedding they 'both went to work in the mill . . . and it was not long before I had a nice little home of my own'.[105] Thomas, Susan and his parents did not need to apply the careful foresight and planning to their wedding that earlier generations had had to respect. Although they had no money to hand when they wished to marry, they and those around them could see that their union had every chance of prospering. The times were changing, and in industrial Lancashire the old rules simply did not apply.

# CHAPTER SIX

# Naughty Tricks on the Bed

> But during this first year I was out of my time we, that is myself and my Harriet, who was to be my wife, done very foolishly. We became too familiar ... ah, this brought guilt into my conscience indeed, and my companion was, by our folly, brought into trouble. (William Swan, p. 49)

THE HISTORY OF marriage delivered on its promise to shed light on both the material and the interior lives of the working poor. As we saw in the last chapter, marriage customs could not withstand the economic and social upheaval that accompanied the industrial revolution. From the turn of the century, some young couples began to enjoy higher incomes. Others found themselves in families and communities less firmly attached to the belief that marriage must be delayed until such time as housekeeping could commence. Both forces undermined the social norms that for several centuries had governed who could marry, and when. Thanks to industrialisation, it seems, getting married was easier than ever before.

But in much the same way as industrialisation picked away at old customs, our writers pick away at the story I want to tell. Time and again, the autobiographers hint at the possibility that all may not be quite as it seems in this account of a new social order in which marital status was becoming ever easier to attain. Grasping what is missing is difficult, as many autobiographers tended to write about their marital and sexual lives in a coded language that can be hard to decipher. Yet the more one reads, the more one becomes convinced that there is something they are not telling.

Take for example the autobiography of James Bowd. According to James, he was twenty-four years old and had 'become a Man', so he followed the advice of Genesis to 'Leave his Father and Mother and Cleave unto His Wife'.[1] But the parish registers reveal that James' young wife Elizabeth gave birth to their daughter Sarah within five short months of their wedding.[2] As with many good stories, there is more than one way to tell it. In one version, the Bowds' marriage was owing to James' desire to obey Genesis chapter 2, verse 24. In another, the Bowds made a hasty trip to the church porch because Elizabeth found herself in a delicate condition.

The discrepancy between the writer's account of his marriage and that reported in parish records is yet greater in the case of Thomas Whittaker, whose marriage to Susan we considered at the close of the last chapter. Thomas gave a lengthy account of the circumstances of his marriage. He took the time to note such small details as the fact that he lacked a decent suit of clothes (and so took those of his brother as he lay sleeping in bed) and the 'nice provision' that his family had prepared for the wedding party on their return from the church. Yet for all his attention to detail, there were some very simple facts that he neglected to mention, such as the name of his wife, or the date of their union. The parish and civil registration records reveal the things that Thomas did not. His wife was named as Susan Scholes, and they married at St Mary's, Stockport, on 15 April 1832. Thomas explained that they had made the long trip on foot from Glossop to Stockport because his wife was under age and her father had objected when the banns were read at Glossop. It was true that she was under age, but she was not that young when they made their trip to Stockport: she was twenty, whilst Thomas was still eighteen. Furthermore, as they both no doubt knew, Susan was three months pregnant at the time of their wedding. In Thomas' account, Susan's pregnancy formed no part of their decision to marry when they did. Whittaker chattered away freely about the ribbons the wedding party wore in their hats and bonnets but he silently passed over Susan's pregnancy and the outcome of this pregnancy, their daughter Nancy. In the process, he hid all evidence of the sexual gratification that he and Susan had snatched before their wedding day.[3]

William Swan, a baker living in east London, gave a slightly franker account of the events that preceded his marriage. He wrote: 'we, that is myself and my Harriet, who was to be my wife, done very foolishly. We became too familiar … ah, this brought guilt into my conscience indeed, and my companion was, by our folly, brought into trouble'.[4] William could not write about these events without resorting to euphemism; but the timeline is not difficult to establish. It was neither their earning power nor new attitudes about the necessity of setting up a home of one's own that brought about William and Harriet's marriage. These two got married because they had embarked upon illicit sexual activity and felt they could not escape the consequences. William's self-chastising tone indicates that he and Harriet had both known that for religious and social – to say nothing of practical – reasons, they should not have engaged in penetrative sex when they did. But sexual attraction can defy logic. However well they understood the potential pitfalls of precocious sexual activity, their bodies, not their minds, had carried the day.

Elizabeth's, Susan's and Harriet's pregnancies remind us of the sexual desire that lies at the heart of human relationships, whether married or not. Working-class autobiographers were, for the most part, extremely reluctant to talk about sex. They, like historians, were far more comfortable talking about marriage than about the sensual pleasures that accompanied, and frequently preceded, it. Yet sex was what it was all really about. It is time to cast away coded references to doing 'foolishly', becoming 'too familiar', and getting into 'trouble'. Sexual desire was integral to every element of courtship and marriage, and it is to this theme that we must now turn.

If we admit that marriage was the only proper place for procreative sex, we immediately see that the marriage customs we explored in the previous chapter were tools to control the sexual desires intrinsic to the human condition. In a world of primitive contraceptive techniques and finite resources, culture had traditionally played an important role in keeping the age of marriage high and the birth rate low. Social disapproval of illegitimacy ensured that marriage was not only about companionship, housekeeping and parenthood; it was also the doorway to procreative sex. The obstacles in the way of marriage were a means of keeping that doorway firmly barred to large numbers of sexually mature young men and women. Viewed in this light, it becomes possible to add another level of interpretation to the changes in marriage patterns described in the previous chapter. There we saw that access to marriage became easier. By the same token, we might add, access to the pleasures of sex was also becoming easier.

But there is another possibility that we need to consider. Society frowned on births outside marriage; but frowning did not stop illegitimate births. 'No less than five now big with Base Children in the Parish Landaff,' grumbled William Thomas, a schoolmaster in south-east Glamorgan, the day following the birth of a 'Base son' to his neighbour, the unmarried Nancy Williams.[5] The following year he primly noted that Elizabeth Lewis was carrying her second illegitimate child, although her first was still being maintained by the parish.[6] The tide of illegitimate births was not of course confined to the parish of Landaff; it spread across Wales, and across England and Scotland too. The parish registers, in their laconic way, have their bit to say about the birth of children outside wedlock. At the start of the eighteenth century, about 2 per cent of all births were illegitimate. By the end of the century that had climbed to 5 per cent.[7] By the middle of the nineteenth century it had crept a little higher, to 6 per cent.[8] Ever more unmarried mothers and their baseborn children. No wonder respectable citizens like William Thomas were grumbling.

And the illegitimate births capture only those women who made it to the end of their pregnancy without tying the knot. A nine-month pregnancy afforded plenty of time for couples to formalise their union before the birth of their child, and so escape the prospect of a bastard birth. Once again, the parish registers contain plenty of information about such goings-on as these. Studies of the registers have indicated that by the end of the eighteenth century between 30 and 40 per cent of all women walking down the aisle were pregnant when they did so. When the pregnant brides and illegitimate mothers are added together, over half of all first-born children were conceived outside marriage.[9] Even this must be less than the true proportion of unmarried couples engaging in penetrative sex. Some parents chose not to baptise their children and some vicars did not record illegitimate births in a readily identifiable way, so some illegitimate children have no doubt been hidden from the official record. Infertility, low levels of fertility, and miscarriage must also have ensured that many other unmarried couples who were having sex did not end up with a child to baptise. Marriage may have been the proper place for sexual intercourse, but it was not the only place. In all, then, we have very good reasons for bringing sex and sexual desire into our discussion of family life during the industrial revolution.

The difficulty is that working-class writers were unobligingly reticent. Some went to considerable lengths to cover up the existence of children conceived before (or born outside) marriage. As for matters of desire and attraction, this was an area of life that many writers could simply not put into words. Yet for all their restraint, there were others who could not reflect on their life without touching upon such themes as the desires and transgressions that had powerfully shaped their younger selves, and upon the large consequences that sometimes stemmed from small sexual acts. It is to these writers that we turn. Those who wrote upon sexual matters form a small proportion of the whole, and we cannot use their evidence to count or measure the incidence of illicit sexual activity in any meaningful way.

But a collection of frank confessions and obfuscated stories provide just enough for us to flesh out the sexual values that governed the courtships of working men and women through the eighteenth and early nineteenth centuries.

Let us begin with John Cannon. John Cannon had been born in 1684 into a Somerset family with some means and pretensions to local status. As such, his outlook during his early childhood appeared rather better than most of the writers we examine here. Yet by his early teens his family had fallen upon hard times, and John spent the next ten years at 'rural and hard labours', first for his father and subsequently with his uncle as an unpaid farm servant. During that decade John learned his work as a husbandman, developed his taste for books and reading, and began to indulge his burgeoning interest in the 'hidden mysteries' of life. In John's narrative, it all began when at age fourteen he and some other boys were taught to masturbate by Henry Scrace, a skill that was sometimes 'put in practice' from then on.[10] At the same time, he embarked upon an ambitious programme of self-education, through the reading of whatever books on sex and pregnancy he could find – Aristotle's *Masterpiece* afforded some insights as did Culpeper's *Directory for Midwives*, though that he soon lost, as his mother, being closer than he had thought, caught him reading it and confiscated it.[11] His interest in the maid followed a less than wholesome turn when, to satisfy his curiosity, he cut holes through the walls of the necessary house 'near the seat' through which he could gaze upon her 'parts'.[12] Such formed the mainstay of John's sexual expression during his teens. It was pleasure of a solitary and unreciprocated variety.

By the age of twenty, John and his friends were trying to fill their leisure hours with more serious contact with the members of the fairer sex; as he put it, 'the time had come to spend time with 'some females to enlarge our pleasure & rouse our spirits'.[13] He entered a few superficial relationships with a succession of Marys (Mary Chapman, Mary Addams and Mary Brown), though none of these dalliances came to much. At the age of twenty-one, however, John was sent to work for his uncle and there began his 'love intrigue' with a new Mary – Mary Rose, his uncle's servant. In a short while John and Mary had progressed from 'jesting complements' to fun and games of a more physical nature. With Mary he shared 'amorous talks & quaint glances, kissing and toying when together in private ... [which] brought on by degrees a more close familiarity even to a plain discovery of such matters & concerns which modesty teaches me to omitt'.[14] Yet Cannon insisted that their adventures fell short of sexual intercourse

– we 'never carnally nor criminally knew each other', he wrote. Once, he admitted, he had had the 'lust to debauch her', but the 'thoughts of the crime … soon quelled that flame'.[15] And given the way both this and subsequent relationships unfolded, we have good reason for believing John's claims of sexual control.

John's stay with his uncle came to an end after about two years. He and Mary had been together throughout most of his term and by now John was sufficiently enamoured to contemplate marriage. Decades after the event, John carefully described how he and Mary had responded to their separation by cementing their relationship with the promise to marry. They met by the common, found themselves a sheltered spot, and there exchanged their promises, breaking a silver shilling in two, each keeping one half in a small bag made by Mary, to remain unopened until they had 'consummated matrimony'.[16] Yet despite these serious promises, the pair did not move towards a consummation of any kind. This was not for lack of opportunity, for they managed regular secret assignations in isolated outbuildings on the uncle's farm, staying closeted together until eleven or twelve at night.[17] Perhaps they realised that with John out of work the wedding bells would not ring soon. With no realistic prospect of marriage and housekeeping, John and Mary erred on the side of caution. Sexual intercourse would have to wait until their hopes could take a more tangible form.

John remained idle at home for a short time before securing for himself a position far better than that of unpaid hind to his uncle. Having found employment as a certified probationer with the Excise, John left the family home in Somerset to take up his post in Watlington, Oxfordshire. With John's prospects having taken a dramatic turn upwards, Mary pushed to formalise the union between them. She did so not by proposing a wedding date, but by sending John a letter suggesting that they meet at Kilmington, on the Wiltshire–Somerset border, 'to consummate our nuptials'. John prevaricated. His promises to Mary were now public knowledge, and on some level he knew he ought to honour them. There can be little doubt that he had genuine affection for Mary. Yet John knew that the onset of penetrative sex with Mary would tie him into marriage as surely as stepping down the aisle, and it must have been that knowledge which caused him to hesitate. John may have been working as a farm servant when they met, but he was not an unlettered labourer, and now ensconced in Watlington as an Officer of the Excise John had perhaps begun to wonder if he might not be destined for finer things than marriage with the maid. It certainly did not help that he had now met Joanna – 'very beautiful …

brisk & airy & of excellent natural parts ... well shaped, of a majestic stature, pale of countenance'.[18] John waited for a few weeks and then fobbed Mary off with a story about being unable to obtain leave. They continued to exchange letters, but it is almost certain that from this time John knew that he would never marry Mary.[19]

John met Joanna shortly after his move to Oxfordshire – she was living in the house opposite his lodgings, working for her aunt as a servant. With her striking looks, she immediately caught John's eye and in little time his frequent visits had developed into a physically intimate relationship. One evening, emboldened by the liquor running through his veins, John went to pay her a visit and, after 'some lovetoyes & amorous expressions', swiftly proceeded to attempting 'a great piece of indecency ... I put my hands under her coats to her knees'.[20] Joanna resisted, but John found that the more she resisted the more he was 'fired', so he attempted a second time. This time Joanna responded by laying out her conditions for access to the terrain under her petticoat. She offered John 'absolute command' over her body, short of 'deflowering or debauching'; in return John must 'be constant to me above all others & in due time to make me your lawful wife'.[21] The offer was too good to refuse and John readily acceded. From then on he frequently used his 'lustful freedom' but refrained from 'any attempt to Carnality'. Perhaps, as with Mary, the realisation that 'carnality' would bind him to marriage helped him to put this self-denying ordinance into practice. Although John never intimated as much, it seems likely that he had no real intention of marriage to a woman with beautiful looks but an 'indifferent fortune'.[22] But if John was happy to strut around town with a beautiful woman on his arm and give full expression to his 'lustful freedom', Joanna certainly did not realise that this was the extent of his wishes. For her, the courtship was supposed to lead to marriage. The affair continued for a further three years, by which time Joanna had perhaps come to repent her original set of conditions, and she now told John she wished she was pregnant so that their marriage could go ahead. Her pleas to set the wedding day became more insistent, and her constant refrain (John appears to suggest) was beginning to grate on his nerves. Despite their shared marriage promise Joanna was not pregnant, and this enabled him to walk away, just as he had done with Mary before.

We learn yet more of the social codes that governed sexuality from John's experiences with a third woman, Ann Heister, which occurred shortly before his split with Joanna. Ann was a servant in the household where he was lodging. But unlike Mary and Joanna, who had halted John's

precipitate forays up their skirts, and placed an embargo on sexual intercourse until such time as a marriage seemed imminent, Ann made a rather
different set of choices. When John found himself alone with her in the
house late one evening he decided to try his luck, slipping his hand 'under
her coat to her knee'. Encountering no resistance, he then 'boldly ventured
higher'. Within a matter of weeks he had had 'Carnal knowledge of her',
and the pair continued at the 'same sport frequently'. The inevitable soon
happened. But for Ann, it was not quite the disaster that we might imagine.
All the while she had been telling John that she would use 'all ways &
means with me till she was with child in hopes to force me to marry her'.[23]
Indeed in Ann's eyes, pregnancy took her directly to the place that Mary
and Joanna had ended up wishing themselves to be. But, as she found to her
cost, she had made a fundamental miscalculation. Ann may have been pregnant, but she lacked certain things that had given John's other relationships
standing and legitimacy. Ann had received none of the tokens and none of
the promises that John had shared with Mary and Joanna. Her relationship
with John was short-lived and secret; it was not publicly acknowledged by
the friends and family around them. John could not be forced into marriage
on the grounds of a pregnancy alone. He refused to marry her and instead
bore the shame and expense of maintaining their illegitimate son.

John, Mary, Joanna and Ann shared the same the same mental horizon,
though they made different choices within that horizon. At the heart of
their values was the understanding that a child should not be born outside
marriage, but none of our writers inferred from this that they should not
engage in sexual intercourse until they were legally wed. In fact, in their
different ways, each indicated that sexual intercourse outside marriage was
perfectly acceptable, so long as both partners were prepared to go ahead
and formalise their union should a pregnancy occur. At some point in their
relationships, Mary and Joanna, realising that a pregnancy would force
John into marriage, signalled their readiness for intercourse. But each time
John realised that matters had progressed too far for him to avoid marriage
should conception take place. At the crucial moment, as marriage loomed
closer, the reality of that choice gave John just the self-control he needed to
ensure that no new life would be created. Ann also thought she could
hasten a marriage by getting pregnant, but she was taking liberties with the
system. John had never promised to marry her, so when she found herself
pregnant John dismissed her claims.

The decisions made by John and his various 'amouresses' help us to
understand why so many firstborn children were conceived outside

marriage. As sexual intercourse began once couples had *agreed* to marry, it stands to reason that many brides would be pregnant by the time they made it to the church. Furthermore, this custom explains the stubborn persistence of illegitimacy within a society that, ostensibly, disapproved of illegitimate births. It is inevitable that some couples would understand the depth of each other's commitment to marriage in different ways. Some women might hope that a pregnancy would turn ambiguous (or non-existent) promises into a firm offer of marriage; some men no doubt uttered crystal-clear promises and later reneged on them. Obviously, plenty could go wrong in a world where couples embarked on sexual intercourse on the basis of their secretly whispered promises to marry rather than publicly witnessed vows in the church.

Many of these ideas are confirmed by a second writer, Edmund Harrold, a wig-maker, barber and small-time bookseller living in Manchester in the early eighteenth century. Edmund's father, Thomas, had owned a reasonably prosperous tobacconist business – it was valued at £371 at his death, when Edmund, his eldest son, was just five years old.[24] Edmund, by contrast, was bent on a course of downward social mobility. He spent just 21 shillings on his wife's funeral, and by the time of his own death his fortune was so depleted that no will was necessary.[25] His heavy drinking no doubt played a role in his slow descent into poverty. Yet somewhere in between the demands of work and the incapacitation caused by his drunken binges – 'rambles', as he termed them – Edmund found time to keep a diary, producing a very rare daily record of the life of a working man between the years 1712 and 1715.

The diary opens in June 1712. Edmund's second wife, Sarah, was three months pregnant with their sixth child. Most unusually for a private diary of this kind, Edmund kept a brief note of each time that he and his wife had sex, and (Sarah's pregnancy notwithstanding) there were plenty such occasions to note. One hesitates to know how to describe what happened in the bedroom (and sometimes elsewhere) between Edmund and Sarah. Edmund recorded each occasion by noting 'I did wife' – a turn of phrase from which it is difficult to conjure images of mutual pleasure and enjoyment. When noting each time he 'did wife', Edmund almost always added a few extra details, usually signalling something about the location and speed of their coitus: '2 tymes, couch and bed, in an hour and ½ time', 'standing at the back of the shop titely', 'new fashion'; 'after a scolding bout', '2 times [in] 4 days', 'titely, old fashion', 'oddly', '2 times finely'.[26] It is not much from which to reconstruct a couple's most intimate moments. Yet there is no reason to doubt that the sex between Edmund and Sarah was of a consensual nature. Sarah stood her ground on other domestic matters, so we might presume that she controlled access to her body as well. Such was certainly the case in the other relationships Edmund described.

In the last month of her pregnancy, Edmund repeatedly noted that Sarah was ill. She continued to decline in the weeks following the birth of their sixth child, and died in December 1712.[27] Their infant daughter was put out to wet-nurse, but she too passed away just four months later. Edmund lost no time in looking around for a new companion. In his thirties, with a household to run and two children to care for, matters moved fast. Within three months of Sarah's death he was visiting a widow, Ellen Howorth, and their courtship turned quickly to the question of marriage. The suit came to nothing. Edmund clearly longed for the companionship and security of marriage, but her temperament and his heavy drinking gave each of them plenty of cause to hesitate.[28] A courtship with a happier ending began when he met Ann Horrocks a few weeks later. Ann was a servant living close by, and as Edmund approvingly noted she was 'very loving and pleasant company, quiet and easie of temper'. Unlike Ellen, the 'maneger . . . [who] wants to be sattisfied', Ann 'submits and talks fine and complying'.[29] Here, Edmund thought, was a union with a much brighter outlook.

Once again, courtship moved directly to thoughts of marriage. Early in their relationship, Edmund and Ann spent the evening with 'a deal of serious discourse . . . about matters', but each still had a number of hurdles to cross before they would be in a position to proceed to the altar.[30] There was the matter of religion – Edmund was concerned about Ann's Nonconformist leanings and hoped to persuade her to convert to the Anglican Church. Meanwhile, his drinking evidently posed difficulties for Ann, who only consented to marry Edmund once he had accepted '3 propositions'; in fact there were four conditions, and each of them circumscribed the timing and quantity of his drinking in some way. Then there was the matter of where her family stood on the prospect of their union. 'Ile incourage her to seek and try how her friends stand affected for marriage soon,' recorded Edmund.[31] As one by one the obstacles were cleared, the nature of Edmund and Ann's relationship changed. And with a distinct prospect of marriage on the horizon, Edmund went from visiting in the daytime to spending the night at Ann's house. He stayed with Ann four times in the weeks before their wedding.[32] With a firm marriage commitment on both sides and the date set, there was nothing to stand in the way of the onset of sexual intercourse.

The writings of John Cannon and Edmund Harrold both indicate that penetrative sex was the privilege of the man who was married, or at least of the man who was prepared to get married should its inevitable consequences occur. So long as they were unmarried, and wished to remain so, both men found sexual enjoyment with their partners in ways that avoided the risk of pregnancy.[33] There were of course other ways of getting sex. Some, we must presume, entered same-sex partnerships, and in a world not simply of room-sharing but bed-sharing these must have been reasonably common. Yet the social taboo on homosexuality was so great that all evidence has been removed from the autobiographical record. In over 350 autobiographies there is not even a whisper of homosexuality, a silence that speaks loudly of our writers' uneasiness with the prospect of same-sex relationships, of the irreparable damage they feared homosexuality might cause to their reputation. Prostitution offered another alternative, its promise of sexual gratification uncomplicated by the risk of fatherhood. How far prostitution posed a serious threat to a man's reputation is difficult to assess, though it did of course pose risks of a different kind. Like most sexual matters, our autobiographers were reluctant to commit their experiences to the page, but one Norfolk diarist, James Zobel, breaks the silence.

James Zobel was a successful window-stainer living in Norwich, whose leisure hours were filled with various romantic intrigues, and who turned to prostitutes in the periods in between. In the spring and summer of 1828, when in his late thirties, James was spending many of his free evenings with his 'sweetheart' Eliza, even suggesting to her that if 'her father and mother would furnish a home, I would marry her'.[34] Yet the courtship clearly foundered, for in December of that year Eliza's wedding banns were published, and they were not with James.[35] In October 1831, with no sweetheart, James attended the annual St Faith's Fair with his friend Robert Barker, noting in his diary that he had 'expended at the Fair (a pros. too) 5 shillings'.[36] Weeks later, he discovered he had a 'gleet'. This could only be explained, he thought, by 'sitting on S. C. Yarrington's Privy Seat, for tis 3 months since connection with Pros., viz., the night of St Faith's Fair' – though as the rendezvous at the fair had occurred just one month earlier one might doubt his self-diagnosis.[37] Despite an unpleasant course of treatment through much of December, he took the risk of consorting with a prostitute once again a year later. After a pleasant evening of ninepins and a dinner, he 'wandered into St Stephens. There I was sufficiently silly and regardless of expense and probability of venereal disease to lay with a prostitute all night. Whole expense with her 6/6.' He later returned to this diary entry and added the words 'no venereal taint' in the margin.[38] A few months later, his affections had turned to 'widow Stannard' and his involvement with prostitution was, for the moment at least, over.[39] By the time his diary resumes in the late 1840s, James was in his late fifties, and was courting Margaret Robinson, whom he subsequently married.[40] Given his involvement with prostitutes it seems fair to suggest that his relationships were far from chaste, though his diary gives no indication of exactly what occurred between him and each of his three girlfriends. Nonetheless, a birth outside marriage was more than he or his partners were prepared to accept, and it seems unlikely that James was engaging in intercourse with these women. Working-class culture did not demand chastity before marriage; its demands were far looser. The social expectation was simply that men and women made sexual choices that did not involve parenthood. For James Zobel the combination of petting and foreplay with possible marriage partners and the occasional night with a prostitute when these relationships fell apart both met his needs for sexual fulfilment and kept his social reputation intact.

One final example from the tail end of our period illustrates the ways in which another young couple negotiated their way through the conflicting demands of sexual desire and the social expectation that procreation should be confined to marriage. Nathaniel Bryceson was a London clerk, living in Richmond Buildings in Soho and working for his uncle at Lea's Coal Wharf. As a literate clerk, he occupied a place in the social order a little above the working class yet Nathaniel had unmistakably humble origins and still lived with members of his extended family in a working-class community. Nathaniel was the illegitimate son of the widowed Mary Bryceson and Nathaniel White, a pauper in the St Marylebone Workhouse: the circumstances of his birth clearly formed something of a family secret, though, as Nathaniel believed he was the son of Mary's first husband, John Bryceson, with whom he shared his name. Meanwhile, his partner, Ann Fox was engaged in the lowest-paid labour the city could offer. Nathaniel never specified exactly how Ann made her living. At the time he met her, she was possibly working with or for Nathaniel's 'granny Shepard', perhaps as a domestic or washerwoman; later in the diary she is working for a Mrs Kennington. Five years later, in the 1851 Census, Ann was still living with Mrs Kennington and was listed as a 'charwoman'; her employer was described as a 'mangler', or washerwoman. Whatever her precise occupation, it seems certain that Ann spent her days at the unskilled scrubbing and charring that helped her richer London neighbours keep clean.

Nathaniel's diary runs through 1846. He had turned nineteen the June before and it seems that his relationship with Ann Fox was in its early stages as the new year began. In the first few months of the year the pair met almost every Sunday, occasionally on other days of the week as well, and took long walks about parts of London far from Soho. Finding a corner that was not overlooked was perhaps more of a challenge in London than it was in smaller towns and rural areas, but Nathaniel and Ann did the best they could. In February, for example, they used a rain shower to '[Shelter] ourselves under arch. Got to wicked tricks'.[41] Whatever they were up to on the bench at St James's Park was sufficient for them to be 'accosted by a policeman'.[42] By April, Nathaniel had taken to paying Ann the occasional visit at Mrs Kennington's on Sundays during her mistress' absence and a change in his living arrangements soon after provided the opportunity for the two to meet privately on a more regular basis.[43] In May, Nathaniel moved into lodgings with his granny Shepard, and immediately began to take advantage of the fact that granny went out every Sunday afternoon. On the last Sunday of May, Nathaniel 'Had Ann up in own room, but there got to naughty tricks on the bed'.[44] Most Sundays between then and the end of the year were spent in much the same way. A new phase of their courtship had begun.

With granny out of the way every Sunday afternoon, Nathaniel and Ann could to engage in whatever form of sexual intimacy they wished. It is interesting to note, however, that they did so in ways that avoided the risk of pregnancy. One Sunday, for example, they 'got to our old tricks in which I got a little further than ever'; but this, it turns out, involved no more than 'catching a glimpse of the hairs covering her c**t'. Nathaniel hoped 'to get on better hereafter in matters of secrecy'.[45] And a few weeks later he noted triumphantly that he had 'Got her drawers off at last'; though he ruefully added that the triumph had been 'to no purpose'.[46] The months passed, but Nathaniel and Ann were obviously not engaging in penetrative sex. One Sunday he noted that he had 'spent a little seed up her petticoat';[47] and another time 'made a terrible mess over Ann's new cloak and my own breeches'.[48] How far Nathaniel really wanted matters to be otherwise is open to question. For all that he cast himself as an intrepid explorer, charting the unknown lands beneath Ann's skirts in search of conquest, it is far from certain what he planned to do if the path suddenly cleared. He was evidently concerned to conceal his relationship with Ann from his family, and had their 'tricks' led to a pregnancy matters between them would be forced into a very public glare. And there is no evidence that Nathaniel entertained even the remotest thoughts of marriage. When their relationship became more intimate, Nathaniel was twenty and Ann was forty-five; he was an aspiring clerk and she was a washerwoman. This was not a union tending towards marriage, which probably goes a long way in explaining their hesitation about indulging in penetrative sex.

The evidence of sexuality contained in the autobiographies is tantalisingly fragmentary and incomplete. Yet these sources permit us to sketch a remarkably coherent picture of the way in which young working people balanced their desires for sexual pleasure and social acceptability. Chastity or sexual purity was not prized at this social level. That 'walking out' would soon lead to some form of sexual exploration was largely taken for granted. Society allowed the young significant freedom, permitting couples to spend time alone together, turning a blind eye to what went on in secluded corners at dusk, complacent about the bumps and bulges that many women carried down the aisle. Yet this permissiveness did not result in an unchecked tide of illegitimate children. Despite the steady trickle of illegitimate births, the number of firstborns baptised by married mothers outstripped those of unmarried mothers by a comfortable margin. Young men and women may have been allowed freedom to explore their sexual selves, but most chose to conform rather than face the disapproval of their family and neighbours. And this indicates that social pressures were effective in extracting conformity from many young adults. We can explore this possibility more fully by looking at what happened to those men and women who failed to abide by their community's expectations.

It is immediately apparent that men and women experienced the responsibility and consequences of illegitimacy in very different ways. Many male writers evidently believed that preventing an unwanted conception had nothing to do with them. That was a woman's job. Decades after the event, John Cannon refused to name Ann in his autobiography, and muttered instead about the 'whore', the 'strumpet' who had ensnared him: their child he labelled a 'bastard'.[49] Thomas Johnson, a carver who managed to impregnate his former master's servant, Mary, responded to his predicament in a similar way. Like Ann, Mary obviously hoped that her pregnancy would precipitate marriage, but in this respect she was to be sadly disappointed: Thomas refused to marry the woman he now described as 'low in stature, and lusty in body ... her complexion inclined to yellow, her face seamed with the small pox'.[50] In his memoirs, Thomas declared that responsibility for the mishap lay with Mary: she was so much older than him, he wrote, that he could 'almost acquit myself of the guilt'.[51]

Yet although both men articulated a distinct double standard that left their partners to carry the blame for what had passed between them, it seems unlikely that their community viewed matters in quite the same way. John Cannon's reputation had suffered badly from the whole affair. In his memoirs he recalled that the affair had brought 'calumny, reproach & scandall'. In an effort to spare his reputation, his friends had used an assumed name when dealing with the courts over the child's maintenance; but John still regretted that his credit had been 'cracked'.[52] And Thomas, in order to avoid the consequences of being sworn as the father of Mary's child, left his situation and travelled 200 miles north, where he had to set about rebuilding his career and his reputation from scratch. Society took a very dim view of men who fathered a child yet refused to marry. John and Thomas may have broken society's codes; but they certainly paid a price for doing so.

The power with which shame could extract obedience from young, sexually active couples is also illustrated in the story of James M'Kaen. M'Kaen was born in Glasgow in the 1750s. Following the death of his father when he was just three years old, he was raised alone by his mother, save for two brief interludes of remarriage, the second of which ended in desertion. While still in his teens and living with his mother in Dalkeith, M'Kaen had married a local girl, but for fear that his mother would object to the marriage, he and his wife kept it a secret and continued to live apart. With the newly-weds living separately the way was clear for James to enter a new relationship with another woman, which he most unwisely did. When news broke of James' adulterous relationship and the illegitimate daughter that it produced, the consequences for him were severe. His wife and her family refused to have anything to do with him. Even his own mother turned him out of her home. Such a carry-on in respectable Dalkeith was more than those close to James could handle.

And the presence of a living, illegitimate child made it very difficult for James to re-establish his reputation within his neighbourhood. When her time came, the young mother of James' child left her place in service and returned home to her family, a few miles away in Libberton. There she gave birth to a daughter. James, wishing to be 'freed from any church scandal, occasioned by my conduct', paid the childbed charges, but quickly found that this did not free him from scandal. The child's mother evidently did not relish the role of unmarried mother, and made a trip from Libberton to deposit her daughter with James. His mother found a nurse to care for her.[53] Yet the affair still weighed heavily on James and his family. He 'wished that scandal to be ever buried in oblivion', but the proximity of his illegitimate child placed an insuperable barrier in the way of the restoration of his marriage and the rehabilitation of his reputation. In the event, his mother took the child to 'an hospital at Edinburgh', paid the fees, and left her in the charge of strangers. James and his family had no further contact with the child, and writing his life story twenty years later, James knew nothing about what had become of her. With his illegitimate child now settled at a distance, it become possible for James to make a reconciliation with his wife. The pair settled their differences, but even together they could not shake off the disgrace and disapproval of James' adulterous affair. The shame was sufficient for him and his wife to leave Dalkeith for Glasgow. Their move, he noted, was 'principally in order to escape the reproach I had incurred by the child'.[54] Dalkeith in the 1770s, it seems, was no place to be contravening the widely held belief that wedlock was the only legitimate place for new life to be created. It is not surprising to find that some couples did not live up to the expectation that unmarried couples should not be baptising children. Of course they failed, over and over again, and in the same old ways. Clearly, however, illegitimacy was a serious matter for all concerned.

Women experienced the consequences of illegitimacy very differently. Most appear to have shared the belief that responsibility for avoiding an illegitimate birth lay with themselves and not with their partners: we have seen a number of times that women were the most active in setting and policing the boundaries for appropriate sexual behaviour. And when women found themselves pregnant and unmarried, it was almost always owing to misjudgement, not the reckless disregard of social mores. How far they aimed to avoid illegitimacy through concern for their reputation is more difficult to assess. Almost all of our accounts of illicit sexual activity have come from male writers, and if women found their reputation wrecked by an illegitimate birth, this was not something that our male writers spent much time dwelling on. What does seem likely, however, is that women were motivated by far more than the loss of reputation. Considerably more serious was the reality of trying to raise a child without a male breadwinner for support, and all of the unmarried women who found themselves pregnant were soon hard at work devising a variety of strategies aimed to ensure that that they were not left raising a child alone.

Ann Heister had believed that a pregnancy would force John into marriage. As the enormity of her error became apparent, she made a desperate attempt to procure an abortion, but was told by the surgeon that the pregnancy was too far advanced. With the birth looming, she took the only option left to her: she named John as the father of her child and left it to the courts to get the maintenance payments she was due.[55] This was almost certainly a case of marriage-planning gone awry, rather than of disregard for society's norms. When the mother of James M'Kaen's child realised that he was already married and that there was therefore no prospect of them raising the child together, she dumped her baby with him 'immediately after its birth'. When James returned their daughter to her, she sent her back a second, and final, time.[56] Once again, becoming a single mother was most definitely not part of her plan.

Mary, the maid carrying Thomas Johnson's child, employed a different (though ultimately no less successful) set of tactics to remedy the situation. Mary's first solution was to tell her employers that she and Thomas had already married, and to then try to convince Thomas that, as she had now claimed they were married, they ought to go ahead and set a date. The plan did not work. Thomas retorted that he had 'never made you any such promise', and instead offered to assist with her lying-in costs and with maintenance for the child. Mary tried again, this time suggesting that perhaps instead of marriage they could just 'live together as man and wife'. Thomas once more refused, and Mary, like Ann, turned to the parish overseers and swore that Thomas was her child's father, leaving 'the rest to their management'.[57] With hindsight we can see the hopelessness of Mary's attempts to regularise matters; yet her desperate efforts also indicate that single motherhood was not something that she found easy to countenance.

These women's actions are echoed by other women in the autobiographies who found themselves pregnant and alone. As a young man living in service, John Lincoln managed to get Ann, his employer's cook, pregnant. They got married, but there was no way for her to raise their child while working as a servant, so she left her place and returned home to her parents. John refused to follow, leaving Ann, in effect, a single mother. The situation was intolerable to both her and her parents. Her mother (according to John) sent forged letters to her daughter 'to inform from time to time – of my carrying on a Criminal conversation With her fellow servant'. The daughter received these and in a fury demanded that he leave the house: 'she flew into a violent passion and said I should leave my service that Very day'. Ground down by their untiring assault, John eventually did leave his employer and moved into the family home.[58] Ann and her parents could not have been motivated by the social stigma of illegitimacy, as the couple were in fact legally married. Both his wife and her parents were keen to force him to leave his place of service and fully assume the role of husband, householder and male breadwinner, presumably fearful that he had too much opportunity to evade his responsibilities so long as he remained in service. Meanwhile Mary Saxby, after an illegitimate birth, endeavoured to persuade her child's father to marry, even though the couple 'had not money enough to discharge the expense', and despite the fact that, in her own estimation, 'he did not promise to prove the best of husbands'.[59] It seems remarkable that Ann and Mary were prepared to go ahead with marriage on such unfavourable terms; but from their perspective, a reluctant or unreliable husband was preferable to no husband at all.

The suggestion that it was single motherhood, rather than illegitimacy, that women were seeking to avoid may be illustrated in one final way. A small number of the autobiographers can be identified as illegitimate children; and in most cases there is also evidence of their mothers seeking an alternative to raising their child alone. In 1841, John Rowland's mother paid a visit to her parents where she was delivered of her illegitimate son. She left him with her parents, they left him with their neighbours, Richard and Jenny Price, and they in turn left him at the workhouse, where he remained for the next nine years.[60] In similar vein, the mother of James Davis paid her parents a visit in 1820, claiming she was married and that her husband would soon follow her. She gave birth within a few weeks, her husband did not arrive, and she left her infant son in the care of her parents.[61] William Milne did not know much about his early years, though it seems that neither of his parents was present and he was in the charge of his father's parents, who had reluctantly assumed responsibility for him. They found a succession of families prepared to take him in for a small payment; he was 'knocked about from one home to another'. At the last of these placements his grandparents paid him a visit and there 'I was found sitting tied to a little broken chair, dressed in dirty old rags, and ravenously eating a piece of dry oaten bread, or Scotch bannock, which had been hastily thrust into my hand when the visitor was announced'. It was too much even for his 'luke-warm guardians'. He was taken in by his father's family, with his mother joining the family a few years later. When his grandmother died, his mother moved out, taking him with her. Where she had been during his early years, though, remained 'an unsolved mystery'.[62]

The choices made by Henry Edward Price's mother also indicate that she had abandoned trying to raise her illegitimate son fairly early in his life. She appears to have been present in Henry's first few years; at least he remembered a young woman 'catching me up in her arms and smothering me in kisses' when he recovered from measles as a very small child. But he remembered more distinctly the time that he spent with his 'Dear old Grandmother'.[63] When Henry was eight, however, 'Gran' decided to emigrate to America and Henry was returned to his mother, who was now married and living in Bristol with her husband and two children. His arrival must have thrown the household into some confusion, as his mother had given her legitimate son the same name as her firstborn – Henry – making it 'necessary to call one little Henry and the other big Henry'. Given this, it seems unlikely that 'big Henry's' mother had expected to maintain a relationship with her illegitimate son. Needless to say, big Henry did not stay long with his new family. He was soon dispatched back to an elderly relative in Warminster, but when she refused to take him in, he too ended in the workhouse.[64]

It is always difficult to deduce the logic that lay behind women's actions. Their actions are revealed to us only through the words of the men with whom they were involved; and it is almost always their actions, rather than their thoughts, that our writers describe. But piecing together the actions and choices of women who found themselves pregnant or, worse still, mothers outside marriage enables us to tender some suggestions about the place of illegitimacy in women's lives. Women found themselves pregnant and alone neither through a disregard of social norms, nor through failure to grasp the seriousness of unmarried motherhood. Illegitimacy was the outcome of misjudgements and mistakes and it was to be avoided at all costs. A woman's first task was to ensure she did not find herself pregnant without any prospect of marriage. If this failed her next tactic was to try to tie her partner into marriage, no matter how poor the material or emotional outlook. When women failed to regularise matters, they frequently found themselves unable to rear their child alone. William Milne did not know when or why his mother had left him, but her own parents were dead and her partner's parents were 'luke-warm' and did not want to help. Without family support it is likely that there was nothing she could do but give her baby to her in-laws to raise as they saw fit. The same was true for most of the women looked at here. Poor families could not afford to maintain an adult daughter at home while she devoted herself to the care of an infant. Most of the unmarried mothers had no choice other than to hand their newborn over to somebody else so that they could get back to earning a living.

There is one final possibility that we need to consider, and that is the extent to which these social and sexual codes changed with the onset of industrialisation. Most parish studies indicate that illegitimacy was increasing over the eighteenth century, forming about 2 per cent of all births at the start of the century, closer to 5 per cent by the end, and continuing to rise until 1850. They also show marked regional variation, with levels of illegitimacy consistently higher in industrial parishes than in rural ones. These findings are suggestive, hinting at the unmaking of the old order in which social disapproval and women's reluctance, and indeed inability, to embark upon motherhood outside marriage helped to keep a lid on illegitimate births. But the parish registers, with their lists of infants marked as 'bastards' and mothers as 'singlewomen', do not have much to say about the choices and experiences that lay behind the changes they document. A handful of autobiographical writers from parts of the industrial north are more forthcoming and allow us to explore the possibility that rapid economic change altered cultural horizons for sexually active women.

Samuel Bamford was born in Middleton in 1788, a small Lancashire weaving village a few miles to the north of Manchester. As an adolescent, he spent brief spells working as a sailor and employed in a Manchester warehouse, but like most of the men in Middleton, he soon settled down to life as a weaver. In the mid-1810s, he became involved in local politics, rapidly emerging as a key figure in the working-class Radical movement and eventually finding himself behind bars for his role in organising the reform meeting on St Peter's Field, Manchester, in 1819. From politics he moved to writing, publishing his first volume of poetry in 1819, and from then on he carved out a modest, sometimes precarious, living as a journalist and writer. But before the politics and before the poetry, Bamford had been an ordinary working man. And like many young people, as he grew to adulthood he discovered a new interest in the opposite sex. As he wrote: 'the young germs of love [began] to quicken in my heart'. Soon he 'abandoned myself to heart-gushings of romantic feelings, bowed in silent but earnest regard to female loveliness, and became soul and heart-bound . . . to more than one, in succession, of the young beauties of my acquaintance'.[65]

The most significant of Samuel's relationships, however, was that with his childhood friend, Jemima Shepherd, whom he ultimately married in 1810. In Bamford's account, he and his 'little Mima' enjoyed an innocent, rural courtship. When she visited him in Manchester, for example, they found a 'secluded arbour' in a 'sweet bowery place', to sit and open their hearts to each other.[66] During the annual wakes, he and Mima left the crowds and went for 'lone walks in the woods'.[67] But it was not all innocent country rambles between Samuel and Jemima. As he frankly admitted in his autobiography, after the wedding Jemima handed him a babe 'just of age to begin noticing things'.[68] Their daughter, Ann, had in fact been born six months earlier.[69]

Although Samuel and Jemima were a little late in regularising their relationship, it is still possible to discern much of the traditional order of events in their pathway from courtship to sexual activity and marriage. Throughout most of a courtship that lasted a number of years, Samuel and Jemima had steered clear of risky sexual behaviour, and when Jemima conceived in spring 1809, the seriousness of their intention to marry was probably understood by both. Samuel did not explain why they did not hasten to the church before Ann's birth so as to avoid the taint of illegitimacy. As neither had living parents with whom they could stay, it may be that they had little choice and were obliged to postpone the wedding until such time as they could set up a household of their own. It is also possible, however, that Samuel and Jemima saw no great reason to hurry. Living in a community of rising illegitimacy, it is likely that the sight of a couple marrying after rather than before their child's birth did not raise too many eyebrows.

Yet there is more to Samuel's story than his overdue marriage to Jemima. Mima's child was not, after all, Samuel's first child. At the same time as courting his 'Little Mima', Samuel was keeping company with a 'Yorkshire lass'. Having returned to Middleton to take up his loom – weaving then being 'a very profitable employment' – Samuel spent his leisure hunting with the other young men and spent his earnings at the alehouse.[70] As he became 'more easy . . . about the sin of inebriety', the path to other transgressions was 'temptingly' laid open.[71] Very soon the 'Yorkshire lass' was in front of the parish authorities, naming Samuel as the father of her illegitimate child and thereby obliging him to pay her a weekly allowance to help in its maintenance. Yet neither Samuel nor his partner had ever had any intention of marrying each other. At the time of his transgression, Samuel was deeply involved with Mima, and even had he not been, he admitted he 'never could have made up my mind to become the husband of the one I had thus injured'. She, for her part (and much to Samuel's relief), felt much the same way and preferred to take his weekly payments than his hand in marriage. In this instance, Samuel and his partner were clearly not following the traditional order of events. It raises the intriguing possibility that the young men and women of Middleton were engaging in sexual intercourse according to a different set of principles to those of earlier generations.

Samuel Bamford was not the only writer to follow a new social code. Anthony Errington was a wheelwright. Born in Felling on Tyne in 1778, he spent his adult life working as a wright on the wagonways of the lower Tyneside coalfields. Anthony married twice: his first wife, Ann, died after nearly eleven years of marriage; ten years later, he married for a second time. Both of his wives were pregnant when they married.[72] His autobiography hints that his second wife may have been living with him as a housekeeper helping to care for his younger children at the time that they married. Either way, there was nothing out of the ordinary about his pregnant brides; we have already seen numerous times that men of Anthony's social status generally started sexual intercourse following the agreement to marry, rather than after the wedding ceremony.

But Anthony Errington's story, like that of Samuel Bamford, also shows that it is quite possible to conform to some social expectations, yet fail to live up to others. Between his two marriages, Anthony spent almost a decade alone. During this period, he may have been unmarried, but he was not always leading a celibate life. Almost eighteen months after the death of his first wife, he and Jane Richardson baptised a daughter, Sarah, at the Catholic St Andrew's Chapel in Newcastle. Why he and Jane did not marry is unknown; Anthony did not discuss the matter in his autobiography. Yet it is interesting that they took the step of baptising Sarah at the Catholic church – interesting because the Catholic church frowned on illegitimate births, so parents in their situation usually opted to baptise them in front of the more complaisant Anglican vicar. Not only did Anthony baptise his daughter in his church, but he subsequently opened his home to her, and his second wife took on the role of 'Mother'.[73] Anthony may have hoped to marry Jane – it would certainly have been timely given that he now had sole responsibility for four small children; perhaps it was Jane who frustrated his plans. What is more certain is that at least one of them had been engaging in sexual intercourse without a serious intention to marry.

A few years later, Anthony, now in his mid-thirties, found himself in trouble once again when a woman he had met briefly gave birth to an illegitimate child. The father of the child was spreading rumours that Anthony had advised the mother, another Jane, to falsely name him as the father. In his autobiography, Anthony hotly denied this: 'It was not mine. I had Nothing to do with the [woman].' But Anthony did know Jane and was sufficiently concerned about the matter to send a friend to look over the child, who reported back that 'it was none of Antys Get, his Children had Strong bone in them'.[74] The truth of the affair has followed Anthony and Jane to their graves. Yet again it seems reasonable to suggest that at least one of them had been engaging in some fairly risky sexual behaviour.

Further detail about personal relationships is contained in the autobiography of Benjamin Shaw, a mechanic living in Preston. Benjamin recounted in exceptionally frank terms the unplanned and unfortunate circumstances of his marriage to Betty Leeming in 1793. Benjamin had got to know Betty two years earlier, shortly after moving with his family to Dolphinholme to take up work in factories there. They were both eighteen years old and this appears to have been the first relationship of any significance in Benjamin's life.[75] After about a year together, she left Dolphinholme to look for work in Preston, prompting Shaw to learn to write, so that he could let her 'know my secrets', and to pay the occasional overnight visit. Within a few months, she wrote to him confiding a rather large secret of her own – 'that she was with child'. Benjamin recalled:

I was now in a Sad Predicament, left in a Strainge place, & aprintice with only 8 Shilings per week, & my parents shifted away, I had 13 months to serve of my time, & trade very bad & the lass quite big, (alass for Poor Ben) I did not know what to do, for I loved her still, though there was no Prospect before us but extream Poverty.[76]

With a heavy heart, Benjamin put up the banns and within weeks the couple duly wed. Betty gave birth six weeks later. Without a penny to set about housekeeping – 'we had neither furniture, or monney, nor friends' – Betty at first continued living with her father and then moved into Benjamin's lodgings, where they 'found their own vituals, & were poor enough'.[77]

Benjamin and Betty fall into the category of improvident marriers – those forging ahead with marriage despite lacking the wherewithal to furnish a home – whom we looked at in the previous chapter. But Benjamin's detailed writing also enables us to unpack the sexual misadventures that played a critical role in his and Betty's fate. Theirs was a shotgun wedding. When faced with the reality of her condition, Benjamin ended up doing what many others before him had done: quickly tying the knot with his heavily pregnant sweetheart to avoid the shame of an illegitimate child. But how had they ever found themselves in this situation?

As Benjamin lamented in his autobiography, everything could be traced back to the night of 11 February 1793.[78] Benjamin had seen Betty just once in the previous four months. Rumours that Betty had been unfaithful had been circulating, so Benjamin travelled to Preston to hear her side of the story. Once there, he almost decided to leave without seeing her, but after a last-minute change of heart, he did go. He ended up spending the night. As he noted decades later, he had 'cause to remember' the date as she wrote to him shortly after to tell him that she was pregnant.

This was an insecure relationship with an uncertain future, and it is very unlikely that Benjamin and Betty had started to discuss their wedding. Even during the pregnancy, Benjamin remained uncommitted: 'I sometimes thought I would not have her.' In a moment of unusual candour, Benjamin admitted that he had found Betty's labour almost as hard as she, wishing, as he heard her groans, 'that she might die I think that if she had died, I should have greatly rejoiced, for we were so poor, & such a dark prospect before us, that it was quite discourageing, however it was not so to be . . .'.[79] It is difficult to escape the conclusion that Benjamin and Betty had fast-forwarded to sexual intercourse far more quickly than they should have. But they had plenty of time to live with the consequences. They remained married for thirty-five years.

The experiences of Benjamin and Betty hint at a change in the speed with which couples progressed to penetrative sex. The personal histories of their seven children illustrate the change with far greater clarity. All of Benjamin's children were put to work in one of Preston's many factories at a young age and reached adulthood in the first third of the nineteenth century. Illegitimacy was part and parcel of the world in which they lived. His eldest daughter, Isabella, gave birth to her first child when she was twenty. She was unmarried so the pair moved in with her parents.[80] His second daughter, Hannah, 'Became with child' when she was eighteen: she too was unmarried and, along with her baby, remained a while with her parents.[81] His third daughter, Mary, similarly had her first child at the age of eighteen, and this too was illegitimate. She married the child's father a month after the birth (the marriage had been delayed as he had been in the house of correction for assault). After spending a few months with her parents, all three 'took a room' and moved out. Mary and the infant were soon back, however, as the marriage broke down before the end of the year.[82] The last of his daughters to reach adulthood, Agnes, also produced a child out of wedlock just as her sisters had done. Agnes had her first child at the age of twenty (it died shortly after birth) and a second, also illegitimate and probably with a different father, two years later. She and her second child lived with a sister, until her own untimely death six months later.[83]

Matters were not much different with Benjamin and Betty's three sons. Though their eldest and youngest both avoided fathering illegitimate children, their middle son, William, managed when he was nineteen to father no fewer than two children out of wedlock in the short space of four months.[84] He married the mother of one of them two years later.[85] In all, then, five of the Shaws' seven children managed to create seven illegitimate children between them. In this family, illegitimacy was part of the normal transition to adulthood.

Yet it is not simply the prevalence of illegitimacy in the Shaw family that is curious. If we look more closely at Benjamin's account we can see that he is not just describing one accidental pregnancy after another. Instead we find adults making very different choices about their sexuality, understanding the connections between sex, parenthood and marriage in novel ways. All five of the children who bore children out of wedlock had entered sexual relationships without any properly formed marriage plans. Isabella got married two years after her child's birth, so marriage had hardly been imminent when sexual intercourse began. William married his child's mother three years later, and of course he only married one of the women he had managed to impregnate. Mary's marriage to Bob Smith occurred more quickly, but it was not a stable union and broke down in less than a year. All three appear to have embarked on sexual intercourse with marriage plans of only the haziest character. Finally Hannah and Agnes did not marry their children's fathers at all. In the case of Agnes, neither father appears to have played any role in his child's upbringing. All five of these adults appear to have displayed an extremely incautious attitude towards the prospect of creating, and potentially raising, a child outside the institution of marriage.

And we can say more. We have seen in this chapter that women usually played by far the most active role in preventing illegitimate births, either by refusing to engage in sexual intercourse when they doubted their partner's willingness to marry, or by doing all in their power to bring about a wedding should a conception occur. Their caution is readily understandable, given the obstacles to raising a child alone. At first sight, it seems surprising that the women in the Shaw family were so careless about the risk of parenthood without the security of a male breadwinner to help them keep body and soul together. But on closer inspection it becomes clear that young women living in early nineteenth-century Preston did not *need* the support of a male breadwinner. The Shaw daughters knew that raising a child took considerable resources. But they also knew they could find those resources without the help of their children's fathers.

Let us look at how each of Benjamin and Betty's daughters responded to the responsibility of a baby to care for. After the birth of her son, Isabella lived with her parents, returned to her work at the factory, and left her mother in charge of the little boy. Hannah did the same after the birth of her daughter, though her return to work was hindered by post-natal ill health. After the birth of her son, and again after her marriage to Bob broke down, Mary moved back into the family home. This now comprised her father, Benjamin, and her younger sister, Agnes, Betty having died two years before. It is likely that Mary stayed at home, cared for her baby and took over the work of the household, while Benjamin and Agnes in return provided her with financial support. Agnes' first child died very shortly after birth, so sadly she did not need to find ways of combining raising a child with earning a living. Following the birth of her second child she moved in with her sister Mary. The plan, no doubt, was that Mary, now reconciled with her husband, would care for Agnes' baby along with her own expanding brood when Agnes returned to the factory, but Agnes suffered serious post-birth complications. She never did return to work and died six months later.[86]

Early motherhood had some sad and complex outcomes in the Shaw family. Hannah and Agnes buried babes-in-arms, and followed their children to an early grave, almost certainly as a result of complications associated with their deliveries. Martha Johnson (the mother of William's first illegitimate child) also died shortly after birth, though her child survived and was raised by her parents. Isabella, Mary and Sarah Coyle (the mother of William's second child) rode out the wave of unmarried motherhood far more successfully, going on to marry their children's fathers and create relatively stable families. Their experiences defy simple summary, though it would certainly be inappropriate to suggest that early and unmarried sexual activity was in some way liberating for the women involved.[87] Like early marriage, the opportunity of unmarried motherhood was a gift double-edged in nature. But this we can say: the combination of abundant female employment at relatively good wages and a dense family network made it possible for the Shaw daughters to raise a child outside the confines of marriage. And with this opportunity came new patterns of sexual behaviour. Since time immemorial, women had guarded the gateway of fertility, rejecting precocious sexual activity, limiting their partners' advances until they were certain that marriage was within their grasp, and desperately trying to corral them into marriage if they did conceive outside marriage. In the factory districts such caution was often unnecessary. Women were not able to raise large families on their own; but one, or possibly two, children outside marriage could be managed, and this knowledge fostered new patterns of sexual behaviour.

If we look over other examples of illegitimate births in the factory districts, we see the choices and experiences that are so vividly illustrated by the Shaw daughters refracted more widely. Let us reconsider, for example, the stories told by Samuel Bamford and Anthony Errington. Samuel's 'Yorkshire lass' was in Middleton when she conceived his child, an area with both domestic weaving and silk factories. The simple fact of living here dramatically raised her chances of supporting herself and her child alone. Jane Richardson, the woman who bore Anthony's illegitimate daughter, may also have had choices beyond marriage. Before the Factory Acts of the 1830s and 1840s there was work for women in the Durham coal mines at quite good wages. Perhaps Jane decided that continuing to work and raising one child in her parents' home was a more attractive prospect than trading her position for unpaid domestic work and the responsibility of raising the four children from Anthony's first marriage, as well as Sarah, and the many more that she was likely to have if they married. In the absence of Jane's version of events, we will never be certain of the forces at work, but the presence of relatively well-paid work for women gave her choices that earlier generations of women had lacked.

Then there is Sally Marcroft, who gave birth to her first child, William, when she was twenty or twenty-one and unmarried. At the time she was living as a servant and weaver in a farmer's family at Pilsworth, a weaving village a few miles south of Bury in Lancashire.[88] She returned to a neighbouring parish for the birth, and spent the following year there lodging with a family and working at the loom. She went on to give birth to a second child by the same man shortly after, though the infant died. The relatively high wages she could command at the loom made the consequences of early sexual activity more manageable than might otherwise have been the case. Indeed, in the eyes of her illegitimate son, William, the standard of living that Sally had enjoyed as a single mother of one child was much higher than that she enjoyed as the married mother of a much larger family. Of course William was not an impartial observer. His mother's remarriage saw him cast out to the workplace, and also may have left him feeling cast out emotionally when a husband and new children began to intrude on the close mother-son relationship that the two had enjoyed for many years. But his contention is certainly plausible. Sally did not need to settle for marriage, housekeeping and a large family. She also had the choice of motherhood in a small, single-parent family.

Let us consider one final example, the case of Ellen Johnston. Ellen was raised in Glasgow in the 1830s. In Ellen's account, her mother had married at the young age of eighteen but her father had emigrated to America soon after her birth, so her mother had returned to her father's house and kept herself and her daughter through dressmaking and millinery. She later remarried and the pair moved out to live with her new husband. At the age of eleven, Ellen started working in one of Glasgow's many cotton factories as a power-loom weaver and by her late teens, she, like the Shaw children, was sexually active. Before long she was involved with a man 'without the form of legal protection' and soon found herself the mother of an illegitimate child. It was not the disaster it might have been. In fact Ellen was delighted by the change in her circumstances. She 'longed for the hour' when her child would be born and was delighted to become 'the mother of a lovely daughter' on 14 September 1852. Ellen lived with her mother, who took care of her daughter while Ellen saw to the business of earning a living for all three.[89] It was an increasingly common way of doing things by the middle of the nineteenth century. With family close by to take care of her child and wages that were good enough to support herself, her child and her mother, Ellen did not have to rely upon a husband. She made choices that simply had not existed for women a century earlier.

As with many of the autobiographical writers, there were things in Ellen's life that set her apart from her peers. Ellen had a creative side, and a few years after the birth of her child she began carving for herself a modest career as a published poet. But if the poetry set her apart, there was not much else that did. Ellen rarely earned enough money from her poetry to live on and was frequently back working in the factories in order to make ends meet. It is possible that she is the 'Helen Johnston' who died in the Glasgow workhouse in 1874. For the most part, Ellen lived a life of poverty and hard work, and for the working women of mid-nineteenth-century Dundee there was nothing unusual about this.

Dundee, unmarried mothers, factory work – these are not the parts of nineteenth-century Britain that we tend to admire. And yet in her poetry and autobiographical writing Ellen is crystal clear: life in a factory town was something to celebrate. In Ellen's eyes Dundee offered her a life of freedom. Industrial Britain allowed her sex without marriage, motherhood without a husband, paid work rather than the drudgery of unpaid housekeeping. They were not the choices that every woman wanted, but they were certainly welcomed by some, and their emergence marked a very real watershed in the lives of working women.

# PART III

## CULTURE

If we have suffered acute privations in the old slave state, so galling that we cannot look back upon them without pain, let us prepare ourselves for the mid-day of freedom, that even now glances her rays upon us. (Thomson, p. 24)

Recounting the familiar milestones of life – entering the workforce, learning a trade, getting married, rearing a family – formed the mainstay of many autobiographies. So it is not for nothing that they have also formed the mainstay of our narrative. But to confine ourselves to retelling the material side of our life during the industrial revolution would be a great disservice to our writers. After all, the autobiographer who confined himself to writing about the daily grind was relatively rare. There, jostling for space with the practical side of earning a living, were all the other things that made a life worth while, and an autobiography worth writing.

Alexander Somerville, in describing his older brother James, captured this other part of life. In the opening pages of his autobiography, and before getting down to telling his own story, Somerville wrote about each member of his family in turn. When he came to James he noted that, as a child, James had been looked upon as 'the most intelligent member of our family'. His fondness and facility for reading and his fine memory had set him apart from the rest of the children in the village. Yet James' childhood talents had never translated into anything tangible in adulthood. He left the family home in early adolescence to take up a position as a cooper's apprentice, and so he continued, making barrels for Britain's ever expanding drinks industry, till the end of his days. Somerville thought his talents had been wasted. He concluded:

Whether the world is the better in having a tradesman who puts hoops upon its barrels, saws its timber, makes its bedsteads, and nails its coffins, and does all those things honestly and to the best of his mechanical ability, instead of contributing to its literature and philosophy with a graceful pen and a strong mind, I shall not determine. But if it be a loss to the world not to have more literature and philosophy than it possesses, it has sustained a loss in the mis-employment of your uncle James.[1]

There was a sentiment behind Somerville's assessment of his brother's fortunes with which many of the autobiographers would have heartily concurred: that working men had more to offer this world than their labour. Running through this extraordinary body of working-class literature was the unshakeable belief that men such as themselves had the capacity to make a contribution to the cultural, religious and political life of the nation. It was accomplishments such as these that turned working men into what one autobiographer called the 'sons of freedom'. And it is to this, the cultural sphere, that we shall now turn.

# SEVEN

# Education

Intellectual bondage is worse than physical ... to be free, we should be in a position to dare the judgement of the wise. (George Holyoake, *Practical Grammar* (1844; 8th edn, 1870), p. 7)

Much of what little I know has been acquired since my school days. (Barr, p. 26)

EMANUEL LOVEKIN was not the kind of man to leave much trace on the historical record. He was born in 1820, the fourth child of Thomas Lovekin, a foundry worker living in Donnington Wood in Shropshire. As a skilled furnace man his father earned a good wage but most of it went on drink, leaving an unhappy wife struggling to raise a family of nine children as best she could. It was an inauspicious start to life and Emanuel was at work in the local coal mines by the age of seven and a half. History does not usually tell us much about ordinary lives like these.

The sources to which historians conventionally turn will not help. Lovekin did not rise high enough in society to lift himself out of obscurity. He never achieved the kind of prominence in business, in the Church or in the arts that might have secured entry to the chattering, record-keeping classes. There again, he never fell so low that he brushed up against such official bodies as the Poor Law or the criminal courts with their tendencies to interrogate, take notes and keep archives. The unexceptional nature of Lovekin's life leaves us with little more than the parish registers – useful perhaps for the outline of his family tree, but unable to tell us much about the interior workings of his life.

In reality, of course, Emanuel Lovekin is not shrouded in obscurity. In his mid-seventies, Lovekin penned an autobiography of around 7,000 words and told us everything about his life he considered worthy of record. It is all there: his hungry childhood, the father who 'took very little interest in home Matters', a spell with the Chartists that brought him perilously close to the wrong side of the law, his time as a navvy in the quarry pits, his long and contented marriage to Edna Simcock, his many years' work for the Primitive Methodists' Sunday school in Tunstall, and much else besides. The thirty-two pages of Lovekin's autobiography contain an embarrass-ment of riches. For once, the historian's challenge is not finding ways to fill in the silences left by an incomplete historical record, but handling the wealth of information the records contain.

Yet if Lovekin's autobiography spared him the oblivion that would otherwise certainly have been his fate, its existence does raise problems of its own. With a father given to drinking and a large number of brothers and sisters, Emanuel's stay at school had inevitably been brief. He was removed from the schoolroom when he was just seven to start minding a trapdoor in the coal pit. So the obvious question arises: how was a man whose schooling had ended at the age of seven and a half able to write an autobi-ography of 7,000 words? In fact the problems do not end there. As Lovekin tells us, not only was his education brief, its quality was dire. He had been born at a time when 'Schooling was not thought very much of among the poorer people'. His mother had found him a place at an 'Old Lady's school', but it was not the teaching he had received there that had provided him with the wherewithal to write down his life story. He could only remember learning one thing at school, and that was a Methodist hymn which she taught all her students to sing. It was hardly an education to make an autobiographical writer.[1]

The problem is not confined to Lovekin: it is writ large across the autobiographies. Industrialisation tended to thrust children into the workplace at ever younger ages. The average age at which the autobiogra-phers started work was just ten years old. Even the most precocious learner would struggle to write an autobiography on the basis of a few years' schooling snatched before the age of ten.[2] And yet at just the moment that the opportunities for working-class schooling became more fragile, the autobiographies begin to flourish. From the 1790s, working-class autobiographies survive in ever increasing numbers, and this should prompt us to ask not simply who wrote them, but how on earth they managed to do so.

The autobiographies contain numerous retellings of Lovekin's story.[3] Although the autobiographers' schooling was highly varied, it all had to be squeezed into the years before they entered the workforce. Over and over again our writers lamented the poor quality, brevity or even complete absence of the teaching they had received in childhood. The Methodist missionary Joseph Barker published an autobiography of several hundred pages, yet he described his younger self as 'a poor ignorant youth who had never in [his] life been a day in any school'.[4] Others made it clear that starting at school did not guarantee that much in the way of learning would follow. Stays could be hopelessly brief. The desperately poor parents of Alexander Bethune did manage to send him to school, but he was there 'never more than four or five months'.[5] Not a few of the autobiographers stated that their schooling had ended before they had even reached the writing class. Elementary schooling could offer a valuable introduction to the written word, but for most working-class children their early schooling was just that – the barest introduction.[6] These brief sojourns in the schoolroom will not carry us far in understanding the creation of this remarkable body of literature.

In any case, there exists a sizeable difference between the ability to hold a pen and the ability to write an autobiography. Admittedly a few of the autobiographies betray their authors' lack of education. There is the work of James Bowd or Joseph Mayett, for example, both of whom wrote largely without punctuation – a missed schooling did not entirely preclude entry to the ranks. Yet others wrote polished autobiographies, published during the author's lifetime, occasionally even achieving a degree of critical acclaim. Certainly, the lengthy and well-crafted narratives produced by some of the most prominent Chartists – William Lovett, Samuel Bamford and Thomas Cooper, for example – rested upon more than the learning provided by the short stints at dame schools, parish schools and (latterly) Sunday schools that their impoverished parents had been able to afford. And when the discrepancy between childhood schooling and written text is fully grasped, the matter of how this body of working-class literature ever came into existence becomes yet more surprising still.

Let us turn back once more to Emanuel Lovekin. After all, his autobiography runs to 7,000 words. Does it offer any clues as to how he had learned to write? Fortunately it does. As an illiterate young man in his teens (Lovekin tells us) he 'began to feel very Strongley the desieries to learn to read'. An accident left him bed-ridden when he was 'about 13teen' and he seized the opportunity to begin learning. His friends got him started on the letters of the alphabet and when his health recovered he began to attend a local 'nights School', where, he thought, he got along 'very nicely'.[7] He also attended the Sunday school run by the Methodists, which ran classes not simply for small children but for teenagers and adults as well. He remained closely connected with both the Methodists and their Sunday schools throughout his adult life, graduating from student to teacher and in due course starting to pass on his rather limited skills to the next generation of young men and women who walked through the doors of the Methodist Sunday school each week.[8] Lovekin may have entered the workforce young but his community had alternative means of education, and, from youth to old age, Lovekin was deeply involved in these as both a student and a teacher. Together, a combination of night school and Sunday schools provided him with just enough literacy to write his autobiography. They were critical in raising him from the historical obscurity to which he was originally destined.

It is alternatives such as these that we shall consider in this chapter. In the early nineteenth century, at just the same moment as the industrial revolution wreaked its most doleful effect on the childhood of the poor, new solutions to the problem of gaining an education began to emerge. Commercial and benevolent night schools, Sunday schools for teenagers and adults, reading clubs, mutual improvement societies and Mechanics' Institutes all played their part in improving the literacy of the working man. Most of the new opportunities were aimed squarely at men, though the Sunday school movement helped to extend literacy to women as well. Let us not for a moment imagine that these developments brought knowledge easily and cheaply into the lives of the working poor. Let us never complacently assume that this compensated for childhoods blighted by long, hard hours in the mill or the mine. As we shall see, picking up an education by these means was difficult and took great commitment on the part of the student. Night schools, book clubs and Sunday schools did not repair the damage caused by early entry to the workforce. They were a different kind of solution altogether. Nonetheless, as we shall see, these new alternatives had much to bring to the cultural life of the working classes.

But let us begin at the beginning. If the nineteenth century was an era of change, what about the century before? What were the traditional routes to enlightenment? In the eighteenth century, the small private day school formed pretty much the only source of education available to the poor. The schools were relatively widespread, but the cost of attending – the fees and lost wages – meant that children's school years were often hopelessly short. Poverty worked its age-old magic: the poorer the family, the shorter the stay. And beyond these day schools, there was very little else. So once their schooldays were over, would-be scholars relied heavily upon friends, parents, and above all their own unassisted efforts, to extend the little stock of learning they had already received.[9]

William Hutton typifies the problem. Hutton rose to prominence as a successful bookseller and writer, but he was born in 1723, one of nine children of a struggling journeyman wool-comber. He received no formal instruction beyond two years at school between the ages of five and seven: After that Hutton never again entered a classroom. His father and a retired schoolmistress lodging with the family did their best to encourage his love of reading, but otherwise Hutton was entirely self-educated, getting hold of whatever books he could lay his hands on and making his way through them as best he could.[10]

The many Methodist and Baptist preachers who penned an autobiography in the eighteenth century also suffered from a lack of teachers. Most of these writers were too busy with the state of their soul to spend much time on such practical matters as how they had learned to read and write. Those who did, however, described simply obtaining the books that interested them and then struggling through them on their own. The spiritual writers never referred to schools or teachers they could draw upon in their endeavour to acquire and understand complex texts once their schooldays had passed.[11] Friends, family and fellow Christians shared the books and what little knowledge they had. Beyond that, each man was very much on his own.

Thomas Holcroft's account of his attempts to extend his literary horizons in the 1750s reinforces the solitary nature of the working man's intellectual endeavour. Holcroft was not certain he had ever attended a school, and concluded that if he had, it must have been 'for a very short time'.[12] He was taught to read by his father and received some lessons in singing and arithmetic while working as a stable-boy at Newmarket, but with these exceptions Holcroft worked entirely without the assistance of those more educated than himself. He made progress by reading whatever he could find.[13] Friends and acquaintances occasionally had books they could share, but books were so scarce that he also kept a close eye on the walls of cottages and alehouses; sometimes he found new songs and ballads posted upon them.

Holcroft, Hutton and other self-taught men were not being perverse in their refusal to turn to more qualified neighbours for help. Their solitary endeavours were a simple reflection of the fact that finding (and paying for) a teacher was often next to impossible. Thomas Tryon wrote a detailed account of trying to learn to read in the early seventeenth century. Although describing a period earlier than that looked at here, his story is interesting in several respects. His schooling had begun at the age of five, but his time in school must have been short because he was at work by the time he was six and had learned little more than to recognise the letters of the alphabet.[14] At the age of thirteen, and mindful of the 'vast usefulness of reading', he bought himself a primer. His friends and neighbours helped him through his primer, but when he wished to learn to write as well, he 'was at a great loss for a Master'. He found a lame man who taught poor children to read and write, but then did not know how to pay him. In the end, he reached an agreement with his master to pay him with one of his sheep.[15] Yet even then Thomas struggled to find time to attend lessons and practise his writing. As a shepherd, he was never free of the responsibility of caring for his sheep so he needed to find others to take over his animals if he was to attend his lessons and practise his writing. It was not until he moved to London that his quest for knowledge took a more modern form – he used his wages to pay a teacher for private instruction. Tryon's difficulties capture the position for poor men seeking to gain an education at the time that he lived: there were few teachers to instruct them, no time for lessons, and no means to pay anyway. For most aspiring but penniless students getting hold of printed material and working through it was the best, and often only, way of learning to read. The matter of writing posed even greater problems: materials and instruction both had to be purchased, and finding the means to do so posed an obstacle that was often simply insurmountable.

Given these difficulties, many poor scholars relied upon the assistance of their wealthier neighbours. Through most of the eighteenth century, the men who rose from humble origins to make a significant contribution to science or the arts usually owed their success to such patronage. This was the means by which William Gifford had been released from manual labour and returned to school to complete his education. Orphaned as a child, Gifford had been placed by his hard-nosed guardian in a shoemaking apprenticeship in the early 1770s. It was literature and mathematics, not shoemaking, that interested Gifford, but his situation rendered any attempt to improve his learning almost impossible. Gifford's employer was hostile to his working at anything other than his trade and, as William explained, 'I had not a farthing on earth, nor a friend to give me one: pen, ink, and paper . . . were, for the most part, as completely out of my reach as a crown and sceptre'.[16] He kept his small stash of books and papers hidden in his garret, and when these were discovered and confiscated, he had nothing but the accoutrements of the shoemaking trade – an awl and scraps of smooth leather – to use in the place of pen and paper. A piece of good fortune came his way, however, when a poem he had written reached the attention of a local surgeon, Mr William Cookesley, who decided to become his bene-factor. He raised a subscription on Gifford's behalf and collected enough to free him from his apprenticeship and return him to school for a further two years. The education he received there enabled him to enter Oxford University and embark upon a career as a writer and editor.[17]

A similar path was taken by James Ferguson. Ferguson was born in a remote part of Scotland and in 'a very low station', but carved out a signifi-cant career as an astronomer and writer of scientific books, and died a wealthy man. He received little schooling as a child – just three months in the grammar school at Keith – and was taught to read and write by his father and a 'neighbouring old woman'.[18] His interest in the workings of the natural world vastly outstripped the learning that these teachers could provide. Fortunately for Ferguson, however, benevolent employers and neighbours stepped in to provide him with the education that neither he nor his family could afford. James Glashan, a 'considerable farmer' for whom Ferguson worked, allowed him time to study and gave him materials to work with.[19] The Reverend Mr John Gilchrist, minister at Keith, lent a map, and a pair of compasses, a ruler, pens, ink and paper so that he could copy it.[20] Thomas Grant, Esq. of Achoynaney, learning of Ferguson's talents, offered him employment and ordered another autodidact in his employ, 'his butler, Alexander Cantley, to give me a great deal of instruction'.[21] And so on. As a poor man living in rural Scotland, Ferguson could not purchase the education he desired. This did not entirely close the door on learning, but it did define the terms on which that learning could be obtained.

What is notable about the course of self-education followed by men such as Gifford and Ferguson is that its progress was largely outside their own control. Once they had exhausted the teaching that family and friends could provide, they had nowhere else to turn. Their further education was a gift, it was not something they were able to access without the interven-tion of their wealthier neighbours. As one literate footman put it, his masters, Mr Hamilton and Lady Anne, were 'the means of my having education'.[22] The difficulty for poor men of talent through most of the eighteenth century was not, therefore, the absence of opportunity. It was rather that they did not control access to opportunities and often remained dependent upon the goodwill of their social superiors to pick up anything beyond an elementary education.

Very little changed before the nineteenth century. Small commercial night schools, offering education in the hours after work for a modest fee, began to make their appearance in the autobiographies in the 1770s. But the spread of such institutions was slow and most of those trying to improve their learning were entering informal agreements with friends, employers or neighbours rather than turning to schools or professional teachers.[23] When James Lackington decided to learn to read in the 1760s, for instance, he paid his master's youngest son three halfpence for each hour's instruction he gave him.[24] David Whitehead took lessons in arithmetic from fellow lodger George Ingham in the evenings after work, and called on neighbours for help when he and George got stuck.[25] Others simply taught themselves in the time-honoured way – getting hold of a primer, finding a quiet corner, and working through it. Allen Davenport was one of a handful of autobiographers who had never received a day's schooling in his life, but he had managed to learn his letters from luckier playmates who attended the village school. He learned to read in the 1780s by buying a printed song which he already knew and comparing the text with his knowledge of the letters and words he knew the text represented.[26] Throughout the eighteenth century, for many uneducated workmen the obstacles to knowledge remained formidable, and very few could count upon a night school to help them get on.

The lack of suitable reading material exacerbated their difficulties. Songs and ballads might help novice readers like Davenport get started, but they were hardly the gateway to learning that many aspiring learners were looking for. Books and newspapers remained expensive, and for those on low incomes they were difficult to procure. The dearth of reading material at a price they could afford was a constant lament amongst the autobiographers. Joseph Livesey, the temperance reformer, was describing the first decade of the nineteenth century when he wrote that there were 'no Penny Publications, no cheap Newspapers, no Free Libraries'.[27] In very similar terms, Timothy Claxton observed that when he reached London in 1810, there were no public libraries or reading rooms, no lectures 'which we operatives could get at, or understand if we did', and no penny magazines.[28] 'No cheap books, no cheap newspapers or periodicals ... to facilitate the acquisition of knowledge', added James Watson.[29]

The lending libraries, which had been established in the eighteenth century, promised no more than a partial solution. Whilst lending libraries certainly contained the kind of literature that the autodidacts sought, most charged fairly hefty fees: they were not intended for, and were indeed largely beyond the means of, the working man. When William Fairburn decided to embark upon a programme of self-education he was helped out by his father, who had 'bought me a ticket in the North Shield's subscription library'.[30] Most autobiographers were not so lucky. In York, there was an entrance fee of 10 guineas to the subscription library and an annual contribution of 26 shillings – charges which, Christopher Thomson sarcastically noted, kept the city's gentlemen uncontaminated by 'the unwashed'.[31] Down to the first decade of the nineteenth century, aspiring students still struggled to get hold of the basic requirements – teachers, books and paper and pen – that promised to open the door to the world of print.

And then, in the 1810s, the world began to change. Slowly at first, soon gathering pace, new opportunities to acquire a little learning began to appear. An expanding network of small, commercial night schools was one element of the matrix.[32] In provincial towns these night schools were largely intended for aspiring apprentices. In Hull, for example, Christopher Thomson profited from 'an evening school' run by a Mr Thompson. It was held during the winter months only and taught 'reading, writing, arithmetic, navigation and other useful branches'.[33] Alexander Bain attended a very similar institution in Aberdeen: William Elgen's school, a 'purely mathematical' establishment, which existed primarily to teach accounting and navigation.[34] Though open to any young man with the means to pay, such schools were in reality most useful to those who already had a fair grounding in the three Rs.

In the industrial districts, night schools played a somewhat different role. Here they aimed to offer a basic education to those who had missed out on elementary schooling earlier in life. Growing up in Heywood, a small Lancashire town nestled between Bury and Rochdale, William Marcroft was one autobiographer who both missed out on schooling during childhood and later benefited from night schools. William had been put to work gathering dung off the roads at the age of six and had graduated to a cotton mill eighteen months later; he had never sat in a classroom in his short life. As a teenager, however, he befriended Jesse Blunt, who encouraged him to come and join him at Job Plant's night school and take his first steps in gaining an education.[35] William Chadwick's family was so poor that attendance at day school was 'out of the question'. He started work at a cotton mill at the age of eight and, like Marcroft, later got what learning he could from night schools instead.[36]

By the 1840s, most of Britain's large industrial towns had a wide range of out-of-hours schooling in place to help fill some of the gaping holes in the workforce's education created by the expansion of child labour. In Leeds, for example, James Bywater spent a few weeks at the free night school provided by his employer. Unfortunately, his love of play got the better of him and he left after a few weeks, 'having struggled hard but in vain' with the work they had set him. When he tried to return later in the year the master refused to readmit him to the school, declaring he had not 'appreciate[d] its gifts'. But it did not stop James getting the education he desired: he went to the evening school in Wortley Lane run by Mr Joseph Smith instead.[37] Night schools were also extending into even relatively remote areas. Robert Collyer, for instance, lived in the tiny village of Fewston on the north Yorkshire moors. There was little in the village besides the church, the mill and the mill workers' cottages – the 1851 Census listed just eighty-eight households containing fewer than 400 inhabitants in all. Yet the demand for schooling was sufficient to prompt one local schoolmaster, Master Hardie, to run a night school in the hamlet during the winter months.[38] In Farsley near Leeds, in the 1840s, two such night schools were in existence, and one proved so popular that a move to larger premises soon became necessary.[39]

Night schools were a market solution to the surge in child employment in the industrial heartlands and the pernicious effect this had on the schooling of the poor. But the market did not have all the answers. The early nineteenth century saw not only an extension of out-of-hours schooling offered on a commercial basis. It also witnessed the growth of new kinds of educational provision emanating from the working class itself: the mutual improvement movement.[40] At its simplest, a mutual improvement society comprised no more than a small group of friends pooling their resources to acquire reading material and meeting on a regular basis to discuss it. Charles Campbell, a cotton-mill worker in the Renfrewshire village of Johnstone, became a member of one such society in the early nineteenth century. His society consisted of just twelve members who met weekly in order to 'to debate on literary subjects'.[41] In 1821, many years before his rise to prominence as a leading figure in the Chartist movement, Thomas Cooper became involved in a similar club in his home town of Gainsborough. A friend of his (he recalled) had 'called together a number of friends and acquaintances' and proposed they should take the *Eclectic Review* and form a '"Mutual Improvement Society" for reading and discussion'.[42]

Within a couple of decades, these small impromptu societies were joined by the larger and more formal Mechanics' Institutes. The first mechanics' institute is usually traced to Glasgow; London (later Birkbeck College), Manchester and Swindon soon followed suit with impressive new institutions of their own.[43] Mechanics' Institutes were generally larger than improvement societies and possessed their own dedicated premises with libraries and reading rooms, though the dividing line between the two was initially not always clear. Yet as the scale of the institutes became more ambitious, they started to differ from the more humble mutual improvement societies in a number of ways. Large and impressive buildings could be erected only at some expense and the money for these projects was not going to be found in the pockets of the unschooled working men they were designed to serve. Ambitious building schemes were sponsored by industrial magnates or other local notables interested in raising the education of the working man. And with middle-class money came a debasement (or so at least it was generally feared) of the mutual improvers' original aims.

Despite their intentions, and to the consternation of those behind them, the Mechanics' Institutes displayed an unmistakable creep towards a better class of client. Charles Shaw observed that any youth wishing to attend a Mechanics' Institute needed both the opportunity to attend and the means to pay its fees. Most of the young men he knew, he darkly noted, had 'neither the one nor the other'.[44] Mechanics' Institutes were certainly not the first port of call for poor men pursuing a course of self-improvement. Most of those who attended their lectures or classes had either received a better than average education during childhood or had already undertaken a programme of self-education through night classes or a mutual improvement society. Almost all of the entrants had learned a skilled trade, though not all had done so by completing a formal apprenticeship. One had entirely quitted manual labour and taken up a position as a clerk before he entered through his local institute's doors.[45]

Not that any of this did much to damage working men's quest for learning. By 1850 there were several hundred Mechanics' Institutes in towns and cities across the UK and it is reasonable to surmise that there must have been some working-class beneficiaries of them. In any case, the existence of these institutions did nothing to harm the more informal and more accessible improvement societies. The two institutions could, and often did, coexist. If working men were not comfortable with the cost or ambience of the Mechanics' Institute, there was nothing to stop them setting up a rival institution of their own. In Carlisle, William Farish and his friends thought the town's Mechanics' Institute had become colonised by 'shop assistants and clerks' and had thereby 'failed somewhat in its mission' to educate the working men of the town. He and his friends set up an alternative institution aimed at what they believed should have been the institute's core constituency.[46] And Charles Shaw, who lacked the 'opportunity' and the 'means' to attend Tunstall's Mechanics' Institute, did not let it trouble him too much: he just set up his own society with a friend instead.[47]

All of these institutions, both large and small, played their part in the spread of literacy. Mechanics' Institutes usually had the advantage of some form of external funding, which allowed them to fill their libraries and offer night classes at relatively low cost. In the smaller clubs members paid their dues weekly: the expense was often counted by the penny rather than the shilling. 'A cheap school of pleasure and profit, well supplied with books, and conducted almost without any expense,' wrote Charles Campbell of his small reading club in Johnstone.[48] Thomson's Artisans' Library asked for just a penny a week from its members.[49] William Farish's newly formed mutual instruction club in Carlisle kept costs down by calling upon its members to provide whatever teaching they could. As Farish recalled, 'Those who could read taught those who could not, and those who could cipher did the same for those less advanced'.[50]

Farish's account of his club's members sharing out their little stock of learning captures the essence of the mutual improvers. Educating the illiterate, both within and without the club and regardless of their means to pay, was part of their mission. The members of Thomas Cooper's small club in Gainsborough did not simply sit around reading and discussing the *Eclectic Review*. They also established an 'Adult School, on Sundays' to teach reading to poor and illiterate adults.[51] John Passmore Edwards was living in rural Cornwall, yet he too became involved in the region's mutual improvement movement. At the age of seventeen he and a friend decided to set up a school to run on two weekday evenings and Sunday mornings to teach 'uneducated men and boys' for free.[52] Timothy Mountjoy and his friends set up a small library in their village. Following its success, the friends decided to set up a night school where 'the young men that went to the pit by day learned to read and write'.[53] At the heart of the mutual improvement ethos lay a commitment to raising the education of working men. As a result, the benefits of these organisations rippled out beyond the enthusiasts with the drive to organise themselves into a reading club.

The mutual improvement ideal may have started in Scotland, but from the second decade of the nineteenth century it had begun to colonise the country south of the border. Thirty-five of the autobiographies mention some form of involvement with a mutual improvement society and twelve more were involved in Mechanics' Institutes. Of these forty-seven institutions, eight were Scottish, the remaining thirty-nine were English.[54] In both countries, their growth was particularly strong in urban areas. For all his ambition, William Lovett had to admit that his efforts at self-improvement had not come to much while he remained in Cornwall: 'I had hitherto made very little intellectual progress'.[55] How different, however, once he had moved to London in his early twenties. He was promptly introduced to a 'small literary association, entitled "The Liberals"'. The members paid a small subscription to purchase books to circulate and discuss among themselves. He joined the newly formed Mechanics' Institute and attended public lectures at Tom's Coffee House in Holborn and Lunt's in Clerkenwell, and before long had joined several associations, 'literary, scientific, and political'.[56]

But if London inevitably offered the finest opportunities for mutual improvement, it was by no means the only place where book clubs and reading groups thrived. Several large cities boasted a host of small improvement societies;[57] as did some provincial market towns.[58] Discussion groups were scattered throughout the factory, industrial and mining regions, in both towns and villages.[59] They were also strong in weaving communities, urban as well as rural.[60] It was only as one moved into rural and agricultural areas that enthusiasm for such collective intellectual endeavour started to wane. As a whitesmith's apprentice in Lowestoft, Richard Gooch had spent his leisure hours practising 'reading and writing'.[61] Rightly did he object to being withdrawn from his position as a footman to work beside his father in the fields: 'I was then a little ambitious of improvement, and thought that a sedate country life would not exactly fit the ideas I had imbibed . . .'[62] Living in the small agricultural village of Fillongley in Warwickshire, David Barr despaired that there were 'no evening schools, mutual improvement classes, or public libraries within reach. The nearest facilities of this sort were at a Mechanics' Institute, but as it was situated six miles distant it was of no practical advantage.'[63] He did manage to find a village schoolmaster two miles away and paid him for some evening lessons but this was soon 'vetoed by my employer', who often required him to work until late.[64] Only two rural autobiographers were actively involved in the mutual improvement movement. One was John Passmore Edwards, whom we have just observed setting up a free evening and Sunday school in Cornwall.[65] The other was William Milne, who joined an improvement society while working on a farm in Lanarkshire. He tried to persuade his four unmarried 'mates' as well as one of the married cottars to attend with him, but regretted that he 'never got a man of them to join our membership, or take any part in the useful and entertaining proceedings'.[66]

Working alongside the clubs to offer reading and writing to those who had missed out on education during childhood were the Sunday schools.[67] The Sunday school movement is usually traced to Robert Raikes, owner and editor of the *Gloucester Journal*, and founder of a Sunday school in his own Anglican parish of St Mary le Crypt in July 1780. Others may have independently opened similar church schools at around the same time, but Raikes was certainly more influential than most in publicising and promoting the new institution. The idea behind the schools was to provide a basic religious education to poor children: most taught reading and some also taught writing as the foundation of that spiritual learning. As the schools' critics have often noticed, however, the early promoters of Sunday schools displayed rather more interest in training the poor to habits of obedience than in opening their minds to the world of literature, science or politics. Raikes once described his purpose as keeping the 'little heathens' off the streets. His preoccupation with a raft of other 'moral problems' – crime, disorder, irreligion – seems to confirm that the gentleman from Gloucester was motivated by something other than altruism.[68]

From small regional origins, the schools grew to become an institution of national importance. By the early nineteenth century, Sunday schools were springing up across the country and their rapid growth continued until the middle of the century. As they grew, the schools shook off the narrow confines in which they had been conceived. Raikes had intended his Sunday school to be controlled by the parish vicar, and so the Anglican schools usually were. But the Nonconformist churches were quick to jump on the bandwagon, setting up their own rival institutions and placing all teaching and management in the hands of men, and increasingly women, drawn from the community rather than the establishment. This network of different schools, conveniently held on the day when children did not work, contributed to very high levels of enrolment: by the 1830s more children were enrolled in Sunday schools than in day schools. By 1851 an estimated three-quarters of working-class children between the ages of five and fifteen attended a Sunday school, and over half belonged to schools outside the control of the Church of England.[69] Sunday schools had emerged as an important institution in the lives of the poor, and dismissing them as dark agents of social control simply will not do.

As one might predict, the autobiographies are chock-full of Sunday schools. Poverty was their lifeblood. Children found themselves on the benches of the Sunday school thanks to their parents' inability to pay for anything better. Richard Buxton's parents were 'much reduced in circumstances' and were unable to pay for more than three months of school. He did, however, attend a nearby Sunday school for more than two years.[70] The autobiographies reveal a sizeable overlap between the children who attended a Sunday school and those who started work at a younger than average age – a Sunday education was clearly an attractive choice to the parents of children who worked during the week.[71] They also confirm that Sunday schooling was the choice of the poor, even when their children were not at work at an early age. By the same token, children whose families could afford a lengthy stint at a respectable day school rarely mentioned attending a Sunday school as well. It all suggests that it was the schooling, rather than the religious instruction, that parents were after.[72]

More surprisingly, however, the autobiographies also reveal that Sunday schools had an important place in the lives of teenagers and adults. Raikes and other early promoters of Sunday schools aimed to reach the poor whilst young and impressionable and so expected their schools to be filled with small children. In their early days, children certainly were their main constituency. But Sunday schools proved extremely elastic with respect to the ages of the students they admitted. Welcoming ever older students was one more way in which they extended beyond their original confines. Samuel Bamford, for example, noted that his Methodist Sunday school in Middleton was attended by children and 'youths . . . young men and women . . . Big collier lads and their sisters'.[73] And William Innes was a strapping lad of nineteen years of age when he first walked through the doors of the local Sunday school.[74]

The connection between Sunday schooling and adults was also laid bare in a Sunday school established by Joseph Livesey and his wife in the early 1820s. In his memoirs he reproduced the notice that they had printed, informing their neighbours of their new venture:

Poor people in Preston and the neighbourhood are kindly informed, that a Sunday school, for youth of both sexes, from fourteen to twenty-one years of age, is kept in a commodious room, No. 4, Shepherd-street.

The scholars are confined to those of the above age; and as every attention is paid to their instruction, with the liberty of going to their own Places of Worship, parents and guardians of youth will find this a

favourable opportunity of providing for the education of those who are
obliged to labour through the week – such as have no learning, or are in
danger of losing that which they have . . . All gratuitous.[75]

For scholars of all ages, the Sunday schools were cheap. Their organisers
borrowed a room from the church and members of the congregation
provided the teaching. There were no membership costs: students simply
paid each time they turned up. Sunday scholars were rarely asked to pay
more than a few pennies and there were even schools which made no
charge at all. In contrast to night schools and reading clubs, they opened
their doors to women, making them the only place where women could
seek to make up the schooling they had not received during childhood.

From the 1810s, the combination of night schools, mutual improvement societies, Mechanics' Institutes and Sunday schools made the prospects for self-improvement brighter than ever before. But it should not be
presumed that these alternatives could substitute for day schools in a simple
and straightforward fashion. Men whose schooling had ended before their
interest in learning had been exhausted, or who had even missed out on
schooling altogether, needed real dedication and energy to make good that
education later in life. Alexander Bain, for example, learned what he knew
by spending the three hours between seven and ten at school each evening
– quite a commitment from a growing boy who had already spent a long
day at his handloom.[76] William Marcroft's journey to enlightenment was
also far from straightforward. He struggled with the embarrassment of
attending school in his 'greasy working patched clothes', with the jeers and
insults of his former playmates, and with disruption to his attendance at
the night school when the needs at home became so pressing that he could
no longer justify the outlay.[77] Thomas Whittaker did not think he 'made
much, if any progress' during his stint at night school, on account of the fact
that his attendance was 'irregular and somewhat spasmodic'.[78]

It was a little easier to fit attendance at a Sunday school around the
demands of a working life, but the education on offer was often limited.
From the outset, some schools had refused to teach writing, arguing that it
was unnecessary for the poor's spiritual instruction. This prejudice persisted
throughout their history. John Bezer deplored the fact that he had spent
nearly fifteen years attending a Sunday school, and yet left knowing
'nothing of arithmetic, and could scarcely write my own name'.[79] Even the
more progressive Sunday schools which aimed to provide a far more
comprehensive education for their students were often constrained by the

fact that they had to rely upon their own students to provide the teaching, and that teaching was squeezed into one day of the week. The educational losses sustained by many individuals because of their early entry into the workforce were serious and real; and those who succeeded in gaining an education in the hours after work later in life must have possessed an uncommon degree of purpose.

Understanding the educational developments we have been looking at here, therefore, requires that we view them not as an alternative route to enlightenment, but as a different kind of experience altogether. Day schools were adroit at drilling poor children in reading, writing and arithmetic, but they cast their pupils as passive learners. They sought to educate through repetition and obedience, not enquiry: children were forced into the desired behaviour by the schoolmaster's rod. At best, the day schools could offer a fairly superficial education to large numbers of the working classes. The number involved in the night schooling movement was always much smaller and night schools simply could not compete when it came to providing a mass education. Yet they did hold the promise of something far deeper for the few that got involved. The adult education movement required commitment and zeal from its members but in return gave access to more complex ideas than an elementary education ever offered its working-class pupils.

It might be argued that an education in itself opens the mind to questions of social organisation and serves to heighten political awareness. Yet it is also clear that the kind of education that was on offer to working men from the 1810s was particularly well adapted to serve as a conduit to other forms of social and political engagement. Book clubs, reading groups, Mechanics' Institutes and Sunday schools all encouraged their members to take an active role in their day-to-day running. The continued existence of these institutions depended upon quickly transforming their most able students into teachers, managers and leaders. In other words, along with raising levels of literacy, these schools and societies gave their students a taste of authority and small-scale power. They instructed their members in the business of governance – knowledge which could easily be transferred to other causes.

A mutual improvement society, no matter how small or fleeting, demanded lots of hard work from its members in order to get operations off the ground. The new recruits were kept busy finding and furnishing suitable premises, stocking a library, managing subscriptions, and devising strategies to retain the rank and file. Indeed, a glance through the autobiographies shows that writers said as much about their part in the routine management of their society as they did on the content of their lessons. John Passmore Edwards, for example, settled upon the local Bryanite Chapel for the small evening school he and a friend decided to establish. But how, they wondered, could the desk-less Chapel be used to teach the pupils writing? Edwards' solution was to use drop-down tables screwed to the Chapel's walls which could be held up with supports during school hours and laid flat against the wall during the services.[80] There was the matter of the books that should fill any new library's shelves. Benjamin Brierley's improvement society in Failsworth entrusted Richard Taylor – 'a great reader . . . well up in not only literature but some of the "sciences"' – to purchase the books for their library. (Brierley and a friend had the less exalted task of carrying the books back from Manchester.)[81] Christopher Thomson and the other founding members of the Artisans' Library in the mining village of Edwinstowe decided that *Tait's*, *Loudon's*, *Gardener's*, the *Penny Magazine*, the *Athenaeum*, *Chambers' Journal* and the *Visitor* 'would form the nucleus of a Library'.[82]

Larger enterprises needed to advertise for new members. On launching his 'Society of Ingenious Working Mechanics', Timothy Claxton wrote a circular, got it printed, and then distributed it around town.[83] And even the smallest society needed to manage subscriptions and abide by a set of rules. Charles Manby Smith's improvement society in Bristol was a tiny club of just six members, yet it still 'had fines for non-attendance, and prizes, paid out of fines, for the best-written productions'.[84] When the initial enthusiasm began to wear thin, members needed to work collectively to devise ways of keeping their institutions alive. Christopher Thomson came up with the idea of a fund-raising ball when the numbers began to fall off at his newly formed Artisans' Library. The villagers, he suggested, should be invited to the library's anniversary tea party and made to listen to talks about 'the importance of education, and the necessity of keeping up the library' before the dancing began![85] These reading clubs were small, humble institutions. Members were often counted in single digits. Yet they deserve to be recognised for the pivotal role they played in enabling working men to acquire the skills necessary to run an organisation.

Inevitably, the larger Mechanics' Institutes required managing on a grander scale. When Alexander Bain looked back at his time at Aberdeen's Mechanics' Institute, he declared that it made 'a most important contribution' to his life. He chose to emphasise that it had 'initiated [him] into the forms of business'.[86] The Mechanics' Institutes required willing members to sit upon their many committees and introduced working men to the nuts and bolts of running an organisation. Record-keeping, accounting, correspondence, annual reports and meetings procedures all had to be learned. And, as Bain pointed out, for a man like him knowledge of such things was hardly less valuable than anything else taught in the institute's classes.

There was also something more intangible that the members of these institutions gained from their involvement. Clubs, societies and a little education gave ordinary working men a measure of status and importance in their own eyes as well as in those of their neighbours. This is why the reading clubs, in their many and various guises, form such a significant chapter in working-class history. It goes without saying that not every recruit of every improvement society went on to become a great politician. Yet as growing numbers of working men began to acquire the skills and confidence needed to engage effectively with the public sphere, the prospect of working-class people working together in pursuit of their own agenda began to change dramatically. The most talented entered the doors in search of literacy, but walked out with the capacity to lead, organise and manage. What is more, they knew it.

The Sunday schools were hardly less effective in imparting both a little education and a quick introduction to the art of leadership. In the Nonconformist churches in particular, the teaching and organisation of Sunday schools was handed over to whichever members of the congregation cared to do it. Very little regard was paid to such details as the status, or even the learning, of those who volunteered. Even within the Anglican Sunday schools, although overall control usually resided in the hands of the vicar, there was often scope for students to rise through the ranks and assume the role of teacher. And we should not underestimate the esteem associated with this role. In working-class eyes, the position of Sunday school teacher carried status. For many men and women, working as a teacher was the first time they experienced having authority rather than being on the receiving end.[87]

As well as teaching the young, Sunday school teachers were expected to play their part in the day-to-day running of the school. The various roles the autobiographers had taken on were frequently, and fondly, recalled. John Wood, for example, spent many years connected with the Sunday school at Allerton Chapel and enjoyed turning his hand to 'almost every kind of school work'.[88] John Harris entered the Sunday school at Troon Chapel when he was five and he was still attending at the age of sixteen. At that point he became a teacher and 'rose from one post to another until I filled the office of librarian'.[89] Larger Sunday schools with several teachers developed suitably hierarchical structures to monitor and manage the work they performed. James Hopkinson was a teacher at the Stony Street Chapel's school in Nottingham. The teachers met regularly to discuss the running of the school and he was appointed 'secretary of teachers meetings'.[90] At the Sunday school at Manchester Road Chapel in Oldham, a select few were appointed 'officers', taking on duties such as reviewing the work of the school or reporting on the visiting teachers.[91] And, of course, somebody had to take overall charge. At the Primitive Methodist Chapel in Great Horton this responsibility fell to Joseph Wilson. Following his success with a particularly unruly class of boys, he was, he proudly noted, appointed 'Sunday School Secretary'.[92] Sunday schools doled out a little bit of education but they also gave some valuable lessons in the way of business. In other words, we are back once again with institutions that helped transform working men into community leaders.

Night schools, mutual improvement societies, Mechanics' Institutes and Sunday schools – these institutions get hardly a mention in most accounts of the industrial revolution. How could such lowly organisations compete with the great working-class movements of that era – the Luddites, the Ten Hours reformers or the Chartists? But these educational establishments should take the place in history that they deserve. They mattered to our autobiographers, to our first-hand witnesses of the world's first industrial revolution. We could probably do worse than grant them a place in our histories as well.

Above all, our writers remind us that the flowering of new educational opportunities at this time offered more than the promise of individual social advancement. They helped to create a workforce with the capacity for *collective* action as well. Let us look back once more at William Marcroft. As a young man, Marcroft had noted that 'men of education had more privileges, did less hard work, and [had] more wages' and this understanding had encouraged him to enter Job Plant's night school with a clear and narrow goal: to get ahead in life.[93] Yet though Marcroft may have sought an education as a means to quit the drudgery of manual labour, long before he had realised his dream of a genteel retirement his education had set him thinking about the way society was organised and prompted his involvement in a wide range of social and political organisations. While working as a grinder in Oldham he joined two friendly societies (the Oddfellows and the Rechabites), the machine grinders' trade union, and the temperance movement.[94] Later he helped found several co-operative trading societies, newsrooms and libraries, and established and taught at Sunday and night schools for 'aged men, whose education had been neglected'.[95] He also began to attend Chartist meetings and to play a prominent role in local politics.[96]

More generally, Marcroft's story reminds us that industrialisation had some surprising outcomes. The combination of poverty and industrialisation had extinguished the chance of schooling during Marcroft's childhood and forced him out to gather dung from the roads at the age of six. But the same forces that had crushed his childhood schooling had helped to create new forms of cheap or free education for adults. Working men proved remarkably adaptable and inventive in the face of the great economic forces that swirled around them. And education opened minds, trained foot soldiers, created leaders. As working men fashioned for themselves new institutions which taught both literacy and governance, they transformed themselves into a social and political force to be reckoned with.

CHAPTER EIGHT

# Gospel Times

I choose to worship God in a temple of my own selection. (Thomson, p. 15)

HAMLET NICHOLSON HAD the impoverished start in life typical of many of our autobiographers. Born into a shoemaker's large family in Rochdale in 1809, he never spent so much as a day at school. Instead he was working alongside his father 'at the cobbler's stool' by the age of eight and he learned his letters from his father and elder sisters. From early childhood, Hamlet attended the weekly service at the parish church, St Mary's, extending his 'stock of words' and deriving a quiet peace from the prayers, psalms and lessons delivered by the church's ministers.[1] He worshipped there, he informs us, 'with comfort and satisfaction from boyhood to youth, and from youth to late in manhood'.[2] At that point, however, he detected the vicar introducing certain Romish practices, and Hamlet's long and harmonious relationship with the parish church was soon shattered.

Matters began to deteriorate when a wealthy parishioner, Mr Jonathan Nield, informed Hamlet of his desire to bring ritualism into the Anglican services. It appears that the vicar, Rev. Dr Molesworth, needed little persuasion and readily introduced a number of ritualistic practices – psalm-singing, bowing and crossing, genuflexion, processions and an offertory held three times a day – all of which Hamlet found highly objectionable. Hamlet signalled his disapproval by walking out of church before the choristers had walked in procession up the aisle to the vestry, but this failed to stem the tide of innovation. It simply 'aroused [the vicar's] indignation'. Molesworth was so incensed by Hamlet marching out of the church before him and the choristers that he asked him for a public apology. He had apparently asked a 'woman' and a 'noted radical' to post apologies 'on the walls of the parish' in the recent past. No doubt he expected Hamlet to do likewise.[3] But Hamlet responded that the vicar 'ought not to be constantly compelling persons to apologise to him like a poor boy', and refused to comply.[4] Molesworth sent his solicitor round for a visit, with the warning that he would take legal proceedings if Hamlet did not apologise. Hamlet simply sent him away, telling him he had no intention of posting a grovelling apology on the walls of the parish. When Molesworth sent a second solicitor around with the same demand Hamlet dismissed him too, objecting to the vicar's attempt 'of degrading me, one of the oldest members of his congregation'.[5]

The battles lines between Hamlet and the vicar were firmly drawn. Each Sunday, Hamlet made his contempt for ritualistic practices known by leaving the church before the choristers had finished their procession to the vestry and the vicar sought various ways of bringing Hamlet back into line. Following the failure of his attempt to extract a more deferential attitude by sending his solicitors, Molesworth set a police constable to sit behind Hamlet in church; summoned him to the magistrates for a breach of the peace; and finally struck him as he made his early exit – though this in the event only succeeded in bringing him in front of the magistrates, accused of assault. But despite scoring minor victories along the way, Hamlet did not succeed in driving ritualism out of his parish church. Although his narrative was not entirely clear on the outcome of his conflict with the vicar, he did refer to having been 'driven from the Parish Church', and in old age was worshipping at St Catherine's in Manchester, where, he noted, the Rev. A. Haworth conducted the service 'in truly Evangelical style'.[6] Hamlet had not changed his ways, but neither, it seems, had Molesworth.

Molesworth and his allies achieved a victory of sorts, but they achieved it with far greater difficulty than they could ever have anticipated. When they set about reforming the service in the parish church, it is doubtful that the possibility that the congregation might oppose their reforms had even occurred to them. Most probably they assumed that a set of parishioners composed largely of weavers and textile workers would hardly notice what they were up to. They certainly believed that any of the more observant parishioners would obediently submit to their reforms. Jonathan Nield, the wealthy magistrate behind the whole affair, had thought that introducing ritualism at St Mary's would be an easy matter: 'as it was largely attended by the poorer classes they would the more readily adopt the changes'.[7] Molesworth had already successfully forced apologies out of parishioners who challenged his authority on other matters. He had evidently imagined the local shoemaker could be made to apologise too. But times were changing, and as Molesworth and his friends found to their cost, deference could not be extracted from the doughty old cobbler.

Hamlet Nicholson's story is complicated in a number of ways. Hamlet may have been born into poverty and worked as a shoemaker, but at the time of his battles with Molesworth he was not a poor man. Since learning how to sole his shoes with gutta-percha, Hamlet had developed a profitable sideline in rubber products and had secured for himself a 'decent social position' in the parish of Rochdale.[8] So this was not a penniless parishioner taking a stand against a well-heeled clergyman. Nor of course was it the first time in history that a vicar had faced difficulties with recalcitrant parishioners. Wherever there are records of parochial relationships there is evidence of clergymen dealing with unruly flocks. Yet despite this, there is something in Hamlet's story that belongs to this particular historical moment. The battle between Molesworth and the shoemaker captures a genuine shift in social relations, a realignment in the balance of power which we might tentatively describe as the decline of deference and the emergence of modern society.

In the first half of the nineteenth century, working-class men and women began to exercise a new independence from their social superiors and in this chapter I hope to show that the sphere of religious belief and worship was a vital arena in which social independence was both learned and practised. Hamlet and his supporters had an alternative to posting demeaning notices on the church walls at the vicar's command and to uttering insincere apologies like 'a poor boy'. Hamlet carried out a campaign of low-level disobedience, organised opposition amongst the parishioners, had recourse to legal counsel, and finally extracted his revenge by printing his own version of the affair in his memoirs. And although Hamlet remained loyal to the Anglican church, another very real alternative for disgruntled parishioners was simply to leave the established Church altogether and go and worship at one of the many nonconformist alternatives instead. It amounted to a seismic cultural shift, and one that deserves to be brought into sharper historical focus.

Nicholson's run-in with Molesworth came at the end of a dynamic period in Britain's religious history – a period known as the evangelical revival. The expression denotes the great wave of religious enthusiasm and missionary endeavour that swept across Europe in the century after 1740.[9] At the forefront of the revival were the Methodists.[10] The Methodists had originally grown within the Church of England, and only split in the 1790s when it became clear that their goals could not be effectively met under the Church's aegis. Having finally split from the mother Church, the Methodists proceeded to split amongst themselves a number of times, but division and secession notwithstanding, Methodism grew rapidly in the first half of the century to become the single most important of the Nonconformist denominations. Outside the Church of England, similar processes of conversionary zeal, growth and schism were also at work. In the early eighteenth century, the most significant of the dissenting churches were the Congregationalists, Presbyterians, Baptists and Quakers, but all were losing members and the once flourishing Dissenters appeared to be entering a state of near terminal decline. In the following half-century, dissenting congregations multiplied rapidly with the Congregationalists, Baptists and Independents doing particularly well. By the end of the century, Dissent had been reinvigorated and the sector continued to grow strongly over the next fifty years.[11] By the early nineteenth century, the supposedly 'national Church' jockeyed for position with a complex patchwork of Churches and creeds. Variously labelled 'evangelicals', 'Nonconformists' and 'new dissent', all denote a new brand of Protestantism which saw the individual's private relationship with God, rather than any outward show of charity or piety, as the key to salvation.

Many of the new converts were drawn in through outdoor revivals, and the autobiographies provide vivid illustrations of the revivals at work. With their open-air services and travelling preachers, revivals brought the word of God to those who seldom crossed the threshold of the parish church. During the summertime, itinerant preachers set themselves up in the fields, on the highways or at the market cross.[12] In the winter months revivalist meetings moved indoors, often into premises of the simplest kind. In Smeeton, Leicestershire, Abraham Deacon joined a prayer meeting in a barn which he described as 'a very common place of worship, the walls being plain bricks roughly painted, and bare thatch at the top'.[13] And Richard Weaver recalled attending Primitive Methodist meetings held in a barn in the village of Hyde, just outside Manchester. In allegorical tones, Weaver sketched the stable and hayloft pressed into service as a Methodist meeting house. As he pointedly added, 'it was not much of a meeting place; but in that lowly hall many a poor sinner found his way to the foot of the cross. We threw in our lot with the congregation that gathered there . . .'[14] Others met in their neighbours' homes, in 'the kitchens of farm-houses and the cottages of labouring men'.[15] The autobiographers frequently referred to the simplicity of the premises in which they first began to listen to the word of God and drew parallels between these simple surroundings and the simple truths preached therein. In the autobiographies, barns and cottages were depicted as a device for drawing in the poor and indifferent, and taken as evidence of a religious form that was free from unnecessary pomp and ostentation.

Naturally enough, the usual expectation that those assembling for prayer would wear respectable clothing was suspended. More than one writer who had stayed away from church owing to the state of his clothes admitted his comfort in finding a place of worship where dress did not matter. Joseph Burdett, an impoverished apprentice working for a framework-knitter in the Nottinghamshire village of Lambley, described himself as 'almost naked' for want of clothes. But his poverty and rags formed no barrier to joining the Ranters' open-air services in the village.[16] And along with their informal premises and dress codes, the preachers who addressed the gathered crowds spoke in a simple language, designed to reach the soul of the poor and uneducated. When Burdett listened to his Lambley Ranters he found the preacher 'engageing and arguments persuasive and language so simple that it was irrisistable'.[17] Mary Saxby had started attending a dissenting chapel in the 1760s, but found she 'could not well understand the minister; his language being too much polished for my weak comprehension'. When the Wesleyan Methodists pitched up at town, however, she delighted in 'hearing discourses . . . levelled to my capacity'.[18] The evangelicals promised a form of Christianity stripped of the social niceties and conventions that structured organised religion. The revival movement offered a point of entry to the Christian fold to those who otherwise rarely entered the doors of a church.[19]

The revivals were the advance guard of the missionary endeavour that characterised the evangelicals. Their success, though, was ultimately measured in the creation of new congregations with custom-built churches of their own. Church-building inevitably worked against the simplicity and openness of the revivals: after all, large donors usually expect some recognition for their munificence, and the Nonconformists were no exception. No sooner had the bricks gone up than old Anglican customs such as pew rents and hierarchical seating crept back in. Richard Cook recalled of the Methodist Chapel in Ferriby, Lincolnshire, that it was the custom of those 'who gave most money to the cause to select their own Pew'. The Waddingham family, he remembered, had chosen a pew in the right-hand corner of the chapel and had it constructed '12 inches higher than the others' – though this, our writer believed, was simply because the Waddinghams were tall, rather than the result of any notions of grandeur or importance.[20]

Yet even as the revivals moved behind doors, the evangelicals continued to prize certain qualities which marked them out from the established churches. Whether out in the fields or inside a newly built chapel, the autobiographers fondly remembered the unpolished working-class preacher – the man in work clothes, the man without schooling or training, the man, in short, like himself. Allen Davenport, for example, recalled feeling 'captivated' in a Methodist Chapel in Aberdeen 'by the splendid eloquence of a popular preacher'.[21] Thomas Burt was raised in a mining family on the Northumberland coalfields and his parents took him along to their Primitive Methodist Chapel from earliest childhood. There he enjoyed sermons 'delivered mostly by local preachers, themselves working men, few of whom had had any advantages of training or possessed any special gifts of eloquence, but all of them earnest, god-fearing men, with a firm belief in the truth of the message they were called upon to deliver'.[22] Israel Roberts singled out William Fox, his father's class leader whose 'ringing voice and hearty singing the writer can never forget. He was a man of no education not being able to read and yet he could line out some of our grand old Hymns in fine style.'[23] Earnest, uneducated and sometimes illiterate preachers delivered eloquent sermons that spoke to their unlettered flock. In many strains of Nonconformity it was common for preachers to share their origins with their congregation and this formed a very noticeable contrast with the social gulf that usually existed between the Anglican vicar and the poorest members of his parish.

The contrast with the alienating wealth, education and status of the parish vicar was stark. William Lea, for example, regretted receiving no 'religious education' while working as a farm servant in Cheshire. The vicars in the surrounding parishes were all 'sporting gentlemen', he ominously noted. None had ever managed to reach his soul.[24] Others depicted their parish vicar as a distant and unsympathetic figure: 'very proud and haughty', recalled one. The 'haughty vicar, who walked through the village as the lord and master' was ruthlessly pilloried by another.[25] This is not to deny that the parish clergy sometimes played a very positive role in the lives of their poorer parishioners. Instances of kindness and charity were also recalled by our writers – helpful and encouraging visits to the sick, and much-needed gifts of food and coal during the winter months. Nonetheless, such largess was distributed within an unequal relationship and did little to dislodge the sense that the Anglican vicar and his poorest parishioners occupied very different places in the social hierarchy.

Nor was this all. It almost went without saying that the parish vicar belonged to a different social class to the humble working families that filled the cheap and free pews in his church. What many writers found more troubling was the way in which the teachings and customs of the Anglican Church sanctioned these social inequalities. The message that John Gibbs, a shoemaker living in rural Sussex, heard repeated from the parish pulpit week after week made him feel decidedly uneasy. John was naturally predisposed to favour the established Church. The cruel neglect he had received as a child at the hands of his father, a self-proclaimed Dissenter, had left him with a strong aversion to all forms of Dissent – 'a dangerous and awful people', as he described Nonconformists to one friend. Working as a domestic servant he noted that the kindness and moral conduct of his Anglican mistress 'far exceeded' that of his father, and from this 'concluded that the High Church of England must be right'. He attended the parish services in search of salvation. But nagging doubts refused to go away. 'The real sentiments of the members of the High Church I could not perfectly understand,' he wrote, 'for they preached nothing but Virtue, Good Works, and Charity; and I often wondered what would become of the poor man who had nothing to give?'[26] He tried to cast these doubts aside, travelling five or six miles to hear services in the neighbouring churches after his day's work was done. But it was all 'to no purpose; of the sermons of some, I could understand scarcely a word, in consequence of their high language'; in others he could hear 'nothing but of Virtue and Works'.[27] In time he abandoned his allegiance to the Anglicans and joined Jenkin Jenkins' congregation at Lewes. His relationship with the Independents was not always easy, but for John it was considerably better than a church which neglected 'the poor man with nothing to give'.[28]

The complicity of the Church in shoring up an unjust social order was also etched in the memory of Joseph Arch, raised in the Warwickshire village of Barford in the 1830s. Later in life, Arch rose to national prominence as the founder of the first national trade union for agricultural workers and as a Liberal MP for North-West Norfolk. Writing his autobiography at the end of his life, he singled out the parish church as the place where he had received his first lesson in social injustice. In St Peter's, Barford, he wrote, 'the poor man and his wife were shown pretty plainly where they came among their fellow-creatures and fellow-worshippers'.[29] The parish poor had some pews set apart for them, but before they could sit in them the women were expected to walk up the church and make a curtsey to the parson's wife.[30] The squire and other parish notables 'sat in state in the centre of the aisle' and erected a curtain around their pews 'to hide them from the vulgar gaze'.[31] Joseph held a vivid memory of the day when he peeped through the keyhole of the church door to see what happened when his father stayed behind to take communion. The procession to the altar perfectly mirrored the local social hierarchy. First the squire walked to the communion rails, then the farmers, the tradesmen, the shopkeepers, the wheelwright, the blacksmith. And finally, 'very last of all, went the poor agricultural labourers in their smock frocks'.[32] The young Joseph was only a child, yet he knew from that moment that the parish church was no place for him.

The Nonconformist churches offered something different. With homely preachers, simple language and a disdain for the most egregious forms of social exclusivity peddled in the parish church, Nonconformity promised a brand of Christianity that was far more palatable to many working people. But Nonconformity provided not simply a more accessible form of religion. It also offered that religion on different terms. In discussing the evangelical revival we must be careful: the movement comprised many denominations, each with its unique brand of theology, forms of governance and commitment to missionary activity. Yet at the heart of the evangelical revival was a tradition of sharing religious experience through Bible-reading, prayer and discussion. Humble men and women, lacking even the rudiments of an education, were invited to share their spiritual journey, to reflect upon the meaning of the Bible, to question and to interrogate their spiritual leaders. In the process, they were transformed from passive recipients of a religion administered by their social superiors to active participants in their own religious culture.

The participatory nature of evangelical Christianity was brought to life by the autobiographical writers. Every denomination had its own form of meeting; many churches held several different kinds of meeting on different nights of the week. But whatever form these meetings took, poverty and illiteracy were no barrier to taking part. Within the Methodists, the class meeting formed the bedrock of membership. The class meeting had originated in the 1740s and comprised a group of twelve members meeting on a weekly basis for Bible study and prayer. A century later, the weekly class meeting still lay at the heart of membership of the Methodist Church. Thomas Wood remembered the class meetings that he attended as a young man in Bingley. The Rev. Jessop led them on Friday evenings and each week either he or one of the group's members prepared an essay which was shared and discussed by the group. The band meeting was a confessional prayer group; members met weekly and confessed any sins they had committed during the week.[33] Israel Roberts fondly recalled the Methodist band meetings he attended on Saturday nights where 'many happy stories of saving grace were narrated'.[34] At experience meetings, members described and discussed their experience of conversion. William Hanson attended a weekly experience meeting at a neighbour's house and, although young, his 'simple' account of his conversion gained approval as a 'thorough conversion' by more senior members of his group.[35] Nor were these small discussion groups the preserve of the Methodists. All the Nonconformist churches encouraged informal meetings, often led by lay members, and attended by any in the congregation who were so inclined.[36]

Up and down the country, the evangelicals invited their unlettered neighbours into their cottages and makeshift chapels to discuss their faith. These gatherings might not seem significant, but let us dwell for a moment longer upon their novelty. After all, the labouring poor were not usually in the business of sharing their views in semi-formal settings. For the most part, working people spoke up in informal situations – in the home or workplace, in the field or street, in the alehouse. Making the transition from speaking informally with friends and family to speaking up in public was not something they had ever been schooled for. Nor did they always find it easy. One Edinburgh baker admitted to feeling 'very timid' the first time he was invited to take a turn at his Sunday school's prayer meeting. Adam Rushton sat in silence through his first two class meetings, but at the third his leader asked him, 'What is the state of your mind?' Adam admitted that the 'question found me entirely dumb. I could not possibly give an intelligent reply, and so I spoke no word'.[37] The farm labourer Joseph Mayett wrote at greater length about the difficulties of speaking aloud.

At the time that Mayett's religious conversion took place, he had given up farm work and joined the army. While living in barracks he had fallen in with a small group of men in his regiment who regularly gathered 'for Religious exercise'. His little set comprised a collection of Methodists and Baptists and they met most evenings after the day's work was done, either in a nearby Independent Chapel or in the fields or woods around their barracks. During a stay at Ottery St Mary in Devon, Joseph's friends were keen that he should speak at one of their evening meetings, but he 'trembled' at the prospect. When his turn to speak eventually came, he 'Coul [sic] not think of a word' to say and fell silent. After further reflection and prayer, Joseph soon 'accomplished the hard task . . . which my friends had laid before me'.[38] Joseph's 'hard task' was simply to speak aloud in front of a small group of like-minded friends, but outside his prayer group there was no forum in which anybody cared to hear Joseph's words. This was the first time in his life that he had been encouraged to speak in a formal setting.

In the context of the lives of the labouring poor, then, there was something highly unusual in these cottage prayer groups. They were part of a process in which uneducated men and women began to find their voice, both literally and figuratively. The prayer groups, class meetings and Bible-study classes of the evangelical revival provided a place where the poor were encouraged to speak. They offered not only the opportunity of learning and practising the art of speaking in public but something more intangible yet hardly less important: the experience of having one's voice heard. As such they are a small yet significant step towards the creation of a working class with the confidence and ability to articulate its views.

Discussion and debate were part and parcel of the evangelical revival. It also, inevitably, was carried away from chapel. In industrial South Wales, Henry Hughes remembered his father 'discussing religious matters' with other members of his Congregational church during the recess between morning preaching and the Sunday school held in the afternoon.[39] In the Scottish Highlands, James Croll recalled that his co-religionists were 'fond of the social prayer-meeting' and 'inclined to speak to one another of their own personal experiences'.[40] In London, Joseph Gwyer remembered how all the Sunday school teachers used to assemble at one member's house in the evenings for singing and discussion of that day's preacher.[41] Other writers indicated that religious discussion throughout the week formed a part of their spiritual life. Francis Mason was raised in a Baptist family in York in the early nineteenth century. Both his father and his grandfather belonged to York's Baptist congregation and the home of young Francis had become the resort of those who wished to join the church or 'discuss its doctrines'. Francis remembered the 'motley group' that would gather around their fireside: 'there was scarcely an article of faith of all the two hundred sects of Christendom, that did not, at one time or another, find an advocate there'.[42] The autobiographers dwelled upon these experiences of meeting, debating and listening. As one writer concluded: 'the whole thing was so novel . . . so totally unlike anything' he had encountered before.[43]

In reality, the cottage meeting in a rural parish was likely to be a very simple affair, its intellectual horizons limited by the illiteracy and poverty of some members. In the cities, some churches took the tradition a step further, encouraging their members to delve deeper into matters of doctrine through the reading of pre-set texts and the writing of essays. In Glasgow in the 1820s, for instance, one autobiographer calling himself the Scotch Lad joined a 'Young Men's Society for Religious Improvement'. The club met every Sunday at seven in the morning, and after singing and prayer a part of the Bible was read, 'questions asked and opinions freely given on the portion read'.[44] Once a month, the group also read and criticised essays that one of the members had written on a religious subject. William Smith thought that Coalbrookdale, an iron-working village in Shropshire, was 'noted at that time for turning out smart intelligent men and hard thinkers and workers'. He joined the 'discussions classes' in the town 'where good preachers were appointed to train [the men]'. Smith also carried on the good work by establishing a Methodist discussion group of his own. It ran during the winter months and was held each week in a different member's home.[45] Such groups borrowed much in inspiration from the mutual improvement societies and like those societies they deserve recognition not simply as a forum for discussion, but as a means for improving the skills of participants. Both the 'Scotch Lad' and William Smith emphasised how much their discussion group had taught them. Smith, for instance, concluded that his participation had been 'a great blessing to me and sharpened me up for discussion and preaching and public speaking'. More generally, these classes of confident readers and writers reflected the better opportunities for self-improvement to be found in urban areas, with Glasgow, London and a handful of industrial districts alone in boasting such organisations.[46]

What we see, then, within these religious communities, is the carving out of a place where a working-class voice was learned, where working-class voices counted. Members of the Nonconformist churches were encouraged to explore arcane matters of doctrine, to discuss their interpretation of the Bible with other members, to find answers for themselves. No especial education or qualification was required to take part in these spiritual endeavours. Some of the autobiographers took particular relish in describing how, through their own efforts, they had managed to unlock a long-standing theological mystery. Here is the account given by Joseph Terry, a boatman working on the waterways in east Yorkshire, of the moment when he found enlightenment on 'the doctrine of the Trinity, which had always perplexed' him.[47] He first read around the subject and then attended lectures given by Joseph Barker, who had recently retired as a Methodist preacher and was now preaching and publishing on a very wide range of religious and political subjects. Terry thought Barker had compelling arguments, and he eventually followed Barker and became a 'thorough believer in the Unitarian Doctrine'.[48]

Joseph Terry's interest in Scripture formed part of his broader intellectual interests. He was fully absorbed in the self-improvement scene as one of the founding members of the Mechanics' Institute at Brighouse, and as a regular contributor of essays, some of which he managed to publish. But activities of this kind were not a precondition of engagement in doctrinal debates. Chapel-goers did not need to be steeped in the culture of self-improvement in order to play an active role in their own spiritual growth. Robert Spurr was a young journeyman shoemaker. He was only just able to keep his family afloat and had neither the time nor the inclination to embark on a root-and branch programme of self-improvement. He did not know much about religious matters, except that he did not want to join the Methodists as he 'did not like that creed'. Yet with attendance at the local Baptist Chapel came a degree of reflection about the things the Baptists stood for. As he wrote in his vernacular way, when he first started attending the chapel at Bramley he was puzzled by some of the Baptists' customs, but 'reading for myself in the [Bible], i found it to be true . . . i agreed with their doctrines such as original sin, regeneration by grace, Baptizam and the Lord Suppor, free justification and adoption, the final perseverance of real believers, the eternal happiness of the rigteous and so on'.[49]

The extent to which the evangelical movement drew in even those with the most impoverished backgrounds is truly striking. Night schools and mutual improvement classes were in theory open to all. In reality, those who took part were usually at some remove from poverty. Most were in full employment and those working in urban and skilled trades were considerably more at home in such institutions than unskilled or agricultural workers. It is undeniable that the Nonconformist churches were also popular with respectable working men following an upward trajectory. But there, sitting in the pews beside them, were men and women whose trajectory was heading anywhere but upwards.

One such convert was Josiah Basset. Josiah had never known anything but hardship and want. His parents had enjoyed comfortable circumstances early in their marriage, but soon after his birth they were 'reduced to abject poverty', a poverty from which they never emerged.[50] Josiah was inevitably sent to work at a young age, turning a spinner's wheel at a ropewalk. Not that this did much to halt the family's decline. When he was twelve, they all retired to St George's workhouse and there Josiah lived out the next five years of his life. He ran away at the age of seventeen, but failed to find anything better on the outside. Unable to find work, he became a vagrant, tramping from town to town, sometimes getting relief from the parish, sometimes successfully begging his meal, and other times finding himself locked up in the bridewell for vagrancy. And so Josiah's life rambled on. He enjoyed several stints of wage-earning – as a shepherd in the Scottish Highlands and as a tinker travelling the country selling 'needles and bodkins', blacklead, and other cheap items. But any prospect of permanent employment or a more settled life eluded him. When he started to attend the Independent Chapel in Union Street he was engaged as a casual day labourer, picking up work from day to day – one day shouting for an election candidate, another walking the streets carrying advertising boards for valentine cards and swimming baths, and the next sweeping the streets. How, he asked, could any church 'receive such a poor outcast as I am'? Yet the Union Street Chapel not only received him, they did so 'with great kindness'.[51] In time, they even admitted him as a full member of the church. Once a member, he was invited to join the Sunday morning prayer meeting and to help teach an evening Sunday school for ragged children.[52] He also joined a weekly meeting on Wednesday evenings for 'mutual religious improvement', remaining all the while a casual, indeed frequently out-of-work, labourer on the margins of a decent existence.[53] Nor was there anything exceptional about Josiah Basset's spiritual, social and intellectual integration in the Union Street Chapel. The Nonconformist chapels were comfortable with poverty. They regarded reaching out to the poor man who (as our shoemaker John Gibbs had phrased it) had 'nothing to give' as a central part of their mission.

The Nonconformist churches were also successful at drawing in women. Wesley's original class meeting of twelve had been envisaged as a class of both sexes and although the evangelical revival expanded and evolved into a complex, and often more conservative, religious force women never lost their place in the Nonconformist community. Female life-writing was not common, nevertheless a handful of women described joining a new religious community, and they usually recorded experiences which were strikingly similar to those penned by men. After her conversion, Caroline Hopwood joined the Methodists, 'went to class and band' meetings, and conversed with preachers about the subjects of their sermons.[54] Mary Saxby joined the Methodists and there enjoyed 'the company and conversation' of other serious Christians.[55] While worshipping with a Baptist congregation in Brough, Mary Smith observed that 'they held that all should use their "gifts", as they called it, at the prayer meetings' and was surprised to find 'women as well as men engaging in oral prayer'. Although initially too timid to speak at prayer meetings, with encouragement she managed to 'venture upon this untried duty', finding as she did so that her 'confidence grew stronger every time'.[56] It was entirely of a piece with the experiences that male writers reported in far greater volume.

It would be easy to exaggerate the place of religion in working women's lives. The chapel doors were in theory open to women, but mothers with young children often found it difficult to get to the chapel at all. In her autobiography, Elizabeth Oakley admitted to quarrelling with her husband over the money he gave to the chapel when 'I so badly wanted it at home'. When a man from her husband's church came to visit and asked if she ever prayed, she replied, 'no I never did I seemed to have so much to think about my family ... my thoughts seemed entirely fixed on my family'. Family cares left Elizabeth with no time to fret over the state of her soul. While her husband spent his evening leisure hours at the chapel or took time off work to attend great Methodist tea parties, Elizabeth necessarily stayed at home with the young children who occupied so much of her thoughts.[57] Yet Elizabeth's initial response to her husband's newfound faith was closely related to her life cycle, in particular to the young age of her children. As her children grew older she responded to the Church's welcoming embrace more positively. Growing churches needed members. Most kept a careful count of their membership and were not too fussy about who filled the pews. As Robert Collyer wryly noted of the Methodists with whom he worshipped for a time in Ilkley, they were not 'over particular' as regards whom they admitted.[58]

The reflection and soul-searching that the evangelicals expected from their members could hardly be more different from the Anglican tradition. The parish church was open to all, but attendance, not engagement, was all that was required. In the parish pews, the labouring poor were encouraged to hear the word of God; they were not invited to share their thoughts or offer up criticisms. The passivity expected from poor parishioners was captured by George Mockford, an agricultural labourer living in rural Sussex in the 1830s. Mockford ended up as a Methodist preacher, but his spiritual journey began in the parish church in the small village of South Malling where he was raised as one of the twelve children of desperately poor parents. The vicar, he recalled, found difficulty in teaching him: 'he would sometimes reprove me by saying I ought not to say this portion of the word of God meant so and so; he was my instructor, and I ought to know nothing but what he taught me'.[59] Another who visited informed him, 'I have been to college . . . and trained on purpose to teach you, and you are taking the place of a teacher to me'.[60] There cannot be much doubt that George took considerable pleasure in recounting these interactions where he refused to play the part of the dumb student. Nonetheless, the essence of his story is no doubt true. In the eyes of the parish vicar there was no role for a poor man like George Mockford, living by the labour of his hands from one day to the next, to question or consider their teaching. The active and enquiring penitent simply had no place in the Anglican tradition.

Part of the difficulty Anglican vicars faced in finding a suitably docile working-class audience for their teaching lay in the fact that they had lost their position as the sole supplier of Christian salvation. As the evangelical revival gained momentum, the religious landscape changed irrevocably. In the eighteenth century, relatively few had anywhere to worship other than the parish church. As John Taylor said of his childhood in the 1740s, there were few Dissenters and 'but little knowledge then of any of the denominations of dissenters'.[61] Very few could claim the same was true a century later. By the 1840s, an extensive religious marketplace was firmly established. Town dwellers could choose between several denominations, and even between different chapels of any given faith. One of the most extreme examples amongst the autobiographers is Alfred Arney, a wheelbarrow-maker who lived in Bristol in the 1850s and devoted most of every Sunday to touring the city visiting churches and chapels and listening to their preachers. In the course of one year covered by his diary he attended at least a dozen different churches, including the 'Catholick chaple' and the 'Latter day Saints Chapple' – sometimes returning repeatedly and sometimes never setting foot in them again.[62] But even more restrained churchgoers made the most of the variety of preachers on offer, occasionally attending sermons almost as form of entertainment rather than as a spiritual experience. Alexander Somerville, for instance, did not represent himself as a deeply religious man but he did describe sampling different preachers in Edinburgh as one of his 'chief intellectual treats'.[63]

The larger the town, the greater the choice; but even those living in rural areas were likely to have some options when it came to where to worship. The agricultural labourer James Nye longed to move from rural Sussex to Lewes where he might 'have my fill of the preached word', but when living in the countryside he had not been without the opportunity to try out a number of different chapels. He had attended the Methodist

Chapel but found several 'bad characters' there, 'all carried away with the sound and missing the substance'.[64] He had also worshipped with the Baptists for a while, but quit before long, declaring it had become 'a dry breast to me'.[65] When the chance to live in Lewes eventually came, James certainly did find a greater variety of churches, but even before getting there he had been able to try out the Methodists and the Baptists. And inevitably the mere existence of alternatives prompted a different kind of relationship between pastor and flock, for no clergyman could be complacent about his congregation's continued loyalty when there were so many other churches from which to choose.

The opening up of the religious landscape which began in the 1790s defies simple summary. On an individual level, Christianity offered solace for a hard life, inner peace, the hope of salvation, friendship and a sense of belonging as well as a myriad other things. Yet collectively the rise of Nonconformity nurtured the working-class voice, a voice that had never been encouraged in the Anglican tradition. There was something intrinsically different about evangelical Christianity. The evangelical revival provided a platform for working-class expression, a new space for working-class spiritual and intellectual activity. Most did nothing with this space, unwilling or unable to exploit these opportunities, given the many other demands in their lives. But its existence represents a historical change of real significance.

One inevitable outcome of this readiness to nurture the religious expression of even the most humble chapel-goer was the rise of the working-class preacher.[66] In part owing to the close connections between autobiographical writing and the confessional narrative, the autobiographies contain a large number of men, and even some women, who took up a life of preaching. One of the most striking aspects of their stories is the sheer ease with which an uneducated working man might embark upon life as a preacher. John Clifford, for example, took his first steps towards preaching in the 'little room in connexion with the Nether Street Baptist Chapel at Beeston'. With four friends, he borrowed the key and 'practised preaching' from a makeshift pulpit made from a box topped with a piece of wood.[67] His minister then encouraged him to 'prepare a sermon as a test and preach it in church', and this went sufficiently well for him to be invited to speak at the young people's prayer meeting, held before the service on Sunday evenings.[68] Before he knew it, John had been admitted to the Midland Baptist College at Leicester. His days in the factory were over and he was well on his way to his new life as a salaried preacher.

John Clifford's entry to a seminary was unusual amongst our working-class preachers. For most, a seminary education was quite unnecessary. Men were able to travel the distance from pew to pulpit in reassuringly small steps, and without recourse to expensive education or training. Here for example is Stephen Brunksill's story. Several years after joining the Methodists, Stephen Brunksill was appointed a class leader, and one night after his class meeting 'gave a word of exhortation'. After he had addressed the congregation 'a few times in this way', his father began inviting his neighbours into his home for prayer and preaching. This gave Stephen new opportunities 'to exhort more publicly', though still on a relatively small scale. Soon the neighbouring societies got wind of the new preacher and invited him 'to visit them and to preach them the word of life', and as his reputation as a preacher grew he was eventually invited on to the circuit as a Methodist preacher.[69] Others simply stood on the street and began to address any who would listen.[70] Despite considerable variation in the ways in which the working-class autobiographers became fully fledged preachers, most described having inched their way along the path slowly and cautiously. Very few had acquired any special training along the way.

Indeed, some autobiographers found themselves propelled into a formal preaching role more quickly than they wished. Several were pushed forward by church officials who lacked anyone better qualified for the task. Isaac Anderson kept telling his church elders that he did not wish to take office as he did not feel capable, but 'they would not heed my requests and ordained me as an Elder by the laying on of hands in David Handley's room at Maldon'.[71] Several of the Methodist preachers recalled that they had not been privy to their call to the ministry. William Lea, for instance, found his name put on the Preston Brook station plan without having so much as been consulted upon the matter![72] Thomas Jackson was even clearer: 'I had never offered myself as a candidate for the itinerant Ministry, nor was I a consenting party to this arrangement.'[73] As he was still an apprentice, Thomas had to borrow the money to purchase his indentures before he was able to take up the offer, though he, like many others who had felt unprepared for the event, recalled the incident fondly as a 'Providential calling'.[74]

The deep social reach of the Nonconformist ministry was remarkable. Men from the lowest rung in society were able to embark upon a life of preaching. John Lincoln, for example, had not simply been raised in dismal poverty by his single mother in late eighteenth-century Suffolk, he was also mired in poverty both at the time that his conversion took place and when he began preaching a few years later.[75] Indeed, such was his poverty that the rent for the cottage in which he began preaching was paid by the parish. Even women occasionally took up a life of preaching, though we should take care not to exaggerate this development. Male preachers always vastly outnumbered female preachers, and the women who preached did so outside the formal structures of the chapels.[76] Yet if they were not present in large numbers, the existence of female preachers is nonetheless significant as yet more evidence of the ability of people on the margins to take up a place at the centre of these churches.

The humble preacher helped to foster a uniquely working-class form of religious culture. Other elements of the Nonconformist tradition also played their part. As many of the young men who joined a chapel in their adolescent years were quick to testify, this usually called for more than attendance on Sundays. Enthusiastic members of a fledging church soon found themselves drawn into a range of activities after the conclusion of the Sunday services. If the revivals were to move indoors, new churches needed to be built and furnished. Congregations had to be maintained and (preferably) expanded, and the Sunday school children taught. The expectation was always that rank and file members would fill these roles. In other words, there was a wide range of ways for working-class men and women to contribute to their churches and this tradition of active service was no less significant than the proselytising and preaching.

For some of those involved, the conviviality of church membership soon acquired social, rather than spiritual, hues. As some writers happily recalled, the chapels welcomed the young of both sexes, and hanging out in the summer evenings with one's chapel friends could be the highlight of a week largely devoted to hard labour. Samuel Bamford even admitted that he and his friends sometimes turned up during the religious observances of the Methodists, seeing them nothing more than an 'opportunit[y] for rude sport'.[77] Even those who described their experience of church membership in less frivolous terms spoke of the opportunities for friendship, fellowship and courtship that went hand in hand with joining a congregation. This sense of belonging could assume particular importance for those who had recently left a life in the countryside and moved to a new town. The Stoney Street Baptist Chapel in Nottingham crops up twice in the autobiographies, and on both occasions played a central role in the writer's social calendar. In the 1820s, after leaving the family farm in Belton to take up work in the nearby great town, Arnold Goodliffe threw himself 'heartily into the work of Sunday School teaching at Stoney Street Baptist

Chapel'. Henceforth, his free hours were fully occupied with 'Religious and Social work'. Sunday school teaching, prayer meetings, tea parties, tract distribution, cricket matches, and setting up new Sunday schools in surrounding villages were just some of the things he enjoyed through his association with the chapel. Not surprisingly, it was also here that he met his wife, Anna Speed, who was, he approvingly noted, 'a very punctual teacher and a member of the Church'.[78] A decade later, James Hopkinson immersed himself in the life of Stoney Street Chapel. He entered as a teacher at the Sunday school and became in time the secretary of the teachers' meetings. He too met his wife in the pews of the chapel.[79] Both men testify to the ways in which membership of a growing religious community offered friendship as well as spiritual growth. At the same time, however, they also indicate the possibility of learning new and useful skills through the church. Stoney Street Chapel and its various institutions needed running and Arnold and James had each in their turn played their part in this work.

This spirit of service characterised all the major Nonconformist churches at every stage of their development. The success of even the most modest revival depended upon individuals being prepared to play their part in helping to establish the new church. During the Methodist revival around Halifax in the 1780s Jonathan Saville became a 'recruiting sergeant', holding prayer meetings on Sundays and other week nights in the villages without chapels. It was his task to train others to hold prayer meetings so that the good work could continue without him.[80] Others opened their houses, either to preach or to accommodate a preacher, once the revival had moved on.[81] As congregations outgrew cottages, some of the autobiographers were even active in the building of new chapels, though not always with the happiest of results.

John Gibbs was one working man who entered the complex world of chapel-building. We encountered Gibbs earlier in the chapter when he finally turned his back on the Church of England and started to worship at Jenkin Jenkins' Independent Chapel in Lewes. Following Jenkins' death, Gibbs began preaching the occasional sermon at the Independent Chapel, but for the most part he preferred to preach to small groups of followers in his own home. By about 1810, he was preaching twice a day. As he had a small house and a large family, he found the situation both 'inconvenient and trying'.[82] When the celebrated Mr M'Culla expressed a willingness to come and preach in Lewes once a month, Gibbs united with ten other men to lease a room and move his followers out of his cottage once and for all.

The plan was that Gibbs and the others would use the room for preaching throughout the week; on Sundays it would be reserved for the exclusive use of Mr M'Culla. The arrangement was satisfactory at first, but as John laconically noted, it was not 'too long before jealousy began to work'.[83] The problem, he explained, was that the locals preferred his preaching to that of the others. The room was packed to the rafters on his nights; half empty the other nights of the week. Despite some half-hearted attempts to resolve their differences the eleven members soon had a catastrophic falling-out. John stopped paying his share of the rent and returned to preaching at home. The new chapel closed not long after his departure. Yet although the enterprise ended acrimoniously, it would be wrong to conclude that it was an unmitigated failure. It certainly taught John plenty about chapel-building, knowledge that served him well when he built a chapel for his exclusive use a few years later.

Once the chapel walls were up, there were a variety of tasks to perform in order to keep the new institution in good health. The running and teaching of Sunday schools emerges as by far the most common duty performed by the autobiographers, and women as well as men frequently took on this work.[84] There was plenty to do besides. George Mitchell was 'proud to say that I have filled every office in that [Methodist] church, except preacher, which a man could occupy'.[85] In small, rural parishes, chapel service was usually conducted on a very small scale, whilst those living in cities were sometimes drawn into more ambitious enterprises. In London, Robert Skeen became a member of the Church of the United Brethren (also known as the Moravians), and later became a steward with responsibility for 'the receipt of all contributions and payment of all expenses'.[86] Samuel Catton set up a Bible Society in West Ham and following its success helped to found an analogous society for the 'Ladies'.[87] In Glasgow, Andrew Aird started up a 'Christian Institute' for young men over the age of sixteen.[88] In the new churches, particularly in the cities, humble, barely educated men learned about local leadership and organisation and in the process gained a measure of importance in their communities.

Even the very poor could find themselves in positions of authority in these chapels, especially at the more humble ones in remote, rural areas. We have already encountered Joseph Mayett, who had joined a small religious sect while serving in the militia. On obtaining his discharge and returning home to his Buckinghamshire parish of Quainton, he resumed work as an agricultural labourer. There he faced chronic underemployment and crushing poverty till the end of his days, often turning to the parish when lack of work or low wages left him unable to earn his food. But poor as he was, Joseph joined with a group of inhabitants – all of them 'poor and in narrow Circumstance of life' – to build a Baptist chapel in the village. He promised to contribute a shilling out of his weekly earnings, though he was, inevitably, frequently unable to pay even this small sum. Over the following years, he also served as a deacon in the church, contributed to debates about eternal election, played a leading role in teaching in the Sunday school, visited the sick, and, after finding that his brother and his wife had 'embazeled the money', installed himself as the chapel's treasurer.[89]

The evangelicals, the Methodists in particular, have often had a bad press. Their dark and forbidding theology, their impatience with the Chartists and other social reformers, their self-satisfaction and tendency to schism – for these and other failings the Nonconformists have been roundly condemned.[90] But whatever the truth of these charges, Joseph Mayett's tale reminds us of the radical and empowering dimension of these grassroots religious organisations. Joseph was a poor man eking out a precarious living as an agricultural labourer. With the exception of a twelve-year stint in the militia, he spent his life in the village where he was born, until his early death aged fifty-six. Yet he still played a very active part in the life of Quainton's Baptist Chapel. The dissenting chapels offered a space for the poor to explore their own souls and exercise authority over others. Once again we are confronted with the fact that the dissenting churches were at ease with poverty. Their ease risked shading into an unpleasant complacency but it also permitted the marking out of new social spaces in which even the very poor could take control of their own lives and those of others within their community.

Of course, the independence that many a dissenting chapel seemed bent on developing in its members could have unintended (and unwished for) consequences. The difficulty is illustrated in the story of John Stradley. The illegitimate child of unknown parents, John had been abandoned as an infant at the London Foundling Hospital in 1757. Following a parish apprenticeship to a blacksmith, he spent most of his adult life working at the Royal Arsenal in Woolwich, semi-literate and wholly outside the influence of any church. When confined to his bed by ill health, however, he began to read through a copy of Harvey's *Meditations* lent to him by a friend. His reading led him to decide to join a church, but he 'never knew aney thing a bout religion before having never heard a Gospel

Sermon' and was therefore 'quite at a loss to know what Demoniation of Profession' to join. He decided to go to 'the place of worship in Plumsted'.[91] But no sooner had he joined than further reflection led him to leave his new spiritual home. As John explained, a friend from the chapel had confided his belief in baptism and John turned to his bible to convince him of his error: 'but to my great surprise as I read the Scripture of Etirnal truth I found indeed it was the command of God'. The minister and other members of the Plumstead chapel tried to dissuade them, but Stradley and his friend stood firm and left the chapel to join the local Baptist church instead.[92]

Many times we may observe the autobiographers joining one church, engaging in its prayer and discussion groups, and eventually turning up evidence that caused them to reject the church that had encouraged them to think about their faith in the first place. William Thomas Swan followed the same path as John Stradley after his Bible study 'led [him] into a firm perssiasion of believers baptism'. He made the mistake of trying to persuade other members of Mr Hyatt's Independent chapel to become baptised as well, which prompted Mr Hyatt to pay him a visit: he 'beg'd me if it was so, to withdraw quietly, and not take a multitude with me'. This, in the end, Swan wisely did.[93] Needless to say though, the autobiographers were as busy deserting the Baptists as they were joining. Samuel Catton set out as a Baptist, but started to become 'very uneasy about the doctrine of predestination'. After much consideration, he resigned as a member and shortly after joined the Society of Friends.[94] On the other hand, Benjamin North's religious conversion had initially led him to the Quakers, but after further consideration, he joined the Wesleyan Methodists instead. North admitted that these two Churches represented two extremes and that some might accuse him of swinging 'from the quiet Quaker to the noisy Methodist'. He stoutly defended his decision by affirming he 'had a right to think and act for myself'.[95]

Not only did the autobiographers abandon one denomination for another, they also flitted around within their denominations, deserting one chapel for another whose pastor and congregation accorded better with their religious views or their temperament, or which was simply easier to get to. Thomas Cooper, for instance, switched from the Primitive Methodists to the Wesleyan Methodists because some of the members of his Primitive chapel had objected to his reading books other than the Bible.[96] It was hardly any less than could be expected. Churches which invited their members to reflect upon their teaching and participate in their running were nurturing skills that could not always be comfortably contained within the institutions in which they had been taught.

Spiritual and doctrinal differences formed the mainstay of most movement between faiths, but a host of more mundane and temporal concerns had the capacity to divide congregations, and as the evangelical revival gathered pace many chapels contained members with the skills to set up rival institutions of their own if their ministers did not provide just the kind of Christianity they desired. Music was a perennial source of conflict. In Haworth, Yorkshire, the peace that John Kitson and his wife enjoyed at Mr Oddy's chapel was disturbed by a dispute which broke out between Mr Oddy and his flock 'over musick'. Six members left the chapel and found themselves a barn for meeting and preaching in. Kitson and his wife joined the secession. For a while the seceders continued to worship in the barn, though in time they built a new chapel at Hall Green, which remains a thriving Baptist chapel today.[97] Meanwhile in London, John James Bezer (like many other autobiographers) taught in his local Sunday school. He found the parson to be 'very proud and overbearing' and took particular exception to his attempts to prevent the scholars from singing. John did not let the overbearing parson tyrannise him for long. He and one of the deacons simply 'headed a little band of malcontents, and opened an opposition shop to preach the gospel of brotherhood in'.[98]

Personalities were at the root of the conflict that John Wood remembered. John described the 'troublesome times' that had commenced in Allerton when the pastor of the Independent chapel had died and Mr Hinchcliffe was elected as his successor. It was a controversial choice. Hinchcliffe's abilities as a preacher were (in Wood's opinion) 'below average' and he soon began falling out with members of the congregation and using the pulpit to make personal attacks on his enemies. His high-handed and authoritarian manner stiffened the resolve of his opponents and when he refused to resign the pastorate, a small party arranged 'to have him forcible ejected'.[99] Church meetings were held. Trustee meetings were held. All to no avail. It was only when the disaffected congregation decided to take possession of the church by changing the locks that Mr Hinchcliffe finally admitted defeat and left the area. But as John Wood noted, though Mr Hinchcliffe may have been removed the damage caused by the affair was more lasting. During the conflict, much of the congregation had fallen away and some had set about building a new Independent chapel in the village. After Hinchcliffe had been removed, those who had remained loyal to the chapel started rebuilding its fortunes by obtaining a preacher, some singers and a new clerk.[100] Those now busy with building their new chapel were in no mood to return. The outcome was a splintered congregation and the whole affair left Wood wishing that 'half the energy displayed in these quarrels was displayed in the charity and good works which adorn the Christian profession'.[101]

Unquestionably, however, the greatest losers were the Anglicans. Loyalty and tradition had sustained the Anglicans through most of the eighteenth century, but as ever more alternatives emerged, loyalty and tradition were losing their power.[102] Some deserted their local parish church over relatively trivial matters. For example, John Bennett and his wife left Dowry Chapel, the chapel of ease to the church of St Andrew in Clifton, Bristol, because they were unhappy with the way their curate, Mr Flaxman, had been treated.[103] Others harboured more fundamental disagreements with a church that failed to meet their spiritual needs. In Preston, Benjamin Shaw was an Anglican in name until his late twenties. He was 'much atatched' to the established Church, though he had to admit that it was 'seldom' that he actually attended its services.[104] In 1799, an acquaintance invited him to accompany him to his Baptist chapel and to his surprise Shaw 'liked the Sermon very well, & thought there was more in religion than I had thought'. Nevertheless, a lifetime's loyalty to the Church of England was not easily discarded and rather than return to the Baptist chapel, he became a more regular worshipper at the Anglican parish of St George's. It was only after many months that Benjamin admitted to himself that there was 'nothing that I wanted there', and began, with his wife, to attend the Methodist chapel instead.[105]

Some writers found that leaving one church for another resolved their religious doubts. Others, inevitably, found that their enquiries led them out of the church altogether. Christopher Thomson owed much of his education to the charity of a wealthy local Methodist, Mr Thompson. Under such guidance, it was no surprise that Christopher soon became an 'accredited Methodist' and 'zealous young sectarian'.[106] But his schooling also instilled a love of reading and to encourage this, his father paid his subscription to one of Hull's private circulating libraries. Thomson was so engrossed in his first book from the library – *Splendid Miseries* – that he was very late for church and called to account for his absence in front of the bench of class leaders. The senior warned him that if he 'did not at once, and unconditionally, renounce all books, except such as they approve of, I was forever lost!'[107] Thomson did not renounce the books. He renounced, after much soul-searching, the Methodists instead. That was the trouble with independent thought. Whilst reading, Bible study and discussion were things to be welcomed, they opened up possibilities that challenged the authority of those who had encouraged them.

Let us close this chapter with one more example from the autobiographies. William Hanson was born in the Yorkshire parish of Soyland. It was a weaving parish, and William spent his life as a weaver, working both handlooms and power looms, regularly moving with his family throughout the district, as one opportunity closed and others opened. At one point, the family settled in Hightown, a village near Cleckheaton. They began worshipping at the Independent chapel, but none of his younger children could enter the Sunday school because they were told it was full. So were the schools at Hightown's Methodist Chapel and parish church. There were vacancies at the parish school at nearby Hartishead, but Hanson hardly thought it was suitable as 'the old clergyman went with a whip on his shoulder to keep the children quiet'.[108] What was a chapel-going man with six children and not a single place available in any of the local Sunday schools supposed to do?

Hanson did the obvious thing: he 'resolved to open my own house for a Sunday School'. The news spread like wildfire and before long some of the 'gentlemen at Cleckheaton' paid him a visit to see what was going on. Hanson told the gentlemen what he thought: 'they did well for the heathen abroad,' he told them, 'but too much overlooked the heathen at home.' They had plenty of qualified teachers at Cleckheaton, why not send a few over to help run a 'branch school' at Hightown? The gentlemen could not but agree. They asked Hanson to scour Hightown for a suitable room, and once he had found one, agreed to pay £3 a year for it. He and a few others 'set things in order' for the opening of the school. Hanson and his friends were now in charge of a Sunday school funded by the gentlemen, but controlled by themselves.

The significance of Hanson's story is easily lost on a modern audience. What could be less remarkable than the Yorkshire weaver and his long-forgotten Sunday school? But this is not simply a story about a school. It is also about a man who did not think too highly of what the local churches had to offer, so set about making a few changes himself. It is about a humble working man telling the gentlemen from Cleckheaton what he thought ought to be done, taking their money, spending it as he saw fit. It is about a man who grasped at the chance to change society. Hanson's actions allow us to glimpse the emergence of a new social order, an order where even the humble weaver had the power to shape his world.

Hanson was a product of the evangelical revival. Throughout his adult life, he was deeply involved in everything Nonconformity had to offer – its prayer groups, experience meetings and a network of like-minded individuals given to lively discourse on matters religious. For all that we might point to precedents or limitations to the evangelical revival, we should recognise the change it brought to working-class communities. The evangelical churches invited male and female, young and old, respectable and very poor to take control of their lives. They empowered their members. And as such, they played their part in the transition to modern society.

# CHAPTER NINE

# Sons of Freedom

In the towns and villages of the south men's minds seemed to be slumbering, until the puff of the steam-engine should awaken them. (Frost, pp. 9–10)

There was no Political Union in the village, there was no Odd Fellows' Lodge, there was no circle of congenial spirits like those with whom he had associated for the last two years; but the young man was not inconvenienced by the deprivation. He became a leader where he had been a follower. (*Scenes from my Life by a Working Man*, p. 68)

JAMES WATSON WAS 'born of poor parents, in an obscure town' and raised by his mother following the death of his father when he was barely a year old. As an adult, however, Watson's life was anything but obscure. Whilst working as a warehouseman in Leeds, Watson's sense of injustice was sparked when he stumbled across a meeting of workmen reading works by Thomas Wooler, Richard Carlile and William Cobbett. He instantly fell in with the Radicals and in the 1820s emerged as a leading figure in the movement. He sold unstamped newspapers, learned typesetting so that he might set and sell his own imprints of radical texts, joined the Co-operative movement, helped to found the Working Man's Association, and sat on the committee appointed to draw up the People's Charter. It was a political career of considerable achievement, one that frequently brought him to the attention of the authorities, and on three occasions it landed him behind bars. Yet Watson's six-page autobiography touched but briefly on the substance of his long and varied political career and concluded instead with the following thought: 'in what I have said, I have had but one object in view – to show my fellow-workmen that the humblest amongst them may render effectual aid to the cause of progress'.[1] Watson had been born into the lowest station of life yet he rose to prominence as an effective actor on the political stage, and it was this – the sheer fact of having engaged in the political sphere – that Watson wanted to emphasise. And it is precisely this transformation of 'humble' men into 'effectual' political agitators that forms the subject of this chapter.

To understand this process, we will need to turn back to the early 1790s and the founding of the London Corresponding Society. Created in January 1792 by a shoemaker named Thomas Hardy, the LCS provides the earliest example of a working man exercising modern political leadership, a novelty that would within a few decades become an accepted part of the political landscape. But in the 1790s, such things were not to be. The government responded to all demands for new political rights with an unflinching nerve. The so-called Two Acts of 1795 attempted to snuff out political agitation by restricting the size of meetings to fifty persons and the Corresponding Societies Act of 1799 outlawed the reform societies outright. By the end of the decade, the LCS and like-minded sister organisations had been crushed, their members dispersed, and the matter of votes for the working man firmly removed from the political agenda.[2]

The political calm that followed proved to be transitory. Although repressive tactics initially weakened the clamour for reform, silencing shoemakers like Thomas Hardy proved a more difficult matter and before long fresh calls for political rights began to surface. By the end of the 1810s they had coalesced into a mass movement that could not be contained. The passing of the Reform Act in 1832, which extended the vote to some better-off property owners but left the working man firmly shut out, added urgency to their demands. In 1838, a committee of six MPs and six working men published the People's Charter, calling for (amongst other things) universal male suffrage. It sparked a new campaign – Chartism – which led a highly effective agitation throughout the 1840s. Although the working man's vote was not obtained until 1867, the political landscape had been transformed by mid-century. 'Humble' men like Watson had entered the political fray.[3]

Arguably, then, the broad contours of the rise of political awareness amongst the working classes are well known. Yet the autobiographies have something to say about why and how working men moved from the margins of the political process to the centre. My suggestion is that the early nineteenth century witnessed a radical change in local power relations, throwing wide open new opportunities for working men to exercise power within their communities. At first they did so on a very small scale, often on matters that were not political in nature – here a man founding a reading group; there one setting up a Sunday school; there another elected the secretary of his trade club. Yet the grasping of such opportunities and the exercise of power in non-political contexts was an important first step towards entering the political sphere, and critical in enabling the emergence of large-scale political movements.

But this is to anticipate. Let us begin at the beginning. Let us start by turning back to the eighteenth century and ask simply: why did so little happen before 1820? If we take it as read that the poor had always had plenty to feel disgruntled about, why had they traditionally failed to articulate that discontent in an effective, or even audible, manner?

These simple questions are difficult to answer because there was very little engagement in the political sphere of any kind by the autobiographers before the 1820s. Just two describe playing a political role before 1800: Thomas Hardy and Francis Place. A further three, Thomas Preston, Samuel Bamford and Allen Davenport became active in the 1810s. Given that around a third of the autobiographers reached adulthood before 1820 (120 in all) the proportion who were politically active was extremely small. Indeed, our writers confirm just what we would expect: in the eighteenth century working men found the world of politics difficult to access. For women it was all but impossible.

Yet if the numbers are small, it is nevertheless interesting to explore how these five men travelled the distance from working man to working-class politician. We should start with Thomas Hardy – the shoemaker who founded the London Corresponding Society in 1792. Hardy was born and raised in Scotland. It was here that his grandfather had taught him shoe-making and it was here that he worked for James Wilson, a shoemaker who had recently moved to Falkirk from London. Wilson's stories of the great metropolis excited Hardy's curiosity and prompted him to migrate to London in 1774. And once there, he did what many migrants do: looked around for things to remind him of home. 'Being of a contemplative and serious turn of mind', he gravitated to the Dissenters and soon became a member of the Crown Court Church, a Scottish Presbyterian church in Covent Garden.[4]

Hardy had worshipped at the church for the best part of a decade when Mr Cruden, their much-loved pastor, died and Hardy found himself drawn into 'some transactions' that he felt deserved a place in his autobiography. A succession of hopeful candidates took the pulpit on Sunday, but it was not until Mr James Chambers took a turn, nearly two years after Cruden's death, that a man of a suitable calibre was found. Members of the congregation had been drifting away, and Hardy saw in the appointment of this charismatic preacher the chance to revive his beloved church's flagging fortunes. He seized the moment. He wrote letters to Mr Chambers and called, chaired and addressed meetings of the congregation. Finally, with the majority of the congregation behind him, he appointed a deputation to request the Elders to call Chambers as pastor. But his request fell upon deaf ears. The Elders were resolutely opposed to giving Mr Chambers the call and after undertaking research into Hardy's candidate, claimed to have discovered that Chambers was a bigamist. More meetings were called and both parties agreed to meet with Chambers in order to determine the truth of the matter. To Hardy's dismay the charge proved true. With his reputation in tatters, Hardy expeditiously let the matter drop.[5]

Hardy's little crusade in his Crown Court Church may not have reached quite the conclusion he had hoped, but it certainly was not effort wasted. It had taught him how to organise an effective campaign, lessons that were valuable when, a few years later, he hit upon the idea of a 'London Corresponding Society'. Having decided that the corruption and greed of politicians elected on a very narrow franchise lay at the root of the nation's ills, Hardy determined upon a society which would work to enhance the political rights of disenfranchised working men such as himself. He 'drew up some rules, with a preamble to them, for the management of the Society' and discussed them with three friends. The four men all agreed to become members and to meet on a weekly basis. At their first meeting, Hardy brought along a book in which new members put down their names and a record of their weekly penny subscriptions was kept. Hardy was appointed treasurer and secretary.[6] From these tiny origins the LCS grew into a national movement with several thousand members organised into dozens of branches in London and beyond. As we have already seen, its existence provoked sufficient concern in government circles to trigger the enactment of some of the most notoriously repressive legislation of the eighteenth century, including, in 1799, an Act which outlawed it by name.

In the early years of its existence, the identity of the founder of the LCS was shrouded in mystery. Hardy did not reveal his role in the society's creation until 1794. Until then the authorities had persisted in regarding it as an offshoot of the Constitutional Society and the creation of a barrister with a long history of involvement in the reform movement: John Horne

Tooke. For how (they no doubt reasoned) could such a pernicious and threatening institution possibly be the creation of a lowly shoemaker?[7] Yet the LCS was indeed the work of Thomas Hardy and to understand how Hardy played a role which was simply unthinkable to contemporaries we need look no further than the dissenting church to which he belonged. Like most such churches, Hardy's Crown Court Church expected its members to play their part in its day-to-day running; it had given Hardy a thorough grounding in the art of campaigning. What Hardy's experiences teach us is that the emergence of working-class politics is not simply a story of new ideas about social and political injustice but also a tale of working men learning about governance. Once shoemakers and other lowly workmen understood how to mount a campaign, a new era of working-class politics became possible.

The London Corresponding Society was Thomas Hardy's creation, but Hardy was not the only autobiographer to play a prominent role in the organisation. Two years after its foundation, Francis Place, a young breeches-maker struggling to escape from poverty and make his way in the world, also entered the LCS as a member. Over the next few years, Place rapidly rose through the society's ranks though he, like Hardy, had not started out as a political reformer at all. Place had become a member of the Breeches Makers Benefit Society in about 1791. The society was a private club into which members paid a weekly subscription to insure them against future ill health or unemployment, and Place initially had little to do with it beyond paying his dues and turning up on the night when new stewards were chosen. After two years of uneventful membership, however, the society struck for an advance of wages and Place stepped forward to lead an ultimately unsuccessful strike.[8]

After the strike and owing to his role in it, Place was unable to find work making leather breeches, so instead he found employment making stuff breeches – trousers made of wool. But his old workmates did not forget how adroitly Place had managed the strike. The following year, a group of them approached him and asked him to set up a strike fund on their behalf; Place agreed and became the 'secretary and confidential manager' of a society which did not (he pointed out) represent the interests of his own trade. Place was then approached by 'the Carpenters' to form another society; and then by the 'journeymen plumbers' to assist in setting up a benefit club. He also 'drew up articles for several other clubs, and assisted in their formation'.[9] Place's skills were sufficient for him to earn an income from his work for these clubs – a useful little sideline that helped him to recover the position he had lost during the catastrophic strike of 1793.

Place had helped several groups of skilled workers to build up their strike funds, so his interest in the London Corresponding Society should occasion little surprise. He was introduced to the society in 1794, at just the moment when Hardy was arrested and put on trial for high treason, and became a member of the Covent Garden division with scarcely a hesitation.[10] By this time, Place was already a skilled and able organiser with proven abilities as a public speaker, treasurer and leader. His fellow members of the Covent Garden division instantly recognised that Place was a man who had more to offer than his weekly dues. Soon they had elected him their delegate and he was representing them at the weekly meetings of the LCS' General Committee.[11] A year later he became chair of the General Committee, and shortly after that the society's assistant secretary. Yet Place's rapid rise within the LCS rested not upon the superiority of his political views, nor even the fact that his views chimed particularly well with those of Hardy and others in the organisation; in fact he left the LCS in 1797 disillusioned by the turn it was taking. The reason that Place briefly emerged as a leading light within the organisation was more mundane: he was one of very few members who had the skills to do so.

A similar tale can be told of the three other men who became politically active before 1820: Thomas Preston, Allen Davenport and Samuel Bamford. Thomas Preston has a place in history because of the role he played in calling the famous meetings at Spa Fields in 1816 to demand (amongst other things) political change. But Preston's political career, just like those of Hardy and Place, did not start with politics. As a young shoemaker in Ireland he had fallen in with striking shop-mates, and he, like Place, had emerged as a leader of the strike.[12] On his return to London in the 1790s, he became a member of the LCS, and there thoroughly imbibed the reform rhetoric, though he did not remain a member for long and appears to have retired from the political scene after leaving the society in the mid–1790s.[13] By 1810, he had returned to public life through membership of some of London's many 'literary societies' intended for the 'improvement of the intellects' of their members through reading and debating. Although Preston did not provide much detail, these societies were probably a cross between a mutual improvement society and a political society – reading groups with a particular interest in political thought.[14] At any rate, through his involvement with trade clubs and strike action, the LCS, and his discussion groups, Preston had a wide range of experience to draw upon when he called the Spa Fields meetings.

The other two writers to become involved in politics before the 1820s also trod a path through various non-political organisations. Bamford helped to found a Hampden Reform Club in his weaving village, Middleton, and became its secretary in 1816. In the years following he emerged as a key figure in reform politics and in 1819 he led Middleton's contingent to St Peter's Fields, where the infamous Peterloo massacre occurred. In his autobiography, Bamford pointed to the Nonconformist Sunday schools, which had in his opinion produced 'many working men of sufficient talent to become readers, writers, and speakers in the village meetings for parliamentary reform'.[15] Meanwhile Davenport had received his political education from his involvement with his shoemakers' trade union. He became a member of the 'fifth division of women's men' (men making women's shoes) in 1813.[16] Soon after, he became their delegate and by the end of the decade he was writing articles for publication in the Radical press and was an active member of a group discussing and promoting the ideas of one of the most influential Radicals to emerge in the 1790s – Thomas Spence.[17]

All five of our politicians moved seamlessly from one form of social engagement to another. Each learned the rudiments of social activism in one context and soon put his learning to use elsewhere. Yet our writers also reveal that men like themselves were few and far between. So much is certainly clear from Francis Place's account of his role as a union organiser in late eighteenth-century London. He (you may recall) had been hired by the carpenters, the journeymen plumbers and 'several others' to set up and manage a strike fund. The carpenters and plumbers had a clear sense of what they wanted: a strike fund which could be built up in prosperous times and then used to support its members when they decided to strike for an advance of wages. But they did not know how to arrange this themselves. Had they not chanced upon Place it is doubtful whether their plans would ever have got off the ground. By the same token, the LCS was hardly awash with competent organisers, and Place ended up near the helm simply because his experiences with the trade clubs had taught him how to get a job done.

Much the same was true of Thomas Preston. With a history of involvement in strike action and Radical politics, Preston's emergence as a spokesman for a group of men opposed to the use of machinery was not entirely uncharacteristic. Still, there was actually something of a mismatch between Preston's agenda and that of the artisans opposing new machines. Indeed, Preston admitted that when he became the spokesman of the 'anti-machinists' he did so 'accidentally', adding that he did 'not accord with all their views'. The drive for Preston's involvement came from the artisans, not from him. He 'grew in favour' with them, he wrote; eventually they 'elected me their secretary'.[18] It seems likely that they decided to work with Preston because they knew there was nobody within their own ranks capable of advocating their concerns. Like Place's carpenters and plumbers, they were looking for a leader and settled upon Preston more because he was competent than for any deeper ideological reasons.

It would be difficult to overestimate the significance of this absence of working-class men able to play a leadership role. Obviously it stood firmly in the way of effective political expression: without a cadre of men competent to run a campaign any attempt at action was doomed to failure.[19] More subtly, however, it helped to colour the action that did take place. Political ideas had to be channelled through the small number of men able to organise action. Whether it is Place setting up a trade club for the plumbers or Preston taking on the anti-machinists' cause, political ideas were finding expression through the efforts of men who had the skill to communicate them but did not necessarily share their views.

It is almost as though Thomas Hardy and others in the LCS understood precisely how the meagre political education of its members hampered their efforts. At least, they were certainly busy trying to remedy the situation. In Place's recollections he described how he would meet with other members of the society for 'readings, conversations and discussions' on Sunday evenings. The chairman chose the week's reading, the book was passed between the members during the week, and on the Sunday the chairman read a portion of it. After his reading, the other 'persons present were invited to make remarks thereon . . . then there was a general discussion. No one was permitted to speak more than once.'[20] It was essentially a mutual improvement society, introducing its members to the ideas that inspired the LCS and teaching them how to debate them. In similar vein, Preston's account of his 'literary societies' elided the educational with the political. Place was already a highly skilled organiser by the time he entered the LCS, yet he nonetheless considered these meetings 'highly useful' and 'very important' and took pains to emphasise the great things which many of its members had gone on to achieve. In part, of course, Place was positioning his discussion group in the self-improving narrative he wished to construct, yet we should not dismiss the truth of his account simply because of this. Reading groups of this nature were important in training a generation of politicians with no prior experience of political leadership. In other words, the LCS was not simply an expression of working-class politics: it was also instrumental in *forming* a new generation of working-class politicians.

Hardy, Place, Preston, Bamford and Davenport were but one very small part of the political scene in Britain around the turn of the century. Yet the detailed reconstruction that each provided of his political awakening enable us to say something about the world in which they lived. All five had cut their teeth on causes other than those for which they became famed. Each followed his own route, but there were three discernible points of entry: the dissenting churches and their Sunday schools; the trade clubs and benefit societies; and mutual improvement societies.[21] Furthermore, political activism was very much the exception rather than the rule. Well over a hundred of the autobiographers reached adulthood before 1820 and therefore might have become involved in politics: only five actually did, a participation rate of less than 5 per cent.[22] For all the achievements of these five men, then, the dominant theme to emerge prior to 1820 concerns the obstacles that stood in the way of an effective working-class politics rather than its achievements. Working-class communities simply lacked men with the ability to lead, organise and manage.

Nor is this entirely surprising. All five of our politicians learned about activism from non-political institutions: unions, Sunday schools and so forth. Yet none of these institutions was well developed in the first two decades of the nineteenth century, so the opportunities for a political education were far from numerous. In fact the autobiographies enable us to demonstrate the extent to which these kinds of societies had penetrated. In all, just six writers (in addition to the above five) had entered the world of public affairs: William Fairburn, Timothy Claxton, Charles Campbell, William Innes, Thomas Carter and Samuel Catton.

Fairburn and Claxton were members of mutual improvement societies. Fairburn described himself as the 'leader' of his discussion group and Claxton helped with some friends to found a 'Society of Ingenious Working Mechanics' with the object of providing a library, lectures and discussion for its members. Both Fairburn and Claxton were living in London at the time and used their respective societies purely as a means of enhancing their education rather than as a springboard to the world of politics.[23] Meanwhile, in a village just outside Glasgow, Campbell became a member of a very small reading group: it was avowedly non-political in intention and like Fairburn and Claxton he never did develop any political interests.[24] Thomas Carter, William Innes and Samuel Catton, on the other hand, had become involved in the Sunday school movement. Catton later promoted Sunday schools, both in Eyke, the Suffolk village whence he hailed, and in Plaistow, just outside London, where he resided.[25] But Fairburn, Claxton, Campbell, Carter, Innes and Catton made up 6 per cent of the autobiographers who reached adulthood before 1820, which suggests that working-class associational activity was still very much in its infancy. Given that clubs and societies which were not political in nature formed an important part of the working man's political training, the slow proliferation of such societies before 1820 helps to explain the difficulties faced by Hardy and other working-class politicians.

These six men were throwing themselves into their improvement societies and Sunday school work in the first decade or so of the nineteenth century. Looking further back into the eighteenth century turns up no evidence of anything that might be regarded as public work. No improvement societies, no trade clubs, no Sunday school teachers. Just as there is no evidence of working-class involvement in the political sphere prior to the 1790s, so are there no examples of working people exercising power in their communities or working collectively in pursuit of common goals. The only possible exception to this was Methodism. From as early as the 1740s, the Methodists had shown a willingness to harness the talents and visions of humble working men, and as the century progressed other Nonconformist denominations proved similarly open to preachers and church-builders in smocks and overalls. Yet Nonconformity stood alone in the encouragement it gave to working-class engagement and leadership, and throughout the eighteenth century the autobiographers who rose to prominence in the Nonconformist movement invariably confined their energies to the church which had nurtured them.

Not that the eighteenth century failed to produce men who made a mark on public life. The earlier autobiographies do contain a number of men who might be considered high achievers: James Ferguson, astronomer and maker of scientific instruments: William Hutton, bookseller and best-selling historian: William Gifford, satirist, editor and translator. These and others managed to gain an education and to enter the world of public affairs once they had done so. Yet by that time, all had left behind the poverty and manual labour which had characterised their early lives. Moreover their journeys from workman to citizen were taken individually. These were tales of individuals striving alone against the odds, not of the disadvantaged combining with others similarly circumstanced in life in pursuit of shared goals. There was, then, something entirely new about the collective endeavours that were starting to take shape in the early nineteenth century. The 1790s saw working men not simply gaining an education and reaping personal benefit, but organising into societies and institutions with committees, secretaries, rules and agendas with the hope of benefiting their kind. It was behaviour with no historical precedent.

Until the 1820s, working-class forays into collective action were experimental, small-scale, tentative, and not wholly successful. After 1820, however, this trend continued at a much accelerated rate. The autobiographies even permit us to put some figures to this process. As we have just seen, before 1820 about 5 per cent of the autobiographers were politically active. Thereafter, the figure always remained above 20 per cent.[26] And it was not just the politics that grew. All forms of social engagement and working-class leadership flourished from the 1820s. If we add together all those writers who played a role in a church or Sunday school, or in the trade union movement or in co-operative adult education, a further 25 per cent are accounted for.[27] Putting the two figures together, we have over 45 per cent of all writers playing a leadership role for some cause, large or small, political or not. The combined figure for the period between 1790 and 1820 was about 11 per cent. And, as already noted, before 1790 there is no evidence of collective social or political engagement at all.

Relating these figures to the actual levels of engagement amongst the working class is of course impossible. Life-writing remained indelibly linked with achievement – years of service to the Sunday school, the trade club or the Chartists provided just the kind of duty that fitted the autobiographical narrative. Little wonder, then, that public service figures so prominently in the autobiographies. The point rather is to find a means of comparing the periods before and after 1820 and of comparing involvement in different kinds of activity. The figures suggest that in the 1820s engagement in the public sphere rapidly ceased to be a marginal activity and moved into the mainstream, with nearly half of all writers playing some kind of role. They also reveal an interesting symmetry between political activism and other forms of social engagement. Throughout the entire period, the number of men involved in politics was roughly matched by an equal number of men involved in a wide range of non-political organisations. It is difficult to escape the conclusion that working-class politics formed just one edge of a broader involvement in the social sphere. Thus understanding the great upsurge in political activity in the late 1830s and 1840s requires us to grasp the shift to much higher levels of social engagement that occurred at just the same time.

Our starting point must be the mutual improvement societies. No other form of club or society was mentioned more frequently in the autobiographies than the humble reading group – thirty-five writers had belonged to a book club and a further twelve had been members of the more formal Mechanics' Institutes. And not only were they numerous, they also enjoyed strong connections with political activism. Between 1820 and 1850 forty-five of the autobiographers were involved in a national political movement in some capacity; a little less than half of these writers, nineteen in all, were also members of a mutual improvement society at some stage.

Several writers made the links between their reading group and their emergence as a politician quite explicit. Take, for instance, Thomas Cooper who led the Chartists in Leicester in the early 1840s. His period of leadership was relatively brief and ended with his imprisonment for sedition in 1843, yet for a few years Cooper had been at the forefront of the movement – a figure of national, as well as local, significance. In his autobiography, he described how, as a young man many years earlier, he had been a member of a small mutual improvement society established by a friend in his home town of Gainsborough. The society, he recalled, 'was valuable to me'. The small club had taught him to read with purpose, collect his thoughts, write an essay, present an argument, and speak in public – all skills which would prove invaluable to the future Chartist leader.[28] Another leading Chartist, Robert Lowery, the Newcastle delegate in the late 1830s, was also involved in a 'debating society'. His society comprised about twenty men and met weekly to discuss a topic introduced by 'the proposer' either 'orally or by a written discourse'. He said: 'I derived much advantage from these discussions; they set us a-thinking and reading on the topics, and accustomed me to try to arrange in a consecutive order all the arguments I could think of.' When he entered he could 'not speak a few consecutive sentences extempore, but I gradually got quicker in arranging my ideas', learning to 'dot down' answers as he listened so as to repeat them 'with more clearness and force'.[29] Both Cooper and Lowery were clear about the education they received from their discussion groups. Of course, it broadened their intellectual horizons by introducing them to the previously closed world of political thought, but it also gave them basic training in the art of public speaking and debate.

And the effects of these small reading groups rippled beyond the great Chartist leaders. Improvement societies played a part in the creation of the Coopers and the Lowerys; they also helped to improve the political skills of working men occupying far less elevated positions in the new working-class political movements of the 1830s and 1840s. Even the most modest education marked a man out from the rest of his peers and small provincial

Chartist societies were not slow to exploit the talents of the most skilled organisers in their midst. John Leatherland, for instance, was a ribbon weaver living and working in the Northamptonshire town of Kettering. In the early 1830s he joined with the seven other men in his workshop to purchase books for discussion, and their endeavours blossomed into a more ambitious 'Mutual Instruction Society' with a programme of lectures and classes, many of them delivered by the society's own members. Leatherland recalled how much he had delighted in the transition from student to 'professor' and described how he had learned to address the small audiences that came to his lectures.[30] It was not entirely surprising, therefore, that when Chartist fervour reached Kettering the reformers endeavoured to persuade Leatherland to play an active role in the local branch.[31] Another autobiographer entered a night school and joined a society for mutual improvement with, initially at least, a view to improving his situation in life. The dream of social advancement proved elusive, but his education did draw him into a new world of political activism. In addition to his mutual improvement society, the anonymous writer attended political meetings and took 'a subordinate part in the agitation of some of the great questions of the day – Reform, the Corn Laws, and Temperance'.[32] Leatherland and our unnamed autobiographer never became leaders of the causes they espoused. Their contributions have long since been forgotten. Yet each played his part at a local level; 'subordinate' players were no less valuable than leaders.

Mutual improvement societies helped to create a cadre of working-class men capable of mobilising political agitation. Yet in our haste to restore these overlooked clubs to their rightful place in history we should not neglect those whose programme of improvement did not take a political turn. Of the forty-seven men who belonged to a book club or mechanics' institute, nineteen had also entered politics. This still leaves twenty-eight men who had entered an improvement society but never engaged in the political sphere. In other words, men were just as likely to leave an improve-ment society with no political interests as they were to move into politics. These twenty-eight writers were engaged in activities that were wholly indistinguishable from the others we have looked at: reading and discussing political and other texts, organising members, collecting dues, issuing fines, and awarding prizes. They simply did not use this experience in order to engage in the political sphere.

For some men, the cultural and intellectual world they accessed through their discussion group was all the reward they desired. As Jacob Holkinson noted, his attendance at public lectures 'opened up a new and very extensive field of discovery'.[33] William Milne thought that attending the meetings of his mutual improvement association and listening to the monthly public lecture it organised 'has been of much service to me ever since'. He just never used his learning to enter politics.[34] So we should not regard mutual improvement societies simply as something that enabled political expression for the working classes. They were a significant development in their own right, providing working-class men with the opportunity to learn about and engage with the society they inhabited, part of the process by which working people acquired a voice for themselves and the capacity for action in the early nineteenth century.

The autobiographies suggest that mutual improvement societies were the single most significant route into politics after the 1820s. There were, of course, many others. In the eighteenth century, Thomas Hardy had gained valuable experience of public affairs through his involvement with the Crown Court Church in Covent Garden, and the dissenting churches remained an important means of political education throughout the nineteenth century as well. As new Dissent expanded rapidly from the 1790s so did the opportunities for working people to learn the art of governance. The range of roles filled by uneducated working men was large. From preaching to building new churches and congregations to distributing tracts and acting as treasurers, there was lots to be done, and performing this kind of service was an excellent way of gaining new and useful skills. Above all, however, the Nonconformists promoted their Sunday schools, and these small institutions played a special role in enhancing the political education of the working classes. At the simplest level, they helped to improve literacy amongst both children and adults, and literacy was of course pivotal to the success of political movements that aspired to be national in scope. Perhaps yet more importantly, however, they encouraged their students to ascend their ranks and take an active part in the day-to-day running of the school. As a result, they enabled humble, barely educated men to learn about local leadership and organisation, as well as to gain a measure of importance within their community.

The autobiographers frequently cited the Sunday schools as a precursor to their political activities: nine of the forty-five men involved in politics after 1820 had been a Sunday school teacher prior to their involvement in politics. John James Bezer spent much of his youth associated with the Raven Row Sunday School in Spitalfields – he attended for fifteen years in all and had inevitably become a teacher by the time he left. By his late teens, he arranged and taught classes in the school, led a singing class, distributed tracts, commenced chapel services, and gave addresses at prayer meetings. Bezer complained that he left Sunday school knowing next to nothing about arithmetic and writing, but he certainly knew plenty about the day-to-day running of a small organisation. He later joined the Chartists after attending a meeting at Lunt's coffee house and became a mid-level organiser, using skills, some of which which had, undoubtedly, been learned at his Sunday school.[35]

Or there is Emanuel Lovekin, working as a miner in the Staffordshire potteries. Following a stint at his Methodist Sunday school in his teens, Lovekin found that he was 'was looked up to as Something alien to the Common Class of young men'.[36] So it was hardly surprising that when a 'Sharp and Strong Agitation' in favour of the Chartists reached his Potteries village he was soon involved, and asked to serve as the secretary. Critics have frequently observed that Sunday schools were not radical in their critique of the social order, and there is certainly some substance to this claim.[37] But these schools did give working men the ability and confidence to interact with their neighbours and opened up the possibility that they might shape the world in which they lived. They remind us of the potential for discontinuity between intentions and outcomes, particularly when dealing with constituencies with no tradition of political engagement. Sunday schools offered their members a basic education and some experience of leadership, an empowering combination which could be put to good use in very different contexts.

Also important in forming working-class politicians were the unions and trade clubs. These had been a training ground for Francis Place and Thomas Preston in the 1790s, and the strong links between trade clubs and the reform societies had not gone unnoticed by the authorities. As a result, the clubs were targeted in the government's crackdown on political activity in the 1790s. The Combination Acts of 1799 and 1800 forbade workmen to 'combine' for higher wages or shorter working hours and forced the trade union movement underground for many years.[38] With their repeal in 1824, however, the trade clubs entered a new era of steady growth and were soon once more playing an important part in developing the political skills and ambitions of their members. A union or trade club needed to be managed, and so had the power to teach a man how to be a politician. Furthermore, by the 1830s the political reform movement had forged strong links with the trade unions. As a result, membership of a union could throw wide open the door to the most active political movements in the land.

Some of these themes are illustrated in the life story of Thomas Dunning, a self-taught shoemaker who served as secretary of the Nantwich Chartist Association between 1838 and 1842. Dunning's political career can be traced back to the early 1830s when, working as a shoemaker in Nantwich, he had joined the Cordwainers' Club, a shoemakers' union of around 500 members. Dunning had risen to prominence within the club when the local magistrates threatened to prosecute all its members on the grounds that the club had administered illegal oaths. The treasurer, the president and several other officers fled the town, leaving Dunning to fill the vacuum their departure created. In the months that followed, Dunning worked closely with the society's solicitor and in the process picked up a considerable and very useful knowledge of the law under which his work-mates were charged and of the workings of the courts. The case ended in the acquittal of all those involved, but landed the shoemakers with a large legal bill, and Dunning was once more active in devising ways to replenish the club's coffers.[39] When the Chartists arrived in Nantwich, then, it was almost inevitable that Dunning should become the secretary of the local association. In that capacity he organised large open-air meetings, presided over weekly shop meetings, collected a thousand signatures for the Charter, and ran a bookshop selling Radical publications.[40] It was a logical extension of the work that he had done for the Cordwainers' Club a few years earlier.

James Dawson Burn's membership of a trade society unlocked the world of politics in much the same way. Burn was born the illegitimate son of an itinerant beggar, at some point, he thought, between 1800 and 1803 – he was unique amongst the autobiographers in admitting to uncertainty about the date of his birth.[41] Burn also provided a particularly fine example of autobiographical writing. The story of his desperately poor childhood, his often absent mother, his intense yet troubled relationship with his stepfather, and his struggle for self-knowledge in the face of uncertain origins gripped the Victorian imagination. It was, unusually, a commercial success in its own time. From unstable beginnings, Burn's life took a more settled turn when he entered an apprenticeship as a hatter in his early twenties. He became involved in politics when he moved to Glasgow in 1831 and joined the hatters' trade club.[42] His hatters' union, he noted, had just amalgamated with other unions, so when he became their representative he was thrust into the midst of a large and highly active trade organisation. Representing the hatters at the general meeting swiftly got him elected to the Central Committee of the amalgamated union. And membership of this committee was a valuable learning experience for a man with almost no prior experience of public speaking. 'The fact was', he wrote, 'the Committee was an excellent school for young beginners in the science of oratory and public debating, and many of the members made no small proficiency in the art.'[43] What is more, at much the same time his amalgamated union was drawn into the orbit of the highly organised Radicals in western Scotland. In a matter of months, Burn had been catapulted from membership of a small hatters' club to the centre of reform agitation in one of the nation's most politicised cities. In his own words: 'I got into the gulf-stream of political agitation, and was carried onwards with amazing velocity.'[44]

Once again, however, although the trade clubs could be, and often were, a point of entry to the world of politics, it would be a mistake to collapse their existence down to little more than training grounds for would-be politicians. Elsewhere amongst the autobiographers were men whose loyalties lay foremost with their union. One such example is Edward Rymer. Rymer, like James Dawson Burn, had spent his childhood in abject poverty. He was seriously injured in a house fire when three years of age, which caused permanent damage to his right eye and to the right-hand side of his body. His father deserted the family three years later. Unsurprisingly, Rymer had been turned out to work at a young age, first as a cowherd, and subsequently as a trapper in a coal mine. He worked as a miner for most of his adult life, and in his late twenties established a branch of the Durham Miners' Union at Thornley – the start of a long and very active career as a trade unionist. For over thirty years, Rymer served as an agent and secretary of various unions, establishing several branches along the way and travelling through the coalfields of Lancashire, Yorkshire, Derbyshire, Durham, Northumberland and Gloucestershire in pursuit of his aims. Yet it was only at the tail end of his career that Rymer became involved in politics when he became a supporter of the Liberal Party, first in the Forest of Dean and thereafter in Yorkshire, where he spent the rest of his life. Rymer reminds us that unions were not simply a conduit to the political sphere. They were important working-class institutions in their own right, part of a broader social transition through which working men were starting to gain control of their own world.

As the nineteenth century progressed, ever more opportunities appeared. From the 1820s, the co-operative movement began to develop and these small institutions soon appear in the autobiographies as yet another source of education for aspiring politicians.[45] In fact, the co-operative movement helped to shape one of the most influential figures in the Chartist movement: William Lovett. Lovett joined the First London Co-operative

Trading Association, a small co-op modelled on a trading society recently established in Brighton, in the late 1820s. Each member paid a small weekly sum, and the combined amount was used to stock a shop with the items of most use to working families, all profits, of course, being ploughed back into the common fund. The movement was in its infancy when Lovett joined his London Co-operative, and a supporting organisation, the British Association for Promoting Co-operative Knowledge, was founded soon after to assist in the establishment of provincial trading associations. When its first secretary resigned, Lovett took up the post and in that capacity organised public meetings and facilitated communication between other associations. It was clearly an arena in which Lovett could learn and practise the skills that would, a decade later, promote him to the very head of the Chartist movement.[46]

Lovett learned about leadership by taking up the reins of a national organisation based in London, but even the smallest provincial co-operative expected its members to help with its running and could introduce them to a previously unknown world of social organisation. When John Wilson attended his first quarterly meeting after joining the Haswell Co-operative Society, he found there were just enough people in attendance to form the committee. Needless to say, he found himself placed on the committee and was soon hard at work trying to revive the co-op's flagging fortunes, even spending a short while as an assistant in the store.[47] Wilson could not but chuckle at the memory of his younger self and his manager, a former miner, trying to run Haswell's co-operative store: 'there never were two men more proficient in bungling,' he recalled. But bungling or otherwise, Wilson was learning new skills as well, no doubt, as building a reputation amongst his neighbours. It is perhaps significant that he described the miner with whom he worked as being 'as highly respected as he was known; a perfect gentleman, upright in conduct, courteous in manner'.[48]

From the 1830s, the temperance movement also became involved in the training of working-class politicians.[49] With its simple conversion narratives and its grassroots rather than top-down structure of organisation, the temperance movement could enhance the political skills of working men in a number of ways. Foremost perhaps was the encouragement it gave to uneducated working men to stand up and speak in public. One anonymous writer who had taken the pledge in the 1850s recalled how he had never liked to address his meeting, 'not being an educated man'. But one night there was no speaker to address them, so 'I stood up and said a few words'.[50] The humble temperance meeting was a rare space in which uneducated working men were thought to have something valuable to say, a small part of the process which helped to nurture the development of a working-class voice.

In addition, the temperance movement relied heavily upon the work of itinerant lecturers, who spread the word through lectures and meetings held in market squares and other public places. Sincerity was valued above polish, so the movement was quick to encourage untrained, working-class speakers. After his arrival in London in the late 1830s, the tailor Robert Crowe divided his time between three organisations: temperance, the repeal movement and the Chartists – but he singled out the temperance organisation in his formation as a public speaker. In Crowe's recollections, so convinced had he become by the teetotallers' rhetoric that he wished to join them in advocating the cause. He was mortified to discover, however, that his 'deficiency as a speaker' would not allow it. Crowe overcame his diffidence by practising his lectures in secluded corners of the city late at night and by this means established for himself a reputation as a 'youthful orator, worthy to be hauked about to public meetings'.[51] John Charles Buckmaster also credited the temperance movement with teaching him the art of public speaking. As a young apprentice, he became involved with a band of temperance reformers and toured the village holding open meetings. He later became a prominent agitator and propagandist for the Anti-Corn Law movement and founded an Anti-Corn Law Association at Tiverton in Devon. It was all thanks to his little band of temperance advocates. Years later, Buckmaster opined that 'whatever little success I may have achieved in after years as a public speaker or lecturer is due to these meetings'.[52]

And the temperance clubs needed their secretaries, fund-raisers and treasurers just like any other voluntary association. William Farish described how his temperance society in Carlisle had selected a new chairman and new committee on a weekly basis so that all members were drawn into running their small affair.[53] Of another society in Chester, he observed that the meetings for 'social intercourse and discussion' were useful in giving the teetotallers 'confidence in expressing their views'.[54] As the movement grew in strength through the nineteenth century, temperance emerged as yet one more way in which men with no tradition of public speaking or social activism learned how to contribute to public life. As with the Sunday schools, there was nothing in the teetotallers' ideas or beliefs that predisposed its members towards Chartism: in fact, their emphasis on the need for individual effort and reform is in stark contrast to the communitarian ethos of the Radicals. But the temperance movement was more than a collection of ideas. It offered its recruits a community and a meaningful role in that community. Although many confined their labours to the temperance cause, others found themselves drawn to new organisations and put their newfound skills to work in different contexts.

There is one final point of entry that we should consider, and that is politics itself. By the 1820s and 1830s working men inhabited a political world. Access to the once closed realm of political ideas and debate was easy to obtain, especially for those living in the great industrial cities. The Chartists and other independent political speakers regularly held meetings open to all-comers and getting involved was not a difficult matter, even for the man with no prior experience.[55] James Watson noticed an advertisement for a meeting to discuss the works of some Radical writers posted on the walls of his town of Leeds and on listening to the men speak was immediately persuaded by their arguments. He made himself useful by going around collecting subscriptions and in no time his career as a Radical and seller of political literature had begun; as he eventually became one of the six working men to sign the Charter it was a career of no little significance. But the really surprising thing about Watson is how unusual his experience was. Of the forty-five men involved in politics, only seven failed to mention any form of social activism before they took up politics (and of course some of these may have been involved in other causes and simply failed to mention the fact). The other thirty-eight had all been busy with some non-political cause or other. And so we are led back once more to the drift towards social engagement which preceded and accompanied the great political movements of the 1830s. Without these grassroots social organisations, it is really an open question whether Chartism as we know it would ever have existed.

Reading clubs, trade clubs, Sunday schools, co-operatives, the temperance movement – they appear as distinct ways for working men to get involved in the political world. In reality, of course, these neat boundaries were illusory and would certainly not have been recognised by our autobiographers. Each writer weaved his own idiosyncratic pathway through numerous different causes before entering politics; often one association shaded seamlessly into the next. Take, for instance, the Newcastle Chartist, Robert Lowery. He attributed much of his political education to a small debating society, yet even before he had entered the society, he had been attending Owenite lectures in the town and sitting 'on a committee connected with political matters'.[56] And later his careers as a Chartist and secretary of the tailors' branch of the Consolidated Trades Union proceeded in tandem. In reality, the dividing line between Lowery's political, union and educational activities is extremely hard to draw.

Other examples abound. John Bates' account of his entry into public life began when he joined a company of men to purchase and read a newspaper on Saturday nights. Bates was often asked to read aloud and through this he 'acquired an interest in public affairs'.[57] Was his newspaper club an improvement society or a political association? Either way, his experiences in the club led him to join a Radical Association and when his association transformed itself into a Chartist centre in 1838 his metamorphosis from newspaper reader to political actor was complete. The autobiographers did not follow neat and tidy paths towards Chartism or any other form of working-class politics. Instead, they were immersed in a world of social activism from which each could map out his own way into the public sphere.

Few of the autobiographers capture the untidy nature of their political enlightenment better than Joseph Barker. Barker had been born into a large weaving family in early nineteenth-century Yorkshire and, like many of those raised in weaving families, he had felt the pinch of poverty only too well in his early years. During adolescence, Barker had undergone a religious conversion and embarked upon a rigorous programme of spiritual and intellectual improvement, an education which proved to be the springboard to an extraordinary career. Through the Methodists he joined a meeting where aspiring young preachers practised their sermons and from there he graduated to delivering sermons further afield. After the usual probation, his name was put on the plan as a Methodist preacher.[58]

But from the outset, Barker had found it hard to submit to the discipline the Church expected. He refused to accept a position as a travelling preacher as he was not prepared to travel abroad and soon left the Wesleyan Methodists for the New Connexion, owing to doctrinal differences which could not be reconciled. And Barker's difficulties with authority did not end with his move to the New Connexion. One of his first actions was to disobey the Church's injunction that its preachers might not marry while on probation, and despite forging a reputation as an excellent and popular preacher, in less than a decade he was expelled for his controversial theological views. Barker promptly set up his own branch of Methodism. Such was his personal charisma that his followers styled themselves the 'Barkerites'. Along the way, he flirted with several other causes. In 1834, he became a teetotaller and was so delighted by the effect on his health that he began delivering temperance lectures – the teetotallers were no doubt equally delighted that such an accomplished working-class preacher had joined their ranks. In 1839, he attended a Socialist meeting. He was so concerned about the speaker's treatment of Christianity that he delivered a series of lectures against socialism in northern England.[59] Then, in 1846, Barker 'began to dabble in politics', throwing himself behind the Irish repeal movement and the Chartists.[60] Two years later, he became a delegate to the Chartist convention. It was the most colourful and tortuous path towards Chartism taken by any of the autobiographers.

There can be no denying that Barker was an unusual case. In his fervent commitment to one religious, social and political cause after another, and in flitting from one political pole to the other, Barker might well be regarded as something of a historical oddity. Yet if his swings from one cause to the next were extreme, the fluidity of his passage was anything but. By the 1830s there were numerous opportunities for the working man to hear and debate novel ideas, especially in those towns in the industrial north of England where Barker spent so much of his time preaching for the Methodists. Barker was supremely effective at engaging with different issues, but he drew upon structures and societies that were already firmly in place.

Barker's story suggests that the associational and political scene was unusually lively in the northern heartland of the industrial revolution. Taken as a whole, the autobiographical literature strongly reinforces this. Indeed, a particular strength of the autobiographies lies in the fact that they enable us to determine those environments which were most favourable to associational, and therefore political, activity. Almost all of those involved in politics or non-political engagement indicated where they lived and how they were employed as they took their first steps towards activism. In all, ninety-four writers were involved in the public sphere: the forty-five who were involved in politics and a further forty-nine who were involved in a wide range of non-political organisations. This provides us with a rich seam of evidence of the connections between living and working conditions and public engagement and even permits us to think about how far the emergence of a working-class politics can be linked to the process of industrialisation.

Turning first to the geography of politics, we find that those entering the public sphere were almost always to be found in areas of industrial and demographic growth. The majority of those who became involved in Radical and Chartist organisations lived either in London, in the big industrial cities (Glasgow, Newcastle, Manchester, Birmingham) or in the industrial villages and townships that dotted Lancashire, Yorkshire and the Midlands. Those living in smaller provincial and market towns were also drawn into Radical politics, though on a noticeably lesser scale. By contrast rural inhabitants were almost never involved in political agitation. Just one of the autobiographers was active in politics when living in the country. This was the anonymous author of *Scenes from my Life by a Working Man*, and he had been involved with the Radicals in Birmingham before moving to take up work in a newly built mill in rural Devon. Finding there was no 'Political Union ... and no circle of congenial spirits' in his new locale, he set up a society of his own and so 'became a leader where he had been a follower'.[61] Later in the century, the farm worker Joseph Arch also entered the political sphere, setting up the nation's first national union of farm workers in 1872, and a decade later becoming a Liberal MP.[62] But this was many years after the decline of Chartism and as a young man Arch had not been involved with the Chartists, despite holding political views that clearly leaned in their direction. His autobiography gives little impression that the Chartists had had any presence in his life or village in the 1840s.

It was not simply the Chartists who found their most congenial home in urban areas. All forms of associational activity fared much better in the most densely populated districts. Take the forty-seven autobiographers who mentioned some form of contact with a mutual improvement society or mechanics' institute. As noted in Chapter 7, all but two of these were based in towns or industrial districts. Much the same story may be told for the unions, co-operatives and teetotallers. Union activity and co-operative stores were both very heavily concentrated in towns.[63] The majority of autobiographers involved in the teetotal movement were also settled in towns, though the temperance advocates did make a serious, and partially successful, attempt to penetrate rural areas too.[64] Only the Sunday schools extended into rural areas, but these were still more widespread in urban and industrial areas and the large schools with several positions for its working-class members to fill were confined to the urban context.[65] With few exceptions, then, most forms of associational activity were to be found in areas of rapid economic and population growth. Pockets of industrialisation, no matter where they were, brought in new and mobile workers and it was they who were most likely to become active citizens in their new communities.

The autobiographies even allow us to probe the relationship between civic engagement and employment patterns. It is helpful to begin with those groups who remained outside the political sphere. The most glaring omission is the very poor. The vagrants, the beggars, the sick and long-term unemployed, though present in some number in the autobiographies, are not to be found engaged in politics, or indeed in any form of public activity.[66] It was also very unusual for farm workers or domestic servants to show much inclination for associational activity. In the case of farm workers, their absence from the politically active is no doubt part and parcel of the general lack of associational opportunities in rural areas. Their close supervision by employers and the general scarcity of employment on the land probably also helped to keep agricultural workers outside the political sphere. It is more difficult to comment on the case of domestic service, as this occupational group is under-represented amongst the autobiographers, though one suspects that the relatively close supervision of domestics helped to restrict membership of clubs and societies in broadly similar ways. One other interesting absence is the army. Although, as might be imagined, throughout the era of the Napoleonic wars military service was a common experience for the autobiographers, it does not emerge as having helped to produce active and engaged individuals. Alexander Somerville was one exception, gaining a degree of fame in the early 1830s after being dismissed from the army for (it was claimed) his public support for the 1832 Reform Bill. His dismissal was the springboard for a modest career as a political agitator and writer.[67] But Somerville was very much the exception to the rule. Most of those who left the army drifted back into some form of unskilled labour, and any skills they had learned proved ineffective in later advancing working-class aims.

By contrast, when we turn to consider who *was* involved in associational activity, two distinct occupational groups are immediately recognisable: skilled workers and industrial workers. The skilled workers hailed from a very diverse set of trades. The humble shoemakers and tailors were present in full force; so too were the most skilled and highly paid cabinetmakers and printers, as were most trades in between. Some had learned their skills through a formal apprenticeship, others outside the apprenticeship system. And their involvement in a wide range of clubs and societies, with both political and non-political aims, was related to the independence they enjoyed from their employers. Although most were working using traditional, unmechanised techniques, they all enjoyed the benefits of having learned a trade, namely full employment and relatively good wages. The skilled workers were generally able to make a decent living from their trade, and this in turn owed much to the economic and population growth that accompanied industrialisation.

Much the same is true of those engaged in industrial employment. Like the skilled workers, the industrial workers were involved in a heterogeneous set of trades. These men were engaged in handloom weaving, a wide variety of work around factories (cotton mills, machine-mending, warehouse work) and mining. Once again, their involvement in the public sphere was closely related to the advantages they enjoyed. In almost all instances, associational activity coincided with full employment and relatively good pay, or at least pay that was regarded as such by the man who earned it. It appears then that the economic growth which accompanied industrialisation, both within and without the new industrial sector, helped to increase workers' independence from their employers and increase the likelihood of their becoming involved in other causes outside their hours of work. The flowering of clubs and societies at this time was not a symptom of the workforce's growing discontent but of new levels of freedom, confidence and autonomy.

By the 1840s the Chartists' presence was felt up and down the country in towns both large and small. So ubiquitous had they become, that the autobiographers were ever more likely to get involved in public affairs by turning up at a branch meeting and getting stuck in. And as Chartism declined after the failed petition of 1842, men who had tirelessly supported their local branch in the movement's heyday simply transferred their energies to other causes. As a result, Chartism was gradually becoming a source of political education, rather than the beneficiary of it. George Cooper took the reverse journey to many of the men born a generation earlier, starting out as a Chartist and then spending several years campaigning on union matters. As a young mill-hand living in Stockport, he had 'taken an active interest in the Chartist movement', so when the town's cotton industry was hit by dreadful depression in the late 1840s he was well placed to take an active role in defending the mill-hands. 'Meetings were called', he remembered, 'and committees formed with the idea of raising subscriptions throughout the country.' A separate committee representing the unemployed was also formed, of which Cooper was made the secretary.[68] A few years later he helped ensure that the more recalcitrant of the Stockport mill owners complied with the Ten Hours Bill. Later still he 'assumed the head of affairs with the object of successfully engineering [a] strike'.[69] Cooper had learned how to agitate from the Chartists and when that movement began to disintegrate he used his skills elsewhere. In slipping from one issue to the next Cooper followed the pattern of earlier writers, but his exact path reflected the changed times in which he lived.

The great flowering of working-class clubs and societies in the 1840s and 1850s owed much to the vibrancy of the Chartist movement and its success in training up the would-be agitator. In the post-Chartist years, working men proved to be ever more confident and competent at organising themselves and began to work as effective campaigners on a great variety of issues. Before long, the autobiographers were involved in causes too many to enumerate. Here an 'Economic Benefit Society' which met in a schoolroom rather than a tavern, for the benefit of colliers who wanted all of their subscriptions paid out in sickness – 'no beer, and no parade, and no music on feast days' eating up the funds.[70] There an allotment society for working men living in a London suburb.[71] A co-operative flour mill in Halifax; a cycle club in Northampton which grew to 185 members; a rambling club for the residents of Bridgeton, Glasgow; a Palestine Exploration Club; and a 'Glasgow Garibaldi Italian Fund' founded with the intention of promoting the unification of Italy.[72] In all of these enterprises we see much the same process at work. Men born poor, and often remaining relatively so, yet nonetheless exercising authority within their communities.

As Chartist fervour dissipated, reforming energies were scattered in many directions, often local in focus. We get a sense of the sheer range of reformist activity from the autobiography of John Wilson. Wilson had been born in Greatham, Durham, and raised by his single father, a hard-living and fiercely independent railway navvy. Following his father's death when he was twelve, Wilson become a miner, and apart from a brief spell as a merchant seaman in the 1850s spent most of his early adult life following that trade. It was a world of long hours, hard labour and heavy drinking and Wilson was wholly removed from the public sphere. The alehouse, not the clubhouse, was where he spent his leisure hours. He was, he ruefully recalled, 'unfit to take a proper part in the public affairs of the nation'.[73] But Wilson's exclusion from 'public affairs' changed rapidly when he underwent a religious conversion in his late twenties. He became a Sunday school teacher at Haswell's Primitive Methodist Chapel and joined the chapel. In little more than a year he had become a lay preacher for the Primitives. There was an 'Improvement Society' connected with the chapel so he was soon attending that as well. At the same time he got involved in numerous other causes: temperance, co-operation, the extension of the franchise, and a trade union for the miners of Haswell all occupied him in the space of a few years in the late 1860s.[74] It is hard not to be struck by the enormous range of organisations in Haswell, which was after all a village with only around 4,000 inhabitants.

As social engagement became normalised, so the autobiographers started to write about it in new ways. Back in the 1790s, our writers had provided agonised descriptions of the structure and regulations of their clubs and societies. There is Francis Place writing about the rules that governed his discussion group right down to such details as the order in which each member might speak and how many times he might do so. Charles Campbell spent more than two pages reminiscing about his small literary society. The number of members, the weekly vote to select the next subject, the rotating 'presidentship' of the meetings, the annual anniversary, and sundry other 'regulations' all got a mention. Down to the middle of the century, several of the autobiographers paid minute attention to the forms and procedures of their clubs. The details mattered. Not only were they curious and interesting in their own right, they provided the writers with a way of underlining their professionalism and the seriousness of the work they did. Later writers, particularly those describing activities in the 1850s and later, simply skipped over the minutiae. That their society had a secretary, treasurer, central committee and a few rules were details too obvious to relate. In little more than a generation, associational activity had become mainstream and knowledge about the ways of doing business could safely be assumed.

We have been looking at the practical side of conducting a campaign – the ability to address or to chair a meeting, to keep a set of accounts, to book a room for meetings, to print and distribute campaigning literature. These are the nuts and bolts of social and political engagement. But along with the ability to perform such sundry tasks came something more intangible, something we might loosely designate 'status'. Many of our autobiographers were acutely aware of the journey they had made from humble workman to community leader. Emanuel Lovekin, for instance, remembered how he had been invited by the local Chartist organisation in his Staffordshire potteries town to serve as their secretary. He had 'got mixted up with some of its great men', he reminisced, and 'even thought myself Somebody, I felt very earnest in the work I had to do'.[75] The Northamptonshire poet, John Leatherland, 'esteemed it an honour' when he was selected as the secretary of Kettering's Chartist association.[76] Occasionally the autobiographers were more self-deprecating about their busy younger selves. James Dawson Burn declared that in his 'little political squad every man was as full of self-consequence and legislative importance as if each were a political Atlas'.[77] But real or imagined, for good or for ill, men like Lovekin, Leatherland and Burn (a miner, a weaver and a hatter) were gaining status in their communities. And it was not just Lovekin, Leatherland and Burn who gained. If we look at the matter the other way around, we can see that miners, weavers and hatters now had leaders of their own to whom they could turn.

Thomas Dunning never indicated whether he felt proud of his stint as the secretary of the Chartist movement in Nantwich. But he did mention it three times in an autobiography that ran to little more than twenty pages, so it is probably safe to assume that he did.[78] Dunning had been born into obscurity. Raised by a single mother and too poor to enter an apprenticeship, Dunning only managed to learn shoemaking thanks to the free instruction he received from a kindly stepfather. Dunning knew he had not been born in this world to lead anything. Yet here he was, as he tells us *three times*, 'secretary to the Nantwich branch of the Chartist Association'. Of course, when the Chartist agitation wound up, Dunning continued to represent the working poor on different concerns – he found himself 'by some means . . . pushed to the front in our movements of local reforms'. So despite the demise of Chartism, Dunning remained a busy man, agitating on matters such as the lighting rates, the church rates, and the suspected embezzlement of the Beam Heath estate charities.[79]

Dunning's metamorphosis from self-taught shoemaker to local leader captures nothing less than a social revolution. The issues that occupied Dunning were not, of course, new. We should not for one moment imagine that eighteenth-century workers had no need or desire to combine in unions or vote in elections. Nor was this the first time that the poor had been concerned about local taxes or cheated of their rightful share of charities set up in their name. As we have seen, eighteenth-century workers suffered chronic underemployment, low wages, and grinding poverty. So we may safely assume that the shoemakers of Nantwich would have welcomed a man like Dunning with open arms fifty years earlier.

No; the discontent was not new. What was new was the ability to express that discontent in effective ways. For the first time in history, working men were learning how to articulate their grievances through peaceful means. Slowly from the 1790s, more rapidly from the 1820s, a raft of new institutions – trade unions and benefit societies, mutual improvement societies, night schools, Sunday schools and Nonconformist churches – cropped up on the social landscape. These small, self-run institutions gave working men the chance to top up a deficient education and learn about the exercise of power. All had their part to play in giving working men a taste of local power and in helping to raise the cultural capital of the working class. Without these early and tentative steps into the public sphere, it is hard to envisage how the mass political movements of the 1830s and 1840s could ever have come into being.

The evidence for working-class engagement is interesting not simply in explaining the emergence of a new form of working-class politics. It is above all testimony to the new intellectual, social and political freedoms enjoyed by the working man. This was an era when a working man could, without any sense of irony, describe his fellows as 'sons of freedom'.

'Sons of freedom' brings us back, of course, to the title of this chapter. The expression was used by William Aitken, who had entered the Manchester mills as a child, risen to the position of overlooker, but ultimately been forced to quit the mills owing to his involvement in the Ten Hours movement. The sons of freedom to whom he referred were his fellow workers and reformers – the men who had fought for the Charter, to the extent even of risking their liberty, during the agitation of the late 1830s.

Aitken knew all too well the dark aspects of early industrial Britain. His life as a factory child had begun before the passing of the Factory Acts; he thought the Manchester of his childhood provided the 'saddest picture of child suffering, of cruelty, and avarice, that can be found in the annals of any human industry in the world'. Yet the undeniable hardships of his early life did not define Aitken's experience of living in early industrial Britain. Far from it. In Aitken's eyes, the industrial revolution was not a simple tale of 'suffering, cruelty, and avarice'. It was not a story of immiseration, degradation and loss. To the contrary, Aitken thought he was living through the 'most industrial age the world has ever seen', and a time of many 'wonderful improvements'.[80] What is more, industry and wealth helped to create a proud and independent proletariat. They had created a class of working men ready to take its place in the cultural and political life of the nation. Aitken's account of life in industrial Manchester was above all a tale of empowerment, of workmen such as himself coming together and working collectively to right wrongs and to take their proper place in society. Those dark days of his childhood? 'All that is changed now.' And that, he poignantly added, was 'thanks to the exertions of the working men themselves'.

CHAPTER TEN

# Conclusion

Looking back sixty years, I cannot help constantly exclaiming 'What a contrast there is betwixt the present advantages of poor people and their children compared to that period [1810]!' (J. Livesey, p. 198)

He is a misanthrope indeed who would wish the old days or customs back again. (T. Wood, p. 11, Bradford Central Library)

Some folks are apt to sigh that the former days were better than these. In some things that may be true; but it certainly does not apply to the hours of labour, and the opportunities for needed rest and recreation. The working classes never had better times than now. (Cooke, p. 34)

CHANGE IS WORKED into the grain of modern life. That our lives differ from those of our grandparents is common knowledge. And whilst none of us know quite what the future holds, we can safely assume that our children will in turn go on to inhabit a world that differs from this one. We can even say something about the general direction of change. Each generation will live longer, enjoy greater levels of material comfort, eat a more varied and exotic diet, and have more possessions. New technologies will change the way in which the next generation lives, works, travels and communicates, though they may pay a price for these advantages by leading lives which are more complex and where time is more scarce. We give our children items that were off-limits luxuries during our own childhoods. In a few decades' time, they will find themselves doing just the same thing. We live in a changing world. It is as evident as night following day.

The autobiographers never spoke of an 'industrial revolution'. But as they entered old age in the 1840s or 1850s, the generation born in the 1790s did display an unmistakable awareness that the times had changed. So what did they make of it all? With so many first-hand witnesses to this transformative moment in world history we can surely do no better than listen to their verdict. What did those at the coalface tell us about their times?

John Bennett, a carpenter born in rural Wiltshire in 1787, was amongst the first to articulate his thoughts about the developments he had lived through. Writing down his memories at the end of his life, he asked his children to 'Look back and see what troublesome times we had during my bringing up'. He told them 'the working classes in my opinion, was never so well off' as they were in the present day. It was just a throwaway comment, a footnote to a much larger retrospective of his life.[1] But there is something to Bennett's remark that should cause us to pause. It was the first time any of the autobiographers had depicted themselves as living in a changing world. Furthermore, Bennett saw the developments he observed in the most positive of terms. He did not think simply that life had changed. He thought it had done so for the better.

John Bennett's memories spanned the years between the 1790s and the 1850s, but we should not think there is anything special about these dates. The point rather is that this period marks the emergence of a new kind of society, a society in which change – dare we call it progress? – over an indi- vidual's lifetime became normal. Writers born in the 1850s were no less struck by the alterations that occurred over their lifetime than Bennett had been, though they inevitably gestured at a new raft of changes. By the early twentieth century, writers could marvel at such developments as tramcars, electricity, a health department, street cleansing, scientific instruments – 'telegraph, telephone, and wireless' – and such 'simple necessaries as matches, watches and umbrellas'.[2] We can draw an unbroken line from the elderly Bennett writing in the 1850s to the present day; at any point indi- viduals will observe that the Britain of their old age no longer resembles the Britain of their childhood.

What is also striking is the degree of agreement between the autobiog- raphers concerning the general tenor of the changes they had witnessed. All through the nineteenth century, writers sound the same celebratory notes of improvements and progress. Benjamin North, for instance, thought that if his parents and ancestors could 'revisit the earth ... and see the domestic alterations, commercial improvements, and the wonderful and astonishing activities of life' they would not be able to 'believe their own eyes'.[3] James Dawson Burn wrote that anyone who cared to compare 'the state of affairs in Great Britain' in the early nineteenth century with the present (he was talking about the 1850s) would have to admit 'that as a nation we have much cause to feel grateful'.[4] Moses Horler, a Somerset miner, thought the life of the colliers in the early part of the century 'was very different to what it is at the present time'. In the 1820s, wages were 'so very much lower . . . Life was very hard for the poor then.'[5]

If wages were higher, what about the possibility that life was simpler and the poor happier back in the old days? James Hawker could not be more scathing about this proposition. He scoffed at the notion that the agricultural labourer 'seemed a Deal Happier 60 years ago'. In his opinion, he 'was merely a Serf'.[6] None of the autobiographers had time for those who fondly reminisced about the past. 'When I hear people talk of the good old days,' thought George Mallard, 'they must be ignorant of what did hapen in those days. I know it was hard times where I was . . .'[7]

The contrasts between then and now were drawn in many ways. Some spoke in general terms about the comforts of the present day compared with those of their past. Others drew attention to some more specific aspect of life. Not a few contrasted the great fortune of the children born after the Factory Acts of the 1830s and 1840s, spared the misfortune of long hours at labour, allowed to enjoy something that resembled a childhood.[8] Then there were the children of today who fussed over the kind of food they would and would not eat – a curious development because in one's own childhood there had been far too little food around to countenance picking at what there was.[9] Samuel Robinson was struck by improvements in the quality and variety of people's diets – the 'universal use of fresh butcher meat', the 'enlarged use of vegetables', and that 'remarkable nutritive agent – sugar'. The change in diet, he concluded, had produced a 'delightful change in the physical improvement of the whole community'.[10]

Small changes in everyday objects were sometimes depicted as emblems of a larger and more significant transformation in life. For instance, the plates, basins and metal spoons which had replaced the clumsy wooden bowl and spoon of his childhood were enough to prompt Thomas Jackson to reflect that 'Society is in a state of constant progress'.[11] Cheap postage prompted Thomas Wallis to observe that 'nearly all the conveniences of life were very limited sixty years ago, compared with the facilities of the present day'.[12]

Whilst many writers stressed the greater material comfort enjoyed by working families, others marvelled at the way the very fabric of life seemed to have changed. No church or chapel and no police was what one remembered about his childhood village. He was 'glad to say things are much better there now'.[13] The wonderful opening of the working man's cultural horizons was frequently noticed: books, libraries, reading rooms, everything that 'distinguishes the present time in favour of the improvement and enjoyment of the masses'.[14] 'I only wish [my parents] had each lived to enjoy and to see the improvements I see,' one man added wistfully.[15]

A charge that is frequently levelled against the autobiographies is that they are biased in some way so as to tell the story of industrialisation's winners. According to this line of argument, any evidence that industrialisation enhanced our writers' lives can be promptly discarded as something that the winners would say, wouldn't they? It's a neat solution, but not wholly convincing. After all, the autobiographers had always been 'winners'. The men who wrote their life story during the eighteenth century had usually achieved something great. Nearly every one of the earlier autobiographers had travelled a journey from obscurity to achieve some kind of distinction in the arts, sciences or the Church. Yet they never claimed that the alteration in their personal fortunes was mirrored in society at large. They had nothing to say about the progress of their times, no sense that their society was in a state of flux. All realised that the dismal poverty of their earlier lives continued all around them. Their life had changed. The times had not and they could not envisage a time when the privations and sufferings they had endured would be eliminated once and for all.

And this was what had changed by the middle of the nineteenth century. Our writers were not simply commenting on the change in their personal circumstances. They were also reflecting upon the strides that other working men and their families seemed to be making. These writers never lamented the passing of the old days – or 'the bad old times', as they were styled by one writer.[16] There were no fond words for the quiet or simplicity that their forefathers had known. To a man, our writers were glad that their grandchildren would never know the life they had once lived.

It must be admitted that the suggestion that many of those who lived and worked their way through the industrial revolution believed their lives had been improved by that process jars with what we think we know. Generations of historians have painted the industrial revolution in relentlessly dark colours: a force which was wholly destructive for the poor, remorseless, unforgiving in its grinding down of the independent labourer of old. This, clearly, is not the assessment of those who lived through it. We have repeatedly seen that working men were extremely adept at grasping opportunities from the turbulent times in which they lived. And now we see them glorying in changes they witnessed. Surely it is time to reconsider the oft-repeated claims that the industrial revolution brought little but misery to those who who did most to produce it.

Understanding the wholly positive assessments of our first-hand witnesses requires that we get to grips with what living in a pre-industrial country was really like. From our eighteenth-century autobiographers we know that in the absence of a fully developed industrial sector, there was just not enough work to go around. Even those with a skill to their name were rarely able to make a good living from their trade, and frequently turned to agriculture to keep themselves and their families afloat. Certainly there were compensations. The quiet state of the economy gave workers more free time, but in reality it was not the kind of free time that anybody wants. Unasked-for leisure was unpaid. It left families without adequate food, lodging or fuel. In much the same vein, having too little work sheltered the very young from the workplace, but as it also left them without sufficient food we should be careful not to idealise their lot. This more than anything is what changed with industrialisation. The industrial revolution increased the amount of work available, for the skilled and the unskilled, for the young and the old. More work. It may not sound exciting, but for those suffering from chronic unemployment, a full-time job was a thing of enormous value. More work meant higher incomes, and for a family living close to the breadline this was very good news indeed.

In emphasising the advantages of economic growth we should not deny that some missed out. Our account has been constructed from the testimony of adult men, and it was undoubtedly this group which did best. By our writers' own admission, early industrial Britain was not a good place for children. More work meant more work for children, and the plight of countless very small children forced into the workplace and stunted by excessive work must constitute one of the most tragic events of our history. It is also notable that the experiences of women are not captured (or at least not directly captured) by the autobiographies. The factory districts certainly did offer more employment opportunities for women and this provided young female workers with greater freedoms. But motherhood grasped back those freedoms and left women even in the most economically vibrant parts of the country living out lives that differed little from those of their grandmothers. It is surely no accident that the emergence of effective working-class feminism was delayed until the advent of effective and accessible forms of family limitation in the twentieth century.

And though I have suggested that adult men had the most to gain from the industrial economy, this does not mean that all men gained in equal measure. This was an economy prone to boom and bust. Gains were tenuous; gains were sometimes lost. Life was still extremely hard and many lived perilously close to the edge of a comfortable subsistence. Yet tenuous gains were preferable to the predictable course of a life devoted to hard labour with no prospect of real improvement. Industrialisation brought immediate and tangible benefits for large sections of the labouring poor. It held out the promise of better wages even to the unskilled and the very poor. Not everybody successfully grasped these possibilities. But before telling the story of those passed by, we should offer a full account of the many who did benefit.

My purpose has not been to substitute the bleak account of Britain's industrial past with a rosy and cheerful account of better and happier times. Nor is my evidence offered as a historical spin on the virtue of trickle-down economics with its assertion that there is no need for political interference to direct the course of growth, its claim that markets can be left to themselves to redistribute the wealth they create. Could things have been better in early nineteenth-century Britain? Undoubtedly. Might different policies have had better outcomes for working people? Certainly. Britain's ruling elites displayed a woeful and lamentable failure to direct economic growth in ways beneficial to the many. Tardy and limited laws to restrict the exploitation of very young children; ineffective market solutions to the problems of sanitation; punitive workhouses as a solution to those who slipped through the net – there is little here to commend. Yet even with a government that did nothing, there is an uncomfortable truth we should confront: industrialisation had remarkable power to put food on the table. And for that first generation, that generation which had expected the hunger of their own childhood to be experienced once more by their children and grandchildren, food on the table was all that really mattered. Autobiographers were not romantic about the old days when their children went hungry. And whatever our views on the rights or wrongs of capitalism, nor should anyone else be.

Nothing stands out from the autobiographers' testimony more strongly than the way in which rising levels of employment pushed up family incomes in meaningful and much appreciated ways. Yet the autobiographies suggest that there was something else at stake. Poverty forced our writers' hand in other walks of life. The decision to marry, the timing and content of their sexual lives – such things could be controlled to some degree by more powerful neighbours when a couple's outlook for raising their children by their own labour was poor. And how did a man challenge the religious or political views of his employer in an era of low employment? Offending one's master meant certain dismissal – a risk that could not be taken when there were no other employers to whom one might turn. Low levels of employment obviously meant low incomes, but it also restricted the personal and political expression of the labouring poor. It continued to restrict working women's scope for self-improvement and political activity well into the twentieth century. And it is perhaps here that we see most clearly the grounds for emphasising the ways in which the industrial revolution enhanced rather than destroyed patterns of life. Critics will argue that the material gains for most families were small. But they were just enough to drag wage-earners out of the servile submission that poverty had forced upon them since time immemorial.

And this brings us back to John Bennett and his thought that 'the working classes . . . was never so well off' as they were now. We might add that the working classes were never so loquacious either. There is after all something astonishing in the fact that Bennett wrote his memoirs at all. In the eighteenth century, autobiographers told their life stories because they had achieved something great. Bennett would not have made such claims for himself. He did enjoy moderate success as a master carpenter, but it was still a life devoted to labour, a life without exceptional or noteworthy achievement. He wrote his memoirs because (he tells us) his children thought his life was of interest and had been on at him for years to write it all down. He wrote also, we might add, because as a young man in Bristol he had sought to extend the woeful schooling of his childhood and had taken advantage of the night classes that the town had to offer. Bennett belonged to a new generation of men who had found their voice. And this is what this book has been all about. This book celebrates the coming of modernity and the role the industrial revolution played in the transition. It celebrates, above all, the creation of a loud and audible working-class voice and invites readers to listen to what the industrial revolution's workers had to say about their life and times.

# Notes

Full bibliographical details of all secondary works cited are contained in the notes below. Autobiographies and memoirs are cited in the notes by surname only and should be cross-referenced with the bibliography for the full citation. Where more than one writer has the same surname, additional detail has been given to enable correct identification of the author. Where items have survived in manuscript form only, I have indicated the archives in which they are stored.

## 1 Introduction: 'A Simple Naritive'

1. R. Anderson, pp. xiii–xxxiv.
2. Bennett, p. 2 (Bristol Record Office); Mayett, p. 2.
3. Lincoln, p. 82 (Norfolk Record Office).
4. Ibid., p. 1.
5. Ibid., p. 5.
6. Ibid., pp. 7–9.
7. Ibid., p. 10.
8. Ibid., p. 13.
9. Ibid.
10. Ibid., p. 21.
11. Ibid., p. 23.
12. Ibid., p. 27.
13. At least this seems a reasonable inference, since John and Sarah gave the name Elizabeth to a daughter in 1826 and again in 1830. See Norfolk Record Office, Oxborough Baptism Registers, 1813–1998, PD 139/56.
14. The starting point for anybody interested in looking at working-class autobiography must be Burnett et al.'s annotated bibliography: John Burnett, David Vincent and David Mayall, *The Autobiography of the Working Class. An Annotated, Critical Bibliography, 1790–1900*, i (New York, 1984). See also Nan Hackett, *Nineteenth-Century British Working-Class Autobiographies: An Annotated Bibliography* (New York, 1985). Many more items have come to light since Burnett et al.'s work in the 1970s and about 20 per cent of the items consulted here are not listed in their bibliography.

15. The broad contours of these debates can be traced in: Maxine Berg and Pat Hudson, 'Rehabilitating the industrial revolution', *Economic History Review*, 45/1 (1992), pp. 24–50; J. De Vries, 'The industrial revolution and the industrious revolution', *Journal of Economic History*, 54/2 (1994), pp. 249–70; M. J. Daunton, *Progress and Poverty. An Economic and Social History of Britain* (Oxford, 1995); Gregory Clark, *A Farewell to Alms: A Brief Economic History of the World* (Princeton, NJ, 2007); Robert C. Allen, *The British Industrial Revolution in Global Perspective* (Cambridge, 2009); Joel Mokyr, *The Enlightened Economy: An Economic History of Britain, 1700–1850* (New Haven, CT, 2010). A simple summary can also be found in Emma Griffin, *A Short History of the British Industrial Revolution* (London, 2010).

16. A useful entry point to autobiographical material, both published and manuscript, is provided by the following edited collections: John Burnett, *Useful Toil: Autobiographies of Working People from the 1820s to the 1920s* (Harmondsworth, 1974); idem, *Destiny Obscure. Autobiographies of Childhood, Education and Family from the Late 1820s to the 1920s* (London, 1982); David Vincent, *Testaments of Radicalism: Memoirs of Working-Class Politicians, 1790–1885* (London, 1977); James R. Simmons and Janice Carlisle, eds, *Factory Lives: Four Nineteenth-Century Working-Class Autobiographies* (Ontario, 2007).

17. This was very clearly the view of the first major study of working-class autobiography. See David Vincent, *Bread, Knowledge and Freedom: a Study of Nineteenth-Century Working-Class Autobiography* (London, 1981), pp. 10, 6. A recent and very robust rebuttal of this view, however, may be found in Jane Humphries, *Childhood and Child Labour in the British Industrial Revolution* (Cambridge, 2010), which subjects broadly the same set of sources that I have looked at here to statistical analysis in an attempt to chart changes in the significance and extent of child labour over the period 1627–1878.

18. Hemmingway, pp. 408–11 (Norfolk Record Office).

19. Oakley, pp. 113–50, p. 148.

20. A useful introduction to female life-writing may be found in Jane Rendall, '*A Short account of my Unprofitable Life*: autobiographies of working-class women in Britain, 1775–1845', in Trev Lynn Broughton and Linda Anderson, eds, *Women's Lives/Women's Times: New Essays on Auto/Biography* (Albany, 1997). Also useful are Eileen Yeo, 'Will the real Mary Lovett please stand up? Chartism, gender and autobiography', in Malcolm Chase and Ian Dyck, eds, *Living and Learning: Essays in Honour of J.F.C. Harrison* (Aldershot, 1996), pp. 163–81; Paula J. Harvey, 'Spreading the wealth: "cultural capital" and modern British laboring women's autobiography', *Women's Studies*, 22/2 (1993), pp. 181–96; Julia Swindells, 'Liberating the subject: autobiography and "women's history": a reading of the diaries of Hannah Cullwick', in the Personal Narrative Group, *Interpreting Women's Lives: Feminist Theory and Personal Narratives* (Bloomington, IN, 1989), pp. 24–38.

21. Tough, p. 6.

22. Frost, p. 42. Contrast with Peter Gurney, 'Thomas Frost', *Oxford Dictionary of National Biography*.

23. E. Johnston, pp. 301–24, 302.

24. Bennett; the quote comes from p. 1 (Bristol Record Office).

25. Ibid., p. 3.

26. These difficulties seem heightened by the fact that literary theorists have been far more active than historians in working with autobiographical material. See, for instance, Karl Weintraub, 'Autobiography and historical consciousness', *Critical Inquiry*, 1/4 (1979), pp. 821–48; William C. Spengemann, *The Forms of Autobiography: Episodes in the History of a Literary Genre* (New Haven, CT, 1980); Robert Elbaz, *The Changing Nature of the Self: a Critical Study of the Autobiographic Discourse* (London, 1988); James Olney, ed., *Studies in Autobiography* (Oxford, 1988); Felicity Nussbaum, *The Autobiographical Subject: Gender and Ideology in Eighteenth-Century England* (Baltimore, MD, 1989); Regenia Gagnier *Subjectivities: A History of Self-Representation in Britain, 1832–1920*

(Oxford, 1991); James Treadwell, *Autobiographical Writing and British Literature* (Oxford, 2005); Sidonie Smith and Julia Watson, *Reading Autobiography: a Guide for Interpreting Life Narratives* (Minneapolis, MN, 2001).

27. Vincent, *Bread, Knowledge and Freedom*, pp. 10, 6. See also W. S. Howard, 'Miners' auto-biography: text and context', *Labour History Review*, 60/2 (1995), pp. 89–99; Nan Hackett, 'A different form of "self": narrative style in British nineteenth-century working-class autobiography', *Biography*, 12 (1989), pp. 208–26; Chris Waters, 'Autobiography, nostalgia, and the changing practices of working-class selfhood', in George K. Behlmer and Fred Marc Leventhal, eds, *Singular Continuities: Tradition, Nostalgia, and Society in Modern Britain* (Stanford, CA, 2000), pp. 178–95; Kevin Binfield, 'Ned Ludd and labouring class autobiography', in Eugene Stelzig, ed., *Romantic Autobiography in England* (Farnham, Surrey, 2009).

28. MacDonald, p. 2.

29. Hutton, pp. vi–vii.

30. Nye, p. 20.

31. Hemmingway, unpaginated introduction (Norfolk Record Office).

32. William Wordsworth, 'Outrage done to Nature', from *The Excursion* (1814); William Blake, 'And did those feet in ancient time', from *Milton: a Poem* (1804–8).

33. Charles Dickens, *Hard Times* (London, 1854).

34. Benjamin Disraeli, *Sybil, Or the Two Nations* (London, 1845).

35. William Cobbett, *Rural Rides* (London, 1830).

36. John Stuart Mill, *Principles of Political Economy*, ed. W. J. Ashley (London, 1909), p. 751.

37. Friedrich Engels, *The Condition of the Working Class in England*, ed. David McLellan (Oxford, 1993) p. 16. See also Tristram Hunt, *The Frock-Coated Communist: the Revolutionary Life of Friedrich Engels* (London, 2010).

38. Published in German in 1845, Engels' ideas remained largely locked away for several decades until the American feminist, Florence Kelley Wischnewetzky, undertook an English translation in the 1880s.

39. Quoted in T. S. Ashton, 'The standard of life of the workers of England, 1790–1830', *Journal of Economic History*, Supplement IX (1949), pp. 19–38, quote p. 20.

40. Arnold Toynbee, *Lectures on the Industrial Revolution in England* (London, 1884), pp. 84, 5. John U. Nef, 'The industrial revolution reconsidered', *Journal of Economic History*, 3/1 (1943), pp. 1–31, p. 1. Toynbee's knowledge of Engels' as yet untranslated work is discussed in D. C. Coleman, 'Myth, history and the industrial revolution', in his *Myth, History, and the Industrial Revolution* (London, 1992), pp. 19–20.

41. John H. Clapham, *An Economic History of Modern Britain: the Early Railway Age, 1820–1850* (Cambridge, 1926).

42. Ibid., pp. 55, 561.

43. The quotes come from reviews by Abbott Payson Usher (*American Economic Review*, 17/4, 1927), pp. 694–6; T. S. Ashton (*Economic History Review*, 5/1, 1934), pp. 104–19; H. L. Beales (*Economica*, 20, 1927), pp. 233–5; and T. H. Marshall (*English Historical Review*, 42/168, 1927), pp. 624–6.

44. J. L. Hammond, 'The industrial revolution and discontent', *Economic History Review*, 2/2 (1930), pp. 215–28, quote p. 219.

45. E. J. Hobsbawm, 'The standard of living during the industrial revolution: a discussion', *Economic History Review*, 16/1 (1963), pp. 119–34, quote p. 119.

46. R. M. Hartwell and S. Engermann, 'Models of immiseration: the theoretical basis of pessimism', in Arthur J. Taylor, ed., *The Standard of Living in Britain in the Industrial Revolution* (London, 1975), pp. 189–213, quote p. 212.

47. E. P. Thompson, *The Making of the English Working Class* (Harmondsworth, 1976), p. 231.

48. S. Horrell and J. Humphries, 'Old questions, new data, and alternative perspectives: families' living standards during the industrial revolution', *Journal of Economic History*, 52/4 (1992), pp. 849–80; C. H. Feinstein, 'Pessimism perpetuated: real wages and the standard of living in Britain during and after the industrial revolution', *Journal of*

*Economic History*, 58/3 (1998), pp. 625–8; Robert C. Allen, 'Engels' pause: technical change, capital accumulation, and inequality in the British industrial revolution', *Explorations in Economic History*, 46 (2009), pp. 418–35.

49. H. J. Voth, *Time and Work in England 1750–1830* (Oxford, 2000); idem, 'The longest years: new estimates of labor input in England, 1760–1830', *Journal of Economic History*, 61/4 (2001), pp. 1065–82; E. Hopkins, 'Working hours and conditions during the industrial revolution: a reappraisal', *Economic History Review*, 35/1 (1982), pp. 52–66; Humphries, *Childhood and Child Labour*; Peter Kirby, *Child Labour in Britain, 1750–1870* (Basingstoke, 2003); P. Huck, 'Infant mortality and the living standards of English workers during the industrial revolution', *Journal of Economic History*, 55/3 (1995), pp. 528–50; Simon Szreter and Graham Mooney, 'Urbanisation, mortality, and the standard of living debate', *Economic History Review*, 51/1 (1998), pp. 84–112.

50. R. Floud, K. Wachter and A. Gregory, *Height, Health and History: Nutritional Status in the United Kingdom, 1750–1980* (Cambridge, 1990), Stephen Nicholas and Richard H. Steckel, 'Heights and living standards of English workers during the early years of industrialization, 1770–1815', *Journal of Economic History*, 1/4 (1991), pp. 937–57; Stephen Nicholas and Deborah Oxley, 'The living standards of women during the industrial revolution, 1795–1820', *Economic History Review*, 46/4 (1993), pp. 723–49; Paul Johnson and Stephen Nicholas, 'Male and female living standards in England and Wales, 1812–1857: evidence from criminal height records', *Economic History Review*, 48/3 (1995), pp. 470–81; Stephen Nicholas and Deborah Oxley, 'The living standards of women in England and Wales, 1785–1815: new evidence from Newgate prison records', *Economic History Review*, 49/3 (1996), pp. 591–9; Robert William Fogel, *The Escape from Hunger and Premature Death, 1700–2100: Europe, America, and the Third World* (Cambridge, 2004).

51. The major exception here is Gregory Clark, whose work suggests sizeable rises in the real wage before 1850. See Clark, 'The condition of the working class in England, 1209–2004', *Journal of Political Economy*, 113/6 (2005), pp. 1307–40, idem, 'Farm wages and living standards in the industrial revolution: England, 1670–1869', *Economic History Review*, 53/3 (2001), pp. 477–505.

52. Lincoln, 'Memoirs', p. 2 (Norfolk Record Office).

53. Ibid., p. 36.

54. Ibid., p. 37.

55. The expression is Hobsbawm's. See his 'The British standard of living, 1790–1850', *Economic History Review*, 10/1 (1957), pp. 46–68, p. 59.

56. Lincoln, 'Memoirs', p. 37.

57. Ibid., pp. 50–2.

58. Ibid., p. 80.


Part I: Earning a Living

2 Men at Work

1. Friedrich Engels, *The Condition of the Working Class in England*, ed. David McLellan (Oxford, 1993), pp. 144–96.

2. Andrew Ure, *The Philosophy of Manufactures, Or, An Exposition of the Scientific, Moral, and Commercial Economy of the Factory System of Great Britain* (London, 2nd edn, 1835), pp. 277–403, esp. pp. 309–13, 379–402.

3. Key works include: Sidney Webb and Beatrice Webb, *Industrial Democracy* (n.p., 1897); J. L. and Barbara Hammond, *The Rise of Modern Industry* (9th edn, London, 1966); E. P. Thompson, *The Making of the English Working Class* (Harmondsworth, 1976).

4. Thompson, *The Making*, pp. 487–8.

5. E. P. Thompson, 'Time, work-discipline and industrial capitalism', *Past & Present*, 38 (1967), pp. 56–97; H. Joachim Voth, *Time and Work in England 1750–1830* (Oxford,

2000); idem, 'The longest years: new estimates of labor input in England, 1760–1830', *Journal of Economic History*, 61/4 (2001), pp. 1065–82. See also, however, E. Hopkins, 'Working hours and conditions during the industrial revolution: a reappraisal', *Economic History Review*, 35 (1982), pp. 52–66; R. Whipp, 'A "time to every purpose": an essay on time and work', in P. Joyce, ed., *The Historical Meanings of Work* (Cambridge, 1987), pp. 210–36; Gregory Clark and Ysbrand Van der Werf, 'Work in progress? The industrious revolution', *Journal of Economic History*, 58/3 (1998), pp. 830–43.

6. Richard Price, *Labour in British Society. An Interpretive History* (London, 1986); Clive Behagg, *Politics and Production in the Early Nineteenth Century* (London, 1990).

7. Sidney Pollard, 'Factory discipline in the industrial revolution', *Economic History Review*, n. s. 16/2 (1963), pp. 254–71; Gregory Clark, 'Factory discipline', *Journal of Economic History*, 54/1 (1994), pp. 128–63; Chris Evans, 'Work and workloads during industrialization: the experience of forgemen in the British iron industry 1750–1850', *International Review of Social History*, 44/2 (1999), pp. 197–215.

8. Suresh Naidu and Noam Yuchtman, 'Coercive contract enforcement: law and the labour market in nineteenth century industrial Britain', *ABER Working Paper*, 17051 (2011); Robert J. Steinfeld, *Coercion, Contract, and Free Labor in the Nineteenth Century* (Cambridge, 2001). Though it should be emphasised that none of these writers position their work within the bleak interpretation of the industrial revolution.

9. Dodd, p. 187.

10. Ibid., p. 221.

11. Ibid., p. 205.

12. *Exposition of a Coiner*, p. 4.

13. Ibid.

14. C. Campbell, p. 23.

15. It is interesting to note that a recent study of agricultural labourers in the period before 1780 suggests that their living standards may also have been higher than previously believed (Craig Muldrew, *Food, Energy and the Creation of Industriousness: Work and Material Culture in Agrarian England, 1550–1780*, Cambridge, 2011). Muldrew's study stops in 1780, but his findings do not of course preclude the possibility of further gains in subsequent decades.

16. Barlow, p. 21.

17. Ibid., pp. 19–20.

18. For an introduction to the history of apprenticeship see J. Lane, *Apprenticeship in England, 1600–1914* (London, 1996); S. L. Kaplan, 'Reconsidering apprenticeship: afterthoughts', in B. De Munck, S. L. Kaplan and H. Soly, eds, *Learning on the Shop Floor: Historical Perspectives on Apprenticeship* (New York, 2007), pp. 203–19; Chris Minns and Patrick Wallis, *Rules and Reality: Quantifying the Practice of Apprenticeship in Early Modern Europe* (LSE Economic History Working Papers, 118/09, 2009)

19. K. D. M. Snell, 'The apprenticeship system in British history: the fragmentation of a cultural institution', *History of Education*, 25/4 (1996), pp. 303–21.

20. Hardy, p. 38.

21. The shoemakers who learned without serving an apprenticeship are: Askham, p. vii; T. Cooper, pp. 42–5; Dunning, p. 214; C. Bent, pp. 5–6; Bezer, pp. 173–7; Gibbs, pp. 45–6; Hardy, p. 38; Holcroft, p. 176; Hollingsworth, pp. 5–6; Jewell, p. 141; Spurr, p. 283; Struthers, pp. xxxiv–xxxvi. Those who entered a formal apprenticeship are: Crocker, pp. ix–xi; Gifford, p. 13; Herbert, pp. 7–12; M'Kaen (though he never completed), pp. 8–9; McAdam, pp. 2–4; W. Smith, p. 180; and Watkins, p. 20. Lackington served an apprenticeship with no premium, pp. 86–7. The fate of Chatterton, p. 2; Nicholson, p. 3; and Younger, p. 103; is not entirely clear.

22. T. Carter, pp. 70–4, 113–14.

23. The other tailors who learned without serving an apprenticeship are [Cameron], pp. 12–13; [Holkinson], 24 Jan. 1857; Lowery, pp. 59–61. The Irish tailor served an apprenticeship ('Life of an Irish tailor', 18 April 1857) as did Robert Crowe, pp. 4–5, though he quit early.

24. Carpenters: formal apprenticeships (Gabbitass, pp. xii–xiii; Jackson, p. 33; Newnham, p. 283; and G. Smith, *Autobiography*, pp. 16–17); uncompleted apprenticeships (Buckley, pp. 78–80, 104–20, and Croll, p. 16); informal arrangements (Bennett, p. 2, Bristol Record Office); Thomson, pp. 165–7). The terms of Murison's apprenticeship are unclear, pp. 212–13. Bakers: formal apprenticeships ('Life of a journeyman baker', 2 May 1857; D. Johnston, p. 31, though it was of only two years' duration; W. Swan, p. 44); informal arrangements (Innes, pp. 8–9; 'Life of a journeyman baker', 13 & 20 Dec. 1856). Whitesmiths: formal apprenticeships (Claxton, p. 5; T. Mitchell, p. 4, Bristol Central Library); and Stradley, [p. 2] (Greenwich Heritage Centre); informal arrangements ([Gooch], p. 16 and [Self-Reformer], p. 284). The fate of T. Wood was not entirely clear, p. 8 (Bradford Central Library). Shipwright: formal apprenticeships (R. Barker, pp. 3–4; Sanderson, p. 22; and Thomson, pp. 59–76); informal arrangement (Thompson, pp. 6–7). Butcher: informal arrangement (J. Taylor, p. 8). Coopers: formal apprenticeships (Hart, 7/2, p. 151; and Nicol, p. 25).
25. Gammage p. 37; North, p. 103; Murdoch, pp. 8–12; Whetstone, p. 60; E. Davis, p. 10. Coach-trimming refers to the painting of horse-drawn carriages.
26. On deskilling, see in particular, Harry Braverman, *Labor and Monopoly Capital: the Degradation of Work in the Twentieth Century* (New York, 1974). See also Stephen J. Nicholas and Jacqueline M. Nicholas, 'Male literacy, "deskilling", and the industrial revolution', *Journal of Interdisciplinary History*, 23/1 (1992), pp. 1–18.
27. Dunning, pp. 120–4. See also Struthers, pp. xxxiv–xxxvi.
28. Dunning, p. 124.
29. Aird, pp. 10–11; *Memoirs of a Printer's Devil*, pp. 91–2; Bertram, pp. 3–28; *Autobiography of Scotch Lad*, pp. 26–33; Adams, pp. 81–90; Leno, pp. 8–9; [Smith], pp. 6–8; Paterson, pp. 60–2; J. Robinson, p. 1; Roper, no pag. (Warwickshire County Record Office); Skeen, pp. 2–6. The exceptions are: Urie, who did not complete his apprenticeship (Urie, pp. 41–2); and *Scenes from my Life*, p. 83. See also Horne, who started as an errand boy in a printers' shop, but left as his father could not afford the premium for an apprenticeship. E. Horne, pp. 30–2.
30. Gilders and carvers (Johnson, pp. 34–6; S. Taylor, pp. 2–3; and Wallis, pp. 23–8); cutlers (Jewitt, pp. 14–17 (Wigan Archives); Longden, p. 10). Consider also the drapers and grocers: Belcher, p. 10; Bewley, pp. 10–11; and Featherstone, p. 10, all entered apprenticeships; Binns, p. 2 (Tyne and Wear Archive Service), learned the work from his uncle. Millwrights (Croll, pp. 15–16, and Haggart, pp. 6–7, entered an apprenticeship; R. White, p. 3. did not). Blacksmiths (Bownas, pp. 1–2; Collyer, p. 21; Hick, p. 5; Stradley, [p. 2] (Greenwich Heritage Centre) all entered apprenticeships). Cartwright and wagon wright (Errington, p. 17, and W. Johnston, p. 13, both entered apprenticeships).
31. Lovett, p. 25. The other cabinetmakers were Hopkinson, pp. 20–1, and H. Taylor, p. 6 (East Riding Archives).
32. Bangs, pp. 11–13.
33. It will be seen that I differ in emphasis from Humphries' recent account of apprenticeship. Humphries has stressed the importance of apprenticeship to industrialisation, but does not distinguish between formal and informal apprenticeships. In order to accept the resilience of apprenticeship during this economic transition, I believe it is necessary to work with a very loose definition of apprenticeship and to recognise that the entry to and substance of 'apprenticeships' did change considerably throughout the period. See Jane Humphries, *Childhood and Child Labour in the British Industrial Revolution* (Cambridge, 2010), pp. 256–305,
34. G. Smith, *Autobiography*, p. 20; [Self Reformer], p. 285; T. Mitchell, pp. 18–22 (Bristol Central Library).
35. Good pay: Collyer, p. 39; Fairburn, pp. 72, 83; Henderson, p. 5; 'Life of journeyman baker', 13 & 20 Dec. 1856; 'Life of a journeyman baker', 2 May 1857; Longden, p. 22; Lowery, p. 61; W. Swan, pp. 50–l; Thomson, pp. 166–7; Wallis, p. 48; Watkins, pp. 23–4; T. Wood, pp. 14–16 (Bradford Central Library).

36. Clothes: T. Carter, pp. 149–50; W. Swan, p. 48. Books: McAdam, pp. 3–4.
37. Gibbs, p. 46; H. Taylor, p. 6 (East Riding Archives); Burdett, p. 8 (Nottinghamshire Archives). See also Burn, p. 134; Corben, pp. 11–12.
38. Burn, p. 152.
39. Claxton, p. 17.
40. Skeen, p. 9.
41. Hick, p. 23.
42. Younger, p. 291; T. Mitchell, p. 18 (Bristol Central Library).
43. Bennett, p. 4 (Bristol Record Office).
44. See, for instance, J. Robinson, p. 1.
45. See, for instance, ibid., pp. 4–8 *passim*; Croll, p. 16. See also, more generally, Humphrey R. Southall, 'The tramping artisan revisits: labour mobility and economic distress in early Victorian England', *Economic History Review*, 44/2 (1991), pp. 272–96.
46. Davenport, pp. 28–30.
47. Ibid., pp. 33–7.
48. T. Carter, p. 152; Crowe, p. 6; [Holkinson], 24 Jan. 1857 (of his father), 31 Jan. 1857 (himself); 'Life of Irish tailor', 18 April 1857.
49. Lowery, pp. 59–61.
50. Chatterton, p. 2.
51. Watkins, pp. 22–3. See also C. Bent, pp. 6–20; 'Life of a journeyman baker', 13 & 20 Dec. 1856; 'Life of a journeyman baker', 2 May 1857. More unusually the East End baker, William Swan, 'found it difficult to get enough for ourselves and the children' owing to unemployment (W. Swan, p. 54). The hatter James Dawson Burn suffered from bouts of unemployment (Burn, pp. 135, 137). See also the shoemaker Robert Spurr (Spurr, pp. 285–6).
52. 'Colin', p. 36.
53. Ibid.
54. Ibid.
55. Writing under the pseudonym John Buckley. See Buckley, pp. 126–8.
56. Lincoln, p. 36 (Norfolk Record Office); Davies, pp. 2–8; Mayett, pp. 85, 92–5; W. T. Swan, p. 15; B. Shaw, pp. 28, 34–6, 37, 45, 47–50.
57. Lackingon, pp. 130–1.
58. Ibid., p. 132.
59. 'Colin', pp. 36, 60, 36.
60. W. Swan, p. 51.
61. D. Johnston, p. 92.
62. It can be seen that I am working with a common-sense understanding of 'skill'. The extent to which factory work in the early nineteenth century was unskilled is challenged in H. M. Boot, 'How skilled were Lancashire cotton factory workers in 1833?', *Economic History Review*, 2nd ser., 48/2 (1995), pp. 283–303.
63. For an introduction to the literature on proto-industry, see Charles Sabel and Jonathan Zeitlin, 'Historical alternatives to mass production', *Past & Present*, 108 (1985), pp. 133–76; Pat Hudson, 'Industrial organisation and structure', in Roderick Floud and Paul Johnson, eds, *The Cambridge Economic History of Modern Britain: Industrialisation, 1700–1860*, i (Cambridge, 2004).
64. J. Bethune, p. 12; Calladine, p. 2; [Moss], p. 5 (Nottinghamshire Archives).
65. Holroyd, pp. 115–16; Livesey, p. 197; Short, [p. 20] (Norwich Castle Museum); Whitehead, pp. 5–6.
66. The most influential account in this vein has been E. P. Thompson, *The Making*; though see also, more recently, John C. Brown, 'The condition of England and the standard of living: cotton textiles in the northwest, 1806–1850', *Journal of Economic History*, 50/3 (1990), pp. 591–614. There have always been critics, emphasising the slow rate of decline and the extent to which factories and mills allowed families to make up the lost wages of the male weaver. See, for example, Duncan Bythell, *The Handloom Weavers. A*

*Study in the English Cotton Industry during the Industrial Revolution* (Cambridge, 1969); J. S. Lyons, 'Family response to economic decline: handloom weavers in early nineteenth-century Lancashire', *Research in Economic History*, 10 (1981), pp. 45–91; Geoffrey Timmins, *The Last Shift: the Decline of Handloom Weaving in Nineteenth-Century Lancashire* (Manchester, 1993).

67. For weavers engaged in farm work: Varley, 5 March 1822, p. 383. For knitters: Woolley, 11 Oct. 1813; 1 April, 17 June 1815 (Nottinghamshire Archives); [Moss], pp. 7–8 (Nottinghamshire Archives). See also the discussion in Carolyn Steedman, *The Stocking-maker, the Magistrate and the Law* (forthcoming), chs 8–9.

68. Bamford, *Early Days*, pp. 225–6; J. Barker, pp. 36–7; J. Bethune, p. 14; Brierley, p. 27; Castle, p. 18 (Essex Record Office); Farish, p. 34; *Short Account of Glasgow Weaver*, p. 4; Gutteridge, pp. 122, 124; T. Hanby, p. 136; Whitehead, p. 31.

69. Hammond, p. 24.

70. Arch, p. 47.

71. Bamford, *Early Days*, p. 226.

72. Brierley, p. 27.

73. Hammond, pp. 24–5.

74. Brierley, p. 27.

75. Bamford, *Early Days*, p. 307; J. Barker, pp. 30–6; J. Bethune, p. 15; Brierley, pp. 22–7; [Butler], p. 12; Castle, p. 21 (Essex Record Office); Farish, p. 34; *Short Account of Glasgow Weaver*, p. 5; Gutteridge, pp. 115–26; Harland extract no. 8 (Bradford Central Library); Holroyd, p. 116; Leatherland, p. 9; 'Life of handloom weaver', 25 April 1857; Livesey, pp. 197–8; Sankoffsky, p. 2 (Cumbria Record Office); Sholl, p. 39; Thom, pp. 21–38.

76. Carnegie, pp. 12–13; Cooke, p. 3; Farish, pp. 6–7; Hemmingway, pp. 2–9 (Norfolk Record Office); 'Life of a handloom weaver', 25 April 1857; M'Gonnagall, p. 2; T. Wood, p. 8 (Bradford Central Library).

77. Calladine, p. 2.

78. Hutton, pp. 63–4; [Moss], no pag. (Nottinghamshire Archives); Ragg, p. vi. The other knitter was Millhouse. His moves between knitting and the Nottinghamshire militia may have been prompted by downturns in the trade. See Millhouse, pp. vii–xii.

79. For more on this process, see Timmins, *The Last Shift*, pp. 17–34, 61–106.

80. See in particular Holroyd, p. 116; J. Bethune, p. 15. Just two of the autobiographers were still weavers when they wrote their autobiography: *Short Account of Glasgow Weaver*, 'Life of a handloom weaver', 25 April 1857.

81. Gutteridge, p. 99.

82. Thom, pp. 21–40, p. 21.

83. Hutton, pp. 63–4.

84. On this see in particular: Maxine Berg, 'What difference did women's work make to the industrial revolution?', *History Workshop Journal*, 35 (1993), pp. 22–44.

85. Factory work: Bates, p. 2; Cooke, p. 5; Farish, pp. 18, 66–84; Hanson, p. 14; Heaton, pp. xxii–xxiii; Hemmingway, p. 385 (Norfolk Record Office); Thom, pp. 47–8. Warehouses and dealing: Bamford, *Early Days*, pp. 187–92; Brierley, pp. 50, 54; Hammond, p. 24; Harland, extract no. 8 (Bradford Central Library); and Whitehead, p. 40. Farish, pp. 78–81 and Hemmingway, pp. 368–74, also worked transporting goods after a stint in the factory. It will be seen, then, that I disagree with Bythell and Lyons, who have argued that factories primarily employed children and wives rather than the displaced weavers. Adult male weavers certainly did take up employment inside, and in support of, the new factories. Bythell, *Handloom Weavers*, pp. 60–4; Lyons, 'Family response to economic decline', pp. 45–91.

86. Livesey, pp. 228–9; Sankoffsky, p. 2 (Cumbria Record Office); J. Wood, p. 20.

87. Their stories are told in: Castle, pp. 21ff. (Essex Record Office); Gutteridge, pp. 99, 115–28, 172–83. John Leatherland and his wife turned to weaving silk vests at this point, and fared a little better. See Leatherland, pp. 31–3.

88. See Heaton, p. xxiii; Leatherland, pp. 9, 31–3; Thom, pp. 8–10, 18.

256  NOTES to pp. 41–4

89. C. Campbell, p. 23; *Exposition of a Coiner*, pp. 4–5.
90. Catton, p. 4. See also Bodell, p. 20.
91. B. Shaw, p. 45.
92. Marcroft, pp. 39–43. See also 'Life of a cotton spinner', 27 Dec. 1856; 'Life of a journeyman baker', 13 & 20 Dec. 1856.
93. Rushton, pp. 66, 82–5.
94. Dodd, pp. 200, 202.
95. Collyer, p. 2.
96. Tough, p. 6.
97. [Wright], no pag. See also Bates, 30 years at Paul Speak's mill, p. 2; Catton, 9 years, pp. 4–5; *Exposition of a Coiner*, 12 years, p. 5; Hanson, 10 years in Messrs Wards' weaving shop, p. 24; Hemmingway, 11 years at Stirling's Mill in Manchester, p. 385 (Norfolk Record Office). Lincoln, 7 years at Woolwich Arsenal, pp. 26–9 (Norfolk Record Office).
98. Gwyer, pp. 8–9; Rushton, p. 54; Teer, p. iv; Townend, p. 22; Watson, pp. 109–10 and references in note 85 above.
99. T. Wood, pp. 8–9,14 (Bradford Central Library).
100. B. Shaw, pp. 38, 42.
101. I. Roberts (bookkeeper), pp. 14–15; 'Life of a handloom weaver' (account collector), 25 April 1857.
102. Hanby, no pag.
103. W. Smith, p. 183.
104. Hemmingway (carrier for 'Fustian Cutters of Lymm'), p. 385.
105. Watson, p. 110. See also Farish, pp. 78–81; Tough, p. 5.
106. Barr, pp. 37–44; Farish, pp. 72–4, 85–6; Langdon, p. 64; Mallard, pp. 11ff. (Northamptonshire Record Office).
107. G. Cooper, [p. 20]. See also Goodliffe, no pag. (Leicestershire Record Office); 'Life of a cotton spinner', 27 Dec. 1856; Oliver, p. 50.
108. Croll (tea), pp. 20–1; Livesey ('cheap cheese'), pp. 228–9; E. Davis (cakes and gingerbread), p. 13. See also the references in note 85 above and 111 below.
109. 'Life of a journeyman baker', 13 & 20 Dec. 1856; 'Life of a journeyman baker', 2 May 1857.
110. See, for example, [Cameron], pp. 15ff.; Love, p. 38ff.; M'Gonagall, pp. 3–8; [Wright], no pag.
111. Chadwick, p. 9; Pearman, pp. 188–91.
112. Hemmingway, p. 408 (Norfolk Record Office). See also Sankoffsky, p. 2 (Cumbria Record Office) and [Porteus], p. 25.
113. For more on social mobility through this period see Andrew Miles, *Social Mobility in Nineteenth and Early Twentieth Century England* (Basingstoke, 1999). Miles' emphasis on the fluidity of nineteenth-century society chimes with the evidence presented here.
114. Tough, pp. 4–6.
115. Powell, p. 10.
116. Whittaker, p. 26.
117. Dodgson, 19 May 1956 (Halifax Central Library).
118. B. Shaw, p. 40.
119. Though rather dated, John Benson, *British Coal-Miners in the Nineteenth Century: a Social History* (New York, 1980), remains a useful introduction to the history of mining. A valuable reminder of the great variation between mining regions is contained in John Langton, 'Proletarianization in the industrial revolution: regionalism and kinship in the labour markets of the British coal industry from the seventeenth to the nineteenth centuries', *Transactions of the Institute of British Geographers*, n.s. 25/1 (2000), pp. 31–49.
120. Burt, pp. 104, 108, 112; Weaver, p. 73; John Wilson, p. 66.
121. Oliver, p. 18.
122. Errington, *passim*. Rymer suggested the pits did occasionally lie idle, but he mentioned just 'days now and then'. Rymer, p. 5. See also the discussion in Burt, p. 112. See,

however, Timothy Mountjoy who noted that at one point 'the summer trade was so bad, we only worked two, sometimes three, days per week, and we could not see when these bad times would come to an end'. Mountjoy, p. 18. For more on the Forest of Dean miners, see Chris Fisher, *Custom, Work and Market Capitalism: the Forest of Dean Colliers, 1788–1888* (London, 1981).

123. Lovekin, no. 4 (Brunel University Library). See also Blow, p. 5; Mallard, pp. 8–9 (Northamptonshire Record Office); W. Milne, p. 173.
124. Arch, p. 50.
125. I. Anderson, p. 9.
126. Lovekin, no. 4 (Brunel University Library).
127. Autobiography of Suffolk Farm Labourer, p. 15 (Suffolk Record Office).
128. [H., Bill], p. 143.
129. John Wilson, pp. 46–7.
130. For more on unemployment, see John Burnett, *Idle Hands: the Experience of Unemployment, 1790–1990* (London, 1994), pp. 54–63, 87–121.
131. Barlow, p. 16.
132. Hopper, pp. 183–4.
133. Chubb, p. iii.
134. Ferguson, pp. 21–2.
135. Ibid., p. 22.
136. Ibid., p. 21.
137. Oakley, p. 139.
138. Nye, p. 20.
139. G. Mitchell, p. 96; Mayett, p. 65.
140. Cook, p. 35 (Lincoln Reference Library).
141. Nye, pp. 12–13; T. Wood, p. 2 (Bradford Central Library); Langdon, pp. 24–5.
142. Bowd, p. 298.
143. Mayett, pp. 61, 72, 73, 76.
144. Younger, pp. 13–14.
145. 'Life of an Irish tailor', 18 April 1857.
146. Edwards, pp. 4–5; G. Smith, *Autobiography*, p. 5.
147. John Burgess, pp. 20, 27, 29, 58, 60, 61, 67, 68. See also Todd, p. 75.
148. Matters were brighter though for those trying to make a living in the second half of the century. See Irving (Carlisle Library); Plastow (University of Warwick); Pointer (Broadstairs Library); Shervington (Worcestershire Record Office).
149. Oakley, p. 139.
150. Catton, p. 4.
151. Ibid.
152. Mayett, pp. 69–70.
153. Ibid., p. 73. See also the incident described on p. 20.
154. Murdoch, p. 2.
155. These include Britton, p. 62; Buckley, p. 78; Croll, p. 16; Crowe, p. 4; Fairburn, p. 69; W. Johnston, p. 13; H. Miller, p. 153; Murison, p. 212; North, pp. 45–6; Paterson, p. 60; Whetstone, p. 60.
156. These include E. Anderson, p. 3; Choyce, p. 3; Davenport, p. 19; Donaldson, p. 23; Haggart, p. 6; B. Harris, pp. 1–2; Hawker, p. 3; Lawrence, p. 18; Mayett, pp. 22–3; Rattenbury, p. 2; Robinson, p. 9 (West Sussex Record Office); Somerville, pp. 124–8.
157. Gibbs, p. 45; [Gooch], p. 16; [Holkinson], 24 Jan. 1857; Jewell, p. 141; [Self-Reformer], p. 284; Struthers, pp. xxxiv–xxxv; Younger, p. 103.
158. I. Anderson, p. 9; Bowes, pp. 9–12; Blow, p. 5; [H. Bill], p. 143; Mallard, pp. 8–9 (Northamptonshire Record Office); W. Milne, p. 173; G. Mitchell, p. 109.
159. Catton, p. 4; Gywer, pp. 8–9; Watson, pp. 109–10.
160. G. Mitchell, p. 96.
161. Ibid., p. 108; See also Bowes, pp. 9–12.

162. G. Mitchell, p. 108.
163. I. Anderson, p. 8.
164. [Self-Reformer], p. 285.
165. Lincoln, pp. 15–25 (Norfolk Record Office).
166. Ibid., p. 27.
167. Ibid., pp. 28–34.
168. Mockford, pp. 14–52, *passim*.
169. The quote comes from E. P. Thompson. See note 4 above.

### 3 Suffer Little Children

1. Charles Dickens, *Oliver Twist* (1838); idem, *David Copperfield* (1850), ch. 11; idem, *Sketches by Boz* (1836).
2. Charles Kingsley, *Water Babies* (1863); Frances Trollope, *The Life and Adventures of Michael Armstrong, the Factory Boy* (1840); Charlotte Elizabeth, *Helen Fleetwood* (1840).
3. The expression was used to particularly good effect by Richard Oastler. See, for example, his letter to the *Leeds Mercury*, 16 Oct. 1830.
4. Coal Mines Act of 1842. For more about this legislation, see Robert Gray, *The Factory Question and Industrial England, 1830–1860* (Cambridge, 1996); Joanna Innes, 'Origins of the factory acts: the Health and Morals of Apprentices Act 1802', in N. Landau, ed., *Law, Crime and English Society, 1660–1830* (Cambridge, 2002), pp. 230–55.
5. The best summary is to be found in Peter Kirby, *Child Labour in Britain, 1750–1870* (Basingstoke, 2003). See also Clark Nardinelli, *Child Labour and the Industrial Revolution* (Bloomington, IN, 1990); H. Cunningham, 'The employment and unemployment of children, 1680–1851', *Past and Present*, 126 (1990); Sara Horrell and Jane Humphries, '"The exploitation of little children": child labor and the family economy in the industrial revolution', *Explorations in Economic History*, 32 (1995), pp. 485–516; Michael Lavalette, ed., *A Thing of the Past? Child Labour in Britain in the Nineteenth and Twentieth Centuries* (Liverpool, 1999); Carolyn Tuttle, *Hard at Work in Factories and Mines: the Economics of Child Labor during the British Industrial Revolution* (Boulder, CO, 1999).
6. Rymer, p. 2.
7. Collyer, p. 15
8. Hopper, p. 182; C. Campbell, p. 2; Hardy, p. 38.
9. Over a hundred of the autobiographers provided insufficient detail to pinpoint the age at which they started work, leaving us with a sample of 251 writers.
10. The figure varies slightly depending upon whether we use the age at which they first started work, or the age at which they started full-time employment, which was often slightly later. If we use the part-time figure, the average age for starting work is almost exactly 10 years. If we use the full-time figure, the average is slightly raised to 10 years and 3 months. As we shall see in more detail below, part-time employment was most heavily concentrated in rural areas.
11. Contrast with Jane Humphries, *Childhood and Child Labour in the British Industrial Revolution* (Cambridge, 2010), table 7.1, p. 176, who finds the average age for starting work is 10.5.
12. Between 1700 and 1749 the mean age for starting work was 10 years; between 1750 and 1799 it was 10.6 years; and between 1800 and 1850 it was 9.8 years.
13. E. Davis, p. 6
14. Belcher, pp. 9–10.
15. Mockford, p. 3.
16. Ibid., p. 2.
17. J. Taylor, *Memoirs*, p. 4.
18. Ibid., p. 6.
19. Of the 31 children who started work at the age of 10, 14 provided evidence of poverty in their family whereas 17 did not. See also Humphries who concludes, in somewhat

similar vein, that fathers' earning capacity is 'not the full story' when it comes to explaining children's age at starting work. Humphries, *Childhood and Child Labour*, pp. 180–3.

20. *Life of a Chimney Boy*, p. 12.
21. Robinson, p. 9 (West Sussex Record Office).
22. By way of context, about 40 per cent of children lived in industrial areas.
23. For instance; Bennett, pp. 9–10 (Bristol Record Office; J. Bethune, p. 6; Cook, pp. 2–3 (Lincoln Reference Library); B. Harris, p. 144; Hogg, p. 5; Mallard, p. 3 (Northamptonshire Record Office); G. Mitchell, p. 96; J. Robinson, p. 7 (West Sussex Record Office); [H. Bill], p. 141.
24. Brown, *Sixty Years*, pp. 12–15; [Gooch], p. 8; Huffer, p. 14; Langdon, p. 28; Shervington, pp. ix–x (Worcestershire Record Office); Shipp, pp. 3–4.
25. See, for instance, Barr, p. 34; Gabbitass, pp. xii–xiii; Featherstone, p. 10; Skeen, pp. 2–3.
26. Barr, p. 34.
27. Gibbs, pp. 27, 30.
28. Ibid., pp. 31–2.
29. Ibid., p. 32.
30. Jewell, pp. 126–8; J. Bethune, pp. 6, 11–12. See also Lea, [p. 4] (Sheffield Archives); John Taylor, 'Autobiographical sketch', p. 7.
31. Hogg, p. 5.
32. Bowcock, p. 8.
33. Bennett, p. 2 (Bristol Record Office).
34. Bowd, p. 295.
35. Jewell, pp. 130–2. See also Mallard, p. 3 (Northamptonshire Record Office). When the farmer who employed him as a child 'got upset he would kick and knock me about one day he was knocking my head against a gate post he said he would knock it untill it was as hard as the post'.
36. Langdon, pp. 29–32.
37. Hogg, p. 6.
38. W. Milne, pp. 109–11.
39. Ibid., pp. 120–2. Joseph Mayett reported a similar tale, returned by his father to a drunken master who beat him, p. 5. See also Nye: when he lost his place in service he was allowed to stay at home 'threshing with my father', but he also 'came back on scanty food again', p. 11.
40. Nye, p. 11.
41. Wallis, p. 16.
42. Ibid., pp. 16–17.
43. See, for example, Hawker, p. 1; Holcroft, pp. 14–17, and Hollingsworth, pp. 4–5 (working for their family); MacDonald, pp. 12–15 (irregular work); Watkins, pp. 11–17 (seasonal bird scarer).
44. Stir(r)up, 22, Nov. 1856. See also 'Jacques', 11 Nov. 1856, who spent a year at home after leaving school 'without finding me in any regular employment'.
45. Hemmingway, pp. 20–5 (Norfolk Record Office). See also Obadiah Short, who was also raised in Norwich in the early nineteenth century and remembered being 'very poorly clothed, and not too well fed' before starting work. Short, [pp. 6, 22–3] (Norwich Castle Museum).
46. P. Taylor, p. 38. Paisley had once been the centre of a thriving weaving industry and offered work for all the family, including small children. But by the 1840s the industry had collapsed so Peter's parents were trying to find him a position as an errand boy, with the usual difficulty that entailed. See also Short, [p. 46] (Norwich Castle Museum).
47. T. Carter, p. 99; Bezer, pp. 162–6.
48. For more detail on child labour in industrial districts, see Per Bolin-Hort, *Work, Family, and the State: Child Labour and the Organization of Production in the British Cotton Industry, 1780–1920* (Lund, 1989); Adam Booker et al., 'Child slaves? Working

260    NOTES to pp. 70–8

children during the industrial revolution, c. 1780–1850', in Michael Winstanley, ed., *Working Children in Nineteenth-Century Lancashire* (Preston, 1995), pp. 25–47.

49. Piecers: Clifford, p. 5; Dodd, p. 187; 'Life of a journeyman baker', 2 May 1857; Teer, p. iii; Rushton, p. 28. Scavenger: Aitken, p. 18.
50. Doffers: Collyer, p. 15; Roberts, pp. 10–11.
51. Aitken, p. 19.
52. Richard Meurig Evans, *Children Working Underground* (Cardiff, 1979); Peter Kirby, 'The historic viability of child labour and the Mines Act of 1842', in Lavalette, ed., *Thing of the Past?*, pp. 101–17.
53. Lovekin no. 2 (Brunel University Library).
54. For example, Hodgson, p. 5; Hughes, p. 7 (Newport Central Library); Parkinson, p. 1.
55. Lowery, p. 45; 'Coal miner's defence', p. 231; Weaver, p. 31; Dunn, pp. 9–10.
56. Lovekin, no. 2 (Brunel University Library).
57. Dunn, p. 17.
58. Brierley, p. 19; 'Life of a handloom weaver', 25 April 1857; Livesey, pp. 196–7; Short, [p. 24] (Norwich Castle Museum).
59. E. Davis, p. 6; Deacon, p. 2; G. Cooper, [p. 14]; Sanderson, p. 13; Hodgson, p. 6; Short [pp. 28, 43–4] (Norwich Castle Museum).
60. Struthers, pp. xviii–xix.
61. Marcroft, p. 33; Rymer, p. 2; Ricketts, p. 121; Marsh, p. 2 (Barnsley Archives); Rushton, pp. 29–31 (clearing brushwood and potato planting).
62. Marcroft, pp. 33–4.
63. C. Bent, p. 4; 'Life of a journeyman baker', 13 & 20 Dec. 1856. See also Hemmingway, pp. 28–9 (Norfolk Record Office).
64. Hemmingway, p. 64.
65. J. Wood, p. 4.
66. Hodgson, p. 5.
67. Marsh, p. 3 (Barnsley Archives). See also Errington, p. 38; 'Life of a journeyman baker', 2 May 1857; Marcroft, p. 33.
68. G. Smith, *Autobiography*, p. 9.
69. Oliver, p. 11.
70. Whitehead, pp. 6–13, *passim*.
71. Hemmingway, pp. 31–2 (Norfolk Record Office).
72. Dodd, p. 186.
73. Hemmingway, p. 29 (Norfolk Record Office).
74. 'Coal miner's defence', p. 231.
75. Dodgson (Halifax Central Library), p. 5
76. A similar observation has been made by Hugh Cunningham in 'The decline of child labour: labour markets and family economies in Europe and North America since 1830', *Economic History Review*, 53/3 (2002), pp. 409–28, esp. p. 419.
77. Hughes, pp. 6–7 (Newport Central Library).
78. J. Harris, p. 28. See also Edwards, p. 6.
79. Gabbitass, p. xii.
80. Clifford, p. 2. See also I. Roberts, pp. 12–13; T. Smith, pp. 6–7.
81. E. Davis, p. 9.
82. B. Shaw, pp. 87–94.
83. Ibid., pp. 43, 44.
84. Ibid., p. 44.
85. Sholl, pp. 37–8; Tryon, pp. 7–8; Hutton, pp. 11–12; D. Taylor, pp. 2–3; J. Taylor, p. 6.
86. Sholl, pp. 37–8.
87. The only exception being Tryon.
88. Better-off families include: Hopper, p. 182; T. Johnson, p. 32; Jaco, p. 260; Staniforth, pp. 147–8.
89. Barlow, p. 15.

90. Ferguson, pp. 4, 11.
91. Hugh Cunningham's suggestion that unemployment was widespread amongst children before 1850 was refuted by Peter Kirby (see the discussion in Hugh Cunningham, 'The employment and unemployment of children, 1680–1851', *Past and Present*, 126 (1990) pp. 115–50; Peter Kirby, 'How many children were "unemployed" in eighteenth and nineteenth-century Britain?', *Past and Present* 187 (2004)) pp. 187–202. My evidence from the autobiographies suggests that availability of work was indeed a factor in determining overall levels of child employment in the way that Cunningham suggested.
92. 'Life of a journeyman baker', 13 & 20 Dec. 1856.
93. T. Wood, p. 7 (Bradford Central Library).
94. Townend, p. 4.
95. Weaver, p. 32. See also Askham, p. vii.
96. B. Shaw, p. 26.
97. Ibid., p. 94.
98. Aitken, p. 18; Hemmingway, pp. 36–7 (Norfolk County Record Office); I. Roberts, pp. 11–13; Rushton, pp. 28–35; T. Wood, p. 7 (Bradford Central Library).
99. Heap, p. 2 (Rawtenstall Library).
100. Lowery, p. 45.
101. 'Autobiography of a Suffolk farm labourer', chapter III (Suffolk Record Office).
102. Todd, pp. 29–35, 44–5, 68, 70, 72; Irving, pp. 2–3 (Carlisle Public Library). For more on the seasonal nature of children's employment in agriculture see Jackson, pp. 27–9; Robinson, p. 7 (West Sussex Record Office).
103. Robinson, p. 7 (West Sussex Record Office).
104. Lea, [p. 4] (Sheffield Archives).
105. Arch, p. 28.
106. Somerville, p. 38.
107. Lawrence, p. 14. See [Loveridge], p. 28; and Adam Rushton, who described working outdoors as a 'rural and free life' and his time at the mill as 'awful factory imprisonment'. Rushton, p. 31.
108. This view has recently been powerfully restated in Humphries, *Childhood and Child Labour*, pp. 172–209, esp. pp. 183–6, 208–9.

## 4 Women, Work and the Cares of Home

1. North, p. 37.
2. Ibid., p. 44.
3. Ibid., pp. 143–4.
4. Ibid.
5. C. Milne, p. 102.
6. Davidson, pp. 27–9.
7. For an introduction to the history of married women's work see A. Janssens, ed., *The Rise and Decline of the Male Breadwinner Family* (Cambridge, 1998); Sara Horrell and Jane Humphries, 'The origins and expansion of the male breadwinner family: the case of nineteenth-century Britain', *International Review of Social History*, Supplement, 5 (1997), pp. 25–64; Sara Horrell and Jane Humphries, 'Women's labour force participation and the transition to the male-breadwinner family, 1790–1865', *Economic History Review*, 2nd ser., 48 (1995), pp. 89–117.
8. Murison, p. 209.
9. Spinners include E. Anderson, p. 3; C. Campbell, p. 22; Davenport, p. 10; Jackson, p. 11; Lackington, pp. 39–42; 'Life of a journeyman baker', 13 & 20 Dec. 1856; Love, p. 8; Ricketts, p. 121.
10. Bobbin-winders include Bain, pp. 12–13; Bezer, p. 159; Myles, pp. 236–7; G. J., p. 5.
11. Younger, p. 8.

12. Fairburn, pp. 56–7, 65–6.
13. 'Life of a journeyman baker', 13 & 20 Dec. 1856.
14. For example Betty Shaw. See B. Shaw, p. 34.
15. Bamford, *Early Days*, p. 101.
16. Marcroft, pp. 28–32. Other weavers include: Bates, p. 1; Cooke, p. 3; Holroyd, pp. 115–16; Short, [pp. 4–5, 9–10, 20] (Norwich Castle Museum); Whitehead, p. 5; J. Wood, pp. 8, 20; T. Wood, p. 5 (Bradford Central Library).
17. Farish, p. 7.
18. J. Wood, p. 8.
19. Dodgson, 19 May 1956 (Halifax Central Library); Fairburn, pp. 56–7. See also however Thomas Cooper, whose mother kept up a small dyeing business after the death of her husband. T. Cooper, pp. 6, 8–11.
20. For women in industrial employment, see Carol E. Morgan, *Women Workers and Gender Identities, 1835–1913: the Cotton and Metal Industries in England* (London, 2002); idem, 'Women, work and consciousness in the mid nineteenth-century English cotton industry', *Social History*, 17 (1992), pp. 23–41; Janet Greenlees, 'Equal pay for equal work?: a new look at gender and wages in the Lancashire cotton industry, 1790–1855', in Margaret Walsh, ed., *Working out Gender: Perspectives from Labour History* (Aldershot, 1999), pp. 167–90; Robert Gray, 'Factory legislation and the gendering of jobs in the north of England, 1830–1860', *Gender & History*, 5 (1993), pp. 56–80.
21. B. Shaw, p. 24. Other women who worked in the factory may be found in: Joseph Burgess, pp. 8–9; Clifford, p. 9; E. Johnston, pp. 306–9; Whittaker, pp. 25–6.
22. This was Joseph Wilson. Living in Great Horton, Manchester, in the 1840s with the Factory Acts in operation, he and his mother swapped roles. He was at home, 'nursing and housekeeping', while his mother went to the factory. See Joseph Wilson, pp. 7, 15.
23. For women in agriculture, see Nicola Verdon, *Rural Women Workers in Nineteenth-Century England* (Woodbridge, 2002); idem, 'The rural labour market in the early nineteenth century: women's and children's employment, family income, and the 1834 Poor Law Report', *Economic History Review*, 55/2 (2002), pp. 299–323; Joyce Burnette, 'Labourers at the Oakes: changes in the demand for female day-laborers at a farm near Sheffield during the agricultural revolution', *Journal of Economic History*, 59 (1999), pp. 41–67; Deborah Valenze, 'The art of women and the business of men: women's work and the dairy industry, c. 1740–1840', *Past and Present*, 130 (1991), pp. 142–69.
24. For mothers working on smallholdings, see Errington, p. 44; Goodliffe, no pag. (Leicestershire Record Office); Hanson, p. 4; Murison, pp. 210–12; Rushton, p. 21.
25. *Short Account of Glasgow Weaver*, p. 5. Other seasonal farm workers include [Cameron], pp. 10–11; Mockford, pp. 21–2; Murdoch, pp. 16–17; Oakley, pp. 131, 141; W. Johnston, pp. 8–9; Shervington (Worcestershire Record Office), pp. ix–x; Somerville, pp. 19–20.
26. Clift, pp. 61–3.
27. Ibid., p. 63.
28. For women in service: Carolyn Steedman, *Master and Servant. Love and Labour in the English Industrial Age* (Cambridge, 2007); Sheila McIsaac Cooper, 'From family member to employee: aspects of continuity and discontinuity in English domestic service, 1600–2000', in Antoinette Fauve-Chamoux, ed., *Domestic Service and the Formation of European Identity: Understanding the Globalization of Domestic Work* (New York, 2004), pp. 277–96; Bridget Hill, *Servants: English Domestics in the Eighteenth Century* (Oxford, 1996); Deborah Valenze, *The First Industrial Woman* (Oxford, 1995).
29. For women who worked in domestic service before marriage, see: Arch, p. 46; Castle, pp. 14–15 (Essex Record Office); [O'Neill], p. 4; Leno, p. 3; Lincoln, pp. 10–11 (Norfolk Record Office); Oakley, pp. 132–9; M. Smith, pp. 1–2.
30. Though a few mothers did find themselves back in service, usually following the death or desertion of their husbands: 'Autobiography of Suffolk farm labourer', p. 3 (Suffolk Record Office); Dunning, pp. 120–2; Watson, p. 109.

31. Spurr, p. 285.
32. Place, pp. 98–9. For other laundry workers, see Adams, pp. 33–5; Arch, pp. 9–10; Hodgson, p. 5; Lincoln, p. 1 (Norfolk Record Office); Munday, p. 111; Sanderson, p. 6; Joseph Wilson, p. 3.
33. For instance Bowd, p. 299; Horne, p. 12; Joseph Wilson, p. 3.
34. Joseph Wilson, pp. 98–9.
35. Adams, p. 33.
36. Sanderson, p. 6. See also John Lincoln, whose mother made up her income from laundry work with a dole from the parish. Lincoln, p. 1 (Norfolk Record Office).
37. Townend, pp. 1–2, 22.
38. Binns, p. 1 (Tyne and Wear Archives Service). See also J. Barker, pp. 35–7; Carnegie, pp. 12–13; Hollingsworth, pp. 4–5; John Jones, 'John Jones', p. 171; Lovett, pp. 32–3.
39. Love, p. 29.
40. Lovett, p. 1; Rattenbury, p. 1.
41. Bezer, pp. 161–2. Other mothers and wives who worked as hawkers may be found in R. Barker, ii, pp. 31–2; Hodgson, p. 3; Holcroft, p. 8; Lomas, p. 156; [Loveridge], pp. 27–31; M'Kaen, p. 21.
42. Hanson, p. 19.
43. Mountjoy, p. 15.
44. 'Life of a handloom weaver', 25 April 1857. Other dressmakers include: Dunn, p. 6; Harland, extract no. 1 (Bradford Central Library); Healey, p. 2; E. Johnston, p. 304; Leno, p. 4; S. Martin, p. 6; H. Miller, p. 24; Nuttall, p. 3 (Flintshire Record Office); Stir(r)up, 22 Nov. 1856; Price, p. 5 (Finsbury Library); Roper, 9 May 1848 (Warwickshire County Record Office).
45. Ashford, p. 20.
46. Leno, p. 4. For other teachers, see also: T. Carter, p. 40; Gough, pp. 3–4, 13; Lowery, p. 45; [Leask], p. 39; H. Miller, pp. 10–11; Starkey, p. 7.
47. Bamford, *Early Days*, p. 15.
48. Nicholson, p. 3.
49. Cook, pp. 9–10 (Lincoln Reference Library).
50. Ibid., p. 10.
51. Pointer, pp. 13–14 (Broadstairs Library). The only other nurse mentioned was the mother of John Castle; see Castle, pp. 1–2 (Essex Record Office).
52. For shops, in addition to the references in note 38 above, see: Goodliffe, no pag. (Leicestershire Record Office); Hemmingway, p. 408 (Norfolk Record Office); Livesey, pp. 228–9; Love, pp. 29–31; Sankoffsky, p. 2 (Cumbria Record Office); [Porteus], p. 25; Sanderson, p. 23. For inns, see Ashford, pp. 14–15; *Exposition of a Coiner*, pp. 5–6; 'Life of journeyman baker', 13 & 20 Dec 1856; 'Life of a journeyman baker', 2 May 1857; Rattenbury, pp. 57–8. William Irving's parents ran a bacon-curing business together, see Irving, p. 12 (Carlisle Library); Thomson, pp. 48–50.
53. Shoemaking: Brown *Sixty Years*, p. 282; Davenport, pp. 42–3; Herbert, pp. 16–17; F. Mason, p. 88; Spurr, pp. 285–6. Tailoring: Hawker, p. 1; [Holkinson], 24, 31 January 1857.
54. Hollingsworth, pp. 8–9; Hopkinson, p. 96.
55. P. Sharpe, 'The women's harvest: straw plaiting and the representation of labouring women's employment, 1793–1885', *Rural History*, 5 (1994), pp. 129–42; Penelope Lane, 'Work on the margins: poor women and the informal economy of eighteenth and early nineteenth-century Leicestershire', *Midland History*, 22 (1997), pp. 85–99.
56. T. Cooper, pp. 8–9; Oakley, p. 139.
57. [H., Bill], pp. 148–9; North, p. 153.
58. Benjamin Shaw had a female cousin who drove a coal cart on the Dentdale coalfields. See B. Shaw, p. 15.
59. Holyoake, ch. 4. See also the various businesses of the enterprising mother of William Hollingsworth. Hollingsworth, pp. 3–5.

60. T. Cooper, pp. 8, 26.
61. T. Mitchell, p. 9 (Bristol Central Library).
62. Ashford, p. 20.
63. Bowd, p. 299.
64. Adams, p. 34.
65. B. Shaw, p. 34.
66. Ibid., pp. 50–2.
67. Oakley, pp. 138–9.
68. [Porteus], pp. 22–3.
69. Ashford, p. 45.
70. Oakley, p. 139.
71. [Porteus], p. 25.
72. Ashford, pp. 78–9.
73. North, p. 153.
74. Joseph Wilson, p. 3.
75. Goodliffe, no pag. (Leicestershire Record Office).
76. Britton, p. 38.
77. Hart, 8/1, p. 68.
78. T. Mitchell, pp. 13–17 (Bristol Central Library). See also Lovett, pp. 32–3.
79. Brown, *Sixty Years*, p. 282.
80. Ibid., p. 293.
81. Murdoch, pp. 16–17.
82. Leatherland, p. 33, Bamford, *Early Day*, p. 308, Lowery, p. 162. See also J. Wood, p. 20;
    [H. Bill], p. 149.
83. Pearman, p. 219.
84. W. Swan, p. 57.
85. Ibid., p. 59.
86. Ibid., p. 50.
87. Joseph Burgess, p. 13.
88. 'Norfolk labourer's wife', p. 28.
89. Langdon, p. 65.
90. Ibid., p. 68.
91. T. Cooper, pp. 8–10.
92. [Cameron], pp. 10–11.
93. Townend, pp. 2–3. See also E. Horne, p. 23.
94. Mockford, pp. 21–2.
95. Carnegie, pp. 12–13.
96. Lowery, p. 45. See also [Leask], p. 39.
97. H. Miller, p. 24.
98. Hanson, p. 4.
99. Somerville, pp. 19–20.
100. Mockford, pp. 52–3.
101. Castle, pp. 1–2 (Essex Record Office).
102. Bezer, pp. 161–2.
103. Marsh, p. 1 (Barnsley Archives).
104. Adams, p. 36.
105. Preston, p. 4.

## Part II: Love

1. Bamford, *Early Days*, p. 169.
2. R. Anderson, p. xxii.
3. Oakley, p. 137.

## 5 A Brand New Wife and an Empty Pocket

1. Harland, esp. extracts nos 7–8 (Bradford Central Library).
2. The themes of this chapter tap into a considerable literature. An excellent starting point is Tim Hitchcock, *English Sexualities, 1700–1800* (Basingstoke, 1997), esp. pp. 24–41. See also David Levine, *Family Formation in an Age of Nascent Capitalism* (New York, 1977); idem, *Reproducing Families: the Political Economy of English Population History* (Cambridge, 1987).
3. Roper, 23 April, 7 May 1848 (Warwickshire County Record Office).
4. [H., Bill], p. 149.
5. Terry, p. 40 (Brunel University Library).
6. Oakley, p. 137.
7. Ibid., p. 138.
8. Lackington, p. 176.
9. Roper, 14 April, 18 April, 12 May, 13 May 1848 (Warwickshire County Record Office).
10. [Gooch], p. 19.
11. Castle, p. 12 (Essex Record Office).
12. Terry, p. 41 (Brunel University Library).
13. Roper, 'Journal', 14 May, 21 May 1848 (Warwickshire County Record Office).
14. Story, p. 140.
15. Oakley, p. 136.
16. Davidson, pp. 27–30.
17. Saxby, p. 5.
18. Ashford, p. 46.
19. Ibid., pp. 47–8.
20. Bryceson, 18 Jan. 1846; 1 Feb. 1846; 13 March 1846; 17 April 1846 (Westminster City Archives).
21. Ibid., 29 Nov. 1846.
22. Cannon, i, p. 55.
23. Ibid.
24. Terry, p. 139 (Brunel University Library).
25. [Gooch], pp. 25–6.
26. Woolley, 19 June 1801; 2 May 1813; Feb. 1813; April 1813; Feb. 1813; 8 Jan. 1813 (Nottinghamshire Archives). For more neighbourly censure in a similar vein see also Huffer, p. 43; Scarfe, 10, 25 Feb. 1828; 21, 23 Jan. 1831.
27. For more on marriage: John R. Gillis, 'Peasant, plebeian, and proletarian marriage in Britain 1600–1900', in David Levine, ed., *Proletarianization and Family History* (Orlando, 1981), pp. 129–62: idem, *For Better, For Worse: British Marriages, 1600 to the Present* (Oxford, 1985); Peter Laslett, *Family Life and Illicit Love in Earlier Generations* (Cambridge, 1977); Wally Seccombe, *Weathering the Storm: Working-Class Families from the Industrial Revolution to the Fertility Decline* (London, 1993); R. M. Smith, 'Fertility, economy and household formation in England over three centuries', *Population and Development Review*, 7 (1981), pp. 595–622.
28. For more on separation, see Joanne Bailey, *Unquiet Lives, Marriage and Marriage Breakdown in England, 1660–1800* (Cambridge, 2003); Pamela Sharpe, 'Marital separations in the eighteenth and nineteenth centuries', *Local Population Studies*, 45 (1990), pp. 66–70; D. A. Kent, 'Gone for a soldier: family breakdown and the demography of desertion in a London parish, 1750–91', *Local Population Studies*, 45 (1990), pp. 27–42; S. Menefee, *Wives for Sale: an Ethnographic Study of British Popular Divorce* (Oxford, 1981); E. P. Thompson, 'Wife sales', in his *Customs in Commons* (London, 1983).
29. G. Smith, *Autobiography*, pp. 19–20.
30. Lovett, p. 31.
31. Wrigley et al., *English Population History from Family Reconstitution* (Cambridge, 1997), table 5.3, p. 134.

32. I. Roberts, p. 35.
33. The question has received considerable scholarly attention. See, for instance, E. A. Wrigley, 'Growth of population in eighteenth-century England: a conundrum resolved', *Past and Present*, 98 (1983), pp. 121–50, p. 127; David Levine, 'For their own reasons: individual marriage decisions and family life', *Journal of Family History*, 7 (1982), pp. 255–64; J. A. Goldstone, 'The demographic revolution in England: a re-examination', *Population Studies*, 49 (1986), pp. 5–33; K. D. M. Snell, *Annals of the Labouring Poor. Social Change and Agrarian England, 1660–1900* (Cambridge, 1985), pp. 345–52; Emma Griffin, 'A conundrum resolved? Rethinking courtship, marriage, and population growth in eighteenth-century England', *Past and Present*, 215 (2012), pp. 125–64.
34. Mather, pp. 158–239, p. 163.
35. Longden, p. 22; Melhuish, p. 17; Nelson, pp. 1–165, pp. 5, 8; Holcroft, p. 177.
36. Bennett, p. 9 (Bristol Record Office).
37. Askham, p. x; Crocker, p. xi; Stir(r)up, 29 Nov. 1856; Struthers, p. lix; Watkins, p. 23.
38. Hick, p. 23; Collyer, p. 42; Jewitt, p. 75 (Wigan Archives Service); [Gooch], pp. 35–7; [Holkinson], 24 & 31 Jan. 1857; J. Taylor, *Autobiography*, p. 8; Goodliffe, no pag. (Leicestershire Record Office); H. Taylor (East Riding Archives), p. 7; Sanderson, pp. 5–41, p. 22; Rattenbury, p. 24.
39. Bezer, p. 178; Munday, pp. 99–121; Place, pp. 100–6; W. T. Swan, p. 6.
40. Dodgson, 19 May 1956 (Halifax Central Library).
41. 'Jacques', 1 Nov. 1856.
42. J. Bent, p. iv; W. Smith, pp. 178–85; Townend, p. 22.
43. Whittaker, p. 25.
44. Hanson, p. 8.
45. Livesey, pp. 213–17, pp. 116–17.
46. Sholl, pp. 37–47; Castle, pp. 15–16 (Essex Record Office).
47. Marsh, p. 12 (Barnsley Archives).
48. Errington, pp. 57, 169.
49. Lovekin, nos 4–5 (Brunel University Library); Rymer, p. 7; 'Narrative of a miner', 25 Oct. 1856.
50. In 1857, Thomas Pointer, an agricultural labourer living at Broadstairs in Kent, married at the age of 20. Pointer, 'Memoirs', p. 12 (Broadstairs Library, Kent).
51. Arch, p. 46.
52. Ricketts, pp. 120–6, p. 123.
53. For example: Carvosso, pp. 38–9; Rodda, p. 129; Staniforth, pp. 109–51.
54. Nye, p. 14.
55. Ibid.
56. Hawker, p. 82.
57. Love, p. 26.
58. Thomson, pp. 159–60.
59. Spurr, p. 282.
60. Mayett, p. 61. See also Love, p. 29.
61. Leno, pp. 29–30.
62. Blow, pp. 6–7.
63. Mockford, p. 14.
64. Burn, p. 129.
65. 'Life of a journeyman baker', 13 & 20 Dec. 1856.
66. Bowd, p. 296.
67. Ibid.
68. Lincoln, p. 10 (Norfolk Record Office).
69. Ibid., pp. 10–12.
70. 'Colin', pp. 29–30.
71. Saxby, p. 8.

72. Nye, p. 14.
73. R. Barker, ii, pp. 31–2.
74. Lackington., p. 191.
75. Lowery, p. 62.
76. Lowe, pp. 24, 45.
77. Ibid., p. 46.
78. Ibid., p. 70.
79. M'Kaen, p. 13.
80. Ibid, p. 14.
81. Bownas, pp. 43–4.
82. Hick, p. 20.
83. Johnson, pp. 47–8.
84. Hutton, pp. 90–1.
85. Lackington, pp. 183–6.
86. There is considerable overlap between those who identified their marriage as improvident and those who resided with their parents after marriage, though the match is not perfect. Those staying with kin are: Arch, p. 46; Bowd, p. 296; Davies, p. 2; Gutteridge, p. 113; [Gooch], pp. 35–7; Harland, extracts 7–8 (Bradford Central Library); Hopper, p. 196; 'Life of a journeyman baker', 13 & 20 Dec. 1856; Lincoln, pp. 10–11 (Norfolk Record Office); T. Mitchell, p. 11 (Bristol Central Library); Mockford, p. 20; Oakley, p. 139; [E. O'Neill], pp. 6–7; B. Shaw, pp. 30–1; Thomson, p. 165; Whittaker, pp. 25–6.
87. Harland, extract 12 (Bradford Central Library).
88. Roper, 23 May, 29 May 1848 (Warwickshire County Record Office).
89. Errington, p. 106.
90. Hollingsworth, pp. 8–9.
91. 'Colin', p. 29.
92. Thomson, pp. 162–3. See also T. Mitchell, pp. 10–11 (Bristol Central Library).
93. Hall, pp. 17–20.
94. Place, p. 102.
95. Ibid., p. 103.
96. Ibid., p. 104.
97. Ibid., pp. 92–3, 121–2.
98. Terry, p. 55 (Brunel University Library).
99. Struthers, pp. lviii–lix.
100. Gutteridge, p. 113.
101. Britton, i., p.74.
102. Ibid., pp. 74–7.
103. Burn, p. 129; Gutteridge, p. 113; Lowery, p. 62; Sanderson, pp. 5–41, p. 22.
104. Hanson, p. 19.
105. Whittaker, pp. 25–6.

## 6 Naughty Tricks on the Bed

1. Bowd, p. 296.
2. Family history pieced together from 1861 Census and Cambridge County Record Office, Elsworth Baptism Register; 26 May 1850 (Sarah, born 15 June 1849).
3. Family history pieced together from Derbyshire Record Office: Glossop Independent Baptism Register, 1812–1837, RG 4/859 (Susan Scholes born Feb. 1812); Cheshire Record Office: St Mary, Stockport, Marriage Register, 1819–1837, MF34/10 (marriage of Thomas Whittaker and Susan Scholes 15 April 1832); Derbyshire Record Office: Glossop Independent Baptism Register, 1812–1837, RG 4/859 (Nancy Whitacre, born 26 Oct. 1832; William Whitaker, baptised 15 Dec. 1833); Lancashire Record Office: St Mary the Virgin, Blackburn, Burial Records, 1658–1837, DRB2 (burial of William

Whittaker, aged 4 months, 24 March 1834). Thomas Whittaker never mentioned the birth of Nancy in his autobiography and implied that William was their only child in 1834. Following the death of Susan in 1837, their daughter, Nancy, appears to have been taken in by her parents. An 8-year-old 'Nancy Whiteker' is recorded in the 1841 Census as living with Joshua Scholes (Joshua and Nancy Scholes were listed as the parents of Susan at the time of her baptism in Glossop in 1812). See also Whittaker, pp. 25–6.

4. W. Swan, pp. 49–50.

5. William Thomas, *The Diary of William Thomas of Michaelston-super-Ely, near St. Fagans, Glamorgan, 1762–1795*, ed. R. T. W. Denning (South Wales Record Society, 11, 1995), p. 80.

6. Ibid., p. 114.

7. The figures are based upon E. A. Wrigley, 'British population during the long eighteenth century', in Roderick Floud and Paul Johnson, eds, *The Cambridge Economic History of Modern Britain: Industrialisation, 1700–1860* (Cambridge, 1997), pp. 75–6. See also Patricia Broomfield, 'Incidences and attitudes: a view of bastardy from eighteenth-century rural North Staffordshire, *c.* 1750–1820', *Midland History*, 27 (2002), pp. 80–98.

8. The figures are based upon my own reworking of the figures presented by Peter Laslett, Karla Oosterveen and Richard Smith, eds, *Bastardy and its Comparative History* (London, 1980) table 1.1, and revised upwards in line with the work of Adair who showed that the earlier work missed many illegitimates (Richard Adair, *Courtship, Illegitimacy and Marriage in Early Modern England*, Manchester, 1996). See also Alysa Levene, Samantha Williams and Thomas Nutt, eds, *Illegitimacy in Britain, 1700–1920* (Basingstoke, 2005). The totals may appear low, but that stems in part from the way that illegitimacy is being measured. The parish registers only reveal what proportion of the total baptisms were of children of unmarried mothers. But this was an era of high marriage rates and married women tended to have much larger families than their unmarried peers, so the children born within wedlock would inevitably greatly outnumber those born outside. An alternative way of grasping the extent of illegitimacy is by looking at the proportion of first births that were illegitimate, or at the proportion of unmarried women giving birth outside marriage. Such measures tell a very different story. Studies of first births in parishes in Kent and in Cheshire indicate that somewhere between 10 and 20 per cent of all first births were illegitimate. Grace Wyatt, 'Bastardy and prenuptiual pregnancy in a Cheshire town during the eighteenth century', *Local Population Studies*, 49 (1992), pp. 38–50, table 6, p. 47; Barry Reay, 'Sexuality in nineteenth-century England: the social context of illegitimacy in rural Kent', *Rural History*, 1 (1990), pp. 219–47, p. 242. A study which relates the number of illegitimate births to the number of unmarried women in mid-nineteenth-century Colyton, Devon, reveals that almost 20 per cent of unmarried women gave birth to a child. Jean Robin, 'Illegitimacy in Colyton, 1851–1881', *Continuity and Change*, 2 (1987), pp. 307–42, p. 309.

9. For more on these themes, see Tim Hitchcock, 'Demography and the culture of sex in the long eighteenth century', in Jeremy Black, ed., *Culture and Society in Britain, 1660–1800* (Manchester, 1997), pp. 69–84; Steven King, 'The bastardy prone sub-society again: bastards and their fathers and mothers in Lancashire, Wiltshire, and Somerset', in Levene et al. (eds), *Illegitimacy*; Adrian Wilson, 'Illegitimacy and its implications in mid-eighteenth-century London: the evidence of the Foundling Hospital', *Continuity and Change*, 4/1 (1989), pp. 103–6; Nicholas Rogers, 'Carnal knowledge: illegitimacy in eighteenth-century Westminster,' *Journal of Social History*, 23 (1989–90), pp. 355–75; John R. Gillis, 'Servants, secular relations, and risks of illegitimacy in London, 1801–1900', *Feminist Studies*, 5/1 (1979), pp. 142–73; Emma Griffin, 'Sex, illegitimacy and social change in industrialising Britain', *Social History* (forthcoming).

10. Cannon, i, p. 26.

11. Ibid., pp. 35–6.

12. Ibid.
13. Ibid., p. 48.
14. Ibid., p. 55.
15. Ibid., p. 63.
16. Ibid., pp. 62–3.
17. Ibid., p. 63.
18. Ibid., p. 88.
19. For more on the making and unmaking of John's pact with Mary, see John Money's excellent summary, ibid., pp. xlv–l.
20. Ibid., pp. 88–9.
21. Ibid., p. 89.
22. Ibid., p. 90.
23. Ibid., pp. 93–4.
24. Harrold, p. xi.
25. Ibid., p. xii
26. Ibid., pp. 5, 20, 26, 27, 31, 33, 35, 42, 44.
27. Ibid., p. 52.
28. Ibid., pp. 74–5.
29. Ibid., pp. 74, 82.
30. Ibid., p. 78
31. Ibid.
32. Ibid., p. 80.
33. The exception here is John's relationship with Ann Heister. We will consider this in more detail below.
34. Zobel, 31 March 1831, p. 4; 23 May 1831, p. 6; 22 June 1831, p. 7; 30 June 1831, p. 8 (Norwich and Norfolk Millennium Library).
35. Ibid., 7 Dec. 1828, p. 11.
36. Ibid., 17 Oct. 1831, p. 21.
37. Ibid., 7 Nov. 1831, p. 22.
38. Ibid., 19 Sept. 1832, p. 31.
39. Ibid., 12, 15, 26 Nov. 1832, p. 34.
40. Ibid, pp. 37–77 *passim.*
41. Bryceson, 22 Feb. 1846 (Westminster City Archives).
42. Ibid., 6 March 1846.
43. Ibid., 3 May 1846; 24 May 1846.
44. Ibid., 31 May 1846.
45. Ibid., 9 Aug. 1846.
46. Ibid., 13 Sept. 1846.
47. Ibid., 11 Oct. 1846.
48. Ibid., 29 Nov. 1846.
49. Cannon, i, p. 104.
50. Johnson, p. 40.
51. Ibid., p. 39.
52. Ibid., pp. 103–4.
53. M'Kaen, p. 15.
54. Ibid., p. 22.
55. Cannon, i, pp. 102–4.
56. M'Kaen, pp. 14–15.
57. Lincoln, pp. 10–11 (Norfolk Record Office).
58. Johnson, p. 39.
59. Saxby, p. 8.
60. Stanley, pp. 6–10.
61. J. Davis, p. 5. It is not clear what her intentions had been and as she died three weeks after the birth it is possible they were never known by her family either.

62. W. Milne, p. 18.
63. Price, p. 1 (Finsbury Library).
64. Ibid., pp. 3–5.
65. Bamford, *Early Days*, p. 169.
66. Ibid., p. 224.
67. Ibid., p. 225.
68. Ibid., p. 294.
69. Ann had been baptised with Jemima's name in January. Lancashire Record Office, St Leonard, Middleton Baptism Register, 1721–1847, DRM 2 ('7 Jan 1810, Ann Shepherd – Daughter of Jemima Shepherd, singlewoman'. Marriage Register 1721–1847, DRM 2; the marriage is recorded on 24 June 1810).
70. Bamford, *Early Days*, p. 225.
71. Ibid., p. 227.
72. Errington, pp. 169, 172.
73. Ibid., p. 109.
74. Ibid., p. 99.
75. Shaw, p. 26.
76. Ibid., p. 30.
77. Ibid., p. 31.
78. Ibid., p. 29.
79. Ibid., p. 32
80. Ibid., p. 90.
81. Ibid., pp. 91–2.
82. Ibid., pp. 104–7. They were reconciled four years later.
83. Ibid., pp. 112, 115–16.
84. Ibid., pp. 96–7; ibid., pp. 87–8.
85. Ibid., p. 89.
86. In fact she did not do so as her own health now began to break down.
87. As was Edward Shorter's controversial thesis. See Shorter, 'Illegitimacy, sexual revolution and social change in modern Europe', *Journal of Interdisciplinary History*, 2/2 (1971), pp. 237–72.
88. Marcroft, pp. 18–22.
89. E. Johnston, pp. 307–10.

## Part III Culture

1. Somerville, p. 22.

## 7 Education

1. Lovekin, nos 1–2 (Brunel University Library).
2. The evidence for trends of literacy, as measured by the ability to sign one's name, is inconclusive. Stephen Nicholas and Jacqueline M. Nicholas, 'Male literacy, "deskilling" and the industrial revolution', *Journal of Interdisciplinary History*, 23 (1992), pp. 1–18, argue for a dip in signing ability between 1790 and 1830. R. Schofield, 'Dimensions of illiteracy, 1750–1850', *Explorations in Economic History*, 10/4 (1973), pp. 437–54 and David Vincent, *The Rise of Mass Literacy: Reading and Writing in Modern Europe* (Cambridge, 2000), indicate very modest improvements. See also R. Crone, 'Reappraising Victorian literacy through prison records', *Journal of Victorian Culture*, 15 (2010), pp. 3–37.
3. Good surveys of education for children may be found in: B. Reay, 'The context and meaning of popular literacy in nineteenth-century rural England', *Past and Present*, 131 (1991), pp. 89–129; M. Sanderson, *Education, Economic Change and Society, 1780–1870* (Cambridge, 1991); Neil J. Smelser, *Social Paralysis and Social Change: British*

*Working-Class Education in the Nineteenth Century* (Berkeley, CA; 1991); David Vincent, *Literacy and Popular Culture, England 1750–1914* (Cambridge, 1989), ch. 3; W. B. Stephens, *Education, Literacy and Society, 1830–1870: The Geography of Diversity in Provincial England* (Manchester, 1987); Phil Gardner, *The Lost Elementary Schools of Victorian England: The People's Education* (London, 1984). The literature for the eighteenth century is more limited, but see Deborah Simonton, 'Schooling the poor: gender and class in eighteenth-century England', *British Journal for Eighteenth-Century Studies*, 23/2 (2000), pp. 183–202; Robert Allan Houston, *Scottish Literacy and the Scottish Identity: Illiteracy and Society in Scotland and Northern England 1600–1800* (Cambridge, 1986).

4. J. Barker, p. 36. See also J. Bethune, pp. 3–4; Bowcock, p. 7; Chadwick, p. 9; Choyce, p. 3; T. Davies, p. 1; W. Johnston, pp. 8–9; Marcroft, p. 41; Nicholson, pp. 1–2.
5. A. Bethune, p. 12. See also Buxton, p. iii.
6. The main exception lies with the Scottish autobiographers, some of whom benefited from a combination of better schools, families and communities that placed greater value on schooling, and (particularly in the more rural and remote areas) the absence of suitable employment for children. See, for instance, H. Miller, pp. 27–144; W. Milne, pp. 35–87; Murison, p. 212; Todd, pp. 25–49.
7. Lovekin, no. 2 (Brunel University Library).
8. Ibid., nos 3, 5.
9. Simonton, 'Schooling the poor', pp. 183–202.
10. Hutton, pp. 9–11, 22.
11. See, for example, Haime; T. Hanby; J. Mason; D. Taylor; J. Taylor, *Memoirs*.
12. Holcroft, p. 22.
13. Ibid., pp. 134–5.
14. Tryon, p. 8.
15. Ibid., pp. 14–15.
16. Gifford, p. 15.
17. Ibid., pp. 15–20.
18. Ferguson, p. 6.
19. Ibid., pp. 12–15.
20. Ibid., p. 16.
21. Ibid., p. 18.
22. MacDonald, pp. 26, 30, 40.
23. Saville, p. 11.
24. Lackington, p. 84.
25. Whitehead, pp. 18–19.
26. Davenport, pp. 10–12.
27. Livesey, pp. 197–8.
28. Claxton, pp. 16–17.
29. Watson, p. 109.
30. Fairburn, p. 73.
31. Thomson, p. 176.
32. The development of adult education remains a very neglected topic. An introduction may be found in W. B. Stephens, *Adult Education and Society in an Industrial Town: Warrington, 1800–1900* (Exeter, 1980).
33. Thomson, p. 61.
34. Bain, pp. 20–1. Other autobiographers to benefit from commercial night schools in urban areas include John Jones, 'Autobiographical extract', pp. 365–6; Herbert, p. 27; *Life of a Chimney Boy*, p. 26; [Leask], p. 95. Those in London include Plummer, pp. xix–xx; Catling, pp. 48–9; Hollingsworth, p. 21; G. Mitchell, pp. 113–14.
35. Marcroft, pp. 38–9.
36. Chadwick, p. 9.
37. Bywater, pp. 5–7.

272         NOTES to pp. 174-7

38. Collyer, p. 13.
39. For Tatsley, see: I. Roberts, p. 21 and Brierley, p. 23. Others in industrial areas to be involved with night schools include: Aird, p. 10; A. Bethune, p. 12; Collyer, p. 13; E. Davis, pp. 11–12; Dodd, p. 213; Farish, pp. 17–18; 'Life of a cotton spinner', 27 Dec. 1856; 'Life of a handloom weaver', 25 April 1857; 'Life of a journeyman baker', 2 May 1857; 'Life of a letterpress printer', 7 Feb. 1857; Livesey, p. 310; Lovekin, no. 2 (Brunel University Library); Rushton; Saville, p. 11; Whittaker, pp. 22–3.
40. Jonathon Rose, *The Intellectual Life of the British Working Classes* (New Haven, CT; 2001), pp. 58–70; John Caskie Crawford, 'The ideology of mutual improvement in Scottish working class libraries', *Library History*, 12 (1996), pp. 49–61; M. I. Watson, 'Mutual improvement societies in nineteenth century Lancashire', *Journal of Educational Administration & History*, 21/2 (1989), pp. 8–17. Also interesting is Anne Secord, 'Science in the pub: artisan botanists in early nineteenth-century Lancashire', *History of Science*, 32 (1994), pp. 269–315, which looks at the routes to scientific learning amongst working-class men.
41. C. Campbell, pp. 3–4.
42. T. Cooper, pp. 46–7.
43. In addition to Rose, *Intellectual Life*, pp. 63–76, see: W. A. Munford, 'George Birkbeck and the Mechanics Institute', in *English Libraries, 1800–1850* (London, 1959); Mabel Tylecote, *The Mechanics' Institute of Lancashire and Yorkshire before 1851* (Manchester, 1957); Edward Royle, 'Mechanics' Institutes and the working classes, 1840–60', *Historical Journal*, 14/2 (1971), pp. 305–21; Gregory Claeys, 'Political economy and popular education: Thomas Hodgskin and the London Mechanics' Institute 1823–28', in Michael T. Davis, ed., *Radicalism and Revolution in Britain, 1775–1848: Essays in Honour of Malcolm I. Thomis* (Basingstoke, 2000), pp. 157–75.
44. C. Shaw, p. 221.
45. Skilled workers involved in Mechanics' Institutes: Bain, p. 16; Bertram, p. 27; Catling, pp. 48–9; T. Cooper, pp. 103–7; [Gooch], p. 81; Herbert, p. 27; Holyoake, pp. 45–50; Lovett, pp. 28–31; P. Taylor, p. 2; Thomson, p. 335; Wallis, pp. 33–4. Others involved in Mechanics' Institutes include: Burland, p. 2; Marcroft, p. 43; Plummer, pp. xix–xx; Terry, p. 63 (Brunel University Library). The clerk was Robert White, see: R. White, p. 9. (Burland, Cooper, Lovett and Thomson had belonged to mutual improvement societies before getting involved in their Mechanics' Institutes.)
46. Farish, p. 46.
47. C. Shaw, pp. 221–9.
48. C. Campbell, pp. 3–4.
49. Thomson, p. 336.
50. Farish, pp. 46–7 .
51. T. Cooper, pp. 46–7.
52. Edwards, p. 10.
53. Mountjoy, pp. 42–3.
54. The Scottish ones are: Bain, p. 16; C. Campbell, pp. 3–4; Myles, pp. 286–7; McAdam, p. 3; W. Milne, pp. 236–40; P. Taylor, pp. 2–9; 'Jacques', 1 Nov. 1856; Urie, pp. 27–31.
55. Lovett, p. 28.
56. Ibid., pp. 28–31. For discussion groups in London, see also Claxton, pp. 23–5; Davenport, p. 68; Fairburn, pp. 83–4; Place, p. 131; Preston, pp. 22–4.
57. For example Goodliffe, no pag. (Leicestershire Record Office); Lowery, pp. 72–3; McAdam, p. 3; [Smith], pp. 14–15; Teer, p. iv; Thomson, pp. 335–44; Urie, pp. 27–31.
58. Adams, pp. 115–19; Barr, p. 26; Buckley, pp. 29–30; T. Cooper, pp. 46–7; Frost, pp. 197–203; p. 81; [Leask], p. 96; Skeen, p. 5; John Wilson, p. 207.
59. Bates, p. 2; Burland, p. 1; C. Campbell, pp. 3–4; Myles, pp. 286–7; Jacques, 1 Nov. 1856; Mountjoy, pp. 42–3; C. Shaw, pp. 221–5.
60. Brierley, pp. 34–6; Farish, pp. 46–7; Gutteridge, pp. 135–6; Heaton, pp. xvii–xix; Leatherland, pp. 9–10.

61. [Gooch], p. 21.
62. Ibid., p. 15.
63. Barr, p. 25.
64. Ibid., p. 25.
65. Edwards, pp. 9–10.
66. W. Milne, pp. 236–7.
67. The definitive history remains: Thomas W. Laqueur, *Religion and Respectability: Sunday Schools and Working Class Culture, 1780–1850* (London, 1976). See also: Keith D. M. Snell, 'The Sunday-school movement in England and Wales: child labour and working-class culture', *Past and Present*, 164 (1999), pp. 122–68; Philip B. Cuff, *The Rise and Development of the Sunday School Movement in England, 1780–1980* (Redhill, 1986); Callum G. Brown, 'The Sunday-school movement in Scotland, 1780–1914', *Records of the Scottish Church History Society*, 21/1 (1981), pp. 3–26; Malcolm Dick, 'The myth of the working-class Sunday school', *History of Education*, 9 (1980), pp. 27–41.
68. *Gentleman's Magazine*, 54 (1784), p. 411.
69. Figures from Snell, 'Sunday-school movement', pp. 125–6, 147.
70. Buxton, p. iii.
71. See, for instance, J. Barker, pp. 31, 34–5; Bezer, pp. 157–9, 161–3, 165–9; Castle, pp. 1–2 (Essex Record Office); Chadwick, p. 9; Collyer, pp. 7–8 15; Cook, pp. 2–3 (Lincoln Reference Library); E. Davis, pp. 6, 11; Dunn, pp. 7, 18; J. Harris, pp. 20–1, 32–3; Heap, pp. 2–3 (Rawtenstall Library); Heaton, p. xvii; Hollingsworth, pp. 3, 21; Langdon, pp. 17, 23–8; Lovekin, nos 2–3, 5 (Brunel University Library); Marcroft, pp. 33, 41; Mallard, p. 5 (Northamptonshire Record Office); Mockford, pp. 1–2; C. Shaw, pp. 6–11; Stir(r)up, 22 Nov. 1856; Teer, p. iii; Terry, p. 7 (Brunel University Library); Townend, pp. 3–4; J. Wood, pp. 4, 12; T. Wood, pp. 6–7 (Bradford Central Library).
72. Also argued in Snell, 'The Sunday-school movement'.
73. Bamford, *Early Days*, p. 108.
74. Innes, p. 11. See also Rushton, pp. 44–7; Teer, pp. iii.
75. Livesey, p. 310.
76. Bain, pp. 15–21.
77. Marcroft, pp. 38–9.
78. Whittaker, pp. 22–3.
79. Bezer, p. 157.
80. Edwards, pp. 9–10.
81. Brierley, pp. 34–6.
82. Thomson, p. 336.
83. Claxton, p. 23.
84. [Smith], pp. 14–15.
85. Thomson, p. 337. See also Barr, p. 26.
86. Bain, p. 16. See also S. Taylor, pp. 2–6; R. White, p. 9.
87. Parkinson, pp. 66–8.
88. J. Wood, p. 10.
89. J. Harris, p. 21. See also Rushton, pp. 49–51.
90. Hopkinson, p. 72. See also Goodliffe who had been a teacher in the same Stony Street Sunday school in the 1820s: 'In 1824 I entered heartily into the work of Sunday School teaching at Stoney Street Baptist Chapel, where for some years a capital School had existed' (Leicestershire Record Office).
91. T. Wood, p. 15 (Bradford Central Library).
92. Joseph Wilson, p. 34. See also Corben, pp. 15–17.
93. Marcroft, pp. 38–9.
94. Ibid., p. 42; part II, pp. 58, 60, 62–3, 65–6.
95. Ibid., p. 67.
96. Ibid., p. 57.

## 8 Gospel Times

1. Nicholson, pp.1–3.
2. Ibid., p. 15.
3. Ibid., p. 25.
4. Ibid., pp. 17–19.
5. Ibid., p. 21.
6. Ibid., p. 52.
7. Ibid., p. 16.
8. Ibid., p. 43.
9. David W. Bebbington, *Evangelicalism in Modern Britain: A History from the 1730s to the 1980s* (London, 1989).
10. John Kent, *Wesley and the Wesleyans. Religion in Eighteenth-Century Britain* (Cambridge, 2002); Mark Smith, *Religion in Industrial Society, Oldham and Saddleworth, 1746–1865* (Oxford, 1994); David Hempton, *The Religion of the People. Methodism and Popular Religion, 1750–1900* (London, 1996); idem, *Religion and Political Culture in Britain and Ireland* (Cambridge, 1996).
11. H. McLeod, *Religion and Society in England, 1850–1914* (London, 1996); idem, *Religion and the Working Class in Nineteenth-Century Britain* (London, 1984).
12. Arch, pp. 21–2.
13. Deacon, p. 19.
14. Weaver, p. 64. See also Barr, pp. 28–9; Arch, pp. 21–2; T. Cooper, p. 37; Farningham, p. 15; Hampton, p. 41; Lea, [p. 6] (Sheffield Archives).
15. Jackson, pp. 24, 25, 64. See also Barr, p. 29.
16. [Moss], no pag. (Nottinghamshire Archives). See also Shervington, p. vii (Worcestershire Record Office).
17. Ibid.
18. Saxby, p. 32.
19. For more on the revivals, see David Bebbington, *Victorian Religious Revivals: Culture and Piety in Local and Global Context* (Oxford, 2012); Ned Landsman, 'Evangelists and their hearers: popular interpretation of Revivalist preaching in eighteenth-century Scotland', *Journal of British Studies*, 28/2 (1989), pp. 120–49; D. Luker, 'Revivalism in theory and practice: the case of Cornish Methodism', *Journal of Ecclesiastical History*, 37 (1986), pp. 603–19.
20. Cook, p. 20 (Lincoln Reference Library). For more on pew rents, see C. G. Brown, 'The costs of pew-renting: church management, church-going and social class in nineteenth-century Glasgow', *Journal of Ecclesiastical History*, 38/3 (1987), pp. 347–61.
21. Davenport, pp. 35–6.
22. Burt, p. 85.
23. I. Roberts, pp. 16–17.
24. Lea, [p. 6] (Sheffield Archives).
25. Hanson, p. 10; M. Smith, pp. 8, 11.
26. Gibbs, p. 34.
27. Ibid., pp. 39–40.
28. Ibid., pp. 53–4.
29. Arch, pp. 16–17.
30. Ibid., p. 17.
31. Ibid., p. 19.
32. Ibid., p. 20. See also Bezer, pp. 170–3; M. Smith, pp. 8, 11–13, 47–8.
33. T. Wood, p. 11 (Bradford Central Library).
34. I. Roberts, p. 28.
35. Hanson, p. 12. For other Methodist meetings see Carvosso, pp. 42–3; Parkinson, pp. 40–1; Saville, pp. 17–20.
36. See, for instance, Dunn, p. 73; Hopkinson, p. 71.
37. Innes, p. 13; Rushton, pp. 55–62. See also Huggins, ch. 3 (Norfolk Record Office).

38. Mayett, pp. 37–42. For a more positive response to being invited to speak see Whitehead, p. 38.
39. Hughes, p. 3 (Newport Central Library).
40. Croll, p. 19. See also Rushton, p. 75; W. T. Swan, p. 7.
41. Gwyer, p. 14.
42. F. Mason, p. 21. See also Hanson, p. 12; Mayett, p. 91.
43. *Scenes from my Life*, p. 83.
44. *Autobiography of a Scotch Lad*, p. 35.
45. W. Smith, p. 184.
46. In addition to the references above, see Aird, p. 15; Basset, p. 132.
47. Terry, p. 63 (Brunel University Library).
48. Ibid., p. 63.
49. Spurr, p. 284.
50. Basset, p. 10.
51. Ibid., pp. 115–19.
52. Ibid., p. 131.
53. Ibid., p.132.
54. Hopwood, pp. 10–11.
55. Saxby, pp. 39–40.
56. M. Smith, pp. 92–3.
57. Oakley, pp. 143–7.
58. Collyer, p. 30.
59. Mockford, p. 12.
60. Ibid., p. 27.
61. John Taylor, *Memoirs*, p. 4. See also Edward Royle, 'The Church of England and Methodism in Yorkshire, *c.* 1750–1850: from monopoly to free market', *Northern History*, 33 (1997), pp. 137–61.
62. Arney, pp. 2–23 (Bristol Central Library).
63. Somerville, p. 72.
64. Nye, pp. 15–16.
65. Ibid., p. 17.
66. Doreen Rosman, *The Evolution of the English Churches, 1500–2000* (Cambridge, 2003), pp. 192–4.
67. Clifford, pp. 15–16.
68. Ibid., p. 17.
69. Ibid., pp. 18–19. See also Featherstone, p. 11; Hampton, p. 58; Harland, extract no. 4 (Bradford Central Library); Huggins, chs III–IV (Norfolk Record Office); Saville, pp. 25–6; G. Smith, *Autobiography*, p. 18; Townend, pp. 24–5, 34–5.
70. See also Flockhart, pp. 76–158, esp. p. 140, *passim*; Weaver, p. 69.
71. I. Anderson, p. 14.
72. Lea, [p. 9] (Sheffield Archives). See also Collyer, pp. 30–1.
73. Jackson, p. 71.
74. Ibid. See also Weaver, pp. 73–4.
75. For more about John Lincoln see introduction, pp. 1–4, 16–19.
76. The female preachers are Evans, Porteus and Davidson. See also D. M. Valenze, 'Cottage religion and the politics of survival', in Jane Rendall, ed., *Equal or Different? Women's Politics in the Nineteenth Century* (Oxford, 1987), pp. 31–56.
77. Bamford, *Early Days*, p. 126.
78. Goodliffe, no pag. (Leicestershire Record Office).
79. Hopkinson, pp. 39, 71–3. See also Aird, p. 15; Barr, p. 31.
80. Saville, pp. 19–20.
81. See, for example, Featherstone, pp. 3–4; Townend, pp. 1–2. See also Mayett, p. 4.
82. Gibbs, pp. 102–14.
83. Ibid., p. 103. See also Carvosso, pp. 45–7, and Mayett, below.

84. See, for instance, G. Mitchell, p. 113; Parkinson, pp. 65–72. For women see, for instance, S. Martin, p. 12.
85. G. Mitchell, p. 115. See also Arch, p. 48; Mountjoy, pp. 3–7.
86. Skeen, pp. 14–15.
87. Catton, p. 15.
88. Aird, p. 15.
89. Mayett, pp. 60–98.
90. Esp. E. P. Thompson, *The Making of the English Working Class* (Harmondsworth, 1976); E. J. Hobsbawm, 'Methodism and the threat of revolution in Britain', in his *Labouring Men: Studies in the History of Labour* (London, 1968). See also, however, James Obelkevich, *Religion and Rural Society in South Lindsey* (Oxford, 1976); W. R. Ward, *Religion and Society in England, 1790–1850* (London, 1972); J. A. Jaffe, 'The "Chiliasm of Despair" reconsidered: revivalism and working-class agitation in County Durham', *Journal of British Studies*, 28/1 (1989), pp. 23–42.
91. Stradley, [pp. 18–21] (Greenwich Heritage Centre).
92. Ibid. [p. 22].
93. W. T. Swan, p. 8. See also *Autobiography of a Scotch Lad*, pp. 52–3.
94. Catton, p. 10.
95. North, p. 75.
96. T. Cooper, pp. 37–9. See also Townend, pp. 34–43.
97. Kitson, p. 6 (Keighley Library).
98. Bezer, p. 178.
99. J. Wood, pp. 13–15.
100. Ibid., pp. 16–17.
101. Ibid., p. 16.
102. Michael Snape, *The Church in Industrial Society. The Lancashire Parish of Whalley in the Eighteenth Century* (Woodbridge, 2003); Geoffrey S. Chamberlain and Jeremy Gregory, eds, *The National Church in Local Perspective: the Church of England and the Regions, 1660–1800* (Woodbridge, 2003); Frances Knight, *The Nineteenth-Century Church and English Society* (Cambridge, 1995); Robert Lee, 'Class, industrialisation and the Church of England: the case of the Durham diocese in the nineteenth century', *Past and Present*, 191 (2006), pp. 165–88; John Walsh, Colin Haydon and Stephen Taylor, eds, *The Church of England, c.1689–1833: From Toleration to Tractarianism* (Cambridge, 1993).
103. Bennett, p. 19 (Bristol Record Office).
104. B. Shaw, p. 38.
105. Ibid., pp. 38–40.
106. Thomson, pp. 61–3.
107. Ibid., p. 66.
108. Hanson, p. 16.

### 9 Sons of Freedom

1. Watson, p. 114.
2. For a useful introduction to the LCS, see H. T. Dickinson, *The Politics of the People in Eighteenth-Century Britain* (London, 1995). See also Benjamin Weinstein, 'Popular constitutionalism and the London Corresponding Society', *Albion*, 34 (2002), pp. 37–57; Iain McCalman, *Radical Underworlds: Prophets, Revolutionaries and Pornographers in London, 1795–1840* (Cambridge, 1988); John Barrell, 'London and the London Corresponding Society', in James K. Chandler and Kevin Gilmartin eds, *Romantic Metropolis: The Urban Scene of British Culture, 1780–1840* (Cambridge, 2005), 85–112; Mark Philp, 'Disconcerting ideas: explaining popular radicalism and popular loyalism in the 1790s', in Glenn Burgess and Matthew Festenstein, eds, *English Radicalism, 1550–1850* (Cambridge, 2007), 157–89; Michael T. Davis, 'The

Mob Club? The London Corresponding Society and the politics of civility in the 1790s', in idem and Paul A. Pickering, eds, *Unrespectable Radicals? Popular Politics in the Age of Reform* (Aldershot, 2008), pp. 21–40.

3. The essential reading on the emergence of Chartism is E. P. Thompson, *The Making of the English Working Class* (Harmondsworth, 1968); Dorothy Thompson, *The Chartists: Popular Politics in the Industrial Revolution* (London, 1984); Gareth Stedman Jones, *Languages of Class: Studies in English Working Class History, 1833–1982* (Cambridge, 1983); Paul Pickering, *Chartism and the Chartists in Manchester and Salford* (Basingstoke, 1995); Miles Taylor, *Ernest Jones, Chartism and the Romance of Politics, 1819–1869* (Oxford, 2003); James Epstein, 'Understanding the cap of liberty: symbolic practice and social conflict in early nineteenth-century England', *Past and Present*, 122 (1989), pp. 75–118; idem, *The Lion of Freedom: Feargus O'Connor and the Chartist Movement, 1832–1843* (London, 1982); Malcolm Chase, *Chartism: A New History* (Manchester, 2007).

4. Hardy, p. 39. See also Alan G. Steinberg, 'Thomas Hardy and the London Corresponding Society: the revolution that never was', *Proceedings of the Consortium on Revolutionary Europe* (1983), pp. 319–417.

5. Hardy, pp. 39–41.

6. Ibid., pp. 44–5.

7. Ibid., pp. 43–4.

8. Place, pp. 112–15. See also (in addition to Thale's fine introduction to his autobiography), James Alan Jaffe, ed., *'The Affairs of Others': the Diaries of Francis Place* (Cambridge, 2007).

9. Place, pp. 125–6.

10. Ibid., pp. 129–31.

11. Ibid., p. 131.

12. Preston, pp. 10–11. See also David Worrall, *Radical Culture: Discourse, Resistance and Surveillance, 1790–1820* (Detroit, MI, 1993), pp. 77–88.

13. Preston, pp. 12–14.

14. Ibid., pp. 20–2.

15. Bamford, *Passages*, p. 12. See also Martin Hewitt and Robert Poole, eds, *The Diaries of Samuel Bamford* (Stroud, 2000).

16. Davenport, pp. 48–51. See also Worrall, *Radical Culture*, pp. 77–88.

17. Davenport, pp. 44–8.

18. Preston, p. 28.

19. It will be seen then that I differ in interpretation to Iain Hampsheir-Monk who has attributed the Radicals' failure to 'linguistic non-performance'. If making a revolution is a 'kind of speech act', he asks, 'might the British have failed through having the wrong kind of speech available or through failing to deploy it adroitly enough, or through mere syntactical incompetence?' See idem, 'On not inventing the English Revolution: the radical failure of the 1790s as linguistic non-performance', in Glenn Burgess and Matthew Festenstein, eds, *English Radicalism, 1550–1850* (Cambridge 2007), pp. 135–56.

20. Place, p. 131.

21. Contrast with Ian McCalman, 'Ultra-Radicalism and convivial debating-clubs in London, 1795–1838', *English Historical Review*, 102/403 (1987), pp. 309–33. McCalman has indicated the importance of debating clubs in sustaining the Radicals during the 1790s and beyond. I would agree these played a significant role, but also wish to draw attention to a wide range of alternative institutions without political focus.

22. The figure has been calculated by dividing five (the number of autobiographers who did play a political role before 1820) by 104 (the number of autobiographers born before 1790 and therefore having the opportunity to become involved in politics before 1820).

23. Fairburn, pp. 83–4; Claxton, pp. 21–5.

24. C. Campbell, pp. 3–4.

25. Later in life he also helped to establish a Bible Society and a school for poor boys in West Ham, and was involved in the Plaistow allotments and temperance movement. Catton, pp. 12–18. See also Carter, p. 166; Innes, pp. 11–15.

26. The figure has been calculated by dividing 45 (the number of autobiographers who did play a political role between 1820 and 1850) by 200 (the number born between 1791 and 1835 and therefore having the opportunity to become involved in politics before 1850).

27. This figure has been calculated by dividing 49 (the number of autobiographers who played a role in a mutual improvement society, Sunday school union or similar organisation but were never involved in politics) by 200.

28. T. Cooper, pp. 46–7.

29. Lowery, pp. 72–3. See also Lovett, pp. 28–9; McAdam, p. 3.

30. Leatherland, pp. 9–10.

31. Ibid., pp. 17–19.

32. 'Jacques', 1 Nov. 1856.

33. [Holkinson], 31 Jan. 1857.

34. W. Milne, p. 237. For similar comment, see Skeen, p. 5.

35. Bezer, pp. 157–9, 165–9, 180–7.

36. Lovekin, no. 3 (Brunel University Library). The others who moved from Sunday school teaching to politics were J. Barker, pp. 77, 286; Burland, pp. 2–3; Goodliffe, no pag. (Leicestershire Record Office); Manton, 22 Nov. 1902, 29 Nov. 1902; Mountjoy, pp. 2–4, 29–30; Terry, pp. 38–41, 62 (Brunel University Library); Joseph Wilson, pp. 33–4, 71. See also Lovett, p. 239 and T. Wood, pp. 10–11, 15 (Bradford Central Library), who moved into Sunday school work after having been involved in politics.

37. Thompson, *The Making*; idem, 'Time, work-discipline and industrial capitalism', *Past and Present*, 38/1 (1967), pp. 56–97 See, however, Thomas Laqueur, *Religion and Respectability: Sunday Schools and Working Class Culture* (New Haven, 1976).

38. For an excellent history of the trade union movement see Malcolm Chase, *Early Trade Unionism: Fraternity, Skill and the Politics of Labour* (Aldershot, 2000).

39. Dunning, pp. 126–34.

40. Ibid., pp. 134–42.

41. A few did not state their date of birth (see, for example, T. Horne, S. Taylor, [Cameron]), but none other stated he or she did not know it.

42. Burn, pp. 138–9.

43. Ibid., p. 139.

44. Ibid. For others who entered by the trade union route, see Lowery, pp. 62–160, *passim*.

45. Very little has been written in recent years about the early history of the co-operative movement. See, however, Peter Gurney, *Co-operative Culture and the Politics of Consumption in England, 1870–1930* (Manchester, 1996); Jennifer Tann, 'Co-operative corn milling: self-help during the grain crisis of the Napoleonic Wars', *Agricultural History Review*, 28 (1989) 45–57; P. Backstrom, *Christian Socialism and Co-operation in Victorian Britain* (London, 1974).

46. Lovett, pp. 33–5. Lovett was also a member of several mutual improvement societies, pp. 28–30.

47. John Wilson, p. 215.

48. Ibid., p. 216. For others who entered politics from co-operative activity, see Castle (Essex Record Office); Marcroft, pp. 66–7.

49. Brian Harrison, *Drink and the Victorians: the Temperance Question in England, 1815–1872* (Pittsburgh, PA, 1971); Lilian Lewis Shiman, *Crusade against Drink in Victorian England* (London, 1988).

50. 'Life of a handloom weaver', 25 April 1857.

51. Crowe, p. 5.

52. Buckmaster writing under the pseudonym John Buckley; Buckley, p. 26. See also Rushton, pp. 92–99.
53. Farish, p. 73. John Bates also entered politics from temperance activity. See Bates, pp. 2–3.
54. Ibid., p. 89.
55. See, for instance, 'Colin', p. 60; Powell, p. 11.
56. Lowery, p. 72.
57. Bates, p. 2.
58. Barker, pp. 86–93.
59. Ibid., pp. 244–6.
60. Ibid., p. 286.
61. *Scenes from my Life*, p. 68.
62. Arch, esp. pp. 65–116, 355–77.
63. For unions, in addition to the references given for James Dawson Burn (nn. 42–44), Thomas Dunning (nn. 39–40), Robert Lowery (n. 56); Francis Place (nn. 8–11) and Thomas Preston (nn. 12–14), see Dodgson, 19 May (Halifax Central Library); 'Life of an Irish taylor', 18 April 1857; Powell, p. 12. For co-operatives, in addition to the references given for William Lovett (n. 46); John Wilson (nn. 47–8), and John Castle and William Marcroft (n. 48); see Terry, pp. 65–6 (Brunel University Library).
64. For temperance advocates, in addition to the references given for 'Life of a handloom weaver' (n. 50), Robert Crowe (n. 51), John Buckmaster and Adam Rushton (n. 52) and William Farish (nn. 53–4), see: C. Bent, p. 24; 'Colin', pp. 85–8; Harland, extract no. 12 (Bradford Central Library); 'Life of a journeyman baker', 20 Dec. 1856; Whittaker, *passim*. See also Blow, pp. 13–24, for temperance work in rural areas.
65. See the references for John James Bezer (n. 35) and Emanuel Lovekin, Joseph Barker, John Burland, Arnold Goodliffe, Henry Manton, Timothy Mountjoy, Joseph Terry, Joseph Wilson and Thomas Wood (all n. 36).
66. See, for instance, Basset; J. Davis; Davies.
67. Somerville.
68. G. Cooper, [p. 18].
69. Ibid. [p. 22].
70. Mountjoy, pp. 38–40.
71. Catton, p. 17.
72. B. Wilson, p. 225; Hawker, pp. 25–6; Hammond, pp. 34–42; Parkinson, pp. 62–3; McAdam, pp. 42–53.
73. John Wilson, p. 207.
74. Ibid., pp. 209–37.
75. Lovekin, no. 3 (Brunel University Library).
76. Leatherland, pp. 17–19.
77. Burn, pp. 140–1.
78. Dunning, pp. 135, 141, 142.
79. Ibid., pp. 142–6.
80. Aitken, pp. 27–8.

## 10 Conclusion

1. Bennett, pp. 9–10 (Bristol Record Office).
2. Freer, p. 9. See also Adams, pp. 42–50; John Wilson, p. 44.
3. North, p. 95.
4. Burn, p. 133.
5. Horler, p. 14. See also Hayes, p. 1.
6. Hawker, p. 76.
7. Mallard, p. 3 (Northamptonshire Record Office).
8. See, for instance, S. Taylor, p. 1. See also Whittaker, p. 24.

9. Weaver, pp. 29–30.
10. S. Robinson, p. 31.
11. Jackson, p. 32.
12. Wallis, p. 22.
13. W. Smith, p. 181.
14. Livesey, pp. 197–8. See also Claxton, pp. 16–17; Watson, p. 109; Joseph Wilson, p. 9.
15. I. Anderson, p. 7.
16. G. Mitchell, p. 100. Except perhaps William Hanson, who was filled with 'wonder and astonishment' at the 'great changes which have taken place in the world'. Many of the changes he admired, 'but not all'. Hanson, p. 3.

# Bibliography

**Manuscripts**

*Barnsley Archives and Local Studies, Barnsley*

Marsh, George, 'A sketch of the life of George Marsh, a Yorkshire collier, 1834–1921', B920 MAR.

*Bradford Central Library (Local Studies collection), Bradford*

Harland, John, Diary, 1810–1815, 1831, 920 Har.
Wood, Thomas, 'Autobiography by Thomas Wood, 1822–1880', 920 Woo.

*Bristol Central Library*

Arney, Alfred, 'Diary, 1851–57', B20208.
Mitchell, Tommy, 'Tommys' Book', TS, B29411.

*Bristol Record Office*

Bennett, John, 'Manuscript autobiography of John Bennett of Bristol', 36907.

*Broadstairs Library, Kent*

Pointer, Thomas, 'Memoirs of Thomas James Pointer of St Peters', 50: Pointer.

*Brunel University Library*

Lovekin, Emanuel, 'Some notes of my Life', 1: 452.
Terry, Joseph, 'Recollections of my Life', 1: 693.

*Carlisle Library (Local Studies Department), Carlisle*

Irving, Thomas, 'Farming and Country Life in Cumberland 100 Years ago', B600.

*Cumbria Record Office, Carlisle*

Sankoffsky, Johan, 'Diary', ex-DX 644/1–2.

*East Riding Archives and Local Studies, Beverley*

Taylor, Hasslewood, 'Untitled MS', DDX1077/11.

*Essex Record Office, Chelmsford, Essex*

Castle, John, 'The Diary of John Castle', B/CAS.

*Finsbury Library (Islington Local History Centre), London*

Price, Henry Edward, 'My diary', 1032 S/HEP.

*Flintshire Record Office, Hawarden, Flintshire*

Nuttall, Samuel, 'My recollections and life', D/DM/742/1.

*Greenwich Heritage Centre, Woolwich, London*

Stradley, John, 'Memoirs of John Stradley, 1757–1825', 920 Strad.

*Halifax Central Library (Local Studies), Halifax*

Dodgson, Joshua, 'Diary of Joshua Dodgson', *Halifax Weekly Courier and Guardian*, 19 and 25 May 1956.

*Keighley Library (Local Studies), Keighley*

Kitson, John, 'Diary of John Kitson of Haworth', 920 HAW KIT.

*Record Office for Leicestershire, Leicester and Rutland, Wigston Magna, Leicester*

Goodliffe, Arnold, 'Memoirs of Arnold Goodliffe', DE7196.

*Lincoln Reference Library (Local Studies Collection), Lincoln*

Cook, Richard, 'The Memoirs of Richard Cook', LOC L.921.COO.

*Newport Central Library (Local Studies Collection) Newport*

Hughes, Henry, 'Autobiography', M380.920.HUG.

*Norfolk Record Office*

Hemmingway, John, 'The Character or Worldly Experience of the Writer from 1791 to 1865', MC 766/1, 795X5.
Huggins, Samuel, 'Some short account of the Birth Life Conversation Travels and Christian Experience of Samuel Huggins Primitive Methodist Preacher', FC 17/148.
Lincoln, John, 'Memoirs of John Lincoln', MC 2669/29, 991X9.

*Northamptonshire Record Office, Northampton*

Clifton, John, 'Day Books, 1763–1784', ZA/8732–46.
Mallard, George, 'Memories', ZA9908/3, X9908/4–15.

*Norwich Castle Museum, Norwich*

Short, Obadiah, 'Recollections, 1861', NWHCM: 1964.590.2.

*Norwich and Norfolk Millennium Library (Norfolk Heritage Centre), Norwich*

Zobel, James, 'Diary, 1827–58', TS. ed. J. K. Edwards, C ZOB.

*Nottinghamshire Archives, Nottingham*

[Moss, Joseph], 'Memoirs of Joseph Burdett, stockinger and sometime apprentice to Mr Kirk of Lambley, Nottinghamshire, 1813–1917', DD1177/1.

Moss, Joseph, 'Recollections of Joseph Moss, a journeyman stockinger, 1817', DD148/1.

Woolley, Joseph, 'Diary of Joseph Woolley, framework knitter, Clifton, Nottinghamshire, 1801, 1813, 1815', DD311/1; DD311/5; DD311/6.

*Rawtenstall Library (Local Studies Department) Rawtenstall, Rosssendale, Lancashire*

Heap, Moses, 'My life and times', TS ed. J. Elliott, LG3 HEAP.

*Sheffield Archives, Sheffield*

Lea, William, 'Autobiography of the Reverend William Lea', MD1900a.

Skelton, Joseph, 'Diary of Joseph Skelton, 1826–1830', MD2064/1–5.

Ward, William, 'Life and Journal of William Ward, Primitive Methodist Minister', MD1490.

*Suffolk Record Office, Ipswich*

'Autobiography of a Suffolk farm labourer', cuttings from the *Suffolk Mercury*.

*Tyne and Wear Archives Service, Newcastle upon Tyne*

Binns, David, Untitled MS, 1203/4.

*University of Warwick, Modern Records Centre*

Plastow, William, 'William Plastow's story', MSS.172/LP/A/115.

*Warwickshire County Record Office, Warwick*

Roper, J. N., 'Journal of some pleasant and comfortable times at Atherstone, Warwickshire, 1848', Z685sm.

*Westminster City Archives*

Bryceson, Nathaniel, 'Diary, 1848', 0730 (transcription available on the archives' website).

*West Sussex Record Office, Chichester*

Robinson, Joseph, 'Joseph Robinson's reminiscences (1820–1917)', MP 2216.

*Wigan Archives Service, Wigan*

Arthur E. Jewitt, 'Passages in the Life of A.E. Jewitt', EHC172/M964.


*Wiltshire and Swindon History Centre, Chippenham, Wiltshire*

Small, William, 'Cherished memories and Associations', 2713/2.


*Worcestershire Record Office, Worcester*

Shervington, Jesse, 'Autobiography of an agricultural labourer', BA 5518 Ref: 970.5: 645 Parcel 1.


## Printed Autobiographies

Adams, W. E., *Memoirs of a Social Atom*, 2 vols (London, 1903).

Aird, Andrew, *Autobiography* (Glasgow, 1899).

Aitken, William, 'Remembrances and struggles of a working man for bread and liberty', in Robert G. Hall and Stephen Roberts, eds, *William Aitken, the Writings of a Nineteenth Century Working Man* (Tameside, 1996).

Anderson, Edward, *The Sailor; a Poem. Description of his Going to Sea, and through Various Scenes of Life . . . with Observations on the Town of Liverpool* (Newcastle, [1800?]).

Anderson, Isaac, *The Life History of Isaac Anderson. A Member of the Peculiar People* (n.p., 1896).

Anderson, Robert, 'Memoir of the author, written by himself', in *The Poetical Works of Robert Anderson* (Carlisle, 1820), pp. xiii–xxxiv.

Andrew, Jane, *Recorded Mercies: Being the Autobiography of Jane Andrew, Living at St Ives, Liskeard, Cornwall* (London, [1890]).

Arch, Joseph, *Joseph Arch: the Story of his Life, Told by Himself*, ed. with a preface by Frances, the Countess of Warwick (London, 1898).

Ashford, Mary Ann, *Life of a Licensed Victualler's Daughter* (London, 1844).

Askham, John, *Sketches in Prose and Verse* (Wellingborough, 1893).

*Autobiography of a Scotch Lad: being Reminiscences of Threescore Years and Ten* (Glasgow, 1887).

Bain, Alexander, *Autobiography*, ed. William L. Davidson (London, 1904).

Bamford, Samuel, *Early Days* (London, 1849).

——, *Passages in the Life of a Radical* (London, [1859?]).

Bangs, Benjamin, *Memoirs of the Life and Convincement of that Worthy Friend: Benjamin Bangs, late of Stockport in Cheshire, Deceased* (London, 1798).

Barker, Joseph, *Life of Joseph Barker, Written by Himself*, ed. John Thomas Barker (London, 1880).

Barker, Robert, *Unfortunate Shipwright: or Cruel Captain, being a Faithful Narrative of the Unparalleled Sufferings of Robert Barker* (London, 1758).

——, *The Second Part of the Unfortunate Shipwright; or the Blind Man's Travels through Many Parts of England, in Pursuit of his Right* (London, 1771).

Barlow, Edward, *Barlow's Journal of his Life at Sea in King's Ships . . . from 1659 to 1703*, ed. Basil Lubbock (London, 1934).

Barr, David, *Climbing the Ladder: the Struggles and Successes of a Village Lad* (London, 1910).

Basset, Josiah, *Life of a Vagrant: Or the Testimony of an Outcast to the Value and Truth of the Gospel* (New York, 1852).

Bates, John, *John Bates, the Veteran Reformer: a Sketch of his Life* (Queensbury, 1895; facs. repr. London, 1986).

Bathgate, Janet, *Aunt Janet's Legacy to her Nieces. Recollections of Humble Life in Yarrow in the Beginning of the Century* (Selkirk, 1894).

Belcher, Richard Boswell, *Autobiography of Richard Boswell Belcher of Banbury and Blockley*, ed. A. W. Excell and Norah M. Marshall (Blockley Antiquarian Society, 1976).

Bent, Charles, *Autobiography of Charles Bent, a Reclaimed Drunkard* (Sheffield, 1866).

Bent, James, 'Introduction', *Criminal Life: Reminiscences of 42 Years as a Police Officer* (Manchester, [1891]), pp. iii–vi.

Bertram, James Glass, *Some Memories of Books, Authors and Events* (London, 1893).

Bethune, Alexander, *Memoirs of Alexander Bethune, embracing Selections from his Correspondence*, ed. William M'Combie (Aberdeen, 1845).

Bethune, John, *Poems by the Late John Bethune with a Sketch of the Author's Life, By His Brother* (London, 1841).

Bewley, George, *A Narrative of the Christian Experiences of George Bewley, Late of the City of Corke* (Dublin, 1750).

Bezer, John James, 'The autobiography of one of the Chartist rebels of 1848', in David Vincent, ed., *Testaments of Radicalism. Memoirs of Working-Class Politicians, 1790–1885* (London, 1977), pp. 147–87.

Black, James, 'Local autobiography: Glasgow in the past century', *Glasgow Herald*, 5 May 1851.

Blacket, Joseph, 'Autobiographical letter', in *Specimens of the Poetry of Joseph Blacket, with an Account of his Life*, i, ed. Mr Pratt (London, 1811).

Blow, John, *Autobiography of John Blow* (Leeds, 1870).

Bodell, James, *A Soldier's View of Empire: the Reminiscences of James Bodell, 1831–92* (London, 1982).

Bowcock, William, *The Life, Experiences and Correspondence of William Bowcock* (London, 1851).

Bowd, James, 'The life of a farm worker', *The Countryman*, 51/2 (1955), pp. 293–300.

Bowes, John, *The Autobiography or History of the Life of John Bowes* (Glasgow, 1872).

Bownas, Samuel, *An Account of the Life, Travels, and Christian Experiences in the Work of the Ministry of Samuel Bownas* (Stanford, CA, 1805).

Brierley, Benjamin, *Home Memories: the Autobiography of a Handloom Weaver* (Manchester, 1886; repr. Bramhall, 2002).

Britton, John, *The Autobiography of John Britton, FSA, Honorary Member of Numerous English and Foreign Societies*, 2 vols (London, 1850).

Broadhurst, Henry, *Henry Broadhurst M.P. The Story of his Life from a Stonemason's Bench to the Treasury Bench* (London, 1901).

Brown, John, *A Memoir of Robert Blincoe, an Orphan Boy (1832)*, in James R. Simmons and Janice Carlisle, eds, *Factory Lives: Four Nineteenth-Century Working-Class Autobiographies* (Ontario, 2007).

Brown, John, *Sixty Years' Gleanings from Life's Harvest: a Genuine Autobiography* (Cambridge, 1858).

Brown, William, *A Narrative of the Life and Adventures of William Brown* (York, 1829).

Brunskill, Stephen, *The Life of Stephen Brunskill of Orton: Sixty Years a Wesleyan Methodist Local Preacher* (London, 1837).

Buckley, John, *A Village Politician. The Life-Story of John Buckley*, ed. J. C. Buckmaster (London, 1897).

Burgess, John, *No Continuing City. The Diary and Letters of John Burgess, a Sussex Craftsman, 1785–1810*, ed. Donald F. Burgess (Redhill, Surrey, 1989).

Burgess, Joseph, *A Potential Poet? His Autobiography and Verse* (Burgess Publications, Ilford, 1927).

Burland, John, *John Hugh Burland by Himself* (Barnsley, [1902?]).

Burn, James Dawson, *The Autobiography of a Beggar Boy, 1855*, ed. with an introduction by David Vincent (London, 1978).

Mrs Burrows, 'A childhood in the fens about 1850–1860', in Margaret Llewelyn Davis, ed., *Life As We Have Known It, by Co-operative Working Women* (1931).

Burt, Thomas, *Thomas Burt: Pitman & Privy Councillor; an Autobiography* (London, 1924).

[Butler, Robert], *Narrative of the Life and Travels of Sergeant B——. Written by Himself* (Edinburgh, 1823).

Buxton, Richard, 'A brief memoir of the author', in his *A Botanical Guide to the Flowers and Plants . . . within Sixteen Miles of Manchester* (London, 1849).

Bywater, James, *The Trio's Pilgrimage: an Autobiography of James Bywater, including Brief Life Sketches of his Wives Maria Thomas, Hanna Maria Jenson*, ed. Hyrum W. Valentine ([Salt Lake City, 1947]).

Calladine, George, *The Diary of Colour-Serjeant George Calladine, 19th Foot, 1793–1837*, ed. Major M.L. Ferrar (London, 1922).

[Cameron, William], *Hawkie, the Autobiography of a Gangrel*, ed. John Strathesk (Glasgow, 1888).

Campbell, Archibald, *The Restless Voyage, Being an Account by Archibald Campbell, Seaman, of his Wanderings in Five Oceans from 1806 to 1812, Written and Published in Edinburgh in 1816 and Supplemented and Re-Edited in 1948* (London, 1949).

Campbell, Charles, *Memoirs of Charles Campbell, at Present Prisoner in the Jail of Glasgow* (Glasgow, 1828).

Campbell, Duncan, *Reminiscences and Reflections of an Octogenarian Highlander* (Inverness, 1910).

Cannon, John, *The Chronicles of John Cannon, Excise Officer and Writing Master*, 2 vols, ed. John Money (Oxford, 2010).

Carnegie, Andrew, *Autobiography of Andrew Carnegie* (Boston and London, 1920).

Carter, Harry, *The Autobiography of a Cornish Smuggler, 1749–1809*, ed. with introduction John Britain Cornish (Truro, 1894).

Carter, Thomas, *Memoirs of a Working Man*, ed. Charles Knight (London, 1845).

Carvosso, William, *The Efficacy of Faith in the Atonement of Christ, Exemplified in a Memoir of Mr William Carvosso* (London, 1836; repr. New York, 1837).

Castle, John, 'Memoirs', in A. F. J. Brown, ed., *Essex People 1750–1900, from their Diaries Memoirs and Letters* (Essex Record Office Publications, 59), 1972.

Catling, Thomas Thurgood, *My Life's Pilgrimage* (London, 1911).

Catton, Samuel, *A Short Sketch of a Long Life of Samuel Catton once a Suffolk Ploughboy* (Ipswich, 1863).

Chadwick, William, *Reminiscences of a Chief Constable* (Manchester, 1900; facs. repr. Longdendale, Cheshire, 1974).

Chatterton, Daniel, *Biography of Dan Chatterton, Atheist and Communist* (London, 1891).

Choyce, James, *The Log of a Jack Tar; or The Life of James Choyce, Master Mariner* (London, 1891; facs repr. 1973).

Chubb, Thomas, 'The author's account of himself', in *The Posthumous Works of Mr. Thomas Chubb*, i (London, [1748]), pp. ii–viii.

Clare, John, 'The Autobiography, 1793–1824', in J. W. and Anne Tibble, eds, *The Prose of John Clare* (London, 1951).

—— 'Sketches in the life of John Clare, written by himself and addressed to his friend John Taylor, esq.', in Eric Robinson, ed., *John Clare's Autobiographical Writings* (Oxford, 1983).

Claxton, Timothy, *Hints to Mechanics on Self-Education and Mutual Instruction* (London, 1839).

Clifford, John, *Dr John Clifford, C. H. Life, Letters and Reminiscences* (London, 1924).

Clift, William, *Reminiscences of William Clift* (Basingstoke, 1908).

'A coal miner's defence', *Potters' Examiner and Emigrants' Advocate*, 11, 18, 25 Jan. 1851.

'Colin', *The Wanderer Brought Home. The Life and Adventures of Colin. An Autobiography*, ed. with reflections by the Rev. B. Richings (London, 1864).

Collyer, Robert, *Some Memories* (Boston, 1908).

Cooke, Noah, 'Autobiography', in his *Wild Warblings* (Kidderminster, 1876).

Cooper, George, *George Cooper, Stockport's Last Town Crier, 1824–1895, Presented by Anne Swift* [n. p., 1974].

Cooper, Thomas, *The Life of Thomas Cooper, Written by Himself* (London, 1872).

Corben, James, *A Langton Quarryman's Apprentice: James Corben's Autobiography*, ed. R. J. Saville (Langton Matravers Local History and Preservation Society, 1996).

Crocker, Charles, *The Vale of Obscurity, The Lavant, and Other Poems* (Chichester, 1830), pp. ix–xii.

Croll, James, *Autobiographical Sketch of James Croll, with Memoir of his Life and Work* (London, 1896).

Crowe, Robert, 'Reminiscences of Robert Crowe, the octogenarian tailor', in Dorothy Thompson, ed., *Chartists' Biographies and Autobiographies* (London, 1986).

Davenport, Allen, *The Life and Literary Pursuits of Allen Davenport* (London, 1845).

Davidson, Margaret, *The Extraordinary Life and Christian Experience of Margaret Davidson (as dictated by herself) . . . To which are added, some of her Letters and Hymns. By the Rev. Edward Smyth* (Dublin, 1782).

Davies, Thomas, *Short Sketches from the Life of Thomas Davies* (Haverfordwest, [1887?]).

Davis, Edward G., *Some Passages from My Life* (Birmingham, 1898).

Davis, James, *Passages in the Life of James Davis, Wandering Musician, Twenty Years on the Road* (Bristol, 1865).

Deacon, Abraham, *Memoir of Abraham Deacon* (London, 1912).

Dodd, William, *A Narrative of the Experiences and Sufferings of William Dodd, A Factory Cripple, Written by Himself (1851)*, in James R. Simmons and Janice Carlisle, eds, *Factory Lives: Four Nineteenth-Century Working-Class Autobiographies* (Ontario, 2007).

Donaldson, Joseph, *Recollections of an Eventful Life Chiefly Passed in the Army. By a Soldier* (Glasgow, 1824).

Dottie, Robert, Autobiographical preface in *The Rambles and Recollections of 'R Dick' (Robert Dottie)* (Manchester, 1898), pp. x–xvi.

Downing, James, *A Narrative of the Life of James Downing, (a blind man), Late a Private in his Majesty's 20th Regiment of Foot* (New York, 1821).

Duke, Robert Rippon, *An Autobiography, 1817–1902* (Buxton, 1902).

Dunhill, Snowden, *The Life of Snowden Dunhill, of Spaldington, East Riding* (Howden, 1987).

Dunn, James, *From Coal Mine Upwards, or Seventy Years of an Eventful Life* (London, [1910]).

Dunning, Thomas, 'Reminiscences of Thomas Dunning', in David Vincent, ed., *Testaments of Radicalism. Memoirs of Working-Class Politicians, 1790–1885* (London, 1977), pp. 115–46.

Edwards, John Passmore, *A Few Footprints* (London, 1905).

Elliott, Ebenezer, 'Autobiography', *The Athenaeum*, 12 Jan. 1850.

Errington, Anthony, *Coals of Rails or the Reason of my Wrighting. The Autobiography of Anthony Errington from 1778 to 1825*, ed. P. E. H. Hair (Liverpool, 1988).

Evans, Elizabeth, 'Memoir of Mrs. Elizabeth Evans', in Z. Taft, ed., *Biographical Sketches of the Lives and Public Ministry of Various Holy Women*, i (London, 1825), pp. 45–58.

*An Exposition of the Nefarious System of Making and Passing Spurious Coin . . . Being the Confessions of a Coiner* (Preston, n.d.).

Fairburn, William, *The Life of Sir William Fairburn* (London, 1877; facs. repr. 1970).

Farish, William, *The Autobiography of William Farish. The Struggles of a Handloom Weaver. With Some of his Writings*, ed. Owen R. Ashton and Stephen Roberts (London, 1996).

Farn, John C. 'The autobiography of a living publicist', *The Reasoner*, 16 Sept.–23 Dec. 1857.

Farningham, M., *A Working Woman's Life* (London, 1907).

Featherstone, Peter, *Reminiscences of a Long Life* (London, 1905).

Ferguson, James, 'A short account of the life of the author', in E. Henderson, *Life of James Ferguson, FRS, in a Brief Autobiographical Account and a Further Extended Memoir* (Edinburgh, 1870).

Finney, John, *Sixty Years' Recollections of an Etruscan* (Stoke-on-Trent, n.d.).

Flockhart, Robert, *The Street Preacher, Being the Autobiography of Robert Flockhart*, ed. Thomas Guthrie (Edinburgh, 1858).

Freer, Walter, *My Life and Memories* (Glasgow, 1929).

Frost, Thomas, *Forty Years' Recollections. Literary and Political* (London, 1880).

G. J., *Prisoner Set Free. The Narrative of a Convict in the Preston House of Correction with a few Remarks by the Rev. John Clay* (Preston, 1846).

Gabbitass, Peter, 'The poet's autobiography', in his *Heart Melodies: for Storm and Sunshine. From Cliftonia the Beautiful* (Bristol, 1885).

Gammage, R. G., *Reminiscences of a Chartist, Robert Gammage*, ed. W. H. Maehl ([Barnsley], 1983).

Gibbs, John, *The Life and Experience of the Author and some Traces of the Lord's Gracious Dealings towards the Author* (Lewes, 1827).

Gifford, William, *Memoir of William Gifford. Written by Himself* (London, 1827).

[Gooch, Richard], *Memoirs, Remarkable Vicissitudes, Military Career and Wanderings* (Norwich, 1844).

Gough, John Bartholomew, *The Autobiography of John B. Gough with a Continuation of his Life up to the Present Time* (Glasgow, 1872).

Green, John, *Vicissitudes of a Soldier's Life* (London, 1827).

[Green, William], *The Life and Adventures of a Cheap Jack by One of the Fraternity*, ed. Charles Hindley (London, 1876).

Gutteridge, Joseph, 'Autobiography of Joseph Gutteridge', in V. E. Chancellor, ed., *Master and Artisan in Victorian England: The Diary of William Andrews and the Autobiography of Joseph Gutteridge* (London, 1969), pp. 75–237.

Gwyer, Joseph, 'Life and Poems of Joseph Gywer', in his *Sketches of the Life of Joseph Gywer, Potato Salesman, with his Poems* (Penge, [1877]), pp. 5–42.

[H., Bill] 'Autobiography of a Navvy', *Macmillan's Magazine*, 5 (1861–2). Extracts repr. in John Burnett, ed., *Useful Toil. Autobiographies of Working People from the 1820s to the 1920s* (London, 1974).

Haggart, David, T*he Life of David Haggart, alias John Wilson, Written by Himself* (Edinburgh, 1821).

Haime, John, 'The Life of Mr John Haime, written by himself', in *The Lives of Early Methodist Preachers, Chiefly written by Themselves*, i, ed. with an introductory essay by Thomas Jackson (London, 1865), pp. 269–311.

Hall, John Vine, *The Author of the 'Sinner's Friend'. An Autobiography*, ed. with an introduction by Newman Hall (London, 1865).

Hammond, William, *Recollections of William Hammond, A Glasgow Hand-Loom Weaver* (Glasgow, [1904]).

Hampton, Richard, *Foolish Dick. An Autobiography of Richard Hampton, the Cornish Pilgrim Preacher*, ed. S. W. Christophers (London, 1973).

Hanby, George, *Autobiography of a Colliery Weighman* (Barnsley, 1874).

Hanby, Thomas, 'The Life of Mr Thomas Hanby, written by himself', in *The Lives of Early Methodist Preachers, Chiefly written by Themselves*, ii, ed. with an introductory essay by Thomas Jackson (London, 1866), pp. 131–57.

Hanson, William, *The Life of William Hanson, Written by Himself* (Halifax, 2nd edn, 1883).

Hardy, Thomas, 'Memoir of Thomas Hardy, Written by Himself', in David Vincent, ed., *Testaments of Radicalism. Memoirs of Working-Class Politicians, 1790–1885* (London, 1977), pp. 25–102.

Harris, [Benjamin], *Recollections of Rifleman Harris, with Anecdotes of his Officers*, ed. Henry Curling (London, 1848).

Harris, John, *My Autobiography* (London, 1882).

Harrold, Edmund, *The Diary of Edmund Harrold, Wigmaker of Manchester, 1712–15*, ed. Craig Horner (Aldershot, 2008).

Hart, William, 'The autobiography of William Hart, cooper', ed. Pat Hudson and Lynette Hunter, *London Journal*, 7/2 (1981), pp. 144–60, and 8/1 (1982), pp. 63–75.

Hawker, James, 'The life of a poacher', in Garth Christian, ed., *A Victorian Poacher. James Hawker's Journal* (Oxford, 1978).

Hayes, Thomas, *Recollections of Sixty-Three Years of Methodist Life* (London, 1902).

Healey, James, *Life and Remarkable Career of George Healey* (Birmingham, n.d.).

Heaton, William, 'A sketch of the author's life', in *The Old Soldier: the Wandering Lover and Other Poems* (London, 1857), pp. xv–xxiv.

Henderson, Robert, *Incidents in the Life of Robt. Henderson*, ed. Rev. J. Martin (Carlisle, 1869).

Herbert, George, 'Autobiography', in C. S. Cheney and B. S Trinder, eds, *Shoemaker's Window: Recollections of Banbury in Oxfordshire before the Railway Age* (Banbury, 1979), pp. 1–38.

Hick, Samuel, *The Village Blacksmith, or Piety and Usefulness Exemplified in a Memoir of the Life of Samuel Hick*, by James Everett (New York, 2nd edn, 1856).

Hobley, Frederick, 'From the autobiography of Frederick Hobley, a nineteenth-century schoolteacher', *Alta: The University of Birmingham Review*, 6 (1968), pp. 331–7.

Hodgson, Joseph, *Memoir of Joseph Hodgson, Glazier, a Native of Whitehaven, Cumberland* (Whitehaven, 1850).

Hogg, James, *Memoir of the Author's Life; and, Familiar Anecdotes of Sir Walter Scott*, ed. Douglas S. Mack (Edinburgh, 1972).

Holcroft, Thomas, *The Life of Thomas Holcroft Written by Himself; Continued to the Time of his Death from his Diary Notes and Other Papers by William Hazlitt* (London, 1852).

[Holkinson, Jacob], 'The Life of Jacob Holkinson, tailor and poet, written by himself', *The Commonwealth*, 24 and 31 Jan. 1857.

Hollingsworth, William, *An Autobiographical Sketch of the Life of Mr Wm. Hollingsworth* (London, n.d.).

Holloway, John William, *An Authentic and Faithful History of the Atrocious Murder of Celia Holloway including the Extraordinary Confessions of John William Holloway* (Brighton, 1832).

Holroyd, Abraham, 'Abraham Holroyd', in Chas. F. Forshaw, ed., *The Poets of Keighley, Bingley, Haworth and District, Being Biographies and Poems of Various Authors of the Above Neighbourhood* (London, 1893), pp. 115–20.

Holyoake, George Jacob, *Sixty Years of an Agitator's Life* (London, 6th edn, 1906).

Hopkinson, James, 'Memoirs', in Jocelyne Baty Goodman, ed., *Victorian Cabinet Maker, the Memoirs of James Hopkinson, 1819–1894* (London, 1968).

Hopper, Christopher, 'The Life of Mr Christopher Hopper, written by himself', in *The Lives of Early Methodist Preachers, Chiefly written by Themselves*, i, ed. with an introductory essay by Thomas Jackson (London, 1865), pp. 179–239.

Hopwood, D. Caroline, *An Account of the Life and Religious Experiences of D. Caroline Hopwood of Leeds, Deceased* (Leeds, 1801).

Horler, Moses, *The Early Recollections of Moses Horler*, ed. M. F. Coombs and H. Coombs (Radstock, 1900).

Horne, Catherine, 'Ramsbottom's oldest lady, lived in six reigns', *Bury Times*, 18 Nov. 1911.

Horne, Eric, *What the Butler Winked At. Being the Life and Adventures of Eric Horne* (London, 1923).

Huffer, Tansley, *The Autobiography of Tansley Huffer of Swineshead, 1828–1901*, ed. with an introduction by Pamela A. Southworth (Boston, 1998).

Huntington, William, *The Celebrated Coalheaver; or Reminiscences of the Rev. William Huntington* (London, 1871).

Hutton, William, *The Life of William Hutton, F.A.S.S., Including a Particular Account of the Riots at Birmingham in 1791* (London, 1816).

Innes, William, 'Autobiography of William Innes', in *Memorials of a Faithful Servant, William Innes* (Edinburgh, 1876).

Jackson, Thomas, *Recollections of My Own Life and Times*, ed. Rev. B. Frankand and with an introduction and postscript by G. Osborn (London, 1873).

Jaco, Peter, 'The Life of Mr Peter Jaco, Written by Himself', in *The Lives of Early Methodist Preachers, Chiefly written by Themselves*, i, ed. with an introductory essay by Thomas Jackson (London, 1865) pp. 260–8.

'Jacques', 'Glimpses of a chequered life', *The Commonwealth*, 1, 8 and 15 Nov. 1856.

Jewell, Joseph, 'Autobiographical memoir of Joseph Jewell, 1763–1846', ed. Arthur Walter Slater, *Camden Miscellany*, 22 (1964), pp. 113–94.

Johnson, Thomas, 'The life of the author', ed. Jacob Simon, *Furniture History*, 39 (2003), pp. 28–64.

Johnston, David, *Autobiographical Reminiscences of David Johnston, an Octogenarian Scotchman* (Chicago, 1885).

Johnston, Ellen, 'Autobiography', in James R. Simmons and Janice Carlisle, eds, *Factory Lives: Four Nineteenth-Century Working-Class Autobiographies* (Ontario, 2007).

Johnston, William, *The Life and Times of William Johnston* (Peterhead, 1859).

Jones, John, 'John Jones, an old servant: an account of his life written by himself', in Robert Southey, *Lives of the Uneducated Poets to which are added Attempts in Verse by John Jones* (London, 1836).

Jones, John, Autobiographical extract in Samuel Smiles, *Men of Invention and Industry* (London, 1884), pp. 364–8.

Joyce, Matthias, 'The Life of Mr Matthias Joyce, written by himself', in *The Lives of Early Methodist Preachers, Chiefly written by Themselves*, iv, ed. with an introductory essay by Thomas Jackson (London, 1866), pp. 109–51.

Lackington, James, *Memoirs of the Forty-Five First Years of the Life of James Lackington* (London, 1795).

Langdon, Roger, *The Life of Roger Langdon, Told by Himself* (London, 1909).

Lawrence, William, *The Autobiography of Sergeant William Lawrence* (London, 1886; repr. Teddington, 2009).

[Leask, W.], *Struggles for Life; or, The Autobiography of a Dissenting Minister* (London, 1864).

Leatherland, J. A. *Essays and Poems with a Brief Autobiographical Memoir* (London, 1862).

Leno, John Bedford, *The Aftermath with Autobiography of the Author* (London, 1892).

'Life of a blacksmith, written by himself', *The Commonwealth*, 17 Jan. 1857.

*Life of a Chimney Boy, Written by himself*, ed. J. Arthur Turner (London, 1901).

'Life of a cotton spinner, written by himself', *The Commonwealth*, 27 Dec. 1856.

'Life of a handloom weaver, written by himself', *The Commonwealth*, 25 April 1857.

'Life of an Irish tailor, written by himself,' *The Commonwealth*, 18 April 1857.

'Life of a journeyman baker, written by himself', *The Commonwealth*, 13, 20 Dec. 1856.

'Life of a journeyman baker, written by himself', *The Commonwealth*, 2 May 1857.

'Life of a letterpress printer, written by himself', *The Commonwealth*, 7 Feb. 1857.

'A light in the gloom; or the politics of the past. An old man's tale', *People's Paper* 8 May–14 Aug. 1852 (ten articles in all).

Lingard, Joseph, *A Narrative of the Journey to and from New South Wales* (Chapel-en-le-Frith, 1846).

Linton, William James, *Memories* (London, 1895).

Livesey, Joseph, 'The author's autobiography', twelve articles in *The Staunch Teetotaler* (1868).

Loisan, Robert, *Confessions of Robert Loisan, Alias, Rambling Bob* (Beverley, [1870?]).

Lomas, John, 'The autobiography of a pedlar: John Lomas of Hollinsclough, Staffordshire (1747–1823)', ed. David Brown, *Midland History*, 21 (1996), pp. 156–66.

Longden, Henry, *The Life of Mr Henry Longden, Compiled from his Own Memoirs* (Baltimore, MD, 1824).

Love, David, *The Life, Adventures, and Experience, of David Love, Written by Himself* (Nottingham, 4th edn, 1824).

[Loveridge, Samson], *No. 747, Being the Autobiography of a Gipsy*, ed. with an introduction by F. W. Carew (London, [1890]).

Lovett, W., *Life and Struggles of William Lovett, in his Pursuit of Bread, Knowledge and Freedom with some Short Account of the Different Associations he Belonged to and of the Opinions he Entertained* (London, 1876; repr. 1967).

Lowe, Roger, *The Diary of Roger Lowe of Ashton-in-Makerfield, Lancashire 1663–74*, ed. William L. Sachse (London, 1938).

Lowery, Robert, 'Passages in the life of a temperance lecturer', in Brian Harrison and Patricia Hollis, eds, *Robert Lowery, Radical and Chartist* (London, 1979).

MacDonald, John, *Travels, in Various Parts of Europe, Asia, and Africa, during a Series of Thirty Years and Upwards* (Dublin, [1791]).

Manton, Henry, 'Alderman Manton's Reminicences', *Birmingham Weekly Post*, 15 Nov. 1902–14 March 1903.

Marcroft, William, *The Marcroft Family* (Manchester, 1886).

Marsden, Joshua, *Sketches of the Early Life of a Sailor, Now a Preacher of the Gospel* (Hull, [1840]).

Martin, Jonathan, *The Life of Jonathan Martin of Darlington, Tanner, Written by Himself* (Lincoln, 1828).

Martin, Sarah, *Sarah Martin the Prison Visitor of Great Yarmouth; with Extracts from her Writings and Prison Journals* (London, n.d.).

Mason, Francis, DD, *The Story of a Working Man's Life: With Sketches of Travel in Europe, Asia, Africa, and America, as Related by Himself* (New York, 1870).

Mason, John, 'The Life of Mr John Mason, written by himself', in *The Lives of Early Methodist Preachers, Chiefly written by Themselves*, iii, ed. with an introductory essay by Thomas Jackson (London, 1873), pp. 307–13.

Mather, Alexander, 'The Life of Mr Alexander Mather, written by himself', in *The Lives of Early Methodist Preachers, Chiefly written by Themselves*, ii, ed. with an introductory essay by Thomas Jackson (London, 1876), pp. 158–239.

Maybee, Robert, *Sixty-Eight Years' Experience on the Scilly Islands* (Penzance, 1884).

Mayett, Joseph, *The Autobiography of Joseph Mayett of Quainton, 1783–1839*, ed. Ann Kussmaul (Buckinghamshire Record Society, 23), 1986.

McAdam, John, *Autobiography of John McAdam (1806–1883): With Selected Letters*, ed. with an introduction by Janet Fyfe (Edinburgh, 1980).

Melhuish, Thomas, *Account of the Early Part of the Life, and Convincement of Thomas Melhuish* (London, 1805).

*Memoirs of a Printer's Devil; Interspersed with Pleasing Recollections, Local Descriptions and Anecdotes* (Gainsborough, 1793).

Metford, Joseph, 'The life of Joseph Metford, 1776–1863', *Journal of the Friends Historical Society*, 25 (1928), pp. 33–44.

M'Gonagall, William, *The Authentic Autobiography of the Poet M'Gonagall* (Dundee, n.d.).

Miller, George, *A Trip to Sea from 1810 to 1815* (Long Sutton, 1854).

Miller, Hugh, *My Schools and Schoolmasters; or, the Story of my Education* (Edinburgh, 5th edn, 1856).

Millhouse, Robert, *The Song of the Patriot, Sonnet and Songs* (London, 1826).

Milne, Christian Ross., *Simple Poems on Simple Subjects* (Aberdeen, 1805), pp. 178–90.

—— 'Christian Milne', in Anon., *Sketches of Obscure Poets: with Specimens of their Writings* (London, 1833).

Milne, William J., *Reminiscences of an Old Boy: being Autobiographic Sketches of Scottish Rural Life from 1832 to 1856* (Forfar, 1901).

Mitchell, George, 'Autobiography and reminiscences of George Mitchell, "One from the Plough"', in Stephen Price, ed., *The Skeleton at the Plough, or the Poor Farm Labourers of the West: with the Autobiography and Reminiscences of George Mitchell* (London, [1875?]).

Mitchell, Thomas, 'The Life of Mr Thomas Mitchell, written by himself', in *The Lives of Early Methodist Preachers, Chiefly written by Themselves*, i, ed. with an introductory essay by Thomas Jackson (London, 1865), pp. 240–59.

M'Kaen, James, *Genuine Copy. The Life of James McKaen, Shoemaker in Glasgow, who was Executed at the Cross of Glasgow on Wednesday the 25th Jan. 1797, for the Murrder and Robbery of James Buchanan, the Lanark Carrier* (Glasgow, [1797]).

Mockford, George, *Wilderness Journeyings and Gracious Deliverances. The Autobiography of George Mockford* (Oxford, 1901).

Mountjoy, Timothy, *The Life, Labours and Deliverances of a Forest of Dean Collier* (n.p., 1887). Extract in *Hard Times in the Forest. Extracts from 62 Years in the Life of a Forest of Dean Collier', by Timothy Mountjoy* (Coleford, 1971).

Munday, John, 'Early Victorian recollections. John Munday's memories', in Reginald Blunt, ed., *Red Anchor Pieces* (London, 1928), pp. 99–121.

Murdoch, James, 'Autobiography', in his *The Autobiography and Poems of James Murdoch* (Elgin, 1863), pp. 1–17.

Murison, Alexander, 'Recollections', in A. F. Murison, *Memoirs of 88 Years (1847–1934), Being the Autobiography of Alexander Falconer Murison* (Aberdeen, 1935), pp. 209–18.

Myles, James, *Chapters in the Life of a Dundee Factory Boy, an Autobiography (1850)*, in James R. Simmons and Janice Carlisle, eds, *Factory Lives: Four Nineteenth-Century Working-Class Autobiographies* (Ontario, 2007).

'Narrative of a miner', *The Commonwealth*, 25 Oct. 1856.

Nelson, John, 'The Journal of Mr. John Nelson', in *The Lives of Early Methodist Preachers, Chiefly written by Themselves*, i, ed. with an introductory essay by Thomas Jackson. (London, 1865), pp. 1–165.

Newnham, Charles, 'Memoirs of Charles Newnham', in John Burnett, ed., *Useful Toil. Autobiographies of Working People from the 1820s to the 1920s* (London, 1974).

Nicholson, Hamlet, *An Autobiographical and Full Historical Account of Hamlet Nicholson in his Opposition to Ritualism at the Rochdale Parish Church* (Manchester, 1892).

Nicol, John, *The Life and Adventures of John Nicol, Mariner*, ed. with introduction Tim Flannery (Edinburgh, 2000).

'A Norfolk labourer's wife', *Eastern Counties Magazine*, 1–2 (1901–2); repr. E. A. Goodwyn and J. C. Baxter, eds, *East Anglian Reminiscences* (Ipswich, 1976), pp. 24–9.

North, Benjamin, *Autobiography of Benjamin North* (Aylesbury, 1882).

Nye, James, *A Small Account of my Travels through the Wilderness*, ed. Vic Gammon (Brighton, n.d.).

Oakley, Elizabeth, 'The autobiography of Elizabeth Oakley, 1831–1900', *Norfolk Record Society*, 56 (1993), pp. 113–50.

Oliver, Thomas, *Autobiography of a Cornish Miner* (Camborne, 1914).

[O' Neill, Ellen], *Extraordinary Confessions of a Female Pickpocket* (Preston, 1850).

O'Neill, John, '50 years experience of an Irish shoemaker in London', *St Crispin, a Magazine for the Leather Trades* (1869).

Owen, Robert, *The Life of Robert Owen, Written by Himself* (London, 1967).

Parkinson, George, *True Stories of Durham Pit-Life* (London, 1912).

Paterson, James, *Autobiographical Reminiscences; including Recollections of the Radical Years, 1819–20 in Kilmarnock* (Glasgow, 1871).

Pearman, John, *The Radical Soldier's Tale: John Pearman, 1819–1908*, ed. Carolyn Steedman (London, 1988).

Pellow, Thomas, *The Adventures of Thomas Pellow, of Penryn, Mariner*, ed. with an introduction and notes Dr Robert Brown (London, 1900).

Place, Francis, *The Autobiography of Francis Place*, ed. Mary Thale (Cambridge, 1972).

Plummer, John, *Songs of Labour, Northamptonshire Rambles and other Poems (with an Autobiographical Sketch of the Author's Life* (London, 1860).

[Porteus, Mary], *The Power of Faith and Prayer Exemplified in the Life and Labours of Mary Porteus, late of Durham* (London, 1862).

Powell, J. H., *Life Incidents and Poetic Pictures* (London, 1865).

Preston, Thomas, *The Life and Opinions of Thomas Preston, Patriot and Shoemaker* (London, 1817).

Prickard, John, 'The Life of Mr John Prickard, written by himself', in *The Lives of Early Methodist Preachers, Chiefly written by Themselves*, iv, ed. with an introductory essay by Thomas Jackson (London, 1866), pp. 170–97.

*The Prisoner Set Free: the Narrative of a Convict in the Preston House of Correction*, ed., Rev. Clay (Preston, 1846).

Ragg, Thomas, *God's Dealings with an Infidel; or Grace Triumphant: being the Autobiography of Thomas Ragg* (London, 1858).

Rattenbury, John, *Memoirs of a Smuggler, Compiled from his Diary and Journal* (London, 1837).

Richardson, William, *A Mariner of England. An Account of the Career of William Richardson* (London, 1908).

Ricketts, Joseph, 'Notes on the Life of Joseph Ricketts, written by himself c. 1858', *Wiltshire Archaeological and Natural History Magazine*, 60 (1965), pp. 120–6.

Riddell, Henry Scott, *The Poetical Works of Henry Scott Riddell*, i, ed. James Brydon (Glasgow, 1871), pp. ix–liv.

Roberts, Israel, *Israel Roberts, 1827–1881: Autobiography*, ed. Ruth Strong (Pudsey, 2000).

Roberts, Robert, *The Life and Opinions of Robert Roberts, a Wandering Scholar as Told by Himself*, ed. J.H. Davies (Cardiff, 1923)

Robinson, John, *A Short Account of the Life of John Robinson* (Torquay, [1882]).

Robinson, Samuel, *Reminiscences of Wigtonshire about the Close of the Last Century* (Hamilton, 1872).

Robson, Joseph Philip, *The Autobiography of Joseph Philip Robson* (Newcastle upon Tyne, 1870).

Rodda, Richard, 'The Life of Mr Richard Rodda, written by himself', in *The Lives of Early Methodist Preachers, Chiefly written by Themselves*, ii, ed. with an introductory essay by Thomas Jackson (London, 1866), pp. 113–44.

Rogers, John, *A Sketch of the Life and Reminiscences of John Rogers* (Southampton, 1889).

Rushton, Adam, *My Life as Farmer's Boy, Factory Lad, Teacher, and Preacher* (Manchester, 1909).

Rymer, Edward Allen, 'The martyrdom of the mine, or 60 years' struggle for life', ed. with an introduction by Robert G. Neville, *History Workshop Journal*, 1 (1976), pp. 220–44; 2 (1976), pp. 148–70.

Sanderson, Thomas, 'The Life and Adventures of Thomas Sanderson, as written by himself, in 1861, in the 53rd year of his age', in *Chips and Shavings of an Old Shipwright; or, the Life, Poems, & Adventures of Thomas Sanderson* (Darlington, 1873), pp. 5–41.

Sanger, George, *Seventy Years a Showman* ([London], 1966).

Savage, John, *Memoirs Containing some Particulars of the Life, Family, and Ancestors of John Savage, Miller, of St. Mary Stoke, Ipswich* (Ipswich, [1900]).

Saville, Jonathan, 'Autobiography', in Francis A. West, *Memoirs of Jonathon Saville* (3rd edn, London, 1848).

Saxby, Mary, *Memoirs of a Female Vagrant Written by Herself*, ed. Samuel Greathead (London, 1806).

Scarfe, William, *The Diary of a Poor Suffolk Woodman*, ed. Pip and Joy Wright and Léonie Robinson (Cromer, 2004).

*Scenes from my Life by a Working Man, with a Preface by the Rev. Robert Maguire* (London, 1858).

[A Self-Reformer], 'A working man's experience', *The Working Man's Friend and Family Instructor*, 1/9 (2 March 1850) pp. 284–5.

Shaw, Benjamin, *The Family Records of Benjamin Shaw, Mechanic of Dent, Dolphinholme and Preston, 1772–1841*, ed. Alan G. Crosby (Record Society of Lancashire and Cheshire, 1991).

Shaw, Charles, *When I was a Child, by 'an Old Potter'* (London, 1903; facs. repr. Wakefield, 1969).

Shipp, John, *The Path of Glory; Being the Memoirs of the Extraordinary Military Career of John Shipp, Written by Himself*, ed. C. J. Stranks (London, 1969).

Sholl, Samuel, 'Short sketch of the life of Samuel Sholl', in *A Short Historical Account of the Silk Manufacture in England* (London, 1811), pp. 37–47.

*A Short Account of the Life and Hardships of a Glasgow Weaver ... Written by Himself* (Glasgow, 1834).

Skeen, Robert, *Autobiography of Mr. Robert Skeen, Printer* (London, 1876).

[Smith, Charles Manby], *The Working-Man's Way in the World, being the Autobiography of a Journeyman Printer* (New York, 1854).

Smith, Cornelius, *The Life Story of Gipsy Cornelius Smith, London, 1890*, ed. Sharon Floate (Romany and Traveller FHS Classic Reprints, 2000).

Smith, George, *The Autobiography of George Smith, 1800–1868. An Autobiography of One of the People* (London, 1923).

Smith, George, *Incidents in a Gipsy's Life, Liverpool, 1886*, ed. Sharon Floate (Romany and Traveller FHS Classic Reprints, 2001).

Smith, Mary, *The Autobiography of Mary Smith, Schoolmistress and Nonconformist* (Carlisle, 1892).

Smith, Thomas W., *A Narrative of the Life, Travels, and Sufferings of Thomas W. Smith* (Boston, 1844).

Smith, William, 'The memoir of William Smith', ed. B. S. Trinder, *Transactions of the Shropshire Archaeological Society*, 58 (1966), pp. 178–85.

Somerville, A., *The Autobiography of a Working Man* (London, 1848; repr. 1967).

Spurr, R., 'The autobiography of Robert Spurr', ed. R. J. Owen, *Baptist Quarterly*, 26 (1976), pp. 282–8.

Staniforth, Sampson, 'The Life of Mr Sampson Staniforth, written by himself', in *The Lives of Early Methodist Preachers, Chiefly written by Themselves*, iv, ed. with an introductory essay by Thomas Jackson (London, 1866), pp. 109–51.

Stanley, Sir Henry Morton, *The Autobiography of Sir Henry Morton Stanley*, ed. Dorothy Stanley (London, 1909).

Starkey, Benjamin, *Memoirs of the Life of Benj. Starkey, Late of London, but Now an Inmate of the Freemen's Hospital, in Newcastle* (Newcastle, [1818]).

Stewart, Alexander, *The Life of Alexander Stewart, Prisoner of Napoleon and Preacher of the Gospel, Written by Himself in 1815* (Oxford, 1947).

Stir(r)up, 'The autobiography of a journeyman shoemaker', *The Commonwealth*, 22 and 29 Nov. 1856.

Storie, Elizabeth, *The Autobiography of Elizabeth Storie, A Native of Glasgow* (Glasgow, 1859).

Story, Robert, *Love and Literature: being the Reminiscences, Literary Opinions, and Fugitive Pieces of a Poet in Humble Life* (London, 1842).

Struthers, John, *The Poetical Works of John Struthers: with Autobiography*, i. (London, 1850), pp. ix–cliv.

Sutton, William, *Multum in Parvo: or the Ups and Downs of a Village Gardener* (Kenilworth, 1903).

Swan, William Thomas, 'The journal of William Thomas Swan, born 1786', in *The Journals of Two Poor Dissenters, 1786–1880*, ed. with preface by Guida Swan and introduction by John Holloway (London, 1970), pp. 1–41.

Swan, William, 'The journal of William Swan, born 1813', in *The Journals of Two Poor Dissenters, 1786–1880*, ed. with preface by Guida Swan and introduction by John Holloway (London, 1970), pp. 42–102.

Taylor, Dan, *Memoirs of Rev. Dan Taylor*, ed. Adam Taylor (London, 1820).

Taylor, John, *Memoirs of Rev. John Taylor*, ed. Adam Taylor (London, 1821).

Taylor, John, 'Autobiographical sketch', in *Poems; Chiefly on Themes of Scottish Interest* (Edinburgh, 1875), pp. 1–48.

Taylor, John, *Autobiography of John Taylor* (Bath, 1893).

Taylor, Peter, *Autobiography of Peter Taylor* (Paisley, 1903).

Taylor, Samuel, *Records of an Active Life* (London, 1886).

Taylor, William, *Diary of William Taylor, 1837*, ed. Dorothy Wise (Westminster City Archives, 1998).

Teer, John, *Silent Musings* (Manchester, 1869).

Terry, Joseph, 'Joseph Terry, Recollections of my life', in John Burnett, ed., *Destiny Obscure: Autobiographies of Childhood, Education, and Family from the 1820s to the 1920s* (London, 1982), pp. 52–8.

Thom, William, *Rhymes and Recollections of a Hand-Loom Weaver* (London, 1844).

Thompson, John, *Memoir of Mr. John Thompson* (Sunderland, [1863]).

Thomson, Christopher, *Autobiography of an Artisan* (London, 1847).

Todd, Adam Brown, *The Poetical Works of A. B. Todd with Autobiography and Portrait* (Edinburgh, 1906), pp. 13–77.

Tough, John, *A Short Narrative of the Life of an Aberdonian* (Aberdeen, 1848).

Townend, Rev. Joseph, *Autobiography of the Rev. Joseph Townend* (London, 2nd edn, 1869).

Tryon, Thomas, *Some Memoirs of the Life of Mr. Tho. Tryon, Late of London, Merchant: Written by Himself* (London, 1705).

Urie, John, *Reminiscences of Eighty Years* (Paisley, 1908).

Varley, Willam, 'Diary of William Varley of Higham', in W. Bennett, ed., *The History of Burnley, 1650–1850* (Burnley, 1948).

Wallis, Thomas Wilkinson, *Autobiography of Thomas Wilkinson Wallis, Sculptor in Wood, and Extracts from his Sixty Years' Journal* (Louth, 1899).

Watkins, Miles, *A Sketch of the Life of Miles Watkins of Cheltenham: wherein is Related the Particular Incidents Related with his History . . . Written by Himself* (Cheltenham, 1841).

Watson, James, 'Reminiscences of James Watson', in David Vincent, ed., *Testaments of Radicalism. Memoirs of Working-Class Politicians, 1790–1885* (London, 1977), pp. 103–14.

Weaver, Richard, *Richard Weaver's Life Story*, ed. James Paterson (London, [1913]).

West, Frank, *The Struggles of a Village Lad* (London, [1880]).

Whetstone, Charles, *Truths. No. 1 or the Memoirs of Charles Whetstone* (n.p., 1807).

White, H., *The Record of my Life: an Autobiography* (Cheltenham, 1889).

White, Robert, *Autobiographical Notes* (Newcastle upon Tyne, 1966).

Whitehead, David, *The Autobiography of David Whitehead of Rawtenstall, 1790–1865, Cotton Spinner and Merchant*, ed. Stanley Chapman ([n.p.], 2001).

Whittaker, Thomas, *Life's Battles in Temperance Armour* (London, 1884; repr. 2009).

Wilson, Benjamin, *The Struggles of an Old Chartist. What he Knows and the Part he has Taken in Various Movements*, in David Vincent, ed., *Testaments of Radicalism. Memoirs of Working-Class Politicians, 1790–1885* (London, 1977), pp. 189–242.

Wilson, John, *Memories of a Labour Leader: The Autobiography of John Wilson, J.P., M.P*, ed. with introduction by John Burnett (Firle, 1980).

Wilson, Joseph, *Joseph Wilson, His Life and Work, with a Foreword by the Rev. H. J. Taylor* (London, n.d.).

Wire, William, 'William Wire, Watchmaker and Postman of Colchester, 1842–57', in A. F. J. Brown, ed., *Essex People 1750–1900, from their Diaries, Memoirs and Letters* (Essex Record Office Publications, 59 (1972).

Wood, John, *Autobiography of John Wood, an Old and Well Known Bradfordian* (Bradford, 1877).

[Wright, William], 'Adventures and recollections of Bill o'th' Hoylus End. Told by himself', *Keighley Herald*, 2 June–8 Dec. 1893.

Younger, John, *Autobiography of John Younger by John Younger* (Kelso, 1881).

# Index